Beyond
Constraint

Shona N. Jackson

Beyond
Constraint

Middle/Passages of Blackness and
Indigeneity in the Radical Tradition

DUKE UNIVERSITY PRESS
Durham and London   2024

© 2024 DUKE UNIVERSITY PRESS. All rights reserved
Project Editor: Bird Williams
Typeset in Merlo by Westchester Publishing Services

Library of Congress Cataloging-in-Publication Data
Names: Jackson, Shona N., author.
Title: Beyond constraint : middle/passages of Blackness and
indigeneity in the radical tradition / Shona N. Jackson. Description:
Durham : Duke University Press, 2024. | Includes bibliographical
references and index.
Identifiers: LCCN 2023058321 (print)
LCCN 2023058322 (ebook)
ISBN 9781478019183 (paperback)
ISBN 9781478016540 (hardcover)
ISBN 9781478023814 (ebook)
Subjects: LCSH: Forced labor—Caribbean Area—History. | Black
people—America—History. | Indigenous peoples—America—
History. | Slavery—America. | Labor—Caribbean Area—History. |
Labor—Philosophy. | Postcolonialism—Caribbean Area. | America
—Race relations—History. | BISAC: SOCIAL SCIENCE / Ethnic
Studies / Caribbean & Latin American Studies | SOCIAL SCIENCE /
Black Studies (Global)
Classification: LCC E29.A1 J34 2024 (print)
LCC E29.A1 (ebook)
DDC 331.11/7309729—dc23/eng/20240511
LC record available at https://lccn.loc.gov/2023058321
LC ebook record available at https://lccn.loc.gov/2023058322

Cover art: *Lost Farm (Billy Goat Hill)*, 2000. © Thornton Dial.
84 × 72 × 13 inches. Courtesy the Thornton Dial Estate. Photograph
courtesy Stephen Pitkin/Pitkin Studio.

Contents

Note on Terminology and Access ... vii
Preface ... xi
Acknowledgments ... xxiii

Introduction ... 1
Relation ... 1
Left and Limit ... 6
Pre-Positions: Grammar, Independence, and Sovereignty ... 16

PART I: LABOUR, WORK, AND MIDDLE/PASSAGES

1 Conversion ... 41
Land as Labour and Labour as Land ... 41
Pessimisms: Invisible Labour versus Visible Work ... 48
Conversion ... 59
Conclusion ... 78

2 Toward a Middle/Passage Methodology ... 83
Drowning the Limit ... 83
The Atlantic ... 92
Passage as Method ... 101
Conclusion ... 120

PART II: NATIVELY RETHINKING
THE CARIBBEAN RADICAL TRADITION

3   Left Limits and Black Possibilities   125
     Working on Water   *125*
     Rupture and Racial Capital   *135*
     Openings   *142*
     Conclusion   *154*

4   Against the Grain   159
     Resisting Inscription   *159*
     Interventions: C. L. R. James and Walter Rodney   *166*
     Conclusion   *188*

5   "Marxian and Not Marxian": Centering Sylvia Wynter
     in the Radical Tradition   191
     Un/Disciplined   *191*
     An Un/Gendered Critique of Scarcity in Capitalist Political Economy *196*
     Indigeneity as Labour Resistance: The Wynterian Critique of
     Land-Labour   *206*
     Of Skins and "Cenes": Relationality and the Epoch   *215*
     Conclusion   *229*

PART III: RIGHTS AND REPRESENTATIONS

6   Work as Metaphor, Labour as Metonymy   235
     Resisting Hieroglyphs   *235*
     Saving Latitudes   *243*
     Metaphor and Metonymy   *255*
     Conclusion   *267*

     Coda: The *Ark* of Black and Indigenous Labour   271

     Notes   297
     Bibliography   339
     Index   357

Note on Terminology and Access

Throughout this book, the terms *native* and *Indigenous Peoples* designate first peoples of Africa or the Americas (as indicated). For readers unfamiliar with the Caribbean, *Indians* refers to South Asians in the modern era, rather than to Indigenous Peoples, as it does in pre-nineteenth century writing on the region. The latter are instead contemporaneously referred to as *Amerindians*. I retain the word sparingly to avoid confusion. The term *Creoles* refers to all non-Indigenous Caribbean peoples. The concept of Creole Indigeneity, developed in my first book, describes processes of becoming native enacted by the descendants of formerly enslaved and indentured peoples in the Caribbean that rest on the displacement of first peoples in the Americas. Beginning in the introduction, I use the term *involuntary settlers*, rather than migrants or arrivants, to refer to the "non-indigenous, 'settler' populations of largely blacks and South Asians in the Caribbean, designated by native peoples in Guyana, for instance, as 'coastlanders.'"[1] In *Creole Indigeneity: Between Myth and Nation in the Caribbean* (2012), I posited *involuntary settlerhood* as a way of recognizing when Creoles articulate settler logics and have the capacity to deploy settler colonialism's constitutional mechanisms. I acknowledge the specific differences of this settlerhood, in which the alienated labour of those denied human rights and the rights of personhood has to be converted into political right. As applied to the discussion of black labour in the Americas, the specific focus of this book, *involuntary settlerhood* captures the burden of two labours borne by the descendants of Africans brought to the Caribbean and the Americas: their physical labour on the land for the white, settler-master's well-being, and a more profound labour for their own being and belonging. This second labour manipulates and rejects the work black bodies do for white humanity. While this latter labour functions as a locus for their new world indigeneities, those that were bound to their flesh rather than their stars and the land, it is overdetermined by a political economy, regional grammar, and postcolonial legal system that valorizes the first labour, the work for the white settler-master. *Involuntary settlerhood* therefore signals key differences from normative, settler contexts and modes of continuity with white, settler colonial power. I, therefore, distinguish Creole indigeneity and processes of involuntary settlerhood from *Black Indigeneity*, which is theorized throughout as a process of both cleavage and relation.

Throughout, I have avoided using "New World" as much as possible and instead use *Americas* to refer both to Caribbean and Latin American countries, collectively, and, at times, to the hemisphere's countries more broadly. I use the term *error* to refer to the Columbian encounter with the Americas and the Caribbean. In the book, the non-American spelling of *labour* signals the cultural and intellectual tradition that is the point of engagement for this discussion of black diaspora histories of coerced work. Although the book's argument rests on a distinction between labour and work, only in chapter 1 do I begin to unpack and adhere firmly to this distinction. Since the terms *labour* and *work* are technically interchangeable, I italicize them in the later chapters when I need the reader to engage with or read for the distinction. I capitalize *Conversion* and *Elimination* throughout to signal them as definitive processes. I also capitalize *Sovereignty* and *Independence*. The term *middle/passage*, written with an interruption, indicates a strategic difference from normative understandings and articulations of the Middle Passage and Atlantic history.

Finally, as someone living with a disability, I daily navigate around constraints placed on my academic work. In particular, I am limited to material that has no other markings than regular typesetting and that can either be scanned and accessed through OCR or which exists in a format that screen readers recognize. At times, I could not use the original source of a term or consider what would typically be a core or essential work. The most glaring way in which this impacted the book is the lack of a reading of Gerald

Vizenor's *Manifest Manners* and Sylvia Wynter's *Black Metamorphosis*. This limitation was exacerbated by the pandemic. Therefore, I heavily reference digital works such as Kindle editions of books or free online digitized texts. I simply could not consider many works because of this limitation, though they would have made the arguments stronger.

Preface

This project is the second of a three-part exploration of how the legacies of coerced labour in the Caribbean shape the social, cultural, political, and economic dimensions of the antagonism between Creoles and Indigenous Peoples.[2] It emerged from questions raised by my first book, *Creole Indigeneity*, where I outlined a central problem in Caribbean history: how the plantation-based labour of primarily enslaved black and indentured South Asian workers under colonialism became the foundation for Creoles' material and political rights to the postcolonial state. I traced narratives in which Caribbean lands were articulated as the patrimony of modern work on the slave and post-slave plantation. Creoles linked labour—their raison d'être for being in the region—to rights by invoking plantation labour as their own prior time in the Americas to supplant Indigenous rights-claims tied to first occupation and belonging.[3] Colonial labour, therefore, became the basis for *involuntary*, settler modes of (Creole) indigeneity.

What repeatedly surfaced in *Creole Indigeneity* was the excision of Indigenous Peoples from the region's most prominent and well-cited labour histories, particularly those in the black radical tradition. This excision, I suggested, was a key structural element of Creole claims to the independent nation state as an outcome of Creoles' own labour struggle. Since labour is both the reason for the subordination of enslaved and indentured peoples and the pathway to rights in the postcolonial state, the historical and cultural depictions of Indigenous Peoples as non-labourers reinforced their political disenfranchisement. Rather than surplus labour, they are instead *beyond* labour, figuring frequently as objects of international, local, and national governments' development discourses that iterate development as uplift and inclusion.[4] Moreover, the constant imperiling of Indigenous lives on their lands by industry incursion necessary for the national good allows the postcolonial government to reinforce Indigenous lack.

Creoles bear continuing responsibility in Indigenous Peoples' dispossession because they inherited imperial and colonial space clearing, treaty making, geographic circumscription of Indigenous space, and the disavowal of Indigenous kinship's sovereign dimensions as a political structure.[5] In addition to the formal mechanisms constraining Indigenous rights, like Guyana's 2006 Amerindian Act or untitled lands, a key feature of involuntary settlerhood is the deployment of a language of extermination, assimilation, and the superseding of Indigenous Peoples' time. That language retroactively recasts Indigenous extermination and supersession not as moments of imperial conquest but as *the post-contact, post-slavery fulfillment of a historically necessary moment of overcoming pre-contact indigeneity, within which indigeneity must be understood as a failure of labour.*

While for Creoles the nation is an outcome of their ancestors' work (in the colonial period) and their own organized labour struggle (in the early twentieth century), they represent Indigenous labour, in contrast, as having neither such *durée* nor terminus. Such labour has only a mere immediacy or a now that registers as a kind of failure, which manages the threat their status poses as both citizens and external sovereigns of the postcolonial. Indigenous Peoples have always worked (in Guyana, for example). Although, not only do they increasingly occupy civil service positions traditionally held by blacks and South Asians, but they work in mining, logging, farming, tourism, etc.), their underrepresentation in our labour histories means that theirs is not a labour for the nation. As *citizens* (domestic subjects of the postcolonial nation-state), Indigenous Peoples' comparative lack of productivity confirms the inability of the telos of modern capital to capture their labours. As extra or *external sovereigns* (occupying spaces whose abridged sovereignty differs from and exceeds that of the nation-state), their presumed failure limits their freedoms by signaling the underdevelopment of their own titled lands.

What is striking about all of this is that in the twenty-first-century Caribbean, we don't have a comprehensive way of talking about Indigenous Peoples' actual work (past and present) *together with* the collective labour of Creoles. We don't have a way of thinking about Indigenous labour outside the need to manage it and its threat to the postcolonial state's originary fallacy, which is generated out of coloniality and resistance rather than what is prior and parallel to both. Any effort to simply (re)write a labour history cannot utilize an additive model to address Indigenous Peoples' own histories of work. Such a move would reduce indigeneity to similitude, making Indigenous bodily labours accessible only by translation through Creole ones. In short, Indigenous Peoples' legibility as workers would depend on their ability to be read through the same lens as all other workers, and *their purchase* on the modern state would still place them in a position of lack. Moreover, the postcolonial state would become the horizon of their extant, *ante*-colonial sovereignties.

The goal of *Beyond Constraint* is to find a more nuanced way to approach Indigenous labour as a central, constitutive part of regional labour history that allows us to understand political economy more broadly and to formulate methods of study. It engages the interwoven histories and legacies of franchise and settler colonialism to offer a way beyond the impasses of black and Indigenous lives around the entrenched and overlapping dialectics of labour and land, and independence and sovereignty. Exploring critical links between blackness and indigeneity, it brings Caribbean, American, Indigenous, settler colonial, and postcolonial studies together with (black) Atlantic studies, the black radical tradition, and particular philosophical strands within black left studies more broadly.

This work engages Indigenous Studies from the explicitly marked, outside position of a nonnative scholar. I use *us* and *we* throughout to designate both my conjoined authorial subject position and my position as a shifting academic reader interested in black and native studies. I also use *we* at times to refer to the collective subordination of black and native peoples without presuming a native perspective, and primarily in order to diagnose features of the black radical tradition specifically and capitalist political economy generally.[6] Since a critical impasse for black and native studies is our textual traditions—that is, where we would and would not read each other—the book offers deliberate and at times *laboured* readings of texts in black and native studies by Caribbean, North American, and other writers, showing just how they have been speaking and can continue to speak to each other. In these readings, I intensively trace my arguments to show divergences and profound alignments between black and native thought.

Like the groundbreaking *Crossing Waters, Crossing Worlds* and more recent works like *Otherwise Worlds*, in this book I am interested in how blacks and Indigenous Peoples relate to each other, where *we* have been forced into antagonism, and where we can begin to create new epistemologies and methods for our scholarship and interactions, particularly around labour and anticapitalist critique. This book does the difficult work of facing both anti-indigeneity in black studies and anti-blackness in Indigenous Studies: the epistemological resuscitation of the very political and economic structures governing our mutual subordination. *Beyond Constraint* indeed moves us beyond the limits imposed by our mutual histories of violent oppression and the academic conventions requiring us to reencounter and redeploy that violence as the absolute breach of our relation.

Beyond Constraint is neither a recovery of postcolonialism, a defense of Afropessimism, an embrace of black optimism, nor an endorsement or rejection of anticapitalist, Marxist critique. It is meant simply as a tool for survival and the breath we were so violently denied under settler colonialism in both its normative and involuntary forms. As I have argued elsewhere, not only were captured and enslaved blacks stolen from the lands they were on; those lands now exist for their descendants only on our skin, and our violent disciplining is the constant forcing of us into and onto our skins. What is urgently needed for blacks is an unfolding into spaces and lands that can house the centuries of packed earth in our flesh: our new breath. However, this unfolding can happen neither on settler lands nor without deference to, respect for, and restoration of Indigenous Peoples' prior sovereignties, which exceed *all* forms of settler right. Our task, then, is as much about challenging global anti-blackness and rejecting settler power as it is about supporting Indigenous sovereignties on a wider scale.

The book is divided into three parts. Its principal intervention is staged in part I, "Labour, Work, and Middle/Passages," which turns to the religious concept of Conversion as an economic analytic to elaborate what I refer to in shorthand as the labour-work dialectic in the Caribbean. That analysis leads to *Beyond Constraint*'s four key arguments, of which two are discussed in part I: First, Conversion was not strictly a religious phenomenon that supported the profit motives of the Catholic Church or the would-be empires of Spain and Portugal in the Americas. It is, instead, a structural element in the institution of a formal split between visible, productive work and invisible, unproductive labour, within which black and Indigenous Peoples, respectively, come to be located. Conversion is, in short, the first formative elaboration of the labour-work divide in the Americas, pitting black and native lives in opposition around labour and land, respectively. This delinking of unproductive labour and productive work is an originary break serving as the wedge between blackness and indigeneity, on the one hand, and independence and sovereignty as the opposed political horizons of blacks and Indigenous Peoples, on the other. In identifying this strategic and historical delinking of *unproductive labour and productive work*, I produce a recuperative method for a regional political economy within which we can read Creole and Indigenous labour together. The second principal argument of part I is that we need to resist the (black) Atlantic and dominant readings of the Middle Passage that sustain this formative break between productive work and unproductive labour. We need to rethink the Middle Passage as a singular origin for enslaved (and indentured) labour, or as originating with black transit across the Atlantic. Instead, the Middle Passage not only begins with Indigenous Peoples; that beginning should be the interpretive lens for later black, chattel movements, and a *continuing* point of entanglement of black and native lives and labours.

Chapter 1, "Conversion," rejects the dominant claim that Indigenous Peoples disappeared from plantation labour—and hence from the history of work in the region—because they were replaced by enslaved and indentured labour. Instead, it argues that Indigenous, post-contact labour vanishes from labour history because it is delinked from the category of just, unfree (or justly bound) labour and sutured permanently with Conversion, the religious-ontological function of the Columbian-era discoveries. As a religious imperative, Conversion fulfills an extractive or devaluing economic function, making Indigenous lands valuable *over* Indigenous bodies, while Indigenous actions are devalued as spiritual *labours*. In contrast, blacks are linked with the Middle Passage, a process that adds value, making their bodies worth more than the lands from which they were stolen. These twin poles of the Atlantic economy (Conversion and the Middle Passage) separate black and Indigenous labours in perpetuity. Moreover, *both* blacks and Indigenous Peoples are involved in processes of adding *and* subtracting value. Both are embedded in Conversion processes *and* middle/passages oriented around the ability to be converted from and to something else.

Conversion is the process that institutes a structural break between productive work and unproductive labour in the Americas, putting in place the labour-work dialectic necessary to proto-capital accumulation. I use Afropessimist and black optimist critical thought to read this distinction between labour and work in Hannah Arendt's critique of Karl Marx. I argue that the labour-work dialectic is *prior* to the land-labour break that disarticulates native and black lives. Initiated at conquest, this dialectic aligns blacks with (regimes of) productive work and Indigenous Peoples with unproductive labours. It is the structural opposition of anti-blackness to anti-indigeneity, which generates and sustains the antagonisms of land *and* labour and Sovereignty *and* Independence. It is also fundamental to the form that global capital will ultimately take, depending not just on black and native subordination, but crucially on the relation of anti-blackness to anti-indigeneity, and hence to the disarticulation of our struggles for freedom. Without the relation of these antagonisms, capitalism loses its accumulative structures and foundational gestures of separating what is productive (and hence can be/come sovereign *after* conquest) from what is not (which resists settler sovereignties tied to work/accumulation). In examining the labour-work dialectic, I use contemporary approaches to primitive accumulation, suggesting that we can rethink labour and land as the purportedly separate spheres of blackness and indigeneity. This allows for recognition of how both Indigenous Peoples and blacks are subjected to common processes of Conversion (the ability to be converted from and to value), and to Elimination as both endure forms of (land) dispossession and (labour) exploitation. Elimination and Death, then, are not the singularly distinct, respective spheres of indigeneity and blackness. Instead, they must be understood in terms of exchange and continuity between initiative and punitive forms of Death/death that sustain anti-indigeneity and anti-blackness as the elaboration of the labour-work divide. By tracking the dialectic as both a structural element of accumulation regimes and the limit of political-economic critique, the chapter sets the stage for confronting the constraints of political economy for representing black labour and recovering Indigenous labour in later chapters.

In contrast to dominant ways of thinking the Atlantic and the Middle Passage as part of its formal constitution (i.e., the relation between process and outcome), chapter 2, "Toward a Middle/Passage Methodology," reads the Middle Passage in terms of its central function, Conversion, arguing that not only blacks undergo a Middle Passage, but so do Indigenous Peoples. Moreover, Indigenous enslavement is a recursively generative context for black enslavement in the Americas. Recognizing the *prior* occurrence of the "wake" and the "hold" for Indigenous Peoples shifts us away from dominant approaches that either omit Indigenous Peoples from Atlantic history or approach them only through the dialectic, including their actions through translation or Conversion. Instead, the chapter reads for the Conversion processes that shape the middle/passage crossings or entanglements of blacks and Indigenous peoples. Understanding Conversion's complexity as the formative structure of the Middle Passage, I suggest, allows us to begin reading

Indigenous labour back into Caribbean history as the history not only of a forgotten Atlantic but of the *first* Atlantic *and* a parallel, contiguous, and continuous mode of work that strategically undoes the telos of the Atlantic proper.

This middle/passage methodology, or reading for *plural* crossings, circumvents the breaches of grammar and time that have disarticulated black, South Asian, and native labour history in the Caribbean, creating a condition of possibility for reading them together. Moreover, if, as critics have suggested, the Middle Passage is interminable for blacks, it is also interminable for Indigenous Peoples, constituting the perpetual Conversion and entanglement of both groups although the contemporaneous middle/passages they endure control blackness and indigeneity for different reasons: for the being of the human same, and to control the sovereign occurrence of non-settler (Indigenous) labours, respectively. The middle/passage, which I write with a pause to signal a distinction from dominant thinking, is what I suggest must literally become the method for our approaches to (labour) history. Passage (i.e., perpetual, epiphenomenal rather than unidirectional crossing) becomes a method through which to read the perpetual entanglement of blackness and indigeneity instead of what have normatively been understood as the breaks between them. Passage, as an alternative way of reading history, thus elaborates our labours and our freedoms in terms of their co-relation.

In part 2, "Natively Rethinking the Caribbean Radical Tradition," I elaborate the book's third major argument: the radical tradition does not deliberately exclude Indigenous Peoples' labour. Rather, their excision results from the affirmation—in works by authors from C. L. R. James to Walter Rodney—of this break between productive work and unproductive labour as a structural element of labour analysis in the region. Until we see how the dialectic operates in the tradition and reject its strategic delinking of our bodily labours, it will remain an impasse for black-native relations in postcolonial and settler states. This part identifies and works through the lingering tensions in the radical tradition between resistant black labours and those labours that were necessary for the colonizer's (white) humanity. These tensions mean that the tradition retains an epistemological account of labour that depends on, and therefore must reproduce, the labour-work break as coextensive with the labour category itself. Ultimately, I demonstrate how the tradition remains open to black and American Indigenous labour despite extant limitations.

Chapter 3, "Left Limits and Black Possibilities," is the first of three chapters to effect a new reading of the radical tradition. It identifies sites of rupture and opening, allowing us to move beyond both the anti-blackness of the labour category and the anti-indigeneity of black left critique. The chapter focuses on close readings of the tensions in Cedric Robinson's *Black Marxism* because he explicitly articulates the tradition in and for itself without reinscribing the labour-work dialectic at key moments, while accounting for (black) indigeneity rather than focusing singularly on black oppression or enslavement as the origin for the radical tradition. These moments or openings are Elimination, Time and Marronage. Robinson's work is critical in demonstrating that to the extent that we see Indigenous Elimination and black Death as the separate spheres of Settler and Franchise colonialism, respectively, we reinforce the break between Exploitation (accumulative work) and Dispossession (unproductive land) undergirding the labour-work divide, which produces anti-blackness and anti-indigeneity as structurally necessary for capital accumulation and to each other. My first intervention in Robinson demonstrates that Elimination is a form of perpetual death that moves across both settler and extractive colonialisms, preventing the re-installation of either bodily or land-based sovereignties. Robinson offers, I also argue, a critical recovery of black labour *before* black work in the resistance of proletarianization as the conscription of blackness for political representation.

Through Robinson's work, I argue that the radical tradition comprises two strands: one affirming black radical critique of capital and the ontological break between the black and the human on which accumulation is based, and another opening toward indigeneity and parallel forms of labour that are not *only* routed through this critique. I also call for resituating enslaved labours in terms of Indigenous Peoples' sovereign labour rather than those of the settler desire that still lingers in the black left's political economic critique. By identifying possibilities for alternative accounts of labour to emerge, the chapter reads *for* the middle/passages within *Black Marxism* that link black and native labour both before and after their conversion(s). The goal is to suggest how the forms of freedom imagined by the black left can resist its sometimes implicit rejection of Indigenous Peoples' non-accumulative labours as the *occurrence* of their sovereignties.

Chapter 4, "Against the Grain," uses this middle/passage strategy of reading for openings in the radical tradition to approach select works by the Caribbean labour historians C. L. R. James and Walter Rodney. This alternative reading of their texts allows us to work through and beyond the limiting pre-positional structure of Caribbean historical materialism; to recover more complex, expansive concepts of the *worker*; and to confront *work* as a unit of analysis in its overrepresentation as time, (productive) land, and social-economic structure. I argue that despite its closures, Rodney's work radically helps to recover the figure of the worker for liberation from both black *D*eath and Indigenous *d*eath because it rescues the category for blacks and Indigenous Peoples from its point of overdetermination by anti-blackness and anti-indigeneity. Reading these texts against the grain allows us to recover a broader view of labour, which shows how the region's black radical tradition not only can speak *to* and *with* the history of Indigenous labour, but also remains critical to current conceptualizations of possibilities for anticapitalist black freedoms and anti-settler Indigenous sovereignties.

Chapter 5, "'Marxian and Not Marxian': Centering Sylvia Wynter in the Radical Tradition," argues that the greatest possibility for thinking Indigenous labour in the radical tradition lies in the weaver, dancer, and philosopher Sylvia Wynter's work.[7] Despite Wynter's fundamental goal to elaborate the conditions of possibility for (and sustaining) *economic* man, and although Marxism serves as an incredibly generative source in her work, Caribbean Studies scholarship has often refused to see her as part of the radical tradition. This chapter suggests that she should be included. It traces Wynter's critique of capitalist political economy to three elements of this project: scarcity, land-labour and primitive accumulation, and black resistance and Death. Mindful of Wynter's work at the edge of the radical tradition, the chapter argues for a cautionary inclusion that recognizes the material critique throughout Wynter's work while recognizing where her critique exceeds and hence partially refuses the black radical tradition, which thus cannot serve as a singular space of interpreting her work.

Finally, the chapter considers openings to indigeneity in Robinson, James, Rodney, and Wynter in light of current discussions of abstract versus concrete labour, black Marxism's future, and the rise of the Capitalocene as an analytic. Thus, while recognizing possibility, the chapter proceeds cautiously, elaborating how this recuperation of the radical tradition *for* indigeneity may risk incorporation into the Anthropocene-Capitalocene debate, that epochal shift (of the last twenty years) in thinking about capital and labour. While this debate reiterates Arendt's planetary concerns, it produces new closures of capital formation by capital's autopoiesis, threatening to reinscribe the big time of capital for all dissident, radical, and still emergent strains of political economy. In addition, the debate risks misreading this recovery of Indigenous labour as though the reading itself were a logical outcome or evolutionary stage of the critique of capital *for* its own sake, rather than for sovereignty. In other words, the debate potentially repositions critique as a new inscription of capital's grammars. The chapter thus looks at these epochal ways of imagining capital's terminus (or "cenes"), opposing them to the refusal of (Fanonian) "skins," or racial capital discussions, together with the Indigenous praxis of "grounded relationality" as a new way of locating and extending this alternative, imaginatively open reading of the black radical tradition. It offers a partial critique of where the appropriation of black strategies of ontological refusal for Indigenous sovereignty risk reinscribing anti-blackness as a critical element.

Beyond Constraint's final argument, in part III, "Rights and Representations," attends to metaphor and metonymy as structures of simulation. It explores when Indigenous labour is doubled or repeated in the land as an expression of Indigenous Peoples' own sovereignty, and when it is doubled and deferred, or read out of the land, in a structural antagonism supporting postcolonial state sovereignties. Attention to the symbolic in this section returns us to previous chapters' discussions of Conversion, the labour-work dialectic, and the settler-master, illuminating the libidinal composition of the division between blacks and Indigenous Peoples. I argue that revisiting the labour-work dialectic as a libidinal structure is critical for understanding how and why settler desire is sustained across time within the global class system, postcolonial political economy, and the radical tradition even when we seek formally to work against it.

Chapter 6, "Work as Metaphor, Labour as Metonymy," formally shifts the discussion to representation by addressing the reproduction or doubling of indigeneity and Indigenous labour. By doubling, I refer to understandings of Indigenous labour not in its immediate context, but in terms of its extraction and re-presentation in other symbolic fields meant to constrain Indigenous sovereignty. This is the logical outcome of the labour-work divide within which Indigenous labour was only visible (read: productive) when it was represented in terms that could be understood in early Atlantic economies.

After establishing how legal and constitutional structures use simulation to constrain Indigenous sovereignty as state-granted rights, the chapter explores how Indigenous Peoples represent or double their *own* sovereign labours by examining one contemporary form of labour by Indigenous Peoples in Guyana: digital mapping of their lands. It centers mapping as one critical way in which Indigenous labour (and land) is doubled, repeated, or represented on its own terms outside the forms of similitude or (metaphoric) doubling required by the labour-work dialectic and its extractive or appropriative logics. The chapter centers one of the 2015 Equator Prize winners, the South Central People's Development Association, a federation of Wapichan Peoples communities in Guyana. It demonstrates that the prize works as an autopoietic moment of capital's attempt to reinscribe the sovereign labours involved in digital mapping within the logic of outcomes driving capital accumulation and re-presentation/re-production. In this case, environmentalism and its savior narratives newly constrain Indigenous sovereignty. However, I suggest that like other Indigenous digital mapping projects, the Wapichan project reflects a strategic *doubling* of their own pre-contact sovereign labours, so their mapping repeats sovereignty's *occurrence* rather than performs a singularly object-oriented act. It is difficult to approach or read this work on its own terms precisely because it is always subject to Conversion, and hence made available or visible through the representative strategies supporting capital accumulation. Thus, to recover this labour as that which can be represented within the radical tradition but *not* converted to it, we must confront both its point of tense incorporation into the labour-work dialectic *and* its absolute difference from the bodily actions that can be represented by the dialectic.

Overall, the chapter focuses on the dialectic's work as a symbolic order or semiotic practice to bring forward conquistador-settler desire from the colonial to the postcolonial period, to continuously reinscribe all bodily actions as manageable, no matter how resistant or contrary. I rely on post-structuralist discussions of psychoanalysis as a semiotic practice to demonstrate how the dialectic works as a symbolic order supporting settler grammars' pre-positional structure (see the introduction) through processes of similarity or metaphor like the law, and processes of contiguity or metonymy like the Equator and similar prizes. I posit that although metaphor is the terrain of work and metonymy that of labour, we can recover Indigenous actions for sovereignty in metonymy only up to a point because it manages, and makes acceptable, the prohibited desire for anti-human domination structures as necessary for the human. The chapter underscores the labour-work dialectic as a relation of incorporation based on metaphor and metonymy, with the latter as the always incomplete point of integration of indigeneity's sovereign occurrences of labour. Therefore, the conquistadorial habit or desire *for* the human forces us to repeat and reinstitute the labour-work dialectic as a structure of anti-blackness and anti-indigeneity in the service of Creole Independence as a form of freedom against Indigenous Sovereignty.

The Coda, "The *Ark* of Black and Indigenous Labour," looks toward extant, imagined possibilities for black labour that do not require such contingency and deferral, placing this labour in relation to that of Indigenous Peoples. I read together the artistic production of three artists: the indigenous, Macushi former teacher George Tancredo, Caribbean American Jean-Michel Basquiat, and the African American Thornton Dial. I argue that the diasporic, black aesthetic tradition offers ways of reading black labour in terms of its openings to indigeneity. The impetuses for this coda are two: an exhibit of Tancredo's balata sculptures in Guyana, which I visited in 2018, and my visit to the coincidental, 2006 exhibition of both Basquiat and Dial's works at the Museum of Fine Arts in Houston, Texas. Basquiat is famous for his postmodern, neoexpressionist drawings and paintings, and has been described as a postcolonial, Afrofuturistic artist. By contrast, Dial, a former farmworker, carpenter, bricklayer, welder, and steelworker, is known for mixed-media creations that have at times been dubbed "folk," "spiritual," and postmodern. The productive disjuncture between Dial's heavy materialism, reflecting both field and factory work, and Basquiat's semiotic wilderness reveals ways of imagining black enslaved and post-slavery labour outside their teleological capture by the nation-state and the limits of late capital. Both artists offer decidedly more than anticapitalist approaches to blackness, slavery, and what, after Basquiat, I refer to as the *Ark* of black labour. They offer new ways of understanding the non-accumulative ends of black labour and new languages for its representation. More importantly, they open up alternatives to labour relations presented as closed off to indigeneity and the possibility of a universal sovereignty. This opening created by Dial and Basquiat allows us to both resist the conscription of Tancredo's labour in the dialectic and place the recurrence of sovereign black labour in dialogue with sovereign Indigenous labour against the grain of their conversion. Together, Tancredo, Dial, and Basquiat show us what black and Indigenous sovereign labour practice can look like.

Acknowledgments

Although this work is primarily in support of the rights of the Wai Wais, Macushis, Wapichan, Potomonas, Lokono, Caribs, Arecunas, Akawaios, and Warraus in Guyana, most of it was drafted on the original homelands of the Tonkawa, Tawakoni, Hueco, Sana, Wichita, and Coahuiltecan in Texas. This is land on which Texas A&M retains the statue of Confederate general Lawrence Sullivan Ross, thereby relying on the role of the symbolic in supporting the violent inscription of politics and right over sovereignty, and reinforcing anti-indigeneity and anti-blackness as structurally necessary to the foundation of the University and its systemic function to reproduce inequality, Elimination, and Death.

Some of the ideas in the book have been presented as papers on various panels: "Natively Rethinking the Black Radical Tradition in the Caribbean" on the panel "Of Blackness, Indigeneity, and Relations of Study" at the Native American and Indigenous Studies Association meeting (Los Angeles, 2018); "Conversion" on the panel "Archipelagic Assemblages, Colonial Entanglements: Rethinking American Studies" at the American Studies Association meeting (Chicago, 2017); "Postcolonial Biopolitics and the Hieroglyphs of Democracy" on the panel "Colonial Agnosia and Biopolitics" at the American Studies Association meeting (Denver, 2016); and "Basquiat after Dial: Bridging the Gap between Black Labor and Critique" on the panel "Afrofuturism" at the American Studies Association meeting (Baltimore 2011). Portions of the book have also been presented at the following invited talks and plenaries: "Work and Water Thinking Indigenous Labour With/In the Radical Tradition" for the Society of Fellows in the Humanities at the Heyman Center at Columbia University (April 2021); "Two Lies and a Truth" at the Harvard University American Studies Workshop (December 2020); "Grammar and Sovereignty" at the Futures of American Studies Institute at Dartmouth University (June 2019); "Middle Passages" for the Department of English and Film Studies at the University of Alberta (October 2018); "Postcolonial Theory" for the Modern Critical Theory Lecture Series of the Unit for Criticism and Interpretive Theory at the University of Illinois, Urbana-Champaign (October 2018); and "'Torpid Creatures' and 'Docible' Bodies: Understanding Indigeneity and Settler Colonialism in the Caribbean" for the Indigenous Geographies and Caribbean Feminisms: Common Struggles against Global Capitalism conference held at the Institute for Gender and Development Studies at the University of the West Indies in Trinidad (March–April 2017). Ideas from the manuscript have been presented at the following discussions or roundtables: at the roundtable on Black Studies and humanism at the Society for Phenomenology and Existential Philosophy (September 2021); at the Blackness and Indigeneity panel discussion for the Black Studies Project at University of California, San Diego (May 2021); "Indigeneity, Settler Colonialism, and the Political Economy of Becoming" as part of the Critical Conversations in Chicano and Latino Studies Speaker Series at the University of Minnesota (February 2017); at the Sawyer Seminar: Interrogating the Plantationocene, at the Center for the Humanities at the University of Wisconsin-Madison (March 2019); and at the roundtable "Other Intimacies: Black Studies Notes on Native/Indigenous Studies" at the American Studies Association in Honolulu, Hawaiʻi (November 2019). Ideas from the book have been or will be published as the following: "Killing *Us* Softly: Conversion and the Arc of Black Death in the Americas" in *Atzlán: A Journal of Chicano Studies* (Fall 2021); "The 'Inadequacies of Marxism' or Black Labor's Pessimism" in "Introduction" to special issue 96 of *International Labor and Working-Class History* on Blackness and Labor in the Afterlives of Racial Slavery (Fall 2019); "Colonialism" in *Keywords for African American Studies* (2018); "Postcolonial Biopolitics and the Hieroglyphs of Democracy" in *Biopolitics-Geopolitics-Life: Settler States and Indigenous Presence* (2023); and "Indigeneity and African Belonging in the New World" in UNESCO General History of the African Diaspora (forthcoming).

I thank the anonymous readers who suggested directions for the development of the manuscript. Thanks to Marilyn Dumont and Stephanie Pruitt

Gaines for permission to reproduce their work. Thanks also to the estate of Thornton Dial, particularly to his grandson, Brandon Dial. Mark Rifkin gave me the courage to seek out a contract and Kyla Tompkins the courage to put my ideas in the world. Jodi Melamed and Angela Pulley Hudson graciously read and commented on an early draft of the proposal. In suggesting a topical and comprehensive list of readings for another project, Josefina Saldaña-Portillo contributed tremendously to revision of chapter 1 and 2. April Hatfield did a thorough and generous reading of chapter 2, providing me with additional sources to strengthen the arguments there. I thank Franco Barchiesi who offered incredibly perceptive and nuanced feedback on chapters 3 and 4. I thank Jodi A. Byrd for the example of her work and for her feedback, and Carole Boyce Davies for insisting that I add a chapter on Sylvia Wynter. I am grateful to Anitra Grisales for editing an early version of the manuscript. All faults and errors that persist, however, are my own. I am sincerely grateful to those who have invited me to share this work along the way, either as a talk or in print, particularly Gabrielle Hosein and Levi Gahman, Keavy Martin and Michael Litwack, Fernando Montero Castrillo, Ricardo L. Ortiz, Michael Ortiz, Yareli Castro-Sevilla, Eve O'Connor, Sandra Harvey, Helen Fielding, Elizabeth Maddock Dillon, Don Pease, Bianet Castellanos, Roderick A. Ferguson, Jeffrey Ogbar, Erica R. Edwards, Alyosha Goldstein, René Dietrich, Kerstin Knopf, Simón V. Trujillo, and Shaista Patel. Thanks to the amazing women whom I had the pleasure of meeting and spending time with—Jean La Rose, J. Sharon Atkinson, Faye Fredericks, Annelita Garcia, Paulette Jacobs, Jacqueline Allicock, Vanda Radzik, Christina Coc—at the Indigenous Geographies and Caribbean Feminisms Symposium in Trinidad in 2017. I thank Joseph Jewell for being a consummate writing companion even as he experienced his own slow loss, and for the Historical Studies in Race and Ethnicity writing group that he convened. I thank its members for their constant presence and encouragement. My editor, Courtney Berger, in addition to her reading and commenting on the manuscript, guided its completion with compassion and patience.

I have been working on *Beyond Constraint* steadily since 2014, though some of the coda was drafted and presented in 2011. The road to its completion, however, has been long and difficult, with a series of debilitating bouts of illness compounded by how the realities of race (and gender) shaped my (in)ability to secure care. As I lay ill, unable to get back to a nearly fully drafted manuscript for months, returning to it only after the murders of George Floyd and Breonna Taylor, and in the midst of the outsized share of death meted out to black, Latinx, and Indigenous Peoples in the COVID-19 pandemic, aspects of the project changed as well as its meaning and urgency. My return to this manuscript was literally in the wake of the quotidian realities of the violence of anti-blackness and the structural violence of the lack of care for aberrant minorities. As I recovered some of my health in the spring and fall of 2020, two texts sustained me and gave me the courage to keep working: Leanne Betasamosake Simpson's *As We Have Always Done* and Frank Wilderson's *Afropessimism*. Without these works and both their forms of truth telling and refusal (and something not like space clearing but a provision of language for the famished), I would not have had the courage to finish. This book, however, would not be in the world without the dedicated and selfless work of my father, Peter Jackson, and my dearest friend, Yael Ben-zvi, who helped me during the last stages of preparing the manuscript for submission. Yael Ben-zvi, Yael Ronen, Faedra Carpenter, Rumya Putcha, Kimberly N. Brown, my brother Shevon Jackson and his wife Yulissa, and Karina Cespedes have all in the course of the loss of self and wholeness that I face shown me extraordinary black girl love. I thank Vismita, Ranjeet, Doug, Jill, Shruti, Prashant, and Sejal for their support. I thank my mom, Jennifer Jackson, for spending months taking care of me as well as my spouse, Robert F. Carley. They both gave of themselves more than they had.

Finally, as with my first book, many family members passed away during its completion, with six alone between November 2020 and August 2021. I am deeply grateful for the care of two in particular, my aunt and uncle, Basil and Evelyn London, who sheltered generations of us moving into the uncertainty of diaspora. Their loss and that of my Aunt Sheila Jackson have been the hardest to bear. This work is for my children, Akir and Amina (Dirty Forever!), and always for Sylvia Wynter, my mentor and friend.

Introduction

Relation

Beyond Constraint: Middle/Passages of Blackness and Indigeneity in the Radical Tradition addresses the excision of Indigenous labour from the Anglophone Caribbean's radical tradition. It examines its root causes in the historical anti-blackness *and* anti-indigeneity of the labour category in political-economic critique that haunts black radical genealogies of Marxism. As a theoretical project, the book seeks to recover Indigenous labour in the tradition from the very point of its foreclosure. *Beyond Constraint* argues that recasting our collective histories and political horizons requires not only developing new approaches to our critiques of capitalist political economy, but also interrogating the flaws and limitations of our base assumptions and categories of analysis. By examining what the labour category *excludes* and hence what labour history can *include*, this project rethinks the black radical tradition, whose origins and reflective articulation emerged in Caribbean discourse as a formative site where Indigenous labour has been eclipsed.

In the Caribbean, the radical tradition must work against its foundational association of Indigenous Peoples with unproductive land, which begins to be transformed only with the importation of productive, enslaved black labour, and the later introduction of indentured South Asian labour. This association sustains a dialectic of land and labour whose establishment instituted proto-capitalist labour coercion tied to regimes of accumulation that positioned indigeneity as labour's excess. It is this excess that must be recentered in a new rereading of our historical involvements. The book is not a history, but argues instead for the *possibility* of a new labour history that stretches the concept of labour within the radical tradition and beyond the limits of the postcolonial state. Such a reading necessarily also stretches the concept of land, positioning Indigenous Peoples *within* the very place they have been denied: the radical tradition.[1] Therefore, the book's approach to regional Caribbean labour history and political economy expands our configuration of both labour *and* what we observe as the objects, economies, and sociopolitical structures in which it is congealed.

As an interdisciplinary project situated at the nexus of black, Indigenous, settler, and postcolonial studies as well as literary and social science methodologies, *Beyond Constraint* reframes the black radical tradition in the Caribbean by asking two questions. First, where and how is Indigenous labour made unthinkable by black labour? Second, how are postcolonial Independence and Indigenous Sovereignty moved into antagonism by the legacies of settler and franchise (or extractive) colonialism?[2] The book's larger social and political aim is to upend labour's role in the material and political disenfranchisement of Indigenous Peoples and to shift the political calculus of Caribbean postcolonial states by recognizing that in addition to deriving rights from what is referred to as prior arrival, Indigenous Peoples also have a place in Caribbean history and Atlantic history more broadly as its *first* workers/labourers.[3] Rejecting the Middle Passage and Kala Pani, respectively, in their overexpression as singularities of black and Indian death and rebirth in and through modern work, I argue that the Middle Passage can be rethought as the time-space of black-native engagement (as a *middle/passage* of relation) and as a method for reading our histories together.

Such a method would account for colonial and plantation-era work in the Caribbean and for Indigenous Peoples' labours and labour history, inclusive of their ante- *and* anti-plantation dimensions. I do not suggest that enslaved and indentured peoples' historical work does not matter, nor seek to reduce Indigenous presence in the Americas and the Caribbean to their modern labour on or off plantations, nor suggest that this expansive approach to labour is antithetical to Indigenous sovereignty based on traditional or customary rights. I hope to provide a way of approaching our histories that better represents those they marginalize. Across the region and with few exceptions, we have staked our political futures on a limited account of our collective bodily actions within and across time: the time of the plantation and its aftermath. Recovering prior and concurrent disavowed actions allows the language of contemporary rights claims to be rendered more equitably and capaciously beyond the settler logics and legal mechanisms they often resuscitate or sustain.

This project contributes to growing efforts in American, Indigenous, and Black Diaspora studies to create sustained epistemological room for dialogue and action outside frameworks that reproduce the very marginalizations they were initially developed to address. It is positioned alongside writings by Jodi Byrd, Kyle T. Mays, Jodi Melamed, Glen Coulthard, Iyko Day, and others who work in and at the intersections of these fields, rethinking the links and ruptures among slavery and settler colonialism, "anti-black racialization," colonization, (state's) rights, and Indigenous sovereignties.[4] In resisting the ways in which the legacies of slavery and genocide continuously set black and native experiences apart, Tiffany Lethabo King writes that "neither has edges. . . . Each form of violence has its own way of contaminating, haunting, touching, caressing, and whispering to the other."[5] This project is in dialogue with hers and other works such as Lisa Lowe's on the imbricated historical structures of racialization and colonization.[6] By reading the radical tradition in terms of not only its closures to but also its non-reductive openings to indigeneity, the project is further linked to critical moves in Indigenous Studies such as *Social Text*'s special issue, "Economies of Dispossession," which aims "to differentiate those forms of inquiry attentive to the dynamics of co-constitution, interaction, and friction from those conventional methods of comparison—comparative literature, comparative politics, and so forth—that insist upon disconnection and equivalence as their point of analytic departure."[7] Not only do the authors not reduce, for instance, black racialization to its intelligibility *through* Indigenous Studies (in parallel with this project's own goal not to have black studies be the interpretive ground for native experience). In keeping with this attempt to think settler and franchise colonialism together, they reframe colonialism as "an ongoing relation of theft, displacement, foreclosure, and violence that cannot be reduced to one determinate relation to racialization."[8] This expansive, relational definition of colonialism is necessary to understand projects like this, which reject the seeming experiential and epistemological disarticulation of black slavery and native genocide.

This effort to move *through* the impasse of labour—configured in extant histories and methodologies as the fissure between (state) Independence and Indigenous Sovereignty—and postcoloniality and decolonization augments current discourses on racial capital that continue to neglect Indigenous labour. While some projects, like King's, effectively reject the overrepresentation of black bodies as labouring bodies, we still need to fully understand the mechanisms that make labour the definitive break between black and native peoples and disappear native labour as a sovereign practice, as well as how to recover and represent *native* labour within the Caribbean radical tradition. Overall, *Beyond Constraint* offers an approach to Indigenous labours past and present so they can be read outside their artificial antagonism with black (and South Asian) labours. This intervention confronts continuing constraints on Indigenous self-determination and the increasingly thanatopolitical consequences of the region's modern labour history and coloniality for Indigenous and non-Indigenous subjects of the Caribbean state. It centers questions about native sovereignty as a politically, economically, socially, and ethically necessary goal of political-economic methodologies that develop out of our plantation-based histories. It demands an account of labour history that acknowledges Indigenous Peoples' labour and rights that derive from *both* prior and continuous sovereignty in the region. Its attempt to rethink labour's possibilities and shortcomings shifts us from the limits of emancipatory politics to the possibilities of sovereign ones.

This book finds that the limit point of indigeneity in the radical tradition expresses a historical relationship between anti-blackness to anti-indigeneity that emerges in the sixteenth century as structurally necessary to both (proto) capital accumulation *and* the language and terminology of capital's critiques. This relational anti-blackness and anti-indigeneity is the arrangement of black and native bodies to the logics of scarcity and abundance through Conversion as both a religious *and* economic phenomenon. To perpetually achieve accumulation and hence meet and manage the desires of both the explorer-conquistador (in their evolution into proto-master and proto-settler) and the sovereign, Conversion establishes a labour-work dialectic. The dialectic places blacks and Indigenous Peoples on opposite sides of work in the Americas. It sustains the evolutionary expression of conquistadorial desire in its material and unconscious expressions, its acceptable and unacceptable functions within social and economic structures in the global class system, and has historically delinked black identities from native ones. The dialectic literally splits the labour category, fixing black and native bodies into a mode of perpetual conversion and exchange. Since the dialectic is intrinsic to both the practice of accumulation and the labour category in political and economic critique, the latter must also function as a scene of libidinal fulfillment for settler-master desire. Finally, the dialectic is central to the biopolitical break between "right" and "sovereignty" in the postcolonial state. That break consolidates the transformation of economic into political right that undergirds Creole sovereignty as a still partial expression of conquistadorial cum settler-master desire necessary for maintaining a mode of power requiring the subordination of Indigenous right.

Beyond Constraint illuminates this problem and offers the middle/passage as a method of reading against the grain of the historical and ongoing conversion of black and native labours and lives for capitalist political economy. It deploys a middle/passage reading to move beyond black Death and native Elimination as they are configured or engineered by the dialectic as the separate, unbridgeable dimensions of our subordination. Across the project, particularly in the first two parts, I suggest that the middle/passage is a space of relation for blacks and Indigenous Peoples and theorize black Death and native Elimination as co-constitutive, relational, and unbound by time. While maintaining Afropessimism's ontological distinction between Death and Elimination, I slightly redefine both in keeping with my reformulation of land *as* labour in order to understand them as a point of middle/passage relation. In this formulation, Elimination is the clearing of the land *from Indigenous bodies*, and Death is the clearing of the land *from black bodies*. Both are what I call *initiative* deaths: the former produces the black enslaved person for work, and the latter makes the land available for settler accumulation. Both deaths are necessary for accumulation as both are managed by the labour-work dialectic that ceaselessly converts black and native labours into their accumulative forms.

I argue, however, that both deaths also have *punitive* forms. Therefore, Elimination operates in the franchise colony (or on any former chattel populations and their descendants, for example, the victims of the Tulsa massacre) to keep blacks from re-entrenching their labour as sovereignty in the land. Death, on the other hand, operates in the settler colony to remove the land from native bodies (e.g., Indian schools) so those bodies cannot impede settler accumulation when native peoples hold onto land that settlers want. These bodies are made available both in conjunction with forms of coerced labour *and* after. If we understand this ongoing structural relation of Death and Elimination, the book argues, then we also understand how black and native pasts and futures remain significantly intertwined. This introductory chapter configures the impasse between blackness and indigeneity in radical, black anticapitalist critique delimiting its constitutive concepts of Independence and Sovereignty. It lays the groundwork for conceptually linking settler colonialism and black enslavement for franchise colonialism as a first step in moving beyond the ways in which capital's real and epistemological structures not only are obscured, but also overdetermine blacks as labour and natives as land and then force us to theorize land (native)/labour (black) outside their fundamental, continued relation.

Left and Limit

In rereading seminal works and authors in the radical tradition, this book engages the black left from the constraint of history, rather than turning to creative or cultural texts that may engage more expansively with indigeneity. I do this because the twentieth-century collective anticolonial and anticapitalist labour struggles that emerged across the Caribbean as a key feature of bids for Independence, the activist writing that captured these struggles, and the histories of enslavement and indenture all directly engaged and reimagined left accounts of exploitation and liberation. They also often embraced socialist principles of political and economic transformation for Caribbean countries. Thus, Marxism, broadly configured as a historical materialist account of capitalist accumulation, class formation, labour exploitation, and possibilities for worker-based, anticapitalist social transformation, has played a critical role in twentieth-century Caribbean political life, in the formation of parties, and in the development of left political philosophies in the region.[9]

However, I engage Marxism as a horizon of both possibility and limitation in our methods and politics, exploring how left ideologies based fundamentally in antislavery and anticolonial politics are positioned in regard to (Indigenous) sovereignty's negotiation, reinvention, and deferral. I look at the robust anticolonial and anticapitalist critique developed by the black left as a strategic pressure on Marxism, but from the *limit* terrain of Indigenous sovereignty, the point at which the tradition necessarily reinscribes both anti-blackness *and* anti-indigeneity. The limit, in short, is where the tradition relies on the entrenched division between labour as the social and political capture of black freedom, and land as the social and political capture of Indigenous dispossession and disenfranchisement. I begin by partially tracing the black left's strategic pressure on Marxism in seeking to account for blacks' bound and unwaged labour, and later their waged labour.

I then elaborate where that pressure fails to challenge settler logics embedded within both capitalist accumulation and left critiques that seek to represent black life and labour history in the face of anti-blackness that exceeds normative categories of political representation.

Bearing in mind the centrality of anticapitalist critique for addressing and upending black exploitation and subordination, *Beyond Constraint* affirms how Black radical thinkers not only developed more nuanced approaches to Marxism-Leninism, Trotskyism, and so on, but were also deeply committed to the Communist Party and socialist platforms. Thus, African American historian Keeanga-Yamahtta Taylor writes that "no *serious* socialist current in the last hundred years has ever demanded that Black or Latin/o workers put their struggles on the back burner while some other class struggle is waged first."[10] However, as she also acknowledges, black activists did become disenchanted with the Communist Party and later attempts at "colorblind" socialism. This constraint on addressing racialization and colonialism as constitutive, ancillary factors in labour exploitation is well-known. For example, in the seminal anticolonial text *Discourse on Colonialism* (1950) by Martinican poet, playwright, and politician Aimé Césaire, we see two different approaches to labour struggle and liberation: enchantment and disenchantment. Throughout *Discourse*, Césaire identifies the creation of the proletariat and the colonized as European societies' two world-historical failures. He squarely positions the destruction of capitalism as the path to end colonialism, writing that "the salvation of Europe is not a matter of a revolution in methods. It is a matter of the Revolution—the one which, until such time as there is a classless society, will substitute for the narrow tyranny of a dehumanized bourgeoisie the preponderance of the only class that still has a universal mission, because it suffers in its flesh from all the wrongs of history, from all the universal wrongs: the proletariat."[11] It is not blacks or the colonized per se (although they are the main focus of *Discourse*) who will effect capitalism's end, but the literal subsumption of their issues to proletarian efforts. Prior to his split from the Communist Party, he therefore resolved the two "problems" he identified (the colonial and the proletariat) in favor of the latter's world-historical function.

Yet in his 1967 interview with Haitian poet, activist, and former communist René Depestre (included at the end of *Discourse*), Césaire changes his position. Following his split from the Communist Party and over ten years after *Discourse*, Césaire illuminates the issues that prompted black left thinkers to reframe the categories of labour analysis for black liberation throughout the twentieth century and which, for some, necessitated a break with communism and with some avenues of Marxist criticism. For Césaire, proletarianization and coloniality are necessarily intertwined, but in the interview, he had to come to terms with the need to theorize anti-blackness beyond both. He is critical of the "assimilationist" tendencies of black communist writers, whom he says neglected "our Negro characteristics."[12] "They acted like Communists," he says, "which was all right, but they acted like abstract Communists. I maintained that the political question could not do away with our condition as Negroes. We are Negroes, with a great number of historical peculiarities."[13] When Depestre presses him on his attempt to "particularize Communism," Césaire responds, "Even then Communists would reproach me for speaking of the Negro problem—they called it my racism. But I would answer: Marx is all right, but we need to complete Marx. I felt that the emancipation of the Negro consisted of more than just a political emancipation."[14] Here Césaire echoes the Afropessimist position on black difference, to which I turn in chapter 1, as that which is prerational and thus cannot be fully expressed within nor achieve redress in political-economic structures.[15] While Césaire's formal withdrawal from the Communist Party in 1956 responded directly to revelations about Joseph Stalin, here we see the key to black left critique: the refusal of abstraction and an insistence on the mutually reinforcing material and extra-material conditions of black oppression. It is an insistence on accounting for the very racialism that political theorist Cedric Robinson tracks in *Black Marxism*, discussed in chapter 3.

While Césaire broadly captures the problems black left thinkers faced with Communist Party politics and anticapitalist critique that was not attuned to black struggle, however, his former student, Martinican revolutionary, philosopher, and psychiatrist Frantz Fanon's engagement with Marxism and its limits is most important for this study. To address labour exploitation, Fanon theorized not simply the slave and the master, but also the settler and the native. Fanon had to unpack blackness as a mode of irrational, sociogenic making that could not be explained in terms of ontology. Thus, he theorizes indigeneity as a social stratum of lack in colonial Algeria in terms of not *only* its material constitution but its own irrational, extra-material processes, theorizing these conditions in terms of ontology's and metaphysics' respective failures. Additionally, while Fanon—like Trinidad and Tobago's prime minister and historian Eric Williams—addresses racism as capitalism's *effect* or outcome necessary to maintain its accumulation structures, as Taylor notes, he also affirms the kind of anteriority (read *cause* here) that Cedric Robinson will probe later.[16] This anteriority, as I suggest in chapter 1, allows us to understand anti-blackness and anti-indigeneity as not only foundational, but intrinsically *relational* elements of capitalist accumulation and anticapitalist critique.

Writing primarily about 1950s colonial Algeria, Fanon saw what scholars critical of capitalism would achieve only later in the century: the colonial peculiarity of the relationship between race and class, wherein race functions as both "cause" and "effect" of the economic structure and its related social relations and institutions whose sui generis condition is the subordination of the racialized native to the white, European settler.[17] For Fanon, while modern racial formation is fundamentally tied to capitalist development, its essentially feudal characteristics reproduce it as both a teleological and anachronistic feature of capitalist development.[18] Fanon rejects capitalism's singular evolutionary narrative in the West because the colonizer exists as both Europe's (progressive) political subject *and* a settler whose power also derives from their extraterritorial (anachronistic) identity, or from the confrontation—rather than shift—of newer and older forms of power. Thus, the "Indigenous Population" (much like the "settler") is produced as always sui generis rather than as evolutionary within capitalism.[19] Moreover, Fanon introduces what we could call a wrinkle in how we explain race in the colonial period when we separate early slave societies from "late" colonies such as Algeria, which had both a native population and a black population constituted through enslavement. While Williams wrote that racism evolved as a *result* of slavery, Fanon suggests that Marxism as an analytic cannot be strictly applied to those colonies first created in the nineteenth century, when race was consolidated scientifically as a biological category of enlightenment humanism because racism is consequential in labour's configuration, suppression, and exploitation at this stage. It thus cannot be explained solely through an account of capitalist development as a singularity of either cause or outcome.[20]

The settler's economic dominance is not a strictly material transformation. It depends on direct and indirect (psychological) violence—rather than ideology—as another form of alienation necessary for the colonial state to exist, and which attaches to or emanates from the settler's whiteness. The latter is secured by its extraterritorial origin and becomes the external validating force for their dominance in the colonies—it comes from somewhere else like the divine right that governs both "serf" and "knight" for Fanon—similarly to God's function as the external validating force of the feudal world.[21] Thus, indigeneity too is not a strictly material phenomenon nor status that can be theorized within narrow, political-economic terms.

Thus, for Fanon, it is not singularly feudal transformation, mercantilism's rise and decline, or capitalism's establishment as a global market system that secures the settler's dominance, but the coextensive link of the settler's evolutionary whiteness with factors considered anomalous to twentieth-century capitalism, which tie the twentieth-century colony to the sixteenth-century imperial outpost cum colony. For this and other reasons, Fanon rejects Marxist orthodoxies, suggesting that Marxist analysis be "stretched" and adapted to the colonial situation. This stretching, however, does not account for slavery and race *alone* (which, as Taylor reminds us, Marx does do to a limited extent).[22] It also allows Fanon to account for *indigeneity* in relation to racialization and settler colonialism. In other words, Marxism must confront race *and* indigeneity as co-constitutive internal and external forces rather than as singularly evolutionary structures of capital formation. While Fanon's engagement with Marxism is critical for this study, as in *Creole Indigeneity*, Fanon's so-called Manichean categories—colonizer/colonized, or putatively normative settler/native—are not the categories of analysis here.[23] For Fanon, the "violence which governed the ordering of the colonial world" is a dialectic that must necessarily culminate in the reversal of these groups' positions as the horizon of political possibility. It "will be vindicated and appropriated when, taking history into their own hands, the colonized swarm into the forbidden cities."[24]

However, if we apply Fanon to the anticolonial Caribbean on the eve of independence, several questions emerge. What does the Creoles' acquisition of "the forbidden cities" mean for the non-African- and non-South-Asian-descended native in the colonies? What does the role reversal of the European colonizer for the descendants of the formerly enslaved and indentured mean for Indigenous peoples marginalized by the analysis of racial capitalism, having been poorly accounted for in the unfreedoms of the colonial state and in anticolonial resistance to it, and who do not accept the nation-state as the political horizon of liberation, making their resistance not just anticolonial but also anti-state? How can we fundamentally account for political-economic transformation not in terms of subsistence, but in terms of indigeneity (either Native American or Wynterian black remaking)? While Fanon restores the critical consideration of settler colonialism and indigeneity to the stretching of Marx by black left thinkers, his writing also reveals where black left thinking remains problematically tied to anticapitalist struggle as a historical change agent for (black)

Creole workers *over* Indigenous Peoples as either workers or subjects whose sovereignty lies outside the (post)colonial state.

Indigenous Peoples in the Caribbean are often seen as not having been eligible to even undergo the transformation from enslaved to free to proletarian to enfranchised, political subject. This is ironic because Marx identifies *both* black and Indigenous American enslaved labour as necessary for the types of capital accumulation characterizing bourgeois dominance in North America and Europe.[25] The nation-state's political economy necessarily checks Indigenous Peoples' right to exist as disalienated subjects. The *limit* of Marxism's radical, black *left* remains the inability to account for indigeneity and more specifically for anti-indigeneity as that which is as necessary as anti-blackness to capital accumulation structures.

However, Fanon points us to an opening allowing that inability to be surpassed from the point of closure of inheritance. In foregrounding violence in the role reversal of colonizer and colonized, Fanon is not talking of simple proletarianization or class transformation. This revolutionary violence stems from more than just class consciousness and therefore exceeds political-economic causality. Therefore, by holding the tradition to account when it comes to indigeneity and Indigenous land-based sovereignties, we can preserve the political and economic excess of Fanonian violence within radical critique as an even more radical mode of stretching yet to be accomplished, rather than stopping short at social transformation. Specifically, the tradition must confront how Indigenous movements resist capitalist economies' fundamentally integrative mechanisms, particularly its countermovements, which they force us to read as part of its modes of conscription.

For example, Yellowknives Dene political scientist Glen Coulthard argues that since capitalism is a fundamentally anti-Indigenous mode of production, native peoples must work to develop political-economic practices on their lands that do not rely on or reinvigorate it.[26] Coulthard rejects proletarianization because it is as much an anti-Indigenous structure as capitalism itself, and is not based on Indigenous Peoples' forms of nonaccumulative, "reciprocal" relationships to land as nature.[27] Yet despite the implications of non-worker-based Indigenous critiques of capitalism and normative strands of opposition not centered on Indigenous sovereignty, becoming proletarian remains critical to and implicit within the thinking of black economic and political theorists in the twentieth-century Caribbean. In his groundbreaking and controversial work *Capitalism and Slavery*, for instance, Williams deliberately linked the rise of capitalist markets in Europe to black primitive accumulation in the colonies to express Marx's position not only that colonial slavery in the Americas was key to "bourgeois industry" but that "it is the colonies that have created world trade."[28] Williams identifies black proletarian identity's precondition and emergence in the late nineteenth and early twentieth century, which was reinforced by the early twentieth-century emergence of the multiracial labour struggle in Trinidad and throughout the Caribbean. Blacks and Indians are thus seen as having resisted colonialism in the Caribbean as definitive proletarians, a status that is at times projected even further back to describe the unwaged enslaved person.

The link between labour, anticolonial struggle, and the independent postcolonial state appears as both causal and teleological in the Caribbean, yet it is precisely this deliberate yoking of class identity and class consciousness to freedom that Coulthard challenges. Coulthard argues that "while it is appropriate to view primitive accumulation as the condition of possibility for the development and ongoing reproduction of capitalism, it is not so to posit it as a *necessary* condition for developing the forms of critical consciousness and associated modes of life that ought to inform the construction of its alternatives."[29] This need is also a root of the disarticulation of black and native futures, he suggests, because primitive accumulation and its teleology continue to "foreclose the possibility of forging radical solidarities in the present" by "[calling] on Indigenous peoples to forcefully align their interests and identities in ways that contribute to our own dispossession and erasure."[30] Writing earlier, the controversial Lakota activist Russell Means put it even more plainly, arguing: "The only manner in which American Indian people could participate in a Marxist revolution would be to join the industrial system, to become factory workers, or 'proletarians.'"[31] Not only did Means reject proletarianization as a mode of anti-indigeneity, but he also argued that socialism "offers only to 'redistribute' the results—the money, maybe—of this industrialization to a wider section of the population." To do this, he suggests, "Marxism must maintain the industrial system."[32]

Means thus offers a double critique of socialism. First, while socialism is about distribution rather than teleologically oriented production and consumption, it emerges from capitalism as a necessary stage of development that must be overcome. It undoes neither capitalism nor the settler state's teleological need for accumulation. Therefore, it is essentially the capture of anti-indigeneity *for* the progressive ends of labour struggle. Moreover, the articulation of telos as need is how capitalist logic produces and reproduces the mode of being human that became dominant as a result of the explorations that commenced in the fifteenth century, if one follows the arguments of Cuban-born Jamaican philosopher and "weaver" Sylvia Wynter, who is herself reading Fanon.[33] Fanon's attention to race, economic structures, and ideology, then, recognizes, as Wynter notes, that within capitalism, "the non-whites, the natives—have to be both perceived . . . and socio-institutionally *produced*" as the limit of white western humanity, materially and ideologically, a point to which I return in chapters 5 and 6.[34] When Wynter writes that the collective nonwhite underclass must be engineered to be "homeless," "jobless," and "relatively low-skilled," she iterates the link between the relations and forces of production in Fanon's "substructure." Reading Fanon, she also iterates the particular way in which these relations and forces are organized and unified by racialization as a tool of the bourgeois class, which had to find a way to externally secure its social order, so it turned to race to replace religion as the externally validating element (sui generis for Fanon) of the capitalist social order.[35]

Means's second critique can be read as a caution about interpretation. Numerous anticapitalist movements are active throughout South and Central America, including the Confederación Nacional de Organizaciones Campesinas Indigenas y Negras (Ecuador), the MST: Movimento dos Trabalhadores Rurais Sem Terra (Brazil), and the trade union Confederación Sindical Única de Trabajadores Campesinos de Bolivia (CSUTCB), which primarily represents the Quechuas, Aymaras, and Tupí Guaraníes. While many of these groups utilize socialist platforms in their fight for land, water, food sovereignty, and worker rights, it would be incorrect to interpret them as primarily class-based. Even where they do not exclusively represent Indigenous Peoples or Black peoples, not only are the peasant communities largely native, but their anticapitalist fight for sovereign labour expression resists anti-indigeneity and anti-blackness (MST). Indigenous sovereignty is not only the historically constitutive force of a worker-based, anticapitalist agenda; it is also not subject to the material and ontological transit that Means rejects (CSUTCB).

Fanon, Wynter, Means, and to some extent Coulthard all emphasize capital's *ontological* function rather than strictly its material or structural functions. This emphasis on ontology and ontological negation is not a rejection of material critique. It is a recognition of the settler-master's evolutionary function as a disciplinary figure essential to the production and maintenance of captive, coerced, and exploited labour. This is more than just a realization that a strict critique of capital, while necessary, is in fact its own limit. It forces a confrontation between the role that a continued critique of capital must play in black liberation, and how the stretching that Fanon envisioned and so many black left thinkers articulated butts up against the need to conceptualize Indigenous labour both in relation to and apart from this particular genealogy of racialized capital.

I work from the point of the uncomfortable position of Fanonian violence and Césairean disenchantment to suggest that, although black liberation can be posited within the tradition that emerged out of Marx's critique of capital, its fundamental and intractable limits are where we can begin to think black and Indigenous labour together in the Americas. I do *not* suggest that we are at the end of Marxism's usefulness for conceptualizing black labour struggle and resistance to capitalism, nor that indigeneity is at the end of Marxist representation. Instead, *Beyond Constraint* reframes some elements of Caribbean Marxist labour history's robust canon in terms of questions about Indigenous sovereignty. It works through the efforts in black genealogies of Marxism to make Marxism legible for black struggle and to make black life and labour legible within the tradition. It reads with and against the grain of the colonial archive, the black radical tradition, and the histories with which they intersect. It also reads with and against efforts to appropriate black anticolonial thought and Atlantic epistemologies for Indigenous Peoples, such as Coulthard's *Red Skin, White Masks* (2014) and Jace Weaver's *The Red Atlantic* (2014), respectively.

In positioning the radical tradition in terms of Indigeneity's limit point, I must clarify that the problems stem not from the tradition itself but from the overall limits of Marxism's emancipatory project that, as Wynter reminds us, is concerned first with the human, rather than with the conditions of those who function as the human's boundary markers (i.e., the human's condition of possibility).[36] For Wynter, Marxism's foundational limit is how its central change agent—class struggle—actually functions as a necessary mode of domination for the production of the (western) human same over and against its human others, and its material conditions of existence. Wynter reformulates Marx's hypothesis that "in all human societies, from their origins, the ... magma of role allocations" had been "generated by each ... society's ... mode of economic production," asking, "how would it have been possible for us not to consider that this hypothesis was perhaps the humanly emancipatory answer to all our issues?" She explains that "this pari passu with the class struggle, as waged primarily over *the ownership* of each such mode's *means of production* ... was nevertheless itself held out to be *the* principle of causality whose imperative transformation would be the very condition of our progressive human emancipation! *That is, the focus is on the expropriation of that ownership, rather than of what that ownership subserves!*[37] Following Wynter, Marxism's flaw is not only that its critique of capital marginalizes blacks and Indigenous Peoples (in keeping with their subordination within capital). Instead, Marxism must first normalize and generalize the western feature of ownership—and hence the role of blacks and Indigenous Peoples as those who can labour but not accumulate—before it posits struggles against it as emancipatory. Wynter's criticism parallels that of, for instance, political scientist Folke Lindahl, who argues that "claims to universal truth ... (over) determine the entire Marxist edifice."[38] Marxism's limit for black liberation, then, is precisely its claims to universality.[39]

Moreover, because Marx affirms the teleological development of human economies and societies, he also has to logically accept "the teleologically determined hegemony of the *bios* (i.e., the material) aspect of our being human" within which nonwhite, western others bear the markers of universal failure and subordination, and within which their redemption can only logically extend the dominant social order that always already requires their failure (i.e., poverty, death).[40] Afropessimist thinker Frank D. Wilderson III makes similar claims in his critique of Gramscian politics, writing that "marxism suffers from a kind of conceptual anxiety: a desire for socialism on the other side of crisis" and the "desire to democratise work and thus help keep in place, ensure the coherence of, the Reformation and Enlightenment 'foundational' values of productivity and progress" for which anti-blackness is foundational.[41]

Marxism thus extends the universality of ownership itself and its intrinsic function to support a western, global order of humans and infrahumans. It affirms capitalist accumulation as central in the very production of the human and the categories that attach to humanity—bourgeois subject, capitalist, proletarian—rather than the categories against which these political economic positions are defined—enslaved person, native, colonized subject, and so on. Since Marx couldn't "see" this, when, for example, he famously argued for the necessity for Asian countries to pass through a capitalist mode of production before achieving socialism, he incorporated ownership's central function into the emancipatory function of evolutionary class struggle as the very site of the inscription of capitalism's global, racialized human order.

This study thus operates from critical awareness of Marxism's limits as realized by Césaire and Fanon, but it also works from another set of limits: how black left studies of racial capital continue to buy into Marxism's restricted human emancipatory potential, which, as Wynter argues, is precisely where the tradition supports rather than challenges the global human order. Therefore, this intervention must be staged *through* and *against* black left Marxist genealogies, which is precisely where the land-labour interface that positions blacks and Indigenous Peoples is continuously reinscribed when Marxism is used to articulate black resistance and entertain possibilities for freedom. Here we encounter the very limit of Fanon's stretching, from which new methods must emerge so that black left analysis, in its inability to even broach the issue of Indigenous labour, stops its own curtailment of Indigenous sovereignty in its enactment of the Marxian limit of freedom for nonwhite non-westerners. Where the radical tradition positions Indigenous Peoples outside labour and posits modern work as the central mode of social evolution, freedom, and earned rights (or enfranchisement) for the formerly enslaved and their descendants, it necessarily rejects concepts of Indigenous sovereignty (and modes of being human) not based in class struggle (recall Coulthard).

This is where, to reiterate Wynter, the radical tradition repeats or extends Marx's mistake. Moreover, when anticolonial nationalisms base themselves on class struggle, as they did in the Caribbean throughout the twentieth century, this flaw in black left discourse takes on structural dimensions in the political economy of the postcolonial state, wherein Creole Independence and Indigenous self-determination remain in conflict. With this conflict in mind, the following section turns to postcolonial Independence as the potential limit of *both* black freedom and Indigenous Sovereignty.

Pre-positions: Grammar, Independence, and Sovereignty

This rethinking of labour as the terrain of rights and freedom in the Caribbean that I propose requires a collective look at (postcolonial) independence and (Indigenous) sovereignty as political modes that capture both anterior and constrained forms of sovereign expression moved into conflict by the legacies of settler and franchise colonialism. Thus, I configure Indigenous Sovereignty and Creole Independence together as a real and conceptual problem space, rather than in terms of a strict opposition. By linking discussions about the constraints placed on Indigenous self-determination in North America, Latin America, and Australia to those in the Caribbean, this section pulls the Caribbean into larger debates about settler and Indigenous sovereignties, exploring the relationship between postcoloniality and settler strategies of control. It situates the Caribbean within wider conversations on sovereignty within Indigenous Studies and rethinks independence from outside its normative logics of postcoloniality and decolonization through its entanglement with sovereignty.

I foreground how Independence and Sovereignty express both the continuity of peoples' sovereign bodily actions as well as ruptured, relational modes of power. I argue that the specific reliance of postcolonial Independence on a conversion of right that valorizes the settler function of the master-settler dyad requires not only the continuous deployment of settler-native relations in the postcolonial state, but also the exercise of settler strategies as a limit for *both* black (Creole) freedom and Indigenous sovereignty. I therefore call for the exercise of postcolonial Independence *with* and *through*—not against—Indigenous sovereignties, as a way to more fully recover the promise of freedom reflected by Independence. I lay out the problematic of Independence through attention to etymology and grammar. Then, I take a comparative look at Indigenous sovereignty, and finally, through Guyana, I highlight how Creole Independence and Indigenous Sovereignty operate as conflicting political modes because of the legacies of settler rather than just franchise colonialism. Throughout, I approach independence and sovereignty not as pure forms of power, but in terms of where they are constrained or overdetermined by the legacies of settler colonial power.

(INVOLUNTARY) SETTLER GRAMMARS OF INDEPENDENCE

Much of the Anglophone Caribbean gained its independence from the 1960s onward. By *independence*, I refer to the legal transfers of power from empire to the local control of Caribbean nation-states.[42] Roughly a dozen countries, however, remain under the administration of former colonizers or later empires, through political arrangements that reflect varying degrees of domination reimagined as political incorporation, such as the territories of the US Virgin Islands and Puerto Rico. Independence transfers of power are of course neither benign nor bloodless, resulting from decades-long struggles and organizing against colonial and imperial, political, and economic manipulation and often brutal repressions. Caribbean examples include the 1930s riots and labour unrest in several countries, a fact often downplayed in narratives by the former colonizers.[43] Together with its political and legal dimensions, Independence represents a culturally elaborated psychic rupture.

However, it also means that former colonies, through alliances such as the British Commonwealth of Nations, are compelled into forms of statehood that are both a break from and a contractual agreement with the (former) colonizer/empire that often retains real and/or symbolic structures of political subordination.[44] The late literary critic Michael Dash wrote of Caribbean postcoloniality, "These new nation states were flawed... but there was no way of imagining alternatives."[45] More than flawed, the Guyanese historian and activist Walter Rodney claimed they represented the extension of colonial power and the continued subordination of Creole populations.[46] Enshrining the geopolitical freedom of formerly colonized peoples yet also supporting global white supremacy and the First World's economic dominance, the postcolonial state necessarily inherits colonial legal and political structures and is compelled into fundamentally unequal, dependent market relationships with the global North.[47] Numerous works address the postcolonial state's limits and its neocolonial, politico-economic status with the First World, often framing neocolonialism as nothing less than a reenvisioned kleptocratic phase of imperialism engineering Third World countries' economic drain.[48]

My interest, however, is not in the status of Caribbean nation-states vis-à-vis the economically and politically dominant global North. I am concerned with a particular feature of postcolonial Independence that inherently restricts it: the reductive maintenance of Indigenous Peoples within postcolonial states as an underclass, or an internal South. Independence is limited in specific ways as postcolonial states require Indigenous Peoples' subordination to a sovereignty that cannot be superseded by any form of Indigenous self-determination. For the postcolonial state, Independence is a stage of the land's evolutionary history, from imperial outpost to colony to home to nation. It is thus part of a teleology in which, for those countries where anticolonial labour struggle was central, labour itself is captured as the universal, forward historical motion that defines and, after Wynter, compromises Marx's critique of capital. The centrality of this infrahuman element of emancipatory politics persists in the postcolonial nation, so we must consider not just the limits of labour struggle but also the settler-master logics tied to positions of dominance within the postcolonial state.

To elaborate how the legal, political, and social mechanisms of the colony cum postcolonial state emerge as the very limit of the independent nation, a brief, etymological approach is warranted. Part of the original meaning of the term "colonialism" is "to cultivate." Colonialism shares its roots with the Latin terms *colōnia* and *colonus*. In the *Oxford Latin Diction-*

ary, *colōnia* is a colony or settlement of conquered or annexed lands by Roman citizens, and *colonus* refers to someone who settles, cultivates, or farms land. In the *Oxford English Dictionary*, the definition of *colony* encapsulates both early Latin terms and meanings, denoting either a "settlement in a new country" or "a body of people who settle in a new locality." Collectively, *colony* articulates land as settlement together and apart from people who presumably do the settling. The term thus effects a suturing and a delinking of the (settled) land as a *political* phenomenon and the settler who performs an *economic* action on the land, while simultaneously extending, and hence relying on, empire's now a priori political right. The plantation itself achieved colonialism's main action or objective: cultivation. This work would be articulated in Caribbean labour history as essential to the rise of capital and to anticolonial struggle, particularly the ways in which colonized peoples resisted colonialism as a proletariat in the twentieth century. As I've traced in *Creole Indigeneity*, cultivation or plantation work itself thus becomes formative for labour history and the postcolonial nation-state's eventual emergence in the region.

With plantation work in the Caribbean, however, the tense break between the land and actions performed on the land and managed through the settler's body becomes aporetic because the person who possessed the land was not the person who cultivated or settled it. When the settler splits his labour (in the functions of master and slave), he effectively not only causes a precarious condition where the enslaved person actually works on the settler's freedom via the settler's right. He also effects the movement between the political and economic, whose eventual integration will of course characterize the biopolitical under capitalism. Slavery turns the settler—the body that manages the split between the land and actions performed on it in the colonies—into a master. The settler's master function produces risk by converting the settler's limited political right into the master's economic right.[49] In essence, in slavery, the settler-master doubles and defers the labours of his own body in the enslaved person, who functions as the master's "surrogate."[50]

The settler retains political right to the land, while the enslaved person performs the cultivation necessary to secure economic right to the land. This economic right (e.g., the Boston Tea Party) becomes the basis for rejecting the political extension of the right of empire into new lands as these figures literally transition to and effect the general shift from *homo politicus* to *homo economicus* as a globally dominant mode of being human.[51] Annexed lands belong to the nation/empire that annexed them, but the settler who works the land can claim that portion of it for himself, and his labour is essential to hold onto it apart from the empire/nation. The settler-master is thus a problematic figure and more so in the Caribbean where Europhilic whites did not settle in large numbers. Caribbean chattel slavery (and later indenture) thus puts the land in political jeopardy if the rights of the people performing the labour on the land cannot be neutralized. Hence, slavery and indenture must function as mechanisms not only to extract and control the labour necessary for cultivation but also to restrict right to the settler-master alone, since all were physically capable of cultivation.

Both slavery- and indenture-based extractive colonies and settler colonies share this emphasis on cultivation and the delinking of the settler-master's body from the cultivated land at different points in their histories. However, it is these Caribbean colonies of exploitation, extraction, and accumulation that we *oppose* to classic settler colonies cum "postcolonial" states such as the United States, Canada, and Australia. Moreover, settler colonial studies overemphasize the settler rather than the bodies that settler societies move into antagonistic relation. The universally necessary break between ownership and labour in modern colonies founded on Indigenous dispossession and black enslavement was achieved not only between the master and the land but also between two bodies: the person who cultivated (the enslaved person) and the Indigenous body in its overidentification with and *as* land that has no economic action performed on it (i.e., uncultivated land). The land (as colony, home, nation) becomes that which has been cleared not of the settler's body per se (which happens at least figuratively with Independence) but of those bodies that don't allow it to be cultivated. This results from the pre-position/al relationship colonialism establishes between blacks and Indigenous Peoples as an effect of settler-master right.

Caribbean history is replete with instances where Indigenous Peoples are identified as the past of the postcolonial nation, and the extinction thesis is routinely deployed within the explanatory apparatus for Creole habitation.[52] Across that literature, a pre-positional relationship, or a grammar, is made possible by and sustained through the standard narrative of Indigenous disappearance: that during the imperial and early colonial periods, Indigenous Peoples perished in the Caribbean and therefore could not participate with great significance in plantation work, thus requiring the importation of first enslaved and then indentured peoples.[53] This supposed fact of either Indigenous disappearance or Indigenous lack of usefulness first establishes a critical difference and distance between Indigenous

Peoples and blacks within colonial space (of the plantation) and time (of the settler-master). Later, it brings forward to the post-Independence period the clearing of Indigenous bodies from the land during the colonial period. Ridding the land of Indigenous bodies, by restricting land titles, for instance, which constrain Indigenous use of and access to homelands, becomes existentially mandated for the postcolonial state.

This pre-position that now governs Creole and native lives operates in two senses: (1) the temporal *pre-position* of Indigenous Peoples to blacks (because of their deaths or after they perished) and (2) in terms of a grammar in which as a unified part of speech, the *prepositional* phrase must express something about the noun and, in this instance, complete its meaning. So the noun/subject—blacks and black labour, for instance—cannot elaborate by or for itself, but must seek consolidation in a causality that always reflexively signals its historical success. In short, the failure of Indigenous labour to be rooted in the plantation is also the register in which the success of black and indentured labour on the plantation occurs. Caribbean historicity depends on this relationship, this grammar. The pre-position (and its function to establish relationships between nouns and reinforce the performative or agential space of the subject noun) is the grammatical unit necessary for (involuntary) settler sovereignties. Within it, the labours of blacks, Indians, and First Peoples cannot exist *at* or *in* the same time, and are now articulated through the substitution or imposition of Being/nonbeing (now based on life/death, productive/unproductive bodily labours) for the pre-contact modes of belonging that served as the immediate and historical contexts for all lives.[54] Moreover, wherever Creoles in the postcolonial state retain colonially mandated relationships to Indigenous Peoples, the prepositional relationship continues to organize Creole and Indigenous relationships to land.

When blacks are said to have worked colonial lands, this is the inscription of colonial time as the effective break between the land (now prior to labour) and the functions performed on it, and therefore between black and Indigenous bodies.[55] The settler possesses the land by establishing a political relationship to it that enacts a new mode of priorness (again via labour), abrogating Indigenous prior occupation and right. The settler essentially conscripts black bodies to undertake or operationalize the function of clearing inherent in possession.[56] When the pre-position is elaborated in anticolonial discourse as a feature of postcolonial nationalisms by black and Indo-Creoles, its continuous deployment brings forward the clearing of land from the imperial to the colonial period as a function of Creole political right. This legally exercised grammar clears the land again, further legitimizing the work that the hands and bodies of the enslaved, the indentured, and their descendants have performed within colonized space and time. It also makes this clearing that was first necessary for settler-master ownership and dominance an essential feature of postcolonial Independence and Creole dominance over Indigenous Peoples. The grammar supports and institutes labour's (colonial) time, which during the anticolonial period becomes the economic right to land that *replaced* the settler-master's political right.

In short, the enactment of the pre-position supports the transformation of the land and right, and it is the peculiar elaboration of the land-labour dialectic as it operates in the Caribbean wherein Indigenous Peoples and blacks, respectively, are fixed on opposite sides of the dialectic. The grammar is thus a real effect of imperial and colonial power formations. Post-Independence Caribbean histories and the territorial nationalisms they supported mobilized this grammatical structure to *reactivate* the definitional breach between the land and the settler-master body, between the economic and the political.[57] Thus, the black (and Indo) Creole citizen-subject, through the conversion of economic into political right, emerges in the postcolonial state as a figure of suture, or the only figure capable of yoking economic and political right, just as the settler had been the only figure previously capable of suture.

Critically, however, the grammar becomes essential for (black) Creoles in another, more urgent sense that even Independence cannot resolve. If we follow the Afropessimist assertion that the dialectic between native and settler differs from that between the enslaved person and human (or master and slave) because the latter serves as the condition of possibility for all other modes of being, we hit upon a key problem that blacks in the postcolonial state face, although Independence in the Caribbean is arguably a more enfranchised position than civil rights in the United States, for example. Wilderson, whose work I return to in chapter 1, writes that "Slavery [like colonialism] is a relational dynamic—not an event and certainly not a place in space like the South," and it "can continue to exist once the settler has left or ceded government power."[58] Moreover, he argues that subalternity is a redemptive position for postcolonial subjects but not for blacks because blackness and being enslaved are always irrevocably linked and because "blacks do not function as political subjects."[59] Wilderson articulates the limit that made Césaire reject class struggle as the single arbiter of black freedom: the absolute, ontological difference of blackness.[60]

Moreover, to the extent that South Asian indenture in the Caribbean is seen as a *kind* of slavery, South Asians experience the same ontological limit without its long *durée*. Thus, in the postcolonial state, even though blacks achieve Independence, the locally expressed and globally articulated antiblackness that produced slavery is still operative for Creoles in general.

Therefore, I suggest that Blacks in the postcolonial state don't simply need to convert right. They must inhabit (this can only ever be partial) the settler's position (and power)—not the master's position, which is fundamentally foreclosed—in order to manage the break between the human (as that which is necessary for civic life and political subjecthood) and the black (enslaved persons). In other words, because both dialectics (master-slave and settler-native) constrain blackness, blacks must enter into and deploy the settler-native relation in order to affirm the political right (based on the ability to be a political subject) that is won from the economic arrangement of the human-slave relation (based on the inability to be a political subject).[61] If the slave/black is the limit of political economy, then the conversion of economic right into political right enables the slave/black to have some form of political right that hinges on the maintenance of settler forms of power. Since postcoloniality allows for the deployment of settler-native relations rather than human-slave relations, it is a position of at least partial overcoming vis-à-vis the enslaved person. However, since postcoloniality structurally emerges out of settler and franchise coloniality, it brings forward the functions of the black enslaved person and the native as the bodies that were originally moved into antagonistic relation that allowed the settler-master to assert his political right.

Here we encounter the conditional nature of independence as a political mode where settler colonialism remains operative because postcolonial freedom for racialized subjects remains contingent on settler colonial legal mechanisms and grammars. These settler features of independence mean that in presenting themselves as the nation-state's true labourers and inheritors, blacks (and South Asians) *must* clear the land again of Indigenous bodies as the only way to approach the position of the human and the political categories to which the human has access. This is the enactment of the causality of the pre-positional grammar. The clearing, however, is still *involuntary* because (1) blacks inherited the franchise colony, and (2) blacks cannot be normative political subjects because their political subjecthood is achieved through the conversion of economic right *into* political right, rather than through the conversion of (the empire's) political right into economic right.

The limits of political subjecthood for the enslaved are clearly spelled out by African American cultural and literary professor Saidiya V. Hartman, on whom Wilderson also relies. Hartman writes, "If the public sphere is reserved for the white bourgeois subject"—in this case the settler-master who functions as the figure of accumulation in the colonies—"and the public/private divide replicates that between the political and the nonpolitical, then the agency of the enslaved, whose relation to the state is mediated by way of another's rights, is invariably relegated to the nonpolitical side of this divide."[62] The conversion of economic into political right that I chart stems from precisely this denial and foreclosure of subjectivity for the enslaved because of chattel slavery's function to encapsulate fungible, object status rather than afford the forms of subjectivity and difference necessary for representation. Thus, not only does Caribbean independence reveal this beholding to the settler-master's inadequate categories of political representation, but our efforts to decolonize remain limited by our political and juridical need to, on some level, take up or inhabit the settler's place from a position of chronic lack in the active conversion of lack into a state of right. It is limited because (our desire aside) we are compelled to enter the already established "forbidden cities" (Fanon) that define political subjectivity.

The historical articulation of this inhabiting as an anti- and decolonial process must therefore be challenged because it relies on limited historical positions and takes on a settler-colonial dimension. It also requires a reevaluation of postcolonial independence as perhaps the *antithesis* of Indigenous sovereignty and even black freedom. Moreover, the grammar reveals that independence and sovereignty, for those in postcolonial states in the global South, are not only pitted against each other, they are the structural outcomes of the land-labour dialectic. Therefore, I locate this project not under the umbrella of Caribbean independence, or attempts to culturally decolonize, but within the ongoing entanglement of postcolonial Independence with native sovereignty. Fully realized Indigenous sovereignty will always be the limit of Independence. Additionally, Independence, and the legal transformation or conversion of settler-master right, will always be the upper limit of black (and South Asian) freedom in the postcolonial state.[63] It is a threshold we can only partially approach through the decolonial process because it requires a radical rupture.

I approach Indigenous sovereignty as that rupture to make visible the continued unfolding of settler and franchise colonial power in the postcolonial state. Rather than offer a strict definition of sovereignty, I discuss it in terms of its epistemological and conceptual constraints in order to force a discussion of settler coloniality within franchise or extractive colonialism. I track Indigenous Sovereignty as both the reflection of precolonial relationships to land based on Indigenous *labour* (especially in chapter 1), and sovereignty's reinvention as a form of right (i.e., customary or traditional right in the Amerindian Act). I therefore approach sovereignty through a tension between Indigenous Peoples as citizens of the postcolonial state with sovereignties that might be negotiated through but exceed that of the state. I admittedly engage Indigenous sovereignty from the legacies of settler and franchise colonialism's violence, seeking to foreground its complexities as an interpretive context for reading postcolonial and settler power in Guyana's dealings with its Indigenous populations. I foreground how settler rather than strictly franchise colonialism in the Caribbean is also the social and political condition under which a variety of actors vie for territory and seek to convert differing conditions of emigration (volitional and coerced) into belonging and right.[64]

CONFIGURING SOVEREIGNTY

The North American context offers several examples of Indigenous sovereignty's complexities—its "confused and confusing" nature, as Lenape American Indian Studies scholar Joanne Barker puts it—concerning the various legal positions of Indigenous Peoples with regard to state and federal governments.[65] For example, during the COVID-19 pandemic, as infections and deaths rose in the Navajo Nation in April 2020, the myriad ways of referring to the nation included references to the Navajo "community" and tribe.[66] Newscasts constantly compared the Navajo nation to states, reporting that *if it were* a state, at one point it would have been the state with the second highest rates of infection/death after New York.[67] Then, Navajo infection rates became the highest in the country, higher, as news broadcasts reported, than individual, true states.[68] Indigenous nations became referential states when safely identified through metaphors that signaled their *difference* from true states.[69] This broadly social way of referring to Indigenous nations on reservation homelands as real, auxiliary, and speculative state structures belies several problems with sovereignty.[70] It reproduces legal precedent (and hence brings forward) the same legalized slippages that denote the subordinate status of Indigenous nations.[71] In particular, it draws attention to the often fundamental incompatibility of Indigenous and liberal governance structures and, as Mohawk political anthropologist Audra Simpson notes, to the seeming "incommensurable" nature of "Indigenous" and "nation" under settler coloniality.[72]

The limits on Indigenous self-determination and sovereignty within the United States have been cohesively spelled out by many scholars who demonstrate how Indigenous Peoples' prior and extant sovereign claims and relationships to lands are restricted by the politics of recognition, and how federal and state laws enact US sovereignty as a direct impingement of Indigenous right.[73] Moreover, these constraints are articulated within the wider context of international law such as the UN Declaration on the Rights of Indigenous Peoples (UNDRIP), which also depends on recognition by individual state actors.[74] It is based on external recognition or validation rather than internal Indigenous recognition.[75] While the Declaration affirms Indigenous right to "self-determination," the term "sovereign" appears only once, in relation not to Indigenous Peoples but to "sovereign states."[76]

Article 46 of UNDRIP states that its "provisions . . . shall be interpreted in accordance with the principles of justice, democracy, respect for human rights, equality, non-discrimination, good governance and good faith," specifying that support of Indigenous rights should not negatively impact "the territorial integrity or political unity of sovereign and independent States." In other words, concepts of right and democracy supersede indigeneity and the particularity of its expression across formally recognized nations *and* unrecognized peoples. Moreover, although the Declaration supports the restoration of land-based sovereignties, such redress can never restrict extant state sovereignties. In short, settler states' territorial integrity must be maintained, although the settler state is formed through the very territorial "dismemberment" that the Declaration prohibits. Thus, the irony of applying the term "state" to Indigenous nations on a provisional and figurative basis socially and epistemically reproduces this distinction, allowing settler states to function through the very breach of native sovereignties.

Writing about Australia, Goenpul feminist and Indigenous studies scholar and activist Aileen Moreton-Robinson sees Indigenous sovereignty as fundamentally opposed to the strategies, structures, and forms of knowledge linked with possession or what she terms "white patriarchal" sovereignty.[77] Moreton-Robinson also asserts that Indigenous modes of ownership or possession are based on ontological relationships to place that are incompatible with those of migrants and settlers.[78] More importantly, she suggests, a substantial amount of political and legal material on Indigenous sovereignty is filtered through a problematic discourse of rights. She argues that since the concept of rights of personhood and property is based on a shift from forms of sovereign to state power enacting race, specifically whiteness, as a biopolitical mechanism for rights' acquisition and distribution, Indigenous forms of sovereignty are more than just antithetical to biologized forms of sovereignty. The latter are based on possessive logics that structurally position Indigenous sovereignty as a threat to the settler state, and this opposition functions as a kind of internal war against Indigenous Peoples, through which state's rights are consolidated.[79] Her work suggests that because Indigenous sovereignty is not based on biopower, the biopolitical discourse of rights and property through which states recognize or affirm their sovereignty first translate and then abrogate Indigenous sovereignty, even where it is granted.

Some consider sovereignty to be such a compromised term for describing Indigenous self-determination under empire and settler colonialism, that it is considered insufficient for designating Indigenous self-governance. Steve Newcomb, a Shawnee-Lenape writer, film producer, and cofounder and codirector of the Indigenous Law Institute, echoes Moreton-Robinson, suggesting that to describe current Indigenous relationships to land as "Indigenous sovereignty" belies the fundamental difference of Indigenous sovereignty within (settler) coloniality wherein Indigenous self-governance is "subordinated" to US sovereignty or dominance.[80] Audra Simpson marks these distinctions and discrepancies, describing Indigenous sovereignty as "nested," noting that "sovereignty may exist within sovereignty."[81] Simpson establishes that "Like Indigenous bodies, Indigenous sovereignties and Indigenous political orders prevail within and apart from settler governance. This form of 'nested sovereignty' has implications for the sturdiness of nation-states over all, but especially for formulations of political membership as articulated and fought over."[82] Rather than seeing the settler state as entrenched, through the politics of "refusal," Simpson sees indigeneity and sovereignty as being in "persistent relation."[83]

Newcomb and Simpson represent two perspectives on Indigenous sovereignty borne out, respectively, in the works of Barker and Mohawk political theorist Taiaiake Alfred. In her introduction to *Sovereignty Matters*, Barker traces the European monarchic and religious origins of the concept that, for instance, lawyer and Lumbee legal scholar Robert A. Williams Jr. identifies as embedded in the concepts of nation and sovereign states as they evolved in pre- and post-conquest European legal efforts to determine just, and hence defensible, versus unjust forms of territorial acquisition.[84] Barker writes that the non-Indigenous concept of sovereignty has been historically used to justify Indigenous dispossession and then to restore right based on dependency on the settler state, so it requires a "translation" to articulate forms of Indigenous self-determination. Against this imperial and colonial concept of sovereignty, Barker offers a definition, based on the work of other Indigenous scholars, as a "contingent" and "embedded" "inherent right that emanates from historically and politically resonant notions of cultural identity and community affiliation."[85]

While Barker redefines sovereignty, Alfred (whose position Newcomb reinforces) rejects the term entirely. Alfred focuses on the application of the terms sovereign/ty to Indigenous Peoples as a means to justify their ongoing "internal colonization."[86] Not only is the concept European in origin, but it poses a "conceptual and definitional problem centered on accommodation of indigenous people within a 'legitimate' framework of settler state governance."[87] Sovereignty is doubly anathema to Indigenous Peoples' self-determination because, he argues, it has been used to justify their legal dispossession, while simultaneously defining and reinforcing the settler state's sovereignty.[88] Because the concept developed and is legally and ideologically exercised through Indigenous dispossession and subordination, Alfred suggests that it needs to be replaced.[89]

Michi Saagiig Nishnaabeg scholar Leanne Betasamosake Simpson describes, in contrast to sovereignty, a practice-based, ontologically rooted concept of Indigenous freedom within which various forms of sovereignty are a component. In *As We Have Always Done*, Simpson echoes those who see Indigenous concepts of *nation* as incommensurable with their liberal western counterpart. Instead, they are based on place, practice, and relationality. Referring specifically to Nishnaabeg concepts, Simpson writes, "Kina Gchi Nishnaabeg-ogamig is connectivity based on the sanctity of the land, the love we have for our families, our language, our way of life. It is relationships based on deep reciprocity, respect, noninterference, self-determination, and freedom.... Our nationhood is based on a series of radiating responsibilities."[90] More significantly, she describes Nishnaabeg governance as forms of practice, as a "how" of practice: "It became clear to me that *how* we live, *how* we organize, *how* we engage the world—the process—not only frame the outcome, it is the transformation. *How* molds and then gives birth to the present. The how changes us.... Engaging in deep and reciprocal indigeneity is a transformative act because it fundamentally changes modes of production of our lives. It changes the relationships that house our bodies and our thinking. It changes how we conceptualize nationhood."[91] For Betasamosake Simpson, who draws on Audra Simpson to articulate a concept of native bodies as "political orders," the body emerges as a site of sovereignty and "self-determination." This self-sovereignty, she argues, is "the very foundation of Nishnaabeg governance."[92]

In other words, the concept of sovereignty she deploys for understanding Indigenous governing structures is fundamentally antithetical to forms of sovereignty deployed by western states that are based on rights—rather than relation—within which sovereignty adheres only in particular figures invested with state or other forms of power. It is based on concepts of individual and collective responsibility and actions that support mutually reinforcing material, cultural, and ontological practices. Betasamosake Simpson offers a concept of nation(hood) for Indigenous Peoples that is fundamentally opposed to settler colonial forms of nation and which is not exclusive to humanity.[93] Also moving beyond singularly human concepts of sovereignty, enrolled member of the Citizen Potawatomi Nation Robin Wall Kimmerer, a plant ecologist and director of the Center for Native Peoples and the Environment at the SUNY College of Environmental Science and Forestry, describes sovereignty as that which attaches to plants as well. In an interview, she says of heirloom corn farmed for centuries by Indigenous Peoples that it is "sovereign": "free," "independent," and not "colonized." Kimmerer says of the corn: "It is itself. It is an untrammeled person."[94] Sovereignty emerges in these works as fraught and multifaceted, including existing and relating reciprocally with humans and nonhumans as the exercise of native political, cultural, and legal mechanisms that do not align with those of the settler state.

Such discussions of Indigenous sovereignty and its relation to the settler state are still largely absent in the Caribbean. Most texts on Caribbean history and society directly address neither settler colonialism nor Indigenous sovereignty. Instead, they divide the region into bounded historical epochs that prioritize colonial labour: conquest, colonization, the establishment of franchise colonialism and enslavement, emancipation, indenture, the rise of class consciousness and anticolonial struggle, Independence, and postcoloniality.[95] This lack of broad, formal consideration of settler colonialism in the Caribbean hampers our discussion of how Creoles constrain Indigenous sovereignty. When these discussions do occur, as with the Iwokrama below, they primarily engage the postcolonial nation-state's constraint of Indigenous right without exploring how settler colonialism, rather than just franchise colonialism, informs this. Thorny issues, such as whether the former franchise colony becomes a quasi-settler state at independence, and what this might mean for Indigenous sovereignties, remain deferred. Below, I explicitly frame the sovereignty issues of Indigenous Peoples in Guyana in terms of settler colonial power and the limits of postcolonial independence. I ultimately suggest that Indigenous sovereignty needs to be enacted differently.

INDIGENOUS SOVEREIGNTY AND SETTLER COLONIAL POWER IN GUYANA

In Latin America and the Caribbean, there are similarities and critical differences in how Indigenous bodies exercise Indigenous sovereignties within their homelands. As with North America, these sovereignties encompass territorial right and control, self-determination, cultural retention and expression, and resource management. They are negotiated within overlapping international and state advocacy groups, conventions, treaties, declarations, acts, degrees of recognition, and different processes for establishing right within (postcolonial) nation-state's legal apparatuses, and through numerous local, national, regional, and international organizations. In short, in Latin America and the Caribbean, even more direct stakeholders are involved in the negotiation, granting, and exercise of Indigenous sovereignty.[96]

NGOs such as COPINH—a nearly thirty-year-old broad association of Lenca groups advocating for "Indigenous autonomy," land titles, resource control, access to health and education, and women's rights—exemplify the multilayered systems of advocacy and governmentality structuring Indigenous rights and self-determination in Latin America.[97] In 2015 in Belize, the Maya Leaders Alliance won a landmark case that granted government recognition of Q'eqchi and Mopan Maya's customary right to land.[98] Yet the Maya still struggle with land encroachments, wider social oppression, and violent repression of their social movements. The struggle of the Maya underscores how land rights and control of resources emerge as the most critical element of Indigenous sovereignty, as the basis for exercising bodily and cultural sovereignties, and as, to borrow language from Betasamosake Simpson, the reciprocal basis for Maya sovereignty.

In Guyana as elsewhere, Indigenous communities struggle with the same central issue of control of land rights as a key element of Indigenous self-determination. They advocate for their rights through Indigenous-led NGOs such as the Amerindian Peoples Association (APA) and the Guyanese

Organization of Indigenous Peoples (GOIP). Like similar NGOs in Latin American states, they work alongside Indigenous nations' governing structures such as (in Guyana) village chiefs, village councils, and the National Toshaos Council, an alliance of Indigenous chiefs mandated, and hence partly constrained, by the Amerindian Act.[99] As a mandated body of chiefs that needs to conduct business in the capital, the Council reveals how Indigenous sovereignty is achieved not apart from, but in coordination with national government.[100] Indigenous communities also negotiate governmental agencies: those that grant land titles (e.g., Ministry of Indigenous Peoples Affairs) and those that must directly balance state resource needs against those of Indigenous Peoples (e.g., Guyana Geology and Mines Commission).

In 2013, founder of the Amerindian Research Unit at the University of Guyana and professor of forestry Janette Bulkan noted that "although the Amerindian population has doubled since 1969, their land claims have reduced by 20%." Moreover, she notes that the Forestry Commission and the Geology and Mines Commission "issue overlapping logging and mining concessions over Amerindian traditional lands in spite of explicit protection."[101] In a report on Indigenous land tenure in Guyana, Tom Griffiths of the Forest Peoples Programme and the Arawakan head of the APA, Jean LaRose, present a consistent claim by Indigenous peoples that land titling does not recognize true Indigenous occupation and land use and is often based on a lack of initial consent by Indigenous Peoples. In one of many such examples, they cite a resident in the Sawari Wa'o Village in Region 9 in the country's southwest who asserts: "The Government of Guyana has an obligation to address our land claims since the time of Independence. This is what our elders and leaders have been saying for years. . . . Many of us live and occupy land outside the small existing village titles that were drawn up without full consultation of our people. . . . We need all of our lands to maintain our way of life, our culture, and our traditional practices."[102] In this claim, land emerges as the intractable basis for Indigenous Peoples' sovereign being. The complex situation of having to apply for title or extensions to title and having rights to land subordinated to state economic needs means that the exercise of land-based Indigenous sovereignty in Guyana is achieved and expressed in part through its very constraint.

Guyana reveals a further way in which Indigenous sovereignty in Latin America and the Caribbean is differently negotiated than in the North American context. Neoliberal governmentality in the underresourced postcolonial state means that the state exercises its own sovereignty through a diffuse network of nonstate actors with which Indigenous Peoples must also negotiate. Gillian Gregory and Ismael Vaccaro write that in Guyana and Latin America, Indigenous Peoples' territorial control is negotiated both with the state and with environmental actors through the very creation of environmentally protected areas.[103] Referring to these areas and to Indigenous-controlled lands as "islands of governmentality," they write that "these islands take the form of indigenous territories targeted for environmental conservation [see chapter 6], that overlap and articulate with— and within—the space of the national territory, and demonstrate that territorial rule is often shaped by slippages or contradictions in the constitution of power."[104] They also crucially observe that the history of granting titles to Indigenous Peoples remains part of long-enduring efforts to dominate the country's interior.[105] Consequently, these "islands" "do not represent changing governmental priorities ... so much as new strategies for the expansion and reiteration of state power—specifically, the re-defining of space and identities through the granting of shared authority over different forms of land-use."[106] This impingement of Indigenous rights through modern conservation works against Indigenous sovereignty both at the level of matter—the land itself—and at that of bodily sovereignty through the forms of contamination, from mining and other industries, that literally leach into Indigenous bodies.[107]

To demonstrate how conservation emerges as a form of "neoliberal governmentality" that constrains Indigenous right through the very granting of titles to Indigenous land, Gregory and Vacarro give the example of the Iwokrama Centre for Rainforest Conservation: 371,000 hectares of rainforest reserve, located almost in Guyana's center (in the southeastern portion of Region 8) are dedicated to sustainable tourism, forestry, and conservation.[108] Gregory and Vaccaro write that, despite its employment of Indigenous Peoples and although its conservationist practices are ideologically aligned with Indigenous land rights and resource control, Iwokrama actually compromises Indigenous sovereignty by allowing the state to exercise governmentality in at least two key ways. First, the Centre is administered through headquarters in the capital, Georgetown (by international actors and funding structures) rather than in Region 8. The Centre describes itself as "an international not-for-profit organisation, governed by an International Board of Trustees and managed by a professional team of around seventy permanent staff in Georgetown and at the Iwokrama River Lodge and Research Centre at Kurupukari. The IIC's Patron is HRH The Prince of Wales."[109] This description reveals the layered structure of administration and, more importantly, the conversion and redeployment of imperial domination and coloniality as redemptive benevolence through the funding structures of international or global conservation.[110] Thus, conservationist benevolence is a redeployment of domination mechanisms.

Gregory and Vacarro's second key point is that the Indigenous Macushi, whose territories border the Centre, not only depend on it for employment, but "are portrayed as intrinsic components of the Iwokrama environment."[111] Thus, within their own homelands, their affiliation with the Centre means that the exercise of Macushi sovereignty fundamentally occurs within the "semi-permanent territorialization of market-oriented conservation and sustainable development."[112] Guyana's government receives international funds for maintaining forested conservation areas that offset "global carbon emissions through forest protections."[113] They therefore argue that the government is actually incentivized to cede portions of its territory to both Indigenous Peoples and non-Indigenous groups in order to secure "the assisted expansion of state sovereign power."[114] Conservation, therefore, allows *right*, the very right that was subordinated to (nation) state integrity in the UN Declaration, to function as the subversion of Indigenous sovereignty.

I spend a good deal of time on Gregory and Vaccaro's findings because they clearly illustrate the limits of Indigenous sovereignty's exercise in the postcolonial state. They demonstrate that Caribbean mechanisms of settler colonialism constrain Indigenous right through its negotiation against nation-state sovereignty, the reorganization of imperial power in international finance networks, and the levels of advocacy of local, nongovernmental, governmental, and international actors. They reveal how settler colonial power is exercised in postcolonial Guyana in a fundamentally different way from other contexts because state governmentality must first be ceded to international actors to be enacted. Moreover, the complex nature of land title in Guyana shows the deep imbrications of imperialism, coloniality, and postcolonialty. The issuance of title to Indigenous lands was a condition of the country's independence in 1966, and the postcolonial government undertook it in earnest in 1976.[115] The British (and Dutch) who had initially restricted Indigenous right to lands became, at independence, the contractual arbiters of the return of Indigenous land in the postcolonial period. Moreover, since the postcolonial state must grant rights, it affirms British (and Dutch) usurpation of Indigenous right as part of the necessary condition of first the colonial and later the postcolonial state's existence. The state itself may perceive land title as an existential threat and so always acts legally to constrain it. As Bulkan notes, the Guyanese state does not grant "Amerindian autonomy outside its sphere of control."[116]

While there are other ways to discuss sovereignty beyond reducing it to land rights, this critical element of its enactment demonstrates how control of land, and hence the achievement of full sovereignty, is directly linked to the institution of a land-labour divide as a feature of settler coloniality's governing mechanisms. The constraint on Indigenous sovereignty through the exclusion of "river and creek banks" and rights to "minerals and ground water" from the land titles granted to Indigenous Peoples in Guyana (as Griffiths and LaRose point out) must be read as a reenactment of coloniality's space clearing through the reinstitution of the land-labour divide. Title granting occurs under a legal distinction (by the Amerindian Act in this case) between the land and productive labour upon it (e.g., state-organized labour to extract minerals). By reserving mineral and water rights (and limiting Indigenous right to water as a state resource), Guyana's government distinguishes the land from its *products* extracted by capital and modern labour power. This distinction between land and labour, between the unproductive and the productive, enacts settler power through the division of the land as a political phenomenon (the settler function) from labour as an economic action on the land (the master function).

In Guyana we see the deployment of the mechanisms of settler coloniality to maintain postcolonial viability for a state sovereignty that is always under threat from underdevelopment, external boundary challenges, and the ceding of internal lands.[117] The strategies of governance impinging on Indigenous right and sovereignty in the face of these threats must be placed in the context of settler colonialism and how it "reentrenches its own power," rather than viewed narrowly as the singular effects of franchise colonialism.[118] Robinson, Simpson, Betasamosake Simpson, and Newcomb clarify that it is settler strategies, rather than just (postcolonial) nation-state actors, that continue to impinge on Indigenous freedom and forms of self-determination and relation to land.

Critically important is Betasamosake Simpson's critique of settler colonialism as that which exists in direct contradiction to the forms of self-determination she describes and which must be eliminated in the process of exercising Indigenous freedoms, self-determination, and governance.[119] She writes, "I understand settler colonialism's present *structure* as one that is formed and maintained by a series of processes for the purpose of dispossessing, that create a scaffolding within which my relationship to the state is contained."[120] If settler colonialism is expressed through a set of structures, we must look at those structures where they exist in countries, not just at the populations of those countries. We must look more broadly beyond the body of the white settler-master and at all the ways and kinds of peoples who have in fact stayed and at *how* they have stayed. We must examine, as Iwokrama demonstrates, the adaptive nature of settler structures of governmentality. Decolonization efforts within the postcolonial state need to be rethought in light of Betasamosake Simpson's argument that any state that either relies on or inherits settler modes of governmentality contributes fundamentally to the dispossession of Indigenous Peoples. Not only are former franchise colonies not free from settler colonial habits, laws, or structures of governance, but the deployment of these mechanisms of rule inside the settler colonial state reflects an adaptation and redeployment of the settler-master position.

My decision to frame this discussion of blackness, indigeneity, and labour within questions about sovereignty and settler colonialism is thus threaded through a desire and a conflict. The desire is to imagine Indigenous sovereignty in terms of its *consequence* for postcolonial independence. The conflict is how to argue for such a mode of sovereignty or right, in support of its expansion, when it is so problematic a concept. According to Alfred, "the next phase of scholarship and activism . . . will need to transcend the mentality that supports the colonization of indigenous nations, beginning with the rejection of the term and notion of indigenous 'sovereignty.'"[121] I have chosen, however, to retain the term despite its problems in order to indicate a specific kind of counter valence to independence and to suggest the consequential way in which I imagine Indigenous rights having real impacts *on* the postcolonial state and for its citizens. When I refer to sovereignty in this book as that which needs to be at the core of postcolonial politics, I do not indicate one form of Indigenous governance. Instead, the collective practices of self-determination of the Wai Wais, Macushis, Potomonas, Arawaks, Caribs, Wapichan, Arecunas, Akawaios, and Warraus in Guyana are what I suggest be writ large in that country. I argue that Indigenous self-determination must be consequential for non-Indigenous Peoples both when they are on what are circumscribed as Indigenous homelands and when they are in the territories of the wider postcolonial state, whether those lands have or have not been marked as non-Indigenous either prior to or after conquest.

The governing concept of sovereignty in this book originates from collective Indigenous Peoples' practices with political consequence for the involuntary settler state, which must constitutionally be subject to Indigenous legal and political structures. In other words, Indigenous sovereignty should be exercised not only on Indigenous lands for native peoples, but together with different Indigenous nations for the postcolonial state. Only in this way postcoloniality can be practiced without constraining both Indigenous sovereignty and Creole freedom. This call for a widening of Indigenous sovereignty is not about newly or more legitimately indigenizing Creole populations. I do not ascribe a redemptive function to indigeneity nor legitimize fantasies of becoming native, which are keenly and structurally tied to Indigenous dispossession. Rather, this is an effort to address the global absurdity where settler and postcolonial states delimit Indigenous Peoples' self-determination without being able to accept that the latter should inform their own governance as well. In formerly colonized Caribbean countries, we have the greatest possibility of reinventing the postcolonial state, ridding it of its settler habits and valences, and affirming Indigenous sovereignties in their priorness to and exceeding of state's rights.

This shift in the exercise of postcolonial politics for which I am calling also means that we must confront narratives of arrival, which I discussed in *Creole Indigeneity*, that are now tied to forms of (post) colonial state power. Moreton-Robinson not only echoes criticisms of postcoloniality and diaspora for their affirmations of "migrancy" over and above Indigenous belonging. Speaking of Australia, she also argues that the term "postcolonial" cannot apply to the entire country because the spaces Indigenous Peoples inhabit are not postcolonial.[122] She writes, "In postcolonizing settler societies, Indigenous people ... position all non-Indigenous people as migrants and diasporic. ... This ontological relation to land constitutes a subject position that we do not share, that cannot be shared, with the postcolonial subject."[123] While Moreton-Robinson argues here about the postcoloniality of a normative settler state, her claims remain applicable for thinking about nonwhite, postcolonial states.[124]

Although in the Caribbean we are talking of populations of color, our postcoloniality is still dependent on the ways that empire and the coloniality out of which the nation-state emerged supported whiteness. Whiteness in this context is more than a racial or cultural designation or ideological position. It is achieved through strategies of governance, retained after independence, supporting and reinforcing the global dominance of whiteness as full political representation and ownership (recall Wynter's critique of Marx). Moreover, slavery and indenture have produced Creole populations that we perceive as native, a becoming that is "incommensurable" with those of its First Peoples, especially where it is secured by non-Indigenous, anti-Indigenous modes of governance.

In Guyana, this is nowhere clearer than where the state must grant titles to Indigenous Peoples, determine who is racially Indigenous, and limit full access to the land and mineral rights of Indigenous Peoples. These "regulatory measures" are defined, Moreton-Robinson writes, by "the possessive logics of patriarchal white sovereignty" in order to "quantify what is recognizable as indigeneity within modernity."[125] States thus fundamentally restrict Indigenous sovereignty by repeatedly placing Indigenous peoples within systems of being and governance that "dispossess the Indigenous subject of an ontology that exists outside the logic of capital."[126] Postcolonial states and their populations of migrants/arrivants still retain the logics of possession and therefore must still act to limit Indigenous sovereignty so that it does not threaten the state itself.[127] Moreover, they continue to deploy not just the legal and political mechanisms of Indigenous dispossession, but a settler-master grammar and structure of power that pulls Creoles into the position of the settler through an inhabiting that is historically and contemporaneously based on their own prior subordination and on that of Indigenous Peoples through the land-labour division essential to the rise of capital.

As theorist Fred Moten reminds us by elaborating the DuBoisian color line in *Stolen Life*, these grammars of difference in which time is both "anoriginal" and anachronistic are not ours.[128] The problem then becomes, how do we confront and reject the grammar? How do we read together two labours (native and nonnative) that cannot operate in nor at the same time because they are now expressed via a biopolitical relation rather than on their own terms? How can we achieve a new approach to labour outside the land-labour dialectic, through which the postcolonial state may act to allow for a fuller expression of Indigenous self-determination with consequential, quotidian impacts for all its citizens? How can Independence become the true practice of freedom rather than the sacrifice of bodily and land-based sovereignties for both blacks and Indigenous Peoples? These are the collective questions to which this book seeks answers.

PART I

Labour, Work, *and* Middle/Passages

1. CONVERSION

Land as Labour and Labour as Land

This project centers three antagonisms that inform black-native relations in the Americas. The first two—land and labour, and independence and sovereignty—are the overarching, interlinked frame of the book. The land-labour dialectic is one effect of the need to clear the land of supposedly unproductive bodies and populate it with those that both produce and (sexually) reproduce themselves so that the settler-master can accumulate.[1] Thus, not only are the historical, social, and political possibilities for Indigenous Peoples and for enslaved blacks and their descendants manipulated initially and continually by the settler's material desires and needs. In addition, both groups are positioned on opposite sides of settler volition. Settler volition and desire are reflected in the postcolonial states' prioritizing of labour (or national development) over land. Thus, as a break from colonial power that continues elements of *settler power*, independence necessarily means greater integration into the global economic order in direct opposition to Indigenous sovereignty. However, the land-labour dialectic is neither foundational nor a fully accurate way of understanding the opposition between blackness and indigeneity. This part, "Labour, Work, and Middle/Passages," explores the background of the land-labour dialectic in order to develop a method for reading and resisting it.

While we often see blacks as identified with forms of primitive accumulation on lands cleared of Indigenous bodies, the land-labour assemblage itself has a more complex history, originating not with the introduction of bound, enslaved labour. It begins when Indigenous peoples are first made to *work* for conquistadors and colonizers in the Caribbean islands and South and Central America, and to have their "bodily actions"—a term I borrow from Hannah Arendt—associated with a particular kind of productive or extractive work that is then opposed to their own actions for themselves (i.e., subsistence). The land-labour dialectic is thus made possible by a third, prior antagonism that is the focus of this chapter: the structural opposition between labour and work. *Labour* reflects a sovereign relation of bodies to land, and *work* is the Conversion of that labour to objective forms that can accumulate and support later settler sovereignties. Unpacking this opposition requires a reassessment of both labour and land in accumulation processes, which I do by rereading colonial texts as well as critiques and clarifications of Marxist concepts. Black-native relations will remain at an impasse until we identify what I see as the macro-structural opposition between *labour* and *work*, articulate how it operates, and learn to work within the break of all three antagonisms.

The land-labour divide between natives and blacks relies on the assumption that Indigenous People did not do the work of later arrivants. However, prior to conquest, those peoples who *become* blacks and natives have transformative relationships to nature, which they affect and by which they are affected. Out of this interaction, this labouring on and in nature, land emerges as a relational space of human activity. As political theorist Robert Nichols makes clear, land for Marx must be understood as an outcome (though not predetermined) of human involvement with nature.[2] Building on Nichols's reading, land, affected by preconquest black and native interactions with it and by their labour on it, emerges as a sovereign home and space of practice for their political modes, cultures, and ontologies.

Enslaved blacks (as first dispossessed natives and later Creoles) are separated not just from the lands they inhabited. They are also separated from the *labour for themselves* they performed on that land, which they transformed into a sovereign home. In the Americas, native peoples, like blacks, are also separated (cleared) from the land and from the forms of labour they performed on it. Thus, franchise colonialism and slavery always create two labour relationships. Black enslaved bodies carry with them into the dungeon and the hold the accumulated exchange between their bodies and lands that slave making tries to eliminate. Additionally, native peoples in the Americas always labour on their lands and continue to do so even when removed to other territories, though that labour does not necessarily produce a new sovereignty.[3] The body of both Indigenous Africans as would-be enslaved peoples and Indigenous Peoples in the Americas is never free of the land. Thus, the land (in Africa and the Americas) is never labour-free.[4]

The land-labour dialectic, which positions blacks and Indigenous Peoples on opposite sides of work in the Americas, assumes a specific correlation between the work performed on the land (the plantation) and the land itself. Stolen land (again imbued with Indigenous labour) becomes reorganized or accessible now only through the productive black labour that has been performed on it. By tying their bodily actions to work on the land in the colonial period, the descendants of the formerly enslaved move forward through time, unlike Indigenous peoples, whose bodies are tied to unproductive land in the past. Blacks, in other words, are tied to exploitative stages of accumulation through labours that are part of capital formation's evolutionary narrative. Indigenous Peoples, by contrast, are fixed in a single moment of accumulation (land acquisition) that has been overcome.

Corrections to this concept of primitive accumulation that is bound to black enslaved labour, however, are not without their limits. In his essay "Disaggregating Primitive Accumulation," Nichols critiques contemporary scholars' problematic extension of primitive accumulation to theorize a range of conditions of exploitation from indigeneity to postcoloniality.[5] Seeking a better account of primitive accumulation, Nichols argues that the key feature seized on by contemporary theorists, "expropriation" or "dispossession," should be understood in Marx's original articulation as a relationship between "exploitation and dispossession" that is evidenced in the land-labour relationship.[6] In elaborating it, Nichols offers key observations for this analysis. First, he writes that "capitalism disrupts our orientation in space, our place-based relations."[7] Second, he clarifies that land for Marx is not strictly an object or commodity that is opposed to labour, but is both "inside and outside of the labour process." Nichols writes that while "Marx's use of the term 'land' is . . . intended to link labour and nature[,] . . . it is not synonymous with either."[8] Teasing out this understanding of land may help reroute and reframe the universalist tendencies in static concepts of primitive accumulation through the recognition that land-labour relationships express diverse peoples' specific sets of interactions with nature.

Emphasizing that dispossession is a feature of primitive accumulation, Nichols posits that while expropriation and dispossession allow the land to become the object of labour or to exist as nature to be manipulated by labour, there is no one-to-one relationship between land and the outcomes of labour. In other words, land and how we interact with it reflect relationships with nature that are not coextensive with those under capital. Nichols recovers from Marx this crucial break between proletarianization and primitive accumulation, where the former is neither the goal nor the automatic product of the latter, making possible contemporary uses of the concept without reinscribing its teleological outcomes.[9] This, Nichols says, allows primitive accumulation to function as a "constitutive and contemporary" concept.[10] Also significant here is Nichols's claim that "if we follow Marx's logic back through the various manifestations of the means of production, we arrive at the insight that the 'separation process' at the heart of dispossession is a separation of the bulk of humanity from the productive power of nature."[11]

I interpret Nichols's rereading of the labour-nature-land relation to mean that what we understand as land in the first half of the land-labour dialectic is always already a labour relationship of all Indigenous Peoples to the earth. However, conquest, settler, and franchise colonialism substitute this relationship for one that separates them from that labour and, I argue, turns their bodily actions *into work* in a transformation that allows that labour to now be marked for and read into (or out of) regimes of accumulation. Consequently, labour is either productive work (for regimes of accumulation) or nonproductive labour: the dialectic at the heart of the labour-land divide. Moreover, if, as Nichols says, "capitalism disrupts...our orientations in space," then what we mark as land for Indigenous Peoples would better be understood as their separation from nature and from their own actions or labours on it. What we mark as labour for blacks would better be understood as both their separation from nature (the disruption of their spatial orientation) and their relationship to land as that which they have invested and transformed by their own Indigenous, pre-slavery modes of labour on it.

If we recognize Indigenous Africans' prior relationship to land, which stems from their own sovereign forms of labour, we undo the teleological link between their bodily forms of labour and the objects of that labour under franchise colonialism as emphasis on marronage seeks to do. When, however, we make a blanket affirmation of and seek to theorize from the land-labour split, we simultaneously identify both groups through the separation germane to primitive accumulation, time (labour, blacks), and space (land, natives). In other words, the identification of Indigenous Peoples with land and blacks with labour reinscribes the telos of primitive accumulation and its presumption of only one relationship each group has with land or labour, respectively. It ignores the fact that plantation work for blacks reflects not just their labour exploitation (what I read as a condition of bare extraction under slavery that generates death out of Death) but also their prior *dispossession* from land imbued with their labour and onto lands that must now only function as an object or "instrument" of their bodily actions within pre- or proto-capital accumulation.[12]

My use of "exploitation" to discuss the extraction of work from black bodies during slavery differs from the Afropessimist position in name only. For Afropessimists, only workers (i.e., those capable of humanity who are therefore not black/enslaved) can be exploited.[13] Here, because I focus on primitive accumulation, I use exploitation to mark not the condition of the worker, but that of bare extraction from black *and* native bodies that is the precondition for the forms of exploitation the worker will face under full-fledged capitalist systems. In *The Groundings with My Brothers*, Walter Rodney argues that the aim of slavery was black death, to which he accords primacy over a simple profit motive.[14] Therefore, exploitation as a form of bare extraction, when applied to blacks, means that slavery is a form of death structured on the ontological Death of the hold and dungeon. The exploitation of native peoples (see Las Casas) is a form of death structured on the ontological death of removal or dispossession.[15] Blacks *and* native peoples must essentially die twice to bring capitalism into being.

When we maintain the break between labour and land, we ignore that for Indigenous Peoples land—as what the spaces they occupy become through the built environment of the plantation and wider colony—reflects their dispossession from nature and from the *labour* that transformed it into land for them outside pre-capitalist accumulation. Therefore, primitive accumulation includes two key, relational dispossessions (not just exploitation and extraction), which we often read out of the analysis. Moreover, to the extent that we continue to see settler colonialism as distinct from franchise colonialism, we reinforce the break between land and labour and Elimination and Death that supports both, when in fact the latter two are forms of dispossession that congeal into post-contact indigeneity and blackness.

Franchise colonialism has to incorporate settler elements (specifically, the clearing of blacks *from their Indigenous lands* so they can function as slaves, and the eliminatory clearing of the land *from black bodies*, which is collectively their *Death* as achieved by the dungeon and the hold of the slave ship). Settler colonialism has to incorporate elements of franchise colonialism (the reduction of native bodies to productive forms and Indigenous *death*, which here is the productive form of their work for franchise colonialism where their labour is insufficient and/or where the need for their land is greater than the need for their labour). To read these dispossessions together, we must explore how the land-labour dialectic results from what this chapter centers on: the original division between what is considered *productive work* (bodily actions that transform land into an object of labour that accumulates) and *unproductive labour* that seems unable to achieve accumulative extraction from the land, even though the latter necessarily already reflects a transformative engagement with nature by Indigenous Peoples. In chapter 2, I suggest that we have misread the origins of primitive accumulation with regard to Indigenous Peoples, which is not, or not only, characterized by land acquisition or theft.

I route the analysis of land and labour here through Marxist critique, which remains useful for thinking through the delinking of black and native lives. Nichols's revision of Marx's account of primitive accumulation allows us to posit that when the land-labour dialectic is instituted, labour becomes, for blacks, a relation to nature (not land), as that which is always already modified by the specific mode of production (now European) under which they engage it. The land, in other words, will always reflect black alienation—even after emancipation and independence. Although independence seeks to suture the land to black labour, those displaced descendants of enslaved (and indentured) peoples cannot be returned to the lands they have lost, to their antecedent sovereignties, because that land, as I wrote in *Creole Indigeneity*, now only exists in/on their skin, which is violently disciplined. In this structural phenomenon, not only are blacks dispossessed from their lands and acts of transformative and sovereign labour on those lands, but post-conquest black labour is never meant to create a metaphysics. Within the postcolonial state, this makes the need to control Indigenous sovereignty (and labour) even more urgent because, to the extent that Indigenous Peoples can claim prior sovereignty on lands, their ontologically sovereign labour does something that black labour cannot do, and it does so always in tension with the state that seeks to curtail or eliminate their sovereignty. The land-labour dialectic and the dialectic of sovereignty and independence it supports are thus the structural relation of anti-blackness to anti-indigeneity, rather than strictly the conflict between blacks and Indigenous Peoples.

This chapter details this foundational separation between labour and work under conquest and colonization, structuring the antagonism of land and labour and hence indigeneity and blackness in the Americas. I outline how the labour-work divide is instituted through a process of Conversion necessary for space clearing and accumulation. I reread the religious principle of Conversion as a core, historical moment when the wider Caribbean's divergent black and Indigenous histories were initiated together rather than seemingly disarticulated. Within this single, Christian monarchic imperative, black and Indigenous Peoples first link up in the fifteenth and sixteenth centuries, and within it Indigenous labour ultimately disappears from Caribbean historiography. I therefore return to Conversion as both limit and optic for moving us beyond the disarticulation of lives, histories, and rights across the time-space of the Americas.

I argue that Conversion, as a *religious-economic* phenomenon, is the concomitant process of the Middle Passage and the particular way in which the mechanism necessary for capital accumulation and later for reading capital (political economy and economics) is established in the Americas: the labour-work dialectic. The dialectic institutes labour and work as antagonistic and agonistic categories necessary for capital accumulation, within which blacks and Indigenous Peoples are positioned on opposite sides of work. Since the categories are based on the literal conversion of black and Indigenous bodily labours *away* from their sovereign expression, they are fundamentally anti-Indigenous and anti-black.

I begin by establishing the labour-work distinction. I then elaborate the process of Conversion and its manipulation of both black and Indigenous Death/death for value, exploring how it forces us to rethink use and exchange as two principle forms of value that are captured by and constitute the commodity, and relatedly the anti-blackness and anti-indigeneity not only of the labour category but of value itself. The chapter begins this middle/passage reading of blackness and indigeneity that the book advances by outlining how black enslavement in the Americas is fundamentally tied to native subordination and enslavement. It theorizes the middle/passage as a concomitant process of native Conversion that adds value to black bodies, while the latter devalues or extracts value from native bodies. It also shows how black Death and native Elimination function as necessary and intertwined processes for accumulation.

Throughout, I will use the term *Conversion* in three ways. First, to designate the spiritual and political process that Indigenous Peoples undergo. Second, to mark the broader *economic* mechanism through which Indigenous labours are literally converted to a state of failure or lack. Finally, to designate the more general process of bringing black *and* Indigenous labours into relation through the labour-work dialectic as their mutual Conversion, although

I use the carceral structures of the Middle Passage (the dungeon and the hold) to distinguish, up to a point, the transformation of black labours.[16]

Pessimisms: Invisible Labour versus Visible Work

In *The Human Condition*, political theorist Hannah Arendt draws on a historical, linguistic contrast between labour and work to develop this distinction:

> Labor is the activity which corresponds to the biological process of the human body, whose spontaneous growth, metabolism, and eventual decay are bound to the vital necessities produced and fed into the life process by labor. The human condition of labor is life itself. Work is the activity which corresponds to the unnaturalness of human existence, which is not imbedded in, and whose mortality is not compensated by, the species' ever-recurring life cycle. Work provides an "artificial" world of things, distinctly different from all natural surroundings.... Work and its product, the human artifact, bestow a measure of permanence and durability upon the futility of mortal life and the fleeting character of human time.[17]

This criticism of Marxism has been dismissed as "banal" and "ideological" by literary, political, and critical theory scholar Warren Montag, who discusses Cameroonian philosopher and political theorist Achille Mbembe's use of it to elaborate his concept of the necropolitical. However, I find that it has not been properly thought for its function in the remaking of black and native peoples as Europe's Others under the mechanisms of racialization and settler colonialism.[18] More recent work such as political scientist Cara New Daggett's *The Birth of Energy* continue to suggest that understanding what is read as work and what is cleaved from it (in her case, "waste") is critical to material planetary transformations, those same large-scale anthropogenic processes to which I turn in chapter 5, which are shaped by capital formation.

I therefore read Arendt's distinction in two ways: as it evolves within her critique of Marx and through the anti-black (and anti-Indigenous) limits of the critique itself. I find that while for Arendt the break between the terms is significant for political economy broadly, there is no account of how that break operates in the Caribbean at the beginning of the modern era, at the moment of the Columbian encounter or error. Moreover, the operation of the distinction in the Caribbean, as a so-called peripheral sphere that profoundly shaped the development of global capital, is in fact strategically central to the eventual collapse between labour and work that, for Arendt, has had devastating planetary consequences. In other words, the introduction of the divide in early Caribbean economies is a globally consequential phenomenon because it is there that the break is first instituted or expressed. It is expressed through a particular pessimism of native *and* black making in which we are placed on opposite sides of a dialectic between labour and work: our labours are understood as a relation between those that are successful or accumulative and hence *visible* and those that are not and hence are *invisible*, just as, for Arendt, work eclipses labour in Marxian analysis.

This invisible labour (Indigenous Peoples) and visible work (blacks) divide secures the excision of Indigenous Peoples from contemporary labour history, which itself works through modern political economy's substitution of unproductive labour for productive work. It also traps blacks in an antagonistic mode of representation premised on anti-indigeneity and anti-blackness. I take up the Arendtian differentiation in order to ultimately read against the grain of its collapse. I demonstrate that the early contrast between the bodily actions of blacks and Indigenous Peoples as work and labour, respectively, eventually delinks their actions in modern labour history and erases Indigenous labour from Caribbean history.

At stake here is not only a better account of a key point in the historical dis/articulation of labour and work in the production of what historian, sociologist, and geographer Jason W. Moore calls "cheap labor,"[19] but also the ability to recover Indigenous actions for Caribbean labour history, and a better recognition of the breaks between the specific labours of Creoles that link up with the time of the now-involuntary settler state and those that do not. Moreover, the distinctions I adapt from Arendt illuminate the global consequences of the opposition between nation-state independence (for former settler and franchise colonies) and Indigenous sovereignty to the extent that each is tied to and affirms different labour outcomes.

At the heart of modern political economy, Arendt claims, is the problematic suture of the economic and the political. Arendt argues that Marx, like his predecessors, recognized the historical distinction between labour and work but could not sustain it, and thus embraced its tautological collapse as "political economy." In Greek thought, the latter term is in fact not concerned with politics proper, but referred initially to household management, which had to be excluded from the political (the realm of freedom) because it encapsulated man's enslavement to necessity.[20] Arendt seems to fault Marx for both sustaining this distinction and accepting the break upon which it is founded: the object's value or "permanence." Because Marx is concerned with the end of private property, he focuses on what man's work produces. In so doing, Arendt says, Marx confuses "animal laborans" for "homo faber," collapsing the man who labours with the man who works or whose work ends in either the production of the object or that of the "potential productivity" of *homo politicus*.[21]

In volume one of *Capital*, although Marx identifies subsistence labour in contrast to productive labour and offers a more expansive view of nature in relation to labour (recall Nichols), he is decidedly focused on labour's objective or productive outcomes. He writes, for instance, "If we examine the whole process from the point of view of its result, the product, it is plain that both the instruments and the subject of labour are means of production and the labour itself is productive labour."[22] Later, he continues, "labour consumes products in order to create products, . . . consumes one set of products by turning them into means of production for another set."[23] Within the capitalist mode of production, productive labour (which depends on waged labour) generates surplus values that transform money or commodities into capital. It is distinct from the reproductive labour through which the worker reproduces the means of his own existence or his "labour power."[24] The labour process, then, as described by Marx, concerns a particular concept of productive labour fundamental to capital, within which labour is always necessarily either captured within the object as product (as a use or exchange value) or fails to be. It prioritizes this rather than retaining and theorizing the distinction between labour that is objective in character and labour that is not.

Modern political theory is largely concerned with the form of productive labour in Marx, which it reifies, according to Arendt, as *work*. For Arendt, political economy emphasizes productive forms of labour because of the world-historical function of "work" or the "world building capacity of man," which requires the valorization of all labour *as* work in order for it to be represented and managed by political economy.[25] Simply put, labour's affirmation as work is the capture of its productivity. For this reason, she suggests, Adam Smith, John Locke, and Marx have all "endowed" labour "with certain faculties which only work possesses" because their political theories are based on labour's permanence as work and its products: wealth and property.

Arendt finds this valorization of work—which obscures its difference from labour—to be fatal on a planetary level for two reasons, which are critical in foregrounding the consequences of the split between black and native labour and lives. First, because our capacity for world, for history, and for the human is now based on a form of alienation in which nature or "matter" is necessarily changed into what is "material" through a fundamentally destructive process. Second, because in its perpetual accumulation (through the "endlessness of production"), capital—despite its terminus in objects rather than life—mimics the interminable nature of the life cycle.[26] According to Arendt, wealth accumulation is now "infinite" like the "life process of the species," so "we have changed work into labour."[27] Summarily, life and livelihoods have been substituted by or taken over by the labour process under capitalist systems.[28] As only one mode of the outcome of human action, the productive form of labour facilitating accumulation processes is now collapsed with and is read as all other forms of labour.

Human possibility is limited, then, not simply by capital accumulation but by our very categories of analysis, which fail to leave room for other expressions of bodily and planetary outcomes. Therefore, Arendt wants not only to remind us of the labour-work distinction but, it seems, to read it back into political economic analysis, to walk back from its catastrophic telos. For this study, we must understand how postcolonial independence that is based on or articulated through the productive outcomes of labour rejects, in Arendtian terms, life processes that do not have an objective character, that do not accumulate. The opposition between independence and sovereignty is thus an opposition between objective death (accumulation under capital) and productive life (subsistence under Indigenous and Maroon economies). Recognizing this, we must unpack Arendt's recovery of labour and address its limitations.

Arendt understands labour as a more generalized form of human action prior to its incorporation into capitalist political economy, which must be recovered because it reconnects with planetary life processes. She contends that "the distinction between productive and unproductive labour contains . . . the more fundamental distinction between work and labour."[29] Her attempt to recover labour from the terminus of work has both a specific relevance and a limitation for thinking the problem of black and Indigenous Peoples' labour in the Americas. Its relevance lies in its clarification that the institution of the division is meant to reorganize *all* relationships to land, past and present, such that they are fundamentally relationships of dispossession. Extending and adapting her criticism, if capital or pre-capital accumulation cannot happen without dispossession, then the primary or initiative reorganization of *sovereign* native (American and African) labour relationships to land is at the core of the split between labour and work that drives or structures accumulation. Arendt thus becomes useful for thinking land theft and Indigenous and black (chattel) enslavement as the primary and therefore antecedent structures of capital accumulation. Thus, the distinction between labour and work is not just a fault within Marxist analysis, nor just a feature of capitalist accumulation. It structurally emerges from black and Indigenous subordination or, more pointedly, from anti-blackness and anti-indigeneity.

The limit, however, of Arendt's distinction is a function of what it seeks to critique: political economy itself. Her differentiation between labour and work is from perspectival man, the limit perspective of what Sylvia Wynter would observe as western man's auto reinvention as a biological organism, a process that Michel Foucault also details. This is a subject that, as *homo narrans*, is always already capable of reason and is the basis for politics.[30] Arendt's concept, in other words, depends on a particular construct of the human as biological, a western understanding deployed as universal within her own criticism while she rejects the universality of labour (as work) within political-economic analysis. Thus, both political economy *and* her criticism of it have an inescapable shared conceit.

Reading Arendt through Wynter clarifies that the specific ways in which, in Darwinian fashion, western man has been reinvented as biological is, after *homo politicus*, coextensive with the evolution of *homo economicus* as a biological being whose hierarchies of blood and phenotype come to index relationships to capital and the products of work. Consequently, Arendt's division does not make sense without the narratologically constructed concept of man *as* biological in specifically western, humanist understandings.[31] Moreover, if it is fundamentally a biopolitical distinction (again based on a western concept of man), then we are forced to address the limits of biopolitics as an ineffective optic for conceptualizing the actions of blacks (and Indigenous Peoples) because it always already refers to political subjects, while blacks are never true political subjects because their Deaths precede subjecthood, and, as discussed in this book's introduction, serve as its threshold. Blacks are, tautologically, political subjects only *after* Death, a foreclosure that makes full representation and enfranchisement impossible. By contrast, for true biopolitical subjecthood, death may be an outcome but not a starting point. Giorgio Agamben's elaboration of *homo sacer*, for example, fails as an optic because it is meant to capture the "after" of normative political subjecthood. Thus, the Death blacks experience has no ontological equivalent within western metaphysics because it produces what Fred Moten refers to as their absolute or categorical "paraontological" difference from the western same and its human (as opposed to black inhuman) others.

Moreover, to the extent that, according to Marx, the specific ways in which the capitalist accumulates means that capital is "dead labor," enslaved blacks involved in (pre) capitalist accumulation are not only ontologically dead (before they work on what will become the products of their labour). Wherever they enter (proto) capitalist political-economic structures they are subjected to another level of death (i.e., killed) because, to the extent they gain some access to representation in this process, it cannot be redemptive nor restorative. This is the second death that I identified as black exploitation above. This second, disciplinary (as opposed to initiative) death always, therefore, occurs because of political economic structures and is simultaneously structurally excessive or "gratuitous" rather than "contingent" or punitive.[32] Thus, black Death from slavery to Jim Crow to contemporary state-sponsored police killings in the United States, for example, remains a functional requirement of western political-economic structures.[33] Black Death means that in seeking recourse to Arendt's useful dichotomy, we must address how work, the opposite side of the labour division tied to processes of accumulation, is not a space or structure of representation for blacks, although they are fundamentally defined by it. Not only is it the site and limit of black representation, but it reflects the fact that the production of blackness through slavery, through Death, places blacks and Indigenous Peoples on opposite sides of Death, on opposite ends of political subjectivity, where one has the capacity for it (Indigenous Peoples) and the other exists only at its limits (blacks).

Frank Wilderson extends the concept of blackness as the zero sum of humanity to argue that blacks are not only the most abject other. They make both humanness and *degrees* of humanness possible for whites (read the settler-master), for those he terms their "junior associates" (less human others who still do not share the position of blacks), as well as for Indigenous Peoples to the extent that their modes of suffering and redress can at least be partially translated in (white) human terms.[34] Religious studies professor William David Hart claims that for Wilderson, "As *dead objects* blacks are haunted by a form of dispossession that places them outside the semiotic systems of humans. They are separated from Marxist and psychoanalytic subjectivity by the hold of the slave ship."[35]

Throughout *Red, White, and Black*, Wilderson is clear that the hold of the slave ship, as a "Human *and* a metaphysical holocaust," cuts blacks off from all subject positions available to the human, both those of dominance and those of grievance; hence, critical and activist discourses that seek forms of redress for the "contingent" violence to which the human is subject rather than the "gratuitous" violence to which blacks are subject actually compound black nonhuman status.[36] In contrast, what distinguishes the settler and "the savage" (a term he borrows from early American writers to signal settler colonialism's remaking of Indigenous identity) from the enslaved person (marking the remaking of blacks through enslavement) is precisely their shared "capacity for time and space coherence," which he terms "cartographic coherence."[37] They both have a "coherent semiotics of loss" around "territorial integrity, political self-determination, economic independence, and religious freedom."[38] Blacks, on the other hand, do not have a "prior space and time" to which they can return and that governs an identity outside blackness, because the space and time of blackness is *always* slavery (or slave status) in its contemporaneity.[39] For Wilderson, although native peoples are structurally subordinated within white supremacy, they are "homunculi" rather than, as blacks are, infrahumans.[40]

This lack of black ability to literally have a geographic space is tied to the fact that for Wilderson, the irrevocable difference between blacks and Indigenous Peoples is that as "dead objects," blacks can possess nothing. native peoples, on the other hand, have land that settlers want, so, he argues, what settlers require from them is consent. Thus for Wilderson, the process of treaty making, for instance, no matter how coercive, represents the "capacity" for representation based on the ability to possess rather than be possessed. In contrast, Blacks function to make consent possible within civil society.[41] According to Wilderson, the processes of becoming "savage" are so fundamentally distinct from processes of becoming enslaved that the settler-native opposition sits structurally atop the black-human opposition, and this positioning is essential to the former's legibility as an opposition between humans and homunculi as a gradation of the human.[42] Some of Wilderson's claims are problematic, especially where land (read: cartography) and time (read: lack of prior space of return) become the main opposition between blacks and Indigenous Peoples because they reinstitute the labour-land divide that separates us.

However, we cannot ignore Indigenous Peoples' uniqueness as political subjects, which Wilderson writes of and which is borne out by, for instance, the UN Declaration on the Rights of Indigenous Peoples. The Declaration codifies Indigenous humanity by recognizing that "indigenous individuals are entitled without discrimination to all human rights recognized in international law" and "possess collective rights which are indispensable for their existence, well-being and integral development as peoples."[43] While it affirms a broad concept of equality in difference at its outset, the Declaration recognizes Indigenous *Peoples* (rather than nations) as having the ability to accrue particular rights. No such affirmation of black human rights appears in any of the documents that ended slavery, in part because blacks lacked global territoriality at the time of emancipation, which makes them fundamentally different from Indigenous groups all over the world.

Moreover, in Article 2 the Declaration affirms Indigenous Peoples' "right to be free from any kind of discrimination, in the exercise of their rights, in particular that based on their indigenous origin or identity."[44] Not only have formerly enslaved blacks lost their indigeneity. Now, that lost indigeneity cannot serve as a basis for an identity than can be broadly protected. Moreover, Indigenous Peoples, in contrast to blacks, can have not only those broadly recognizable, antecedent rights that make them bodies of right (or recipients, vectors, or subjects of rights). They are also entitled to something fundamentally denied blacks: forms of reparations. Article 20 states that "Indigenous peoples deprived of their means of subsistence and development are entitled to just and fair redress."[45] Even the Dominican Friar Bartolomé de Las Casas, writing in the sixteenth century, acknowledges this right as one of would-be human status by stating that "they had, from the very beginning, every *right* to wage war on the Europeans, while the Europeans never had just cause for waging war on the local peoples."[46] During slavery in Guyana, the Dutch, and later the British, restricted Indigenous rights but also liaised with Indigenous People and "recognized" Indigenous leadership.[47] Moreover, despite their failure to grant land titles, the British created Indigenous reservations in order to return Indigenous Peoples to lands that they *could* possess, after conquest. Keeping this in mind, the distinctions between blacks as infrahumans and Indigenous Peoples as homunculi (with the always already deferred potential to become fully human), supports Wilderson's distinctions between having land and not having anything but the ability to exercise labour on that land for the master-settler.[48]

For both Wilderson and Hart, Indigenous Peoples do not suffer the categorical Death of blacks that positions the latter not just as objects, or even things, but as nonbeings who have crossed the threshold into the absolute Difference of "nothingness." The Declaration technically bears out Hart's observations about Wilderson's argument: that the figure of the "savage" remains potentially intelligible under forms of sovereignty even if only in terms of loss, because the capacity for loss and return makes Indigenous Peoples essentially only "half dead."[49] Arendt herself, in *The Origins of Totalitarianism*, also refers to "natives" as savages (differently than Wilderson does): although they reflect a kind of irrationality for her, they represent an evolutionary stage of European culture, society, and peoplehood in contrast to blacks. Despite her attempt to critique European colonialism and its blind and intrinsic violence, Arendt uses the "savage" as, after Chinua Achebe, a "foil" for European humanity.[50] She also distinguishes the term (black) "savage" from the worker (who is black in the colonies) and who, like the native, also has evolutionary capabilities.[51] The "savage" in her work represents an irredeemable position unlike the native. The black in Arendt is redeemable only as other than itself, that is, as native or worker, while the latter allows the enslaved person or the black, but not the savage, to aspire to humanity. Though premised on a condition of subordination, this capacity for political life and sovereignty makes politics accessible to Indigenous Peoples, but not to blacks.

The limits of subjecthood for blacks leave us with Fred Moten's assertion that biopolitics (with its affirmation of life) is not the terrain of blackness because it rests on a conceptualization of man as a "political animal," while blackness is conceived in the break of these terms rather than their suture.[52] Defining blackness as "the anoriginal displacement of ontology," Moten asserts that "black life—which is as surely to say *life* as black thought is to say *thought*—is irreducibly social; that, moreover, black life is lived in *political* death or that it is lived, if you will, in the burial ground of the subject by those who, insofar as they are not subjects, are also not, in the interminable ... analysis, 'death bound.'"[53] Since blacks, for Moten, experience the hold as an originary or initiative displacement (read: Death as elaborated by Wilderson and, below, Hartman), there "is a certain black incapacity to desire sovereignty and ontological relationality whether they are recast in the terms and forms of a Lévinasian ethics or an Arendtian politics, a Fanonian resistance or a Pattersonian test of honor."[54] This, on the one hand, is the foreclosure of Arendtian categories for blacks because Arendt speaks of the political animal, not those experiencing political subjecthood as its foreclosure. Moreover, since the labour-work division Arendt employs is based on biological subjects who are already political subjects/animals, this division is in one sense *internal* to the human as a political animal.[55]

Yet, precisely because Arendt tries to carve out and elaborate a distinction inside the always already of *homo economicus*'s labour (as a pure reproductive biological life) and work (as the field of the political animal), we can read the phenomenological "exhaustion" that Moten finds useful in her writing. Although she represents what he terms a "dissident strain of phenomenology," in *The Universal Machine*, Moten identifies in Arendt's writings an "antiblack refusal to see black political subjectivity" that allows us to more clearly realize how blacks refuse such modes of (single being) subjectivity.[56] It is thus the limits of Arendt and her inability to recognize blacks or Indigenous Peoples as rational political subjects, rather than the normative, celebratory way in which she is taken up by most thinkers, that becomes useful. With this in mind, I return to her criticism of Marx in *The Human Condition*.

Despite its limits, Arendt's distinction creates space for thinking about the actions or labours that Indigenous Peoples and blacks do for themselves versus the work they must do for Europeans. This terminological break offers a way of approaching and making visible how the constant reinscription of liberal subjectivity in postcolonial studies belies the "mimetic" desire (Wynter) for whiteness (as a relation to class and as an expression of a genetically redeemed status) in the capture of all of our labours as and through work.[57] In other words, although Arendt's distinction between labour and work unwittingly points to the lack of a priorness for the analysis of human action within political economy, she offers a useful mode of reading for understanding the capture of bodily actions that would be instrumental to the uneven recognition of black and Indigenous peoples in Caribbean labour history. It allows us to read labour correlatively, first through this internal division that represents failure (or exhaustion, after Moten), and second, through an external priorness and sovereignty of relation. An example of what this means occurs in the work of Métis artist Marilyn Dumont's poem, "Not Just a Platform for My Dance," which reads:

this land is not
just a place to set my house my car my fence

this land is not
just a plot to bury my dead my seed

this land is
my tongue   my eyes   my mouth

this headstrong grass and relenting willow
these flat-footed fields and applauding leaves
these frank winds and electric sky

are my prayer
they are my medicine
and they become my song

this land is not
just a platform for my dance

Dumont's assertion that land is not simply a space on which the phenomenological is staged "but instead "is" or exists as "my tongue my eyes my mouth," opens up what Arendt's use of the labour-work distinction productively *failed* to open onto: nothing less than the equal relation of body and land, which Arendt can only apocalyptically approach as a return *within* political economy, rather than as a beginning.[58] In Dumont's work, this equal relation does not mean that the land is fixed or that it doubles the Indigenous body or substitutes for it, as in capitalist political economy. It is movement and this is sovereignty, in stark contrast to what will become reservations that are based, legally, on the lack of movement.

Arendt's sticky distinction between labour and work thus becomes a way, within political economy, to mark the labours that might belong to the animal that is not pre-political, the political animal embedded in capitalist political economy, and the infrahumans and *potential* political animals (blacks and natives, respectively) captured within capitalist political economy in the postcolony as success (blacks) and failure (native).[59] Her work becomes useful for apprehending what actually shapes the pre-positional relationship between blacks and Indigenous Peoples. It allows us to understand that the contemporary break between them (where the latter is essentially a failed market identity and the former successful) is not only the absolute inverse of their relationship to Death.[60] It is strategically a function of how their precapitalist subordination hinges on the imminent collapse of labour and work within modern political theory. Moreover, Arendt's writing reminds us that, although political subjecthood may be differently un/available to blacks and native peoples, it does not mean, as Afropessimism holds, that all forms of relation are foreclosed.

Nor does it mean that the structural antagonism—imposed by black chattel slavery and settler colonialism—of Indigenous Peoples as subjects of rights to blacks as objects of Death is insurmountable. Instead, I argue that black Death and Indigenous "half" death must always be understood as being in relation. In other words, while for Afropessimism the black as abject human other makes possible all other forms of human relation, black Death arises out of a relationship to nativities past and present. Black

Death is therefore a specific form of nonequivalent *relation* to indigeneity and to Indigenous Peoples, rather than just a radical and unbridgeable break from all (possible) humans.

Conversion is the historical phenomenon that institutes the labour-work dialectic. It is an analytic that foregrounds blacks' and Indigenous Peoples' movements to and within these vectors of un/productive work, and the acts of being mis/read that they represent. Emphasizing this movement allows us to go beyond the limits of Death—of being truly dead or only half dead—as the no less limited articulation of a superimposed difference between blacks and Indigenous Peoples, in which the possibility of Indigenous sovereignty (for Afropessimism) necessarily remains elaborated through (to reference Hart and Wilderson) the very limits imposed on it. I now turn to outline how Conversion and the Middle Passage emerge as concomitant processes that value and devalue native and black bodies, respectively, and elaborate what this means for understanding black and Indigenous Death/death in terms of their relation, not exclusion. I begin with early writings about the region in which two modes of labour emerge to eventually be falsely captured by the labour-work division.

Conversion

It is possible to read Caribbean history in terms of at least two concurrent, divergent modes of *labour* from the moment the region first entered what I have referred to as the discursive or symbolic economy imposed by Europeans at the time of the Columbian error.[61] This economy, evident in Christopher Columbus's texts about the Americas, has two dimensions: scarcity (and hence needs) and abundance (or excess). In his first letter about the Caribbean, written after he arrived back in the Canary Islands, Columbus writes, "And I gave a thousand handsome good things, which I had brought, in order that they might conceive affection, and more than that, might become Christians and be inclined to the love and service of their highnesses and of the whole Castilian nation, and strive to aid us and to give us of the things which they have in abundance and which are necessary to us."[62]

Columbus identifies Indigenous Peoples with a surplus of resources while essentially identifying Europeans with scarcity and needs. Twice in the letter, he refers to lands and people as "innumerable" or "without number."[63] Indigenous Peoples thus come to be associated with "abundance" and excess, which Columbus subordinates to European needs, and so the labour they do, and have done, to produce their own innumerability cannot be recognized as such.[64] Consequently, in every instance where Columbus references Indigenous Peoples' labours, either through direct physical work he witnessed or its products, it is always already subordinated to a language (read: discursive economy) external to them. In that economy, their labour for themselves, for their very reproduction as an innumerable population—which has occurred within the mandate of their own cosmogonic narratives and the social-political systems they produced—becomes misread as "necessary" (things/objects/work) for European survival. As such, Indigenous labour is immediately linked to the principle of scarcity that attains because of the sea voyage to the Americas, the precarious, unsustainable microcosm the caravels represent, and Columbus's mandate to find spices and precious metals for the Spanish kingdom whose resources had been depleted by the nearly eight-centuries-long Reconquista.

Through this collective, sustained scarcity, Columbus records (i.e., translates) in his letters what he observes of Indigenous labour. He refers to Indigenous Peoples who "carry their goods" or the products of their labour, and observes cane-made weapons harvested at "seeding time." He records boats "made of a single log of wood," whose "speed is a thing incredible," in which "they navigate among all those islands, which are innumerable, and carry their goods."[65] He further believes that "the women work more than the men."[66] Columbus sees Indigenous labour and its products, neither of which is part of the pre- and proto-capitalist economies of which he is a part. Read counterintuitively, Columbus's letters contain the beginnings of labour history in the Americas/Caribbean; in this history, an extant, parallel, nonaccumulative form or mode of labour is misread through its "conversion" within and to the global economies that will emerge from this encounter. Native labour for themselves is misread through its (later failed) conversion within and to *work*. This Conversion is effected precisely by the superimposed dialectic of abundance and scarcity/needs, the two modes or forms of capture (or failure of capture) of pre-contact Indigenous labour.

Conversion is understood in Columbus's era largely as a religious principle, the indoctrination into and acceptance of another faith as a mandate of Europe's Christian monarchs in their efforts to acquire overseas territories. As a political and (canonical) legal mechanism of conquest, Conversion has a complex history both before and after conquest of the Americas, and its ramifications unfolded differently across Latin America and for Caribbean territories as a whole, as the first place in the Western Hemisphere where its mandate was exercised and fulfilled by the Columbian voyage.[67] As a requirement, the refusal of which legitimated "just war" and conquest, Conversion facilitated the direct usurpation of Indigenous lands.[68] While religious Conversion and Indigenous vassalage did yield some protections for Indigenous Peoples, throughout Latin America those protections led to continued forms of Indigenous labour exploitation and bound labour.[69] Indigenous Peoples' forced labour continued under their vassalage, and enslaved blacks also had to be "converted" to Christianity, and manipulated it where possible. However, I focus on how Conversion literally cleaved Indigenous Peoples from blacks so that their labours could not be understood together, and the ramifications of this within Anglophone Caribbean labour history.[70]

Conversion, as I consider it here, is expressed in a host of texts, including Columbus's letters, Pope Alexander VI's Papal Bull of 1493 (the "Inter Caetera"), and Las Casas's work. The Papal Bull explicitly mandates the need to "instruct" the "inhabitants and residents"' of "discovered" "islands or mainlands" "in the Catholic faith and train them in good morals."[71] In his first letter, Columbus invokes it as the overarching justification for his voyage, writing that he will seek the Spanish sovereigns' permission for the "conversion to our holy faith" of the peoples he has encountered.[72] The need to convert Indigenous Peoples is accompanied by Columbus's pointed assertions about their absolute difference, in particular, from those non-Christians already known for nearly half a century since Portugal's African discoveries below Cape Bojador. He declares, "In these islands I have so far found no human monstrosities, as many expected, but on the contrary the whole population is very well-formed, nor are they negroes as in Guinea, but their hair is flowing, and they are not born where there is intense force in the rays of the sun."[73]

This need to convert newly discovered peoples to extend Europe's Christian social order—a well-known part of the Old World logic—helped maintain a way of being dominated by religious-monarchic rule. In *The American Indian and Western Legal Thought*, Lumbee legal scholar Robert A. Williams Jr. details the canonical arguments through which the Old World established and retained its rights to newly encountered territories, and which have eventually become foundational for international law and right regarding territorial acquisition and possession. However, the established rights to conquer non-Christian peoples attached to the conversion imperative were challenged in 1514. Then, the secular priest, *encomendero*, and later Dominican Friar, Protector of the Indians, and Bishop of Chiapas

Las Casas argued that Indigenous Peoples, though subordinate and fallen, should not be enslaved like the "negroes" of Guinea that Columbus mentioned, but instead be made "vassals" of the Spanish Crown.[74] This shift in Las Casas's thinking has been robustly theorized in Latin American and religious studies as the first of Las Casas's three major auto-conversions (his second conversion was his entrance into the Dominican Order in 1522, and his third was his eventual recognition that black slavery was unjust, beginning around 1547).[75]

Sylvia Wynter, who first theorizes Las Casas's conversion for Caribbean Studies, argues, in keeping with the general consensus on his transformation(s), that he came to recognize "the *relativity of all human systems of perception including our own*; as the reality, not of a single absolute reason, but of culturally determined modes of reason, as the reality of the cultural-historical relativity of our own."[76] In her two-part essay in *Jamaica Journal* in 1984, Wynter outlines the logic that led Las Casas to see the conquest and importation of blacks to the Americas as both "just" and necessary for the salvation of Indigenous Peoples, and to see the latter's conquest as "unjust." This "conversion" was essentially Las Casas's ability to reject prevailing reason; it was first a religious-ethical transformation to the *idea* of Indigenous humanity coextensive with the affirmation of black infrahuman status.

My interest in Las Casas lies in the arguments that allow blacks and natives to be delinked: not only do these arguments become generalized across the region's literature regardless of discipline, but Las Casas is their significant, outsized source. As a theological shift that disconnects earthly material gain from Christian spiritual gain, Las Casas's conversion is responsible for the rationale (not the initial cause) for wide-scale black enslavement in the Americas as a definitive substitute for native labour. He lays this rationale first in a 1516 "Memorial de Remedios" and again in a 1518 "Memorial de Remedios para Las Indias."[77] Arguing that "en muy breve tiempe quedarán las islas todas despobladas si muy presto no se sacan los indios del poder do los cristianos," Las Casas proposes the following to solve the Indigenous depopulation problem for then "Española, Cuba, Sant Juan y Jamaica":

> Lo tercero, que vuestra alteza haga merced a los cristianos que agora están en las islas, que puedan tener cada uno dos esclavos negros y dos negras y no debe de haber duda de la seguridad dellos, y darse han las razones para ello.

Later he continues,

Item, que cualquiera que hiciere ingenio para hacer azúcar, que vuestra alteza le mande ayudar con algunos dineros, porque son muy costosos, y les haga merced a los que los hicieren, *que puedan llevar y tener veinte negros y negras, porque con ellos ternán otros treinta cristianos que han menester por fuerza*, y ansí estarán los negros seguros.[78]

This conversion of Indigenous Peoples to partial humanity emerges as a poetic-cum-structural aporia that places Indigenous Peoples and blacks on opposite sides of labour. Blacks must do physical labour for material gain, while Indigenous Peoples, no matter what work they do in building missions and in their continued labour for the Spanish, are relegated to spiritual labours because for Las Casas they are firmly tied to the Christian goal of Conversion that justified the Spanish and Portuguese conquest. In short, Conversion devalues Indigenous bodily labours by essentially extracting value from them. They literally cannot work productively (or be seen as doing so) because it would undercut the religious imperative. Their labours for themselves, like that of Indigenous blacks transported for slave labour, become antecedent.

Read within black diaspora studies, the primacy of Caribbean/American, Indigenous Conversion over sub-Saharan, black enslavement exemplifies the difference between Indigenous Peoples and blacks that has led to the general position—within black studies and Afropessimism specifically— that blacks are in fact the *only* group ever entirely denied humanity. I suggest that this conversion's goal is not simply religious. Indigenous Peoples' bodies are read differently enough, so although blacks are already converted in Europe before being allowed to work there or in the Americas, during the period of slavery, blacks will not be admitted to the kind of partial humanity that made Indigenous Peoples servants of the crown. Its goal is also *economic*: Conversion is a mechanism of economic incorporation for proto-capitalist markets that increasingly relies on accumulation and is based on the precondition of Indigenous, eliminatory (i.e., initiative) death.

Thus, Indigenous *labour* could never be understood as anything other than *surplus* in the precapitalist and eventually capitalist economies that emerged (a point to which I return in chapter 2).[79] Their labour resulted in the creation and maintenance of "ecclesiastical plantations" throughout Latin America and the Hispanophone Caribbean, which are often not analyzed as contributing to world economic development as black plantation work, because Indigenous colonial labour/work was absorbed into and *as* the foundation (read: base) for the newly created, independent Latin American states in the early nineteenth century.[80] This process instituted an antagonism that involuntary settler states like those in the Caribbean can resolve for their black, South Asian, and Creole populations broadly, but not for Indigenous populations. The state, then, came to redirect and embody the futurity of Indigenous labour, delinking it from the Indigenous body and Indigenous cosmogonic narratives. Moreover, we can see in Latin America at the dawn of independence (early nineteenth century), the same equation in Fanon—"you are rich because you are white, you are white because you are rich"—used to stretch Marxist analysis for late colonies.[81] Therefore, there is a clear link between colonial Latin America, colonial Africa, and the early Caribbean with regard to race and economics. However, because subordinated classes have already been historically delinked in categories of analysis, the similarity of their positions is lost both historically and contemporaneously.

Las Casas's conversion that justified the importation of black enslaved labour was effective not only because it found a more reliable and in theory endlessly renewable labour source. It worked because it froze Indigenous labour in time-space and, by fixing and thus disappearing that labour, usurped their sovereignty. It rendered Indigenous Peoples' "work" invisible (prior to and at conquest) whether it was for their own well-being (labour) or for the continued well-being of the European cultural-economic system that supplanted theirs. In other words, while the conversion is identified as Las Casas's own recognition of Indigenous humanity (vis-à-vis Africans' infrahumanity), it is also part of that original Conversion that Columbus achieved in the discursive economy that rendered their labour invisible against Europe's needs (scarcity). In this latter Conversion, Indigenous labour is again rendered invisible against Europe's needs (scarcity), but this time it is spiritual scarcity that will continue to organize them as a material underclass. Within the latter form of scarcity, Indigenous work as a supersession of their labour is, again, rendered invisible *against* the scarcity Europeans experienced. Moreover, when blacks are eventually imported as slaves, they come to be associated with needs and scarcity: conditions satisfied by work. They are tied, therefore, to work rather than abundance (a misreading of Indigenous labour systems), so their labour becomes visible *as* work because it is on the other side of the dialectic.

Although she does not articulate it in these terms, Wynter directs us to this process of making Indigenous labour invisible. In her essays on Las Casas's conversion, Wynter notes that Las Casas's suggestion of importing people to be enslaved was part of the same logic that led him to argue that Indigenous Peoples should not be enslaved. As scholars on "just law" and Las Casas also observe, she writes, "Las Casas is not here proposing the substitution of White and Black slaves for Indian slaves per se, but instead the substitution of enslaved men and women who can be categorized as 'justly enslaved' within the system of classification legitimated by Catholic Christian doctrine, for a group of enslaved men and women who cannot be so classified."[82] With this distinction, Wynter points to something fundamental about the exchange of blacks for Indians. It was never the same exchange, and it excises Indigenous Peoples from the fact and language of "just" labour. In other words, their labour could no longer be understood within the new governing logic of the Indies because it could not be captured even by the category of unfree labour, which would come to be associated with the rise of capitalism and the eventual class consciousness of the formerly enslaved and indentured.

Thus, Indigenous Peoples' labour disappears along with the Indigenous body in the Caribbean in particular, not singularly because of the narrative of extinction—which originates with Las Casas and other priests—that dominates the region, as we are led to believe. It disappears because of its *delinking* from the category of just, unfree labour and its permanent suture with the religious-ontological function of the discoveries. The development of the plantation mode of production allowed blacks to outstrip this suture, whereas the substitution of the *repartimiento* for the *encomienda* did not do the same for Indigenous Peoples. This is the real significance of Wynter's argument that the exchange of blacks for Indians was not equivalent. Both groups continue to work for European humanity and economies, but that work is not only understood and articulated differently; it is also ideologically divergent in the religious-secular dialectic that produces blacks and Indentured Peoples (e.g., South Asians) as modern subjects. In this context, Las Casas's work is central for rethinking the history of labour in the Americas and the Caribbean. Although he operates in what was then the single religious-monarchic context for understanding that history (the papal granting of discovered territories first to Portugal's sovereigns and then, with the Americas, to Spain), his work chronicles Indigenous Peoples' religious *and* economic conversions.

In *A Short Account of the Destruction of the Indies*, Las Casas writes that Indigenous Peoples are naturally predisposed to receive the Catholic faith because of their "docile," kind natures. The text is a plea to Charles V, whom Las Casas supposes has not yet had time to read, and therefore act on, his earlier, longer appeal to stop the brutalization of Indigenous Peoples in the Americas and the Caribbean. A busy Charles V (Holy Roman Emperor) has "perhaps allowed it to slip to the back of your mind."[83] In the shortened appeal, Las Casas chronicles the brutal and often gratuitous extermination of millions of Indigenous Peoples from the Caribbean islands and Latin America's mainland territories, thus simultaneously producing the region's foundational extinction narrative as a function of his salvific efforts. He repeatedly contrasts Indigenous (or more aptly Bartolomean) docility with the barbarism of the Spanish conquistadors and settlers. The former in fact have such "delicate constitutions" that he compares them to Spanish nobility who are "born with a silver spoon in their mouths . . . shielded from the rigours of the outside world."[84] In the same passage, he also claims that they have absolutely no desire for "material possessions."

Moreover, not only are Indigenous Peoples unsuited to function as slaves, but they seem to live in a "paradise" (a term he uses several times) that requires no work. Las Casas describes the islands as "more fertile and more beautiful than the Royal Gardens in Seville."[85] With his goal of ending the Spaniards' extermination and torture of Indigenous Peoples, he presents an image of Indigenous Peoples as owing their existence to God's benevolent design rather than their own labour since the lands they inhabit are so fertile. Indigenous Peoples possess "intelligence," but only to the extent that they are predisposed to receive the Christian doctrine.[86] Their status as "gentle lambs" means that their intelligence and hard work could not have developed those fertile lands. Joyce Caplin has argued that the concept of Indigenous Peoples' hereditary or "lineage"-based bodily weakness was an old Roman idea about noncitizens as "feminized" and weak. This idea was later recuperated by the English to demonstrate that Indigenous Peoples could have no claim to lands because they were too weak to cultivate them.[87]

Without undermining Las Casas's aims (or immediate context), it is possible to read a record of Indigenous Peoples' *work* (the reorganization of their bodily actions for Europeans) even in his descriptions of their supposed docility and aversion. At one point, he notes that Indigenous Peoples supply Europeans with food (and that Europeans' personal daily food requirement is equivalent to the amount that three indigenous families eat in a month).[88] Later, speaking of the gold-rich province of Santa Marta, he writes that its native inhabitants had "the will and the know-how to extract it."[89] In denouncing the barbarism of one "commander" in Trinidad, he further claims that the "local people" "had done everything they could for him."[90] The text includes specific references to their extensive work for Europeans throughout the Caribbean islands and South and Central America's mainland territories, including building "temples and houses for the friars," working as domestic servants, working in mines and in the "fields on their master's estates," and serving as "beasts of burden" carrying "baggage," "excessive loads," "burdens of three and four *arrobas* for distances of up to a hundred or even two hundred leagues," as well as carrying "their Christian masters in hammocks."[91]

In these instances, Indigenous Peoples work for Europeans, but their labour is presented in terms of Europeans' voracious capacity for it rather than their own production. Though "the will and the know-how" above are premised on the fact of abundance, this knowledge can instead be read as native industry, a status Las Casas does not accord it here. European need, stemming from initial scarcity, obscures both Indigenous labour and Indigenous work in the narrative. Moreover, because Las Casas frames Indigenous Peoples' bodily food requirements as substantially less than that of Europeans, their food production is automatically cast in terms of their docility in a land that is so fertile that it spontaneously achieves an aesthetic height that no physical labour could re/produce. Since the Spanish "royal gardens" are less beautiful than the lands inhabited by Indigenous Peoples in the Americas, it appears that in the latter location, work is antithetical to beauty. Work as a social need or good is thus necessary for Europeans but not for Indigenous Peoples. Therefore, at every moment that natives' labour for themselves and their work for Europeans rises to the foreground in Las Casas's writings, it is necessarily substituted both by the view of them as docile (and hence unable to labour, thereby requiring providentially abundant nature) and by the capture of their labour as excess (not scarcity) for European desire.

Las Casas uses docility as a strategy to show how unsuited Indigenous Peoples are to a life of slavery. However, his own documents also provide ample evidence of pre-contact, Indigenous *labour* (bodily actions for themselves), unconnected to and preceding their enslavement and work under the Spanish. By reading against the grain, we see in Las Casas's descriptions the labour required to obtain their food, the labour that populated the islands and mainland with "teeming millions" and at least ten kingdoms, "each . . . larger . . . than the whole of the Iberian Peninsula."[92] We need to read against the grain statements such as this about New Spain (present-day Mexico City): "This area had originally boasted four or five great kingdoms, each . . . as large as Spain and . . . inhabited, as the Almighty had ordained, by more people than the combined population of Toledo, Seville, Valladolid, Saragossa and Barcelona, even when these Spanish cities were at the very height of their fortunes."[93] Las Casas's goal is to communicate the devastation and loss of "four millions souls" in that region, which he does well. However, plainly evident here is the tremendous amount of Indigenous labour that went into building such vast, densely populated kingdoms. Labour by Indigenous Peoples for themselves is literally hidden behind Las Casas's own conversion and desire to have them under the Crown's protection.

Further, phrases like "done everything they could" gesture to native labour that results in objects for Europeans. That labour is performed within a native worldview, but because it is what "they" (Indigenous Peoples) could *give* (i.e., what was extracted through exploitation as bare extraction), Las Casas foregrounds the cause and result of the labour, which leads to the misreading of *all* Indigenous labour as though it were only for Europeans. In another instance of their labour for themselves within their worldview and socioeconomic systems, Las Casas notes Indigenous Peoples "living and working with their families,"[94] and the "gourds" of gold that an Indigenous king "gifted" to the Spanish sovereigns. This latter is not work in the mines for Europeans, but labour for native well-being whose product is then presented to Europeans. This gold cannot be viewed solely in terms of its value for Europeans and their later enslavement of Indigenous Peoples to extract it. It is fully produced within a native economy, which does not value it *as* money in a system of exchange. It is akin to the cultivation of crops, the mining of metals, the making of building materials for temples and other structures, the building of homes, and the development of irrigation systems that native peoples engaged in prior to and after the Columbian error.[95]

Labour for the (well) being of Indigenous Peoples themselves, which precedes the encomienda system and the torture of Indigenous Peoples to produce wealth for Europeans, is increasingly made to intersect with labour for Europeans through the gifts of cloths, food, precious metals, and other items given voluntarily to Europeans before being taken or extracted by force. This process is the "conversion" of Indigenous Peoples from their systems of well-being to those of Europeans, which are tied to wealth accumulation. Thus, Indigenous Peoples labour/work in two parallel economies. In one, they *labour* for themselves and live in cities and towns supporting a "denser population" than many in Spain or Portugal.[96] In the other economy, Indigenous Peoples not only were traded for goods but were forced to *work* in mines, build ships, and carry Europeans' possessions. While both economies are eclipsed in Caribbean labour history, the latter, which settler colonialism eventually captures (in Latin America, for instance), allows only two outcomes, each revealing something about the conversion of Indigenous labour.

The first is the subordination of Indigenous Peoples' well-being to the European economy that at that moment used both money and barter. This outcome is graphically represented, for instance, in the image of women forced to abandon infants on the road because they could not carry both their children and the Spaniards' possessions.[97] Another example Las Casas recorded is Indigenous Peoples' idols, which were first confiscated because they were believed to be made of precious metals, and then sold back to them when they were found not to contain gold nor silver.[98] The idols' transformation into goods with measurable value is the translation and conversion of labour for Indigenous well-being within a European economy to serve European needs. This is the capture of Indigenous labour for European well-being as a function of the market.

The second outcome is the conversion of their pre-conquest, sovereign labour for their own well-being into labour for well-being in God, which Las Casas contrasts to labour for the well-being of Europeans, which he reads as destructive. This outcome is tied to Las Casas's conversion and is based on their ecclesiastical *labour*, which he distinguishes from secular *work*. Las Casas records Indigenous Peoples building churches for the friars who were teaching them the word of God. He sees this work, which serves Europeans, as *labour* for God (the parallel of the market), hence for their own well-being, differentiating it from the real work that soldiers, governors, and others make them carry out. Moreover, even his criticism of conversion does not entail a rejection of this ecumenical economic value.[99] Therefore, from both these conversions—market and God—I argue that Indigenous Peoples' actual work must be read back into regional histories of capital's development starting with the middle/passage and its historical narratives that disappear Indigenous labours.

Las Casas's chronicling of Spanish abuses reveals a history of Indigenous Peoples' labour in the Americas that has not been understood because of these conversions, in which they either work until extinction (hence lack of future usefulness and the need for importing people to be enslaved), or labour for God, a spiritual work sitting outside the economies that will matter for capital's rise. Incidentally, this labouring until extinction is, to recall, the same goal of slavery according to Walter Rodney, and thus they are subject to the same death as blacks in the second (punitive) instance of its occurrence. The first economy, in which Indigenous Peoples cease to function through extinction, is conveniently trumped by the second, which hides their continuing work for European well-being. Since, however, it is the first that matters for the rise of capital, and in it they cease to be productive, especially in the Caribbean territories where extinction is seen as having been definitive, Indigenous Peoples are simply left out of Caribbean narratives of capital's development and rise that track its prehistory to the introduction of enslaved blacks to the region. Since Indigenous Peoples' work only remains through religious conversion and salvation, it effectively ceases to matter at all.

What further distinguishes Indigenous Peoples from those brought to the Americas to be enslaved is that the religious-economic "conversion" is their extraction from their systems of social well-being. For blacks, this extraction occurred *with* the middle/passage; with all its attendant economies, the middle/passage converted blacks into valuable labour, so blacks' (or their labours') conversion *to* value. Hartman reinforces this for us: "In the company's view," she writes, "the dungeon was a way station for human refuse and a cocoon for labourers. The miracle of the slave trade was that it resuscitated useless lives and transformed waste into capital."[100] The dungeon, like the hold, is a key element in the transformation of blacks because it strips them of what devalues them: their indigeneity. It is essentially the death of their Indigenous selves (of their non-accumulative sovereign labour on sovereign lands) that they undergo when they emerge from the dungeon and the hold. This death in fact *adds value* to their bodies, a process that is then completed by the plantation as a "machine" into which they are placed.[101] Because Death in this instance is not biopolitical (as discussed above), it allows for their transformation into commodities. This Death is not only the foreclosure of blacks' ontological sovereignty, but also the specific requirement of their productivity for the settler-master. The Middle Passage, as that which adds value to black bodies, thus emerges as the counter process of native Conversion in the Americas, devaluing their bodily labours.

Even where they were bought and sold to be enslaved rather than rounded up and made to work, Indigenous Peoples seemingly lacked this middle/passage process of adding value to their persons because, as Las Casas notes, their bodies expired when they were too weak to work. If work produces wealth and property (which Arendt claims are labour's permanent and accumulative form, rather than its consumable or ephemeral one), and

Indigenous Peoples were thought to have no private property, then by necessity they had to be seen as having no work, no permanence to their labour on their own lands.[102] This perception of Indigenous lands is borne out in Lockean theory, as Audra Simpson demonstrates in *Mohawk Interruptus*, noting that for Locke "the origins of property reside in that which is mixed with labour. Thus, that which does not appear to have been mixed with labour is alienable. But only certain forms of labour, those which are perceptible to certain viewers, matter."[103] The identification of Indigenous lands in the Caribbean with abundance rather than scarcity allowed colonizers not to "see" the prior, sovereign, and possessive labour that went into these lands. Indigenous labour could accumulate and, were it to be recognized, it would have threatened the alienability of their lands, as Simpson demonstrates.

In contrast, even though blacks themselves could not accumulate, precisely because of their middle/passage transformation—their conversion to value—their labour was transformed into work that would not be immediately productive but would lead to the accumulation of the settler-master's wealth. The only way Indigenous Peoples could have value in and of themselves would be through Death, from which they are already foreclosed by eliminatory processes. Rather than transformative Death, they undergo—from Las Casas to the anthropologist Patrick Wolfe—"elimination" and that can be read as, ironically, the productive form of Indigenous Peoples' labour, that is, their work, the object-outcome of which is now the potential productivity of the land that has been cleared.[104] In short, because *labour* is the non-accumulative term in the dialectic that has to be overcome, Indigenous Elimination (through physical death or assimilation to remove native entrenchment in the land) is the Conversion of their non-accumulative labours to *work*. The dialectic renews itself through this constant and contemporaneous operation. Although, like the hold for blacks, Elimination is an initiative form of death for Indigenous Peoples, it is a proximate death rather than a categorical one.

The emphasis on Indigenous Elimination (to which I return in chapter 3), however, obscures the ways in which Indigenous Peoples also experience a middle/passage. At several places in the text, Las Casas notes Indigenous Peoples' forced relocation to work on other islands in the modern-day Caribbean, movements that are not significantly factored into regional labour history. According to Las Casas, non-Bahamians were "drafted in from other parts of the New World," and "shipload after shipload of natives" were offered "for sale in Santa Marta or on the islands of Hispaniola,

Jamaica, and Puerto Rico."[105] By Las Casas's account, over one million Indigenous Peoples were thus forcibly relocated and sold into slavery, a trade in which, according to him, they more often "perished" than survived.[106] Since they died in large numbers, indeed, no value was added by their capture and enslavement, as happened with blacks.

Cherokee/Assateague-Gingaskin scholar Ron Welburn argues that this capture and enslavement should be read as an "other middle passage" that he distinguishes from Indian removal in North America. In his *Roanoke and Wampum*, Welburn defines this middle passage: "the trafficking of indigenous peoples from homelands along the Atlantic coast and the interior of the Western hemisphere into transoceanic slavery, a dreadful and painful legacy that begins with Columbus, who captured *Indios* to display in Spain, . . . is a middle passage because of how captive Indians must have rationalized it; a middle/passage which . . . precedes the wrenching of Africans from their continent for slave labor in the Americas."[107] Critical in Welburn's assessment is the emphasis on the experience of the space of the transition from labour to work and, more importantly, his locating of that experience not just in terms of black experience, but within an Indigenous worldview. He combats the fact that "Natives are easily obscured by the dynamics attending western hemisphere African history, culture, and affairs, whether . . . motivated by Europeans or Africans themselves."[108] Of captured Wampanoag he asks, "What did they imagine had happened to them, . . . the name of their people signifying People of the Dawn, by being taken from home by people like those who overcame them and were now shipping them deeper into the Dawn's origins?"[109]

Despite the fact of Indigenous transport and enslavement, the problem is that Indigenous Peoples are first linked with (religious) Conversion—a process we can reframe as extractive or devaluing—while blacks are linked with the Middle Passage—a process that adds value, or realizes the value held in black bodies.[110] These twin poles of Atlantic economy separate black and Indigenous work. However, both blacks and Indigenous Peoples are embedded in processes of Conversion that subtract value, just as both are involved in middle passage processes of adding value that orient around the ability to be converted from and to something. Conversion, as the mirror process of the Middle Passage, should thus be understood as a point of entanglement of Indigenous labour with Caribbean/American economies, as its facilitator, beyond land theft.

Within this framework, Indigenous Peoples' forcible relocation is not only another middle/passage. It is constitutive of a *prior* or foundational middle/passage without which—and largely because of its presumed failure (though on one level it had to have worked for it to be duplicated)—the black middle passage would not have come into being. This middle/passage links Africa to the Caribbean and what would become the Americas, and is formative for how those territories will come to look and what populations they will have in the future. Thus, I argue that it is as foundational for European modernity as the African middle/passage, and should be read along with that as a history of Indigenous work (which Welburn does not emphasize) within modernity and for capital's rise. It must, however, also be read alongside the history of Indigenous labour for their *own* well-being, which runs parallel to middle/passage transformations of sovereign labour.

Moreover, this labour for self can be equated to subsistence living that enslaved blacks and indentured peoples performed on the land. Thus, theirs is also a history of labour for self *within* that antagonistic work for Europeans. The lesser visibility of this middle/passage results not only from the extinction narrative but also from the linked nature of physical and ontological uprootedness. For blacks captured and transported to the region, both occurred together. For Indigenous Peoples, one could occur without the other, most notably where they were made to labour *in place* or were converted to the Catholic faith so that their labour was for God and the feeding of the spiritual self (i.e., building churches, etc.). Though distinctive, these tandem movements of Indigenous Peoples represent a middle/passage that is already the Caribbean Sea, so Indigenous Peoples' middle/passage is part of the history of forced labour in the Americas. It also represents another passage, asking us to rethink the normative ends and beginnings of regional labour history.

The sale and purchase of Indigenous Peoples—the hallmark of this middle/passage—is similar to that of blacks. Las Casas notes that not only were Indigenous Peoples rounded up and displayed similarly to later slave auction blocks, but they were actually traded to those seeking labour for European goods that ranged in value from a block of cheese to clothing and other items. What Las Casas views in their careless extermination (the logic behind "perish"), which supposedly did not happen with black enslaved people who were valuable chattel, is not simply the failure of conversion to the Spanish faith. It is also the failure of conversion to value because, like the land, they were associated with abundance (their own labour for self, which cannot be understood in a system that only recognizes abundance in its ability to be converted). This sixteenth-century unsuccessful conversion to value (across some Caribbean territories), however, will be accomplished with the rise of capital, so that today, Indigenous Peoples are a labouring underclass in the Americas or are associated not with fertility (representing potential conversion) but with poverty.

Moreover, Las Casas makes a significant distinction, as Anthony Pagden notes in his introduction to *A Short History*, between the papal-granted sovereignty over the new lands and Indigenous sovereignty over their own bodies and the lands they inhabited (for Las Casas, the latter is more likely the freedom to be full servants of God). He describes them as "natural masters and dwellers in those vast and marvelous kingdoms," repeatedly noting that they are "legally" free. Within that sovereignty we can read their labour for themselves, which, again, is unproductive both for sixteenth-century empire and the rise of capital. If we follow Amy Turner Bushnell's tripartite division of Indigenous engagement with the Atlantic into coerced labour, and semi-autonomous spheres of influence (see chapter 2), then we can suggest that it is precisely the fact that Indigenous pre-contact labour systems remained robustly concurrent with European ones that led to the failure of attempts to enslave them. Even Las Casas's conversion and attempt to admit Indigenous Peoples to a higher degree of humanity than Africans does not recover their labour for themselves from this misreading, and it remains wedded to the very labour he tries to excise them from because both occur within the always already of their primary conversion. Both labours still occur within Europeans' new cosmogonic order and its shift from God to man, from religious to more secular modes of being human. Reading Indigenous subsistence and plantation labour through their Conversion in the discursive and political economy of the Old World allows us to see Indigenous Peoples' labour as a parallel or corollary of black slave labour, which was also for God, but man first, "propter nos."[111]

The focus, then, is not singularly on slavery or slave labour and what escapes it (e.g., marronage or the slave plot) as the only viable way of thinking about the work that built capital. Such a reading largely privileges or supports the dominant labour episteme it occurs within, revealing the profoundly European concept of labour that drives Atlantic histories. Moving around and beyond the Atlantic and its privileging of this labour as the only space/place/time in which black and Indigenous histories meet and disarticulate, what becomes formative is "conversion" itself. Conversion as Europeans' religious *and* economic motive links blacks and Indigenous Peoples, and is also the point where their linked histories are misread. Both groups were subject to conversion as a religious motive, but blacks' religious conversion is largely seen as second to their economic one, while the reverse is true for Indigenous Peoples.

Finally, Conversion is both how the mechanism necessary for capital accumulation (the labour-work dialectic) is established in the region and the (later) method for reading capital (political economy and economics). It is also essential to value in Marxist critique, so Marxism and its revision in the radical tradition bring forward this origin of value in anti-blackness and anti-indigeneity as fundamental to the commodity. If we accept that primitive accumulation is an ongoing structure of capital accumulation, that it involves both labour and land extraction, which are inseparable from anti-blackness and anti-indigeneity through the Conversion of black and Indigenous bodily labours, and that efforts to understand the fundamentally transformative accumulative relationships with nature that begin well prior to the industrial revolutions commencing in the eighteenth century, then it is not a stretch to assert that the forms of value that we understand in capitalism, particularly use value and exchange value, are based on and are thus fundamentally structured in/by antiblackness and anti-indigeneity.[112] Therefore, it is not just the labour category that is antagonistic because it retains the foundational association of anti-blackness to anti-indigeneity, but value itself. We do not need to understand Indigenous and black Conversion to value retroactively nor seek to reconcile it with the predominant concepts of value in critiques of capitalism. Instead, we need to chart how Conversion creates what will be valuable, the categories of value within capitalism, and then how Marxism reads for this. Thus, Conversion essentially creates the structures of accumulation *and* what Sylvia Wynter refers to as the "master" disciplines for reading capital: economics and political economy.[113]

At the outset, I looked at Marx's emphasis on productive labour, which generates the surplus values necessary to capital formation. To elaborate this claim, I shift here to two of the most familiar categories of value within his work, illustrating how an attention to Conversion impacts these categories. In the section titled "Commodities and Money" in *Capital*, volume 1, Marx lays out a theory of value with regard to labour under capitalism as a global phenomenon. Rather than focus on the labour theory of value as a whole, I want to narrow the discussion to the two categories of value essential to the commodity form and therefore intrinsic to the theory of value: use and exchange. Marx defines *use value* as both independent of the labour required to produce the commodity and dependent on the object's consumption or use. In contrast, *exchange value* allows the labour in the commodity to be abstracted, so that commodity can circulate within markets. Moreover, he notes that "to become a commodity a product must be transferred to another, whom it will serve as a use value, by means of an exchange," adding that "nothing can have value without being an object of utility. If the thing is useless, so is the labour contained in it; the labour does not count as labour, and therefore creates no value."[114] In other words, value is determined by human labour (power) in the first order and by its ability to be represented both concretely by and abstracted within the commodity in the second.

Additionally, the commodity's ability to be exchanged because of the conversion of concrete forms of labour into "abstract labor or value" for the market is, overall, what I index as the productive form of value, which capital requires and in which, by necessity, Marx's analysis is grounded.[115] Even where use value does not correspond to the labour time and skill put into the commodity, it is still tied to exchange value through the very process of becoming a commodity, because without use value the commodity lacks exchange value. Thus, commodities' use value also depends on human labour, albeit in a somewhat different manner than exchange value. Common to productive value forms, Marx repeatedly emphasizes, is human labour and value within capitalist economies, which is fundamentally based not only on human labour but also on its ability to be transformed into use and exchange values in the commodity.

While a more detailed study could examine different forms of labour and kinds of value from the fifteenth century through the early industrial era, I suggest that the value that is the subject of Marx's writings in the nineteenth century is already rooted conceptually in (and hence repeats) the real exchange/conversion that happens *to* and *between* black and Indigenous bodies and which is necessary for the commodity to emerge.[116] I am not arguing, as Susan Buck-Morss does about Hegel, that he must have had real enslaved peoples in mind when he developed his ideas on lordship and bondage.[117] Marx repeatedly lambasts slavery in *Capital*, but he also recognizes native "enslavement and entombment" and black slave labour as instrumental to "bourgeois industry" (*Capital*, volume 1).[118] Critical here is the recognition of both black and native captive labour as key in capital transformation, rather than a singular emphasis on one over the other. However, it is also key that in this same movement of recognition, we have the Conversion initiated by Las Casas, which turns native labour into its failed status as "entombment." I therefore suggest that use and exchange value in Marx's writings express the labour-work dialectic itself as capital literally writes its terms of expression and critique. The kinds of exchange of labour for and to value that will characterize capital as Marx sees it started in the early sixteenth century in the Americas in efforts "to make human bodies abstractable into value forms."[119]

If, as this chapter argues, the division between productive work and unproductive labour is fundamentally exercised or realized through this prior process of adding and subtracting value from black and Indigenous bodies, and the Atlantic economies are globally consequential, then we must revisit the *categories of analysis* within capital, in this case these specific categories of value. We can thus read back into them this a priori exchange in order to understand both the fundamental anti-blackness and anti-indigeneity of categories of value as categories of analysis, as well as how what may seem to be abstract and/or broadly applicable categories are rooted in something that is in fact not abstract: Death/death. We cannot use political economy's terms to retroactively describe geologic transformation (see Moore). Instead, we must understand that if such transformation is based on the rendering of biology as matter (via property relations), as (in)human geographer Kathryn Yusoff illustrates in *A Billion Black Anthropocenes or None*, then it is instrumental to later modes of value transformation and abstraction, which render concrete human labour into both abstract labour and its nonequivalent form *as matter* in the commodity. To this end, use value (central to wealth as elaborated by Marxist economist and geographer David Harvey) is logically the process of the transformation of blacks, the addition of value to their bodies so they could be used as objects/commodities subject to exchange, while exchange value is logically the process of the transformation of Indigenous bodies, the removal of (useless/nonproductive) value from their bodies and the deposit of such value in the land for useful extraction.[120] Use value and exchange value in Marxist critique are logically related to processes of exchange for consumption.

I argue that we should rethink this conceit of value in which those who can consume are privileged, yet those who make consumption possible (and hence the categories used to express it) are not. Use and exchange value are then categories for the reproduction of an *original* domination. Moreover, they develop through their opposite processes: use for exchange (blacks) and exchange for use (Indigenous Peoples). These transformations precede the forms of alienation that are the point of resistance to capitalist exploitation. My argument is not about value in general, nor about the commodity as a "universal" component of capitalist economic systems (which for Marx, as Harvey reminds us, is premised on its accessibility to everyone regardless of any kind of status that might cleave one from the family of man—literally an abstraction that blacks and Indigenous Peoples cannot afford).[121] My argument is specifically about the forms of value with which the commodity is imbued. If capital is a global-economic system that develops from feudalism through its protocapitalist phases to literally transform the earth, and that transformation is rooted in slavery, settler colonialism, and racialization, then the forms of creating value that are specific to these systems are those from which capital first develops, and which are then used to create the categories used to read capital.

Moreover, if the labour-work dialectic, as Arendt argues, is a formal part of capitalist critique and the forms of value intrinsic to capital that it produces are fundamentally dependent on the ability of human labour to be transformed—that is, to be other than what it is—and as I argue the dialectic is a vehicle for capital accumulation by putting in place a fundamental form of human transformation, then the value form within capital is dependent on this, and this is what we must reject by challenging both capitalism and the blindness of its descriptive apparatus. The latter allows it to continue to work through invisible forms of conceptual value production that continuously reinscribe inequality. Why then can we not look at the whole edifice of Marxist critique from this vantage point, rather than from attempts at conceptual reconciliation, expansion, or correction?

Conclusion

This chapter offers an alternative reading of labour for Caribbean history. With the introduction, it forms the stage in establishing a method that recovers Indigenous labour for Caribbean historiography and particularly the region's radical tradition. Its focus is the labour category and the specific ways it manages a distinction germane to modern political economy: the contrast between unproductive labour and productive work. This distinction, I argue, is central to the disappearance of Indigenous Peoples' labour histories, so I approached their bodily actions not from the point at which they are already foreclosed by teleological capital, but instead as they operate, in Arendtian terms, through an ongoing labour-work dialectic that organizes actions, bodies, and histories into productive and unproductive outcomes. Moreover, the association of Indigenous Peoples with unproductive labour is crucial for settler and postcolonial sovereignties because it is the specific way in which Indigenous sovereignties can be controlled (or read *out of* the land; see chapter 3).

The distinction is responsible for delinking Indigenous and black labour in the Caribbean. Their labours should be understood as opposed not because of the standard narrative of Indigenous disappearance, but because of the specific ways a labour-work dialectic is instituted in the region with the Columbian error, within which blacks and Indigenous Peoples are positioned on opposing sides of the dialectic of scarcity/productive work versus abundance/reproductive labour. The chapter exposes how this labour division is instituted in the Caribbean's early economy through the process of Conversion. As the ideological and material transformation of both blacks' and Indigenous Peoples' (unproductive) bodily labours for their physical work, Conversion is their mutual, ongoing middle/passage that emerges before the sea as history.[122] It is where Indigenous labour is disappeared and misread, and where black labour emerges as its eclipse in the binary opposition of re-productive to productive labour that maintains and advances inequality within capitalism. It is thus a crucial point at which to begin reading material history against the grain in order to link the struggle of racialized labour within globalization for equity.

Reading for the processes of Conversion rather than its terminus undoes the causal link between the labour (as work)-rights relation that reproduces the postcolonial state as an outcome of a singular effort. It allows us to introduce a pause between the plantation, its modes of labour/work, and the postcolonial state's capture of the latter. Moreover, if we reread the radical tradition in the Caribbean in terms of the space between labour and work (see chapter 4), we can foreground how the postcolonial state— as an inheritance of the colonial state—has a parallel, imminent existence in terms of a not yet or becoming within which we can recuperate black and Indigenous labours rather than just elaborate their histories of work. This *imminence* or "not yet" is the capture of indigeneity against the settler state's *immanence*, and it allows us to see how Caribbean political economy contains within it fundamentally interruptive units of being/existence/ labour rather than units of production.

In seeking, however, to uncover the labour-work divide, the chapter had to address an additional problem: the limits of the categories of labour that forced us to confront the fundamental, ontological, and therefore structural difference between blackness and indigeneity, infrahumans and homunculi. For the West, the latter category marks an aspirational distinction from true humanity, while the former is completely irredeemable. For Afropessimism, whose elaboration of blackness as slaveness I take seriously, the ontological difference between blacks and natives cannot be resolved. Afropessimism defines blacks and Indigenous Peoples, respectively, through two kinds of structural deaths: Death and a kind of "half" dead status that retains the possibility for life as representation within civil society and political economy. Moving slightly away from ontological death to focus on the labour-work divide, however, clarifies a few things. First, Death/death is the new relation to land and labour that slavery and settler colonialism effect, respectively. Black Death, specifically, is the cutting off of our labour from sovereign lands and the imposition of a new objective relation to labour. Indigenous Peoples' so-called half-dead status should be understood as a similar process. However, while for blacks dispossession (separation from sovereign land and labour) must precede their becoming black, for Indigenous peoples this separation is contingent. This cannot be changed. There is no way for black labour to become sovereign on stolen Indigenous land or to recover a lost, antecedent sovereignty. To participate in civil society is to accept or maybe even desire our Death, and (postcolonial) Independence is the conscription of our Death via its constitutionality.

What we can address, however, is the fact that black labour in the Americas, its conversion as work, is only possible because of the making of the "savage" as able to be dispossessed (read: continuing and contingent). It is only possible because any labour performed on this land is necessarily objective or object-oriented. Thus, as I have demonstrated, the labour-work divide is not just necessary to capital accumulation. It is a specific way in which labour under capital accumulation is fundamentally created as anti-black and anti-indigenous and requires this relation in order to support accumulation. It is the yoking of regimes of racialization to regimes of (settler) colonialism rather than their disarticulation.

The distinction between productive and unproductive work that regimes of proto-capital accumulation institute and sustain, and for which political economy reads, does not make sense without the division it imposes between black and native bodies and sovereignties, and its effort to manage black and native lands and labours. This is the real pessimism we must engage and work back from, not the seeming impossibility of relation that leaves blacks and Indigenous Peoples on opposites sides of freedom struggles. Moreover, within Afropessimism there is a way for black and Indigenous struggles to move forward together without translating black struggle, as Wilderson warns, into legible yet antagonistic terms.[123] Wilderson argues that in order for all subhumans (recall his use of the term "junior associates") to work with infrahumans, the point of engagement must be black Death. He also fundamentally suggests that civil society cannot be the stage of black struggle, so, in short, what is warranted is a turning away from a political landscape in which blacks could never have full representation.

While he is right that we must confront anti-blackness within Indigenous thought (and as I discuss in this book, anti-indigeneity in black thought) he does not actually discuss Indigenous systems of governance in their difference from that of civil society. Though some Indigenous systems of governance may in fact contain anti-black elements, we must remain aware of the fact that (1) they are not coextensive, but remain in conflict, with civil society, and (2) the universality of antiblackness does *not* precede Indigenous sovereignty at contact.[124] Thus, anti-blackness was never structurally tied to Indigenous forms of sovereignty, and is extant now where those sovereignties are forcibly redefined for Indigenous Peoples *by* the settler state. Moreover, since Christian cosmogonic systems held religious others as the then liminal category for the human, their supplanting by secular, bodily differences that congeal into race is still a change specific to the global human order deployed by Europeans. It is still neither internal nor foundational to Indigenous systems.

Despite his seemingly irreconcilable approach, Wilderson in fact shares the position of Glen Coulthard and Leanne Betasamosake Simpson, who argue that Indigenous Peoples must essentially refuse forms of representation based on recognition. This *same* (Fanonian) refusal is the point where black and Indigenous struggles can move forward together. Both the "black" and the "native" (where the latter is read as the redeemable "savage" disposed to dispossession) represent forms of dispossession that continuously bring forward and execute the logics and practices of slavery and settler colonialism. Yet Indigenous labour (on Indigenous lands) does something that black labour (on stolen lands) cannot do. Juan Ginés de Sepúlvada's homunculi and Las Casas's lambs have a type of sovereignty that is repeatedly recognized, even as they are simultaneously enslaved and killed: the sovereignty that documents like the UN Declaration on the Rights of Indigenous Peoples seek to restore.[125] In contrast, for blacks, the only space of true labour is now our flesh and its recovery, while for native peoples it is both their bodies *and* lands. When Wilderson writes that "the slave's reference to his or her quarters as a 'home' does not change the fact that it is a spatial extension of the master's dominion," this must signal to us that there is no sovereign space for black labour, especially if slavery is, as he says, always a contemporaneous context for blackness.[126] However, if we recognize that in the postcolonial state Independence—as a form of objective death that is opposed to sovereignty as a form of productive life—codifies the land-labour divide, anti-blackness and anti-indigeneity, and Death/death, we come to the need for a collective point of refusal.

Beginning by exploring the limits of Atlantic conceptualizations that privilege dominant understandings of its economies, the next chapter mobilizes the labour-work dialectic in a revision of Atlantic history. As I argue, understanding the complex nature of Indigenous Conversion(s) in the Caribbean and recognizing their own prior middle/passage allow us to begin reading Indigenous labour/work back into Caribbean history as the history not only of a forgotten Atlantic but of a parallel mode of work that is contiguous and continuous, and that challenges the Atlantic itself as a category of analysis.

2. TOWARD A MIDDLE / PASSAGE METHODOLOGY

Drowning the Limit

In *The Repeating Island,* Cuban writer and theorist Antonio Benítez-Rojo exclaims, "Let's be realistic: the Atlantic is the Atlantic (with all its ports and cities) because it was once engendered by the copulation of Europe—that insatiable solar bull—with the Caribbean Archipelago."[1] Benítez-Rojo's violent copulatory metaphor reflects the dominant academic perception of the Atlantic as an economic political body of world historical development that becomes such by its entanglement with Europe. The heteropatriarchal image of a Caribbean vagina and phallic Europe keenly depicts the dominant epistemological approaches to the Atlantic, with Europe as the primary actor effecting change in a passively waiting Atlantic world. As a sustained field of inquiry and historical organization, Atlantic studies deploys the "ocean sea" as an epistemological tool for the study of race, labour, culture, and society.[2] Its generative fields of inquiry have emerged as an important place to think and account for different sets of historical actors, particularly Europeans and blacks.

However, the Atlantic is also a limiting epistemological space that cannot support this more expansive reading for the labour-work dialectic. It operates from the founding conceit elaborated by Benítez-Rojo: that the Atlantic comes about *because* of Europe. This conceit has fractured the histories of black and Indigenous peoples in the Americas, with the latter most often left out of various configurations in a critical myopia that sees Indigenous Peoples only in terms of land masses and placedness, rather than oceanic or sea movements and fluidity.[3] Indigenous Peoples in the Americas are not typically associated with the kinds of middle passage crossings that produce and reproduce the Atlantic. Contemporary, more inclusive explorations that expand Atlantic studies have their own limitations. Many revisionist approaches end up reinscribing the Atlantic as an organizing trope, and still operate within the breach of black and Indigenous labour in the Americas. In particular, conceptualizations of the Atlantic as a given outcome that is then reinscribed as a historical entity continue to restrict other ways of imagining movements and lives that challenge its unificatory causality. In her critique of Atlantic and black Atlantic studies, Michelle Wright argues that they more often than not suffer a "qualitative collapse," where the multispatial and multitemporal histories of peoples circulating in the region are subjected to a linearity that affirms progress (or its lack) and certain bodies over others, especially cis, straight men.[4]

Moreover, attempts to extend these frameworks to consider other parts of the (black) diaspora (as those I explore below) are still fundamentally limited by the Atlantic's organizing, heterotrophic (read: consuming) time-space. In proceeding from the root assumption that European action is very much the modern or progressive (i.e., Renaissance/Enlightenment) solar bull acting upon the feminized, vaginal Other (i.e., backward, racialized, and underdeveloped), Atlantic studies reinscribes and works through the very racialism generated out of the Atlantic encounter, reproducing the Atlantic's peoples and knowledges within the ordering hierarchy of the Atlantic itself. As Wright observes, "In the strict logic of cause and effect, white racism is the agent that sets the historical agenda for the Black progress narrative because it initiates the Atlantic slave trade (as opposed to slavery within Africa), Atlantic slavery, segregationist laws, racist violence, terrorist acts against Black communities, and exploitation by the state, medical professionals, science, industry—the list goes on, and in each moment, whiteness is the actor and Blackness the reactor."[5] In *Creole Indigeneity*, I critiqued how black and Indian middle passage narratives were used to support definitions of rights and access that exclude Indigenous Peoples because they did not have a Middle Passage origin in the Atlantic's "dark waters."[6] Here, I return to and work from the limitations of this Atlantic and the nationalist narratives that reach back to capture it as a telos for enfranchised, racialized subjects in what Wright defines as a "middle passage epistemology." Within this epistemology, Atlantic crossings become "linear progress narratives" that approach blackness as a "vertical," hierarchically ordered phenomenon rather than a "horizontal" one that dis/articulates across a variety of contexts and within specific spaces and times.[7] Working at the limits of Atlantic studies and dominant Middle Passage narratives against the Middle Passage as structure, this chapter continues to develop a method for a new labour history of the Caribbean that began in chapter 1. It reads together black and Indigenous forced labour in the Caribbean as a new starting point for regional labour history. I bring the interrelated considerations of Conversion and the labour-work dialectic to bear on an analysis of Atlantic epistemologies that constrain a recovery of Indigenous labour. I show how we might pursue an alternative focused on movements and processes of relation that can be developed into a perspective and method for future study.

After highlighting significant textual moments in Atlantic studies around black and Indigenous labour, the chapter returns to the conceptual elaboration of Conversion as a co-making process of blackness and indigeneity. Shifting away from the Atlantic, it returns to the Middle Passage in order to complicate the origins, actors, and outcomes it generates and supports. My goal is to formulate a new way of thinking of not only the Middle Passage such that it is not exclusive to groups crossing the Atlantic into chattel slavery and indenture, but also those who circulate throughout the region in related and different ways, whose movements challenge the dominant time of the Middle Passage. I develop the *middle/passage* as a methodology that circumvents breaches of grammar and time such that they are no longer the break between black, Indian, and native labour history in the Caribbean. Instead, they constitute a condition of possibility for reading them together through the movements, currents, and processes of engagement that mutually shape anti-blackness and anti-indigeneity in the production of seemingly absolute black and native difference.

Caribbean literature is replete with images that approach the Atlantic and the Caribbean Sea as fluid rather than deterministic horizons for Creole life. These texts reveal the ocean and sea as spaces of both the forced remaking of enslaved and indentured peoples and these peoples' *deliberate* movements and transformations in the Americas, outside the nationalistic and diasporic narratives into which they are often pulled. This approach is evident, for instance, in works by numerous writers and cultural critics including Édouard Glissant, M. NourbeSe Philip, Derek Walcott, Grace Nichols, Mahadai Das, and Kamau Brathwaite. Collectively, these creative efforts think with, through, and against (rather than being constrained by) the Middle Passage as a space where racialized actors are manipulated by historical forces beyond their control.

Many critical approaches to Caribbean and black diaspora cultural production work with/in these creative engagements, rejecting outcomes and fixity and privileging fluidity instead, including Elizabeth DeLoughrey's *Routes and Roots* and, more recently, Tiffany Lethabo King's *The Black Shoals*. Both are concerned with how our ability to understand the links between black, native, and other racialized peoples is severely restricted by land-based methods, or, in Atlantic studies, with methods that apprehend the presumptive and productive knitting together of land masses. King, for example, not only thinks about black studies' responsibilities to native studies, but also resists the entrenched associations of native identities with land and black bodies with "rootlessness" and the kinds of movements that for Wright (in the case of the Middle Passage) become teleological. Taking up the geomorphologic shoal, King writes that it "creates a rupture and . . . opens up analytical possibilities for thinking about Blackness as exceeding the metaphors and analytics of water and for thinking of Indigeneity as exceeding the symbol and analytic of land."[8] Both she and DeLoughrey develop frameworks that engage Brathwaithe's "tidalectics." DeLoughrey uses the same investment in movement to foreground passages and different spaces and confluences shaping blackness, Indigeneity, and other ethnic and Creole identities, shifting the framework for reading these literatures from the vertical ones Wright rejects to more horizontal, geo-relational ones that allow them to be interpreted within their own similar regional contexts.

Together, these and similar critical interventions perform the kind of "epiphenomenal" approach to our histories for which Wright has argued. Critiquing middle passage epistemologies that restrict blackness and shape our criticisms of black cultural production, Wright holds that we must understand cultural objects or formations within their own time and space, their "epiphenomenal time," rather than from our own temporal concerns, biases, and epistemological structures. For Wright, this time rejects "linear" "causality" through a "concept of spacetime that takes into account all the multifarious dimensions of Blackness that exist in any one moment, or 'now.'"[9] Epiphenomenal time engages with but does not directly evolve from the fundamentally restrictive and exclusive notions of "middle passage blackness."[10] Wright's temporal and spatial approach to blackness (in terms of its titular "physics") is clearly deployed, for instance, in Black Studies scholar Christina Sharpe's theorization of the "wake" to describe the black experience and the contemporaneity and immediacy of slavery's violence.[11] Sharpe's concept also rejects restrictive approaches to the Middle Passage that tie it to entrenched (material) rather than phenomenal outcomes for blacks. In other words, Sharpe's "wake" does not reinscribe the linearity of middle passage time because it reimagines time through the now's ever-present wakefulness, disturbance, and possibility. Her work elucidates Wright's claim that we should attend to blackness not as a "what" but as a more inclusive "when."[12] In suggesting that we need to move *beyond* the ways that "middle passage epistemologies" force us to privilege outcomes and identities that cannot be sustained by its temporality, Wright envisions this postwar approach as a critically necessary rupture and new framework for viewing black history, actors, aesthetics, and critical traditions.

While I agree with Wright and have pointed to the Middle Passage's limits as a singular vision for Creole identities, I do not want to jettison the term. Rather than approach it as a singular point of (black) becoming or genesis into nonbeing (Fanon), however, I reengage it as a point of entanglement with Indigenous Peoples and their own transformations that occur in relation to blacks during the imperial and early colonial period. I contend that we have poorly understood what the Middle Passage is, what it does, and what it produces. Because the Middle Passage is key in the positioning of blacks and Indigenous Peoples on opposite sides of slavery and genocide, of labour and land, it is to this that we must return to rethink their co-making. Moreover, I argue that understanding the complex nature of both black and Indigenous conversion(s) in the Americas, and the recovery of the latter's own *inaugural* middle/passage allows us to begin reading Indigenous labour-work back into Caribbean history as the history not strictly of a forgotten Atlantic but of a parallel mode of labour that is contiguous, continuous, and challenges the Atlantic as a category of analysis. It also allows us to challenge dominant ideas about primitive accumulation. I do not argue that Indigenous crossings should be understood through the framework of black middle passage crossing, the dominant form of translation to which their histories are subject in attempts to make them supposedly more consequential. Instead, I extend and develop my claim in the preceding chapter that black crossings actually occurred in the context of Indigenous ones. Thus, the narratives of political and economic progress and development tied to the Middle Passage as a structure of accumulation owe their very basis to what they exclude.

I therefore foreground native enslavement in the Caribbean and the movements that relate to that enslavement. I then deploy a newly imagined middle/passage against the macro-configuration of the Atlantic to suggest that we should pursue neither the ocean nor even the (Caribbean) sea as fully realized historical, aesthetic, and critical formation. Instead, we should engage a concept of the middle/passage based in the shared physical movements of blacks and Indigenous peoples and their real, conceptual, and ideological conversions that have been necessary for settler and franchise colonialism, the making of the Atlantic as a world-historical phenomenon, and the rise of capital. These movements remain open and ongoing, rather than closed and teleological.

A better way of visualizing this return to the middle/passage and the terminological break I signal by writing it with a forward slash is to apprehend it geospatially from one constitutive point of entanglement for the Caribbean Sea and Atlantic Ocean: the Anegada Passage at the upper point or northern portion of the Lesser Antilles, separating the British Virgin Islands from Anguilla, another UK territory (see figure 2.1). This is one of two places where the depth of the passage or channel allows the Atlantic Ocean to empty or spill into the Caribbean Sea.[13] Growing up in my second Caribbean home of the US Virgin Islands and traveling to Virgin Gorda and Tortola, I have long been familiar with the passage. However, sifting through the overabundance of tourist images in a quick web search pulled up its negative associations, with one calling it the "bitch" passage because opposing currents and winds make it difficult to cross.[14] The name itself, meaning "flooded," "drowned," or "submerged" passage, stems from the Spanish *anegar*, directly capturing both the tectonic formation and the dangers of navigating the strait.[15] The passage can be understood in terms of contemporary movements (economic, cultural, population, etc.) and the hierarchies of race and economic access that define them, specifically those that map the passage and Anegada island in the British Virgin Islands as destinations that satisfy touristic desires arising out of the conquistadorial habit (see chapter 6). However, as an ocean-sea formation rather than a manmade one, the passage existed prior to conquest, prior to slavery, and prior to the middle/passage.[16] This point where the ocean and the sea meet predates the meanings that have been placed on them and the presumed directional movements (the penetration of the vaginal Sea by the phallic Ocean) informing conquest, enslavement, genocide, coloniality, and postcoloniality.

I return to the concept of the passage as the friction or resistance created out of the mutual encounter of different bodies of water to signal not history itself but, first, the kind of difficult encounters or crossings that

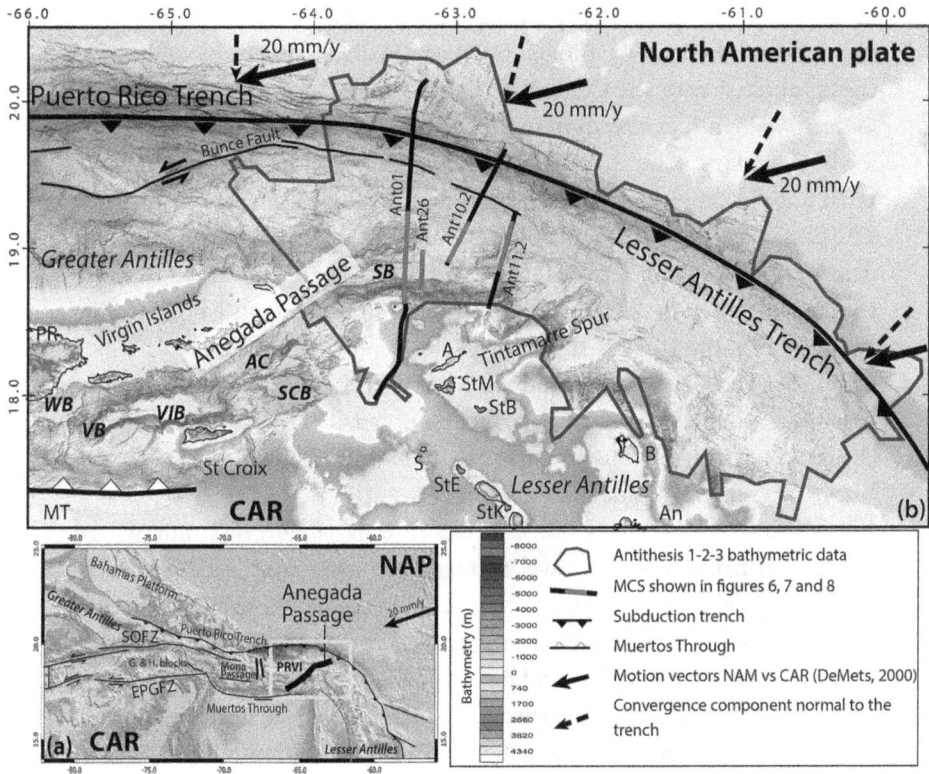

FIGURE 2.1: Map of the Anegada Passage.

must be made within black and Indigenous studies for us to fully under-stand how black and native lives, subordinations, and freedoms intersect and inform each other. Second, the passage, within which the dark blue of the Atlantic is read with, alongside, and through its contact and con-trast with the turquoise of the Caribbean Sea, points to the very conver-sions that I suggest structure black-native relations in labour history. The Atlantic waters do not strictly dominate or penetrate; they are converted by the encounter like the waters of the Caribbean Sea. The passage itself is situated near other underwater geologic formations, which are as much its horizontal and epiphenomenal articulation as the hierarchically ordered, racialized history that emerges from it.

Those other formations pictured in the map—including channels, pas-sages, trenches, and plates—are co-constitutive but not fully deterministic of the Anegada Passage in both its past and contemporary formation.[17] As an extant, ongoing tectonic event, the passage captures encounters, processes, and crossings by Indigenous Peoples that predate conquest *and* those initiated with the Columbian error, which continue to shape black and native identity in relation to each other, not specifically in relation to a white, settler-master. It is thus a liminal and limit space with which we must engage, from which this act of methodological recovery proceeds. The passage, geologically and epistemologically, is both the realization and drowning of the limit between the Atlantic and the Caribbean Sea, a space that represents both the constraint of black and Indigenous labour as they straddle opposite sides of the strait in the deployment of the dialectic of labour/Sea and Work/Ocean, and the point where those labours necessarily meet as the limit is approached and submerged. This reengagement with the middle/passage is thus an active engagement with and drowning of the historical and geographic limit as method.

This middle/passage is not one where only some cross, nor where blacks and native peoples travel through and away from each other. Instead, they cross and recross in perpetual entanglement. It is the point where the ocean and sea exist in terms of their co-making, where we can read the co-making of blacks and native peoples. Such co-making, through processes of conversion, also reflects the material and "lexical" "plasticity" of blacks that literary and feminist studies scholar Zakiyyah Iman Jackson outlines, *and* the forms of plasticity (to extend her work) to which Indigenous Peoples are subjected. Indigenous Peoples do not experience anti-black racialization. Yet, prior to the introduction of black chattel slavery, their bodies endured forced labour *and* extermination that generated forms of "plasticity" including, for example, "tearing" by wild dogs, "floggings," basting and "roasting," the creation of "sores"—all forms of breaching the body's somatic-ontological integrity in order to remake them as legal subjects of western jurisprudence, and which still leaves them meta/physically *open* to subsequent forms of remaking.[18] Moreover, their bodily puncture and trauma occurs, in the narratives of Bartolomean docility, as a partial humanization through their semantic transmogrification from "beasts" to injured animals. They are, in other words, humanized through animals, rather than strictly as or against them, though the latter is crucial for their subordination.

We have misread the bodily injury of enslaved Indigenous Peoples as charted, for instance, by Las Casas's appeals, as though they were a result of their bodily weakness and therefore through the lens of his conversion, rather than as the result of their own prior economic conversion and juridical (read: the abrogation of sovereignty) remaking. Like blacks, they are subject to forms of bodily and "ontological plasticity," although their racialized outcomes are different.[19] In other words, while Indigenous Peoples' eventual vassalage means that they are, legally, fundamentally different from blacks, it also means that Indigenous slavery (like black slavery) and attempts to control, transform, and abolish it are the context within which Indigenous Peoples are remade both bodily and ontologically into something they never were before, which governs not anti-blackness in this case, but anti-indigeneity as the telos of settler colonialism. Moreover, both Indigenous slavery, in its multitude of forms, and black chattel slavery have this remaking of indigeneity as their origin. Thus, there is no mutual exclusivity of anti-blackness and anti-indigeneity, especially when considering, as *Beyond Constraint* does, how attempts to discipline Indigenous Peoples lead to forms of movement and conversion that are implicated in and reshaped by black enslavement. Although both forms of plasticity produce homunculi and infrahumans as the respective objects of anti-indigeneity and anti-blackness, that of the former is equally the context for the remaking of blacks, as are the specific but not exclusive injuries and violations (bodily, juridical, psychic, ontological) to which the latter are subjected under chattel slavery.

To foreground this mutual point of black and Indigenous remaking in the Americas, I write middle/passage as a kind of interruption, with a pause, a form of *caesura*, signaling engagement and articulation rather than absolute break, genesis, or movement in any particular direction. I retain the distinct and capitalized term "Middle Passage" only when referring to dominant ways of conceptualizing it. Following Brent Hayes Edwards's concept of décalage, the forward slash inserts a pause in our extant understandings of the middle/passage, suggesting that a different iteration of it needs to be engaged, which focuses on it as a space of both gap or break *and* a horizontal articulation of black and native histories and bodies. I do not wish to deploy a new term for this method, but simply work toward a better understanding of the term(s) we already have. The forward slash indicates the difficulties and possibilities that emerge from passage, process, conversion, and our ability to recognize this as both the site of black-native loss and the place from which we can remake ourselves in terms of more volitional relations. A middle/passage methodology privileges not crossings *into* the hierarchies of political, economic, and historical formations, but *relations* of exchange in meaning, value, and being. Passage is thus a method of encounter and differential relation. This chapter's ultimate goal is to articulate and deploy a middle/passage methodology that can recover the subject/ed positions and labours that have fallen into the Atlantic's waters.

The Atlantic

A critical turn in Atlantic history has sought to open up its conceptual reach away from older, narrower approaches that foreground white actors and reinforce global hierarchies of culture and capital by privileging the histories of the North and First World over those of the South and Third and Fourth Worlds. This turn includes work by historians David Armitage, Thomas Benjamin, Peter Linebaugh, Marcus Rediker, J. H. Elliott, and others. However, despite attempts to expand the Atlantic as an epistemological tool, it remains limited because of the constant reinscription of its founding conceit, the temporal bias, the overemphasis on the Anglophone world, the continued bifurcation of (black) racialization and (settler) colonization, the consignment of black and Indigenous Peoples to separate spheres of influence, and the acts of translation and relational similitude it requires for black and native actions.

While important and necessary, these attempts to critique and expand the Atlantic fail both to fully capture Indigenous historical action or to bring together black and native labour within the same time-space, a move that is critical for disrupting the pre-positional structure of Caribbean history and producing new, regional labour histories that neither support narrow state nationalisms nor extend settler colonial strategies into postcolonial state governance. This failure stems in large part from the fact that as a macro-formation that arises to study the productive outcomes or formations that develop out of European involvement in the region, the Atlantic is an analytic structure designed to capture one half of the labour-work dialectic—work and its products—as an interpretive, evaluative model. The result of this valorization of work (and its related formations) is that the pre-position separating blacks and Indigenous peoples (see the introduction to this book) becomes an epistemological trope of history even in more expansive, necessary approaches to the Atlantic. European actors are still privileged above others; black actors are subject to inclusion in an additive model that reinvigorates European agency; and Indigenous actors are subject to fitful acts of translation while their actions and lives remain bracketed off from those of enslaved blacks. Where the latter is not the case, studies still retain the pre-positional supersession of African to Indian labour. Not only does European culture (and myth in particular) act as a hermeneutic for understanding Indigenous Peoples' historical realities, but native sociopolitical differences, whether in the Old or New Worlds, often disappear into their translation as antecedents of modern, global economic formation within which Indigenous Peoples reemerge as workers engaged in the types of labour leading to the rise of capital.[20]

As opposed to such broader approaches, other methodological circumscriptions to the racialized Atlantic(s) account for elided groups' agency and the realities of their forced labour. Signal in this emphasis is the work of Afro-British historian and cultural theorist Paul Gilroy, illuminating black actors in the time-space of the early Atlantic. In his seminal *The Black Atlantic*, Gilroy studies African-descended peoples' cultural and historical movements across the region. In many ways, the book does for diasporic black cultures what works like Eric Williams's *Capitalism and Slavery* and Joseph Inikori's *Africans and the Industrial Revolution in England*, together, do to demonstrate enslaved blacks' greater role in global, capitalist economic formation. Gilroy not only foregrounds black actors, but holds that their movements construct a deeply politicized "counter culture of modernity" operating within and across national boundaries, resisting "ethnic absolutism," and offering African-descended peoples a "critical, intellectual, and moral genealogy."[21] In the three decades since its publication, Gilroy's work has been both roundly criticized for its narrowness with regard to time and gender, and simultaneously adapted for its reach to other diasporic formulations resulting from enslavement and forced dispersal for labour. Many have expanded its interpretive framework to rethink this oceanic hermeneutic away from its exclusivity regarding blackness and black movements originating with capture in continental Africa and dislocation, particularly to the Anglophone Americas. The selected adaptations, extensions, and criticisms of Gilroy's work discussed below are especially useful for charting the limits of the Atlantic's necessary extensions to racialized actors.

Some approaches address the linguistic myopia of American-dominated black Atlantic studies, arguing that it should also function as an analytic for understanding the movements and resistances of black Lusophone, Francophone, and Hispanophone worlds in the Americas, the Caribbean, and Africa. In a 2012 issue of *Comparative Literature Studies* dedicated to extending Gilroy's framework, for example, editors Jossianna Arroyo and Elizabeth A. Marchant essentially ask why, if colonization in the Americas began with Spanish and Portuguese explorers, is Gilroy's and other black Atlantic formulations limited to only the Anglophone world? In the issue,

Ruben A. Sánchez-Godoy centers on an early sixteenth-century African and Indigenous Maroon community in modern-day Ecuador. By noting that, according to Gilroy, one of Columbus's shipmates on his first voyage was black, Sánchez-Godoy establishes the presence of a non-Anglophone black diaspora at the inception of European Atlantic crossing, which was not defined by chattel labour status. Gilroy is thus critical for establishing early African strategies of resistance to enslavement and colonization. With special relevance for this study, Sánchez-Godoy suggests that Gilroy's work can also be used to foreground black-native relations that emerged despite "the mechanisms of separation between African captives and indigenous people imposed by the Spanish authorities in the new territories."[22] More significantly, he uses the presence of "African-Amerindian subjectivities" to suggest that the black Atlantic has both other origins and other outcomes. In the same *CLA* issue, Brady Smith similarly suggests that the existing black Atlantic formulation represents a "hegemony" in black diaspora studies and should extend to other regions, such as Cape Verde. Smith finds Gilroy's formulation problematic both for its "narrow" understanding of blackness and for its geographic framing, which eclipses non-Anglophone regions that played a significant part in transatlantic history.[23] Together, Sánchez-Godoy's and Smith's works indicate that other geographies and linguistic and ethnic groups—with their attendant social and cultural histories of resistance—are missing from the formulation of the black Atlantic. However, they still write within the Atlantic analytic they extend, adapt, and open up.

In contrast, two of the most significant rejections of Gilroy's framework come from Brent Hayes Edwards, an African American scholar of the Francophone black diaspora, and Paul Tiyambe Zeleza, Malawian historian and creative writer. Both writers' works are part of a critical turn that rejects additive approaches to the black diaspora in order to get beyond the ways that the (black) Atlantic time, space, and geography elides numerous black historical and cultural trajectories. Edwards's "The Uses of Diaspora" claims that Gilroy's term "black Atlantic" "often usurps the space that might otherwise be reserved for *diaspora*."[24] The latter, for Edwards, is a more historically specific and effective analytic against the Atlantic's limits as both geographic and "oceanic frame."[25] Although the concept is still grounded by "classic diasporas," he finds diaspora's "epistemological work" nuanced enough to engage with the broad range of cultural, political, and historical differences and disarticulations constituting the black diaspora.[26] Edwards's conceptual deployment is further distinguished by his insistence on approaching the black diaspora in terms of its constitutive breaks rather than just forged connections.[27] He contends that "articulations of diaspora demand to be approached . . . through their *décalage*. For paradoxically, . . . exactly such a haunting gap or discrepancy . . . allows the African diaspora to 'step' and 'move' in various articulations."[28] This emphasis on trajectories of movement that do not fit neatly is a critical, anti-essentialist push in keeping with later works like Michelle Wright's. It rejects narrow concepts of diasporic identity that might still depend on hegemonic interpretive modes that, as with Atlantic studies more broadly, do not challenge the organizing assumption of a bounded unification, racial essentialism, or monolingualism, nor extend to address other critical modes of engagement, resistance, and intellectual genealogies that emerge from a conception of diaspora as "intervention" rather than unification.[29]

Like Edwards, Zeleza seeks to replace Gilroy's black Atlantic with a more dynamic framework in keeping with works such as *The African Diaspora in the Indian Ocean* or *Routes of Passage*, which reconfigure the (black) Atlantic's time, space, and dominant political, economic, and cultural formations. In "Rewriting the African Diaspora," Zeleza utilizes then extant criticism of Gilroy's work, arguing that although Gilroy seeks to reject the "snobbery of African American analytical exceptionalism," he simply reinscribes it.[30] Zeleza argues that *The Black Atlantic* utilizes a limited notion of diaspora that contributes to Africa's "homogenization and racialization." Citing Laura Chrisman's oft-mentioned critique of *The Black Atlantic*, he argues that the African diaspora is articulated as a thoroughly modern formation "*imposed* upon African populations."[31] Thus, Gilroy's limited concept necessarily reinscribes the central Enlightenment principle of African backwardness remedied by European entanglements. As an alternative to the Atlantic's singular oceanic framework Edwards rejects, Zeleza also offers a more nuanced concept of diaspora, broader in its geographic and temporal reach. He argues for a continental and oceanic framework comprising "four dominant dimensions of the global African diasporas": "intra-Africa, Indian Ocean, Mediterranean, Atlantic diasporas."[32] Further, he rejects the Atlantic's singular time, using Colin Palmer's work to argue that the African diaspora experienced its first dispersal 100,000 years ago (the date given for the first, significant migration of modern humans), and thus *precedes* Africa's incorporation into European modernity and global economic systems.[33] Zeleza's expanded diasporic analytic thus works fundamentally differently from previous concepts by engaging a productive antimony containing both blacks (a post-European engagement marker of continental African origins) and diverse *indigenous*, African peoples, who have moved globally while still within their own cosmogonic systems and modes of identification. Together, Zeleza and Edwards successfully reject the European conceit that has predominated Atlantic studies. Challenges like Zeleza's, in particular, are advanced in other newer assessments of the Atlantic, expanding its scope and offering up a more nuanced historical field by working within its ruptures (*décalage*).

Of particular concern for this book are approaches privileging a third set of actors in the Atlantic: Indigenous Peoples. One of the most significant of these newer assessments in attempts to define a "red Atlantic" is *Atlantic History*, which approaches the region from several perspectives: imperial, Indigenous, African, and a more broadly conceptual angle. In the introduction to this multinodal project, editors Jack P. Greene and Philip D. Morgan foreground long-standing issues surrounding the Atlantic's cohesion and delimiting as a space of history and analysis configured by time, language, imperial power, race, and so on. Rather than seek to resolve these issues, they embrace the Atlantic as "an anachronistic concept."[34] Amy Turner Bushnell's chapter in the same volume, "Indigenous America and the Limits of the Atlantic World, 1493–1825," argues not only that Atlantic history is "Eurocentric" because it positions non-European actors as "adjuncts or obstacles" to colonization and empire building.[35] Like Arroyo and Marchant, she suggests that it also operates through a particular intra-European bias that fails to consider Spanish colonialism, which saw greater entanglement with Indigenous Peoples. Thus, Spanish colonialism's exclusion by dominant studies misses a key site in which to look at Indigenous peoples' lives and labour in and at the edges of the Atlantic world.[36] Rather than an Atlantic perspective, Bushnell argues that only a more *hemispheric* worldview could account for Indigenous Peoples' movements, forced labour, and, critically, their agency and freedom within the colonial era.

Bushnell argues for another way of understanding Indigenous Peoples' lives during that time by dividing them into three groups that shaped the Atlantic world in relation to European settlements and incursions: Incorporated Peoples (Indigenous Peoples as labour), Extractive Frontiers (where Indigenous Peoples generated "products of value"), and Autonomous Peoples (who resisted Europeans).[37] The strength of Bushnell's argument is the recognition of Indigenous Peoples' multiple forms of engagement with the Atlantic as a structure of contact and, in keeping with my elaboration of the labour-work dialectic, the recognition of at least two types of Indigenous action that can be identified as their labour *and* work. Its limitation, however, is that Indigenous Peoples necessarily enter the Atlantic within the particular time of discovery. For instance, Bushnell mentions precolonial Arawakan flood management techniques (which I discuss in chapter 3), in order to note European entanglement with the Moxos, thereby refiguring their pre-Columbian time for Atlantic history.[38] While Bushnell challenges the Atlantic's space (read: reach) and repositions Indigenous peoples as actors and agents, the Atlantic paradigm still limits the time of her investigation. The difficulty of challenging the Atlantic axis on both its *temporal* and *spatial* fronts means that even attempts to push against this framework almost always invoke one axis or the other, leading to a persistent marginalization of Indigenous Peoples, a problem that preoccupies the work of historian Paul Cohen, which reveals the lack of a method for truly decentering the Atlantic.

In his essay, "Was There an Amerindian Atlantic? Reflections on the Limits of a Historiographical Concept," Cohen examines how Atlantic history's varying methodological approaches marginalize Indigenous Peoples. For Cohen, dominant analytical frameworks such as empire, military, capital, and migration are all inadequate because they cannot account for Indigenous Peoples' "agency" or "perspectives" to which, in fact, European lives and economies were subject. At one point, Cohen suggests possible ways of looking at Indigenous Peoples in the Atlantic that dovetail with normative modes of analysis, including labour. In iterating, for example, how Indigenous Peoples' lives in the early Atlantic, colonial world fit dominant interpretive frameworks, Cohen notes that "Amerindians could also be studied as sources of labour in the Atlantic economy" because "existing narratives of Atlantic history do not always recall that most slaves in the Americas before 1700 were Amerindians rather than Africans—and that, like Africans, Amerindians both practiced slavery and furnished slaves to Europeans."[39] Yet it seems that for Cohen the limits of the "Atlantic paradigm" do not outweigh its benefits as an analytic. Thus, although he asks whether "we need the Atlantic to make sense of the history of Amerindians and of their interactions with other peoples in the early modern period" and cautions that "historians should remain careful not to annex" Indigenous history into the Atlantic, he concludes that "the history of the Atlantic would best be written as one shaped by a multiplicity of centers and peripheries, rather than as a simple, Atlantic-centered process."[40] In other words, for Cohen, the Atlantic must first be displaced in order both to be recentered and to center Indigenous Peoples' histories. It is the impetus of such displacement that, I argue, most Atlantic scholars struggle to retain as, like Cohen, they continue to embrace the Atlantic as a causally necessary explanatory tool for social and economic regional change.

Like Cohen's essay, Robert Stam and Ella Shohat's *Race in Translation* tries to expand the concept of the Atlantic to think other histories within it and directly incorporate (or apply it to) Indigenous Peoples. More pointedly arguing for a red Atlantic than the preceding texts, the authors intervene in existing Eurocentric methodologies and limited nationalisms. They seek a "fluid transnational and translational methodology" that allows them to bring the Lusophone, Francophone, and Anglophone Atlantics into a single interpretive framework.[41] With culture rather than race as the primary point of connection, their "multicolored Atlantic seascape" allows them to

> advance, in conjunction with the well-known work on the "Black Atlantic," the idea of the "Red Atlantic" and, on a different register, the "White Atlantic." Although the expression "Red Atlantic" has ... refer[red] strictly to the indigenous peoples of the Americas, we conceptualize it in a broader sense to suggest that the entire Atlantic world is "Red" and indigenized, in that it has been impacted not only by the Conquest that enriched Europe materially but also by indigenous modes of thought and sociability that triggered a salutary epistemological crisis by provoking European thinkers—from Montaigne and Diderot to Pierre Clastres—to question the dominant social norms.[42]

The authors read the Atlantic in terms of these dominant metaphors of color as an effect of raciality/racialization. Moreover, noting American slavery's origin with enslaved Indigenous Peoples and the substitution of 100,000 enslaved Indigenous peoples for blacks in Brazil during a seventeenth-century twenty-five-year "suspension" of the slave trade, they argue that "colonialism, conquest, slavery, and multiculturality are thus inextricably linked."[43] Key in advancing a "syncretic" rather than disarticulated Atlantic concept is their emphasis on the shared temporality of Indigenous and Black enslavement and the porosity of these identities. However, Stam and Shohat are still limited terminologically by the Eurocentrism at the heart of postcolonial studies, and seem caught in the discursive play and lack of positionality that has haunted the "post." In defining the Atlantic in terms of color and the three dominant linguistic spheres mentioned above, into which they interject a red Atlantic as part of the "race/coloniality problematic," they not only defer to and privilege the constitutive histories of these blocs, but subject the entire region to a single framework of racialization.

Additionally, the Enlightenment emerges as a pivot point in their argument. By tracking its reach, they necessarily reinscribe the nation-state they hope to transcend with an emphasis on fluidity. "Race" becomes not possibility, but the limit of their intervention even where they seek to subtend it with culture and action.

While Stam and Shohat acknowledge Europeans' inability to affirm Indigenous Peoples' pre-contact modes of existence, they too cannot recognize them as anything more than a counterpoint to terms already extant in the race-culture Atlantic debate. For instance, they write, "Although native agricultural practice had sustained indigenous people for millennia, it was not recognized by Europeans as authentic agriculture but only as a kind of animal-like foraging. The fact that a densely populated and culturally remolded land was seen as 'virgin' reflects a kind of mental 'ethnic cleansing,' a discourse of imaginary removal."[44] They focus on European perception of Indigenous Peoples and the transformation of Indigenous modes of being and sustaining, situating such modes neither outside the dominant terms of their analytic nor within the terms of an Indigenous worldview. They are also framed not in terms of sovereignty—its possibilities and foreclosures—but in terms of imperialism and coloniality. Thus, by eschewing the notion of "a single European Enlightenment" in favor of "multiple transatlantic enlightenments," they put in place the Haitian Revolution and its dialectical engagement with the French Revolution, leaving out Indigenous Peoples either because it is a dialectic that only impacted the latter negatively, or because a non-European engaged Atlantic would be anachronistic and specious.[45] Moreover, as in the passage quoted above, in numerous places the authors evacuate the black Atlantic of its materiality and indigeneity precisely because they read it through race's discursive rather than material structures. They continue to mobilize the Atlantic as a macrostructure within which the sea knits together lands that are then pulled into a modern history.

Dismissing Stam and Shohat's work as simply a postcolonial exercise, the Cherokee legal, religious, and Indigenous Studies scholar Jace Weaver faults attempts to stretch the Atlantic framework because, as he writes in the preface to *The Red Atlantic*, "When other scholars—nonspecialists in indigenous studies—seek to expand [Gilroy's] vision of the black Atlantic to include other Others, they only end up reinscribing the marginality of the indigenes of the Western Hemisphere."[46] Weaver's red Atlantic is aimed at "restoring" indigenous peoples to the center of discussions of Atlantic world modernity as "equally important to, if not more important than, the

Africans of Gilroy's black Atlantic."[47] He critiques Gilroy's elision of native peoples: "other than his reference to the 'Indians' they slaughtered, Native Americans make no further guest appearances in the pages of *The Black Atlantic*."[48] Partially echoing Elliot's disregard of a singular history of Atlantic modernity, Weaver reads the Atlantic as a "contact zone" where "American indigenes engaged in trade and supplied maritime labour, worked alongside non-Natives in legitimate enterprise and in piracy."[49] He also acknowledges that while Indigenous Peoples "experienced nothing in transoceanic shipment as horrific as the middle passage" (a point somewhat disproved by the historical record and both Wendy Warren's and Andrés Reséndez's works discussed below) and were not involved in the "Triangle Trade," they were also captured and transported "abroad." He defines the red Atlantic as a space of Indigenous persons' movement, material resources, and ideas and cultural exchanges "encompass[ing] the Atlantic and its major adjacent bodies of water," beginning nearly five hundred years before Columbus (including pre-Columbian contact) and running through 1927, though this year did not end native peoples' real or imaginative engagement with that space.[50] Importantly, this timeline looks at the Atlantic in terms of native peoples' own cosmogonic narratives, sovereignty, and agency (e.g., Weaver notes Inuit, Cherokee, and Choctaw creation myths that engage the "sea") and their forced transport both prior to and during black slavery. In charting these movements, Weaver does not confine his work to the Atlantic basin, but engages distant continental regions such as Peru, whose peoples and products entered and circulated in the Atlantic. Crucially, Weaver defines this Atlantic differently for Indigenous Peoples, saying that while Africans were "indigenous to Africa," for Indigenous Peoples the Atlantic is a space of "mobility while still being rooted in place."[51]

Weaver's and similar works represent a distinctive refashioning of the Atlantic world's history and theory through which we may understand how Indigenous Peoples' existence in the Americas shaped the Atlantic *outside* and *within* Benítez-Rojo's copulatory construction/production. For the purposes of this book, most significant is Weaver's reclamation of the Atlantic as a space produced *initially* within Indigenous Peoples' worldviews, not out of Greco-Roman myth or European voyages. This native emergence is always (at least through the book's end in 1927) concurrent with its evolution despite its eclipse by Europe's remaking of the space within capitalist modernity. Weaver's interests, he says, lie not in detailing Indigenous movements, as others have done, but in "center[ing]" Indigenous Peoples.[52] This gesture and critical strategy significantly distinguish his work from studies that might affirm Indigenous Peoples as participants in or denizens of the Atlantic world but not as actors moving through, within, and out of their own social and economic systems, acting from their own ontological volition as well as from forced or compelled movements.

Weaver's reclamation of the Atlantic might be best understood as first an erasure and then a reinstituting from a point of radical difference, anchored by the fundamental act of movement. While his is still the Atlantic's most expansive reconceptualization and the first to actually affirm its pre-contact, extra European origins, it still does not conceptually bring together black and native histories and labours. In one sense, it is a pre-expansion that takes the Atlantic in other directions; while this work is necessary, it does not achieve what I think must happen for the Caribbean. Below, I read with Weaver but move further to mobilize not the Atlantic but the middle/passage and movements that might be named/unnamed/grouped/ungrouped to mobilize points of relatedness and conversion that articulate both with and against the black middle passage. I formally consider Black and Indigenous labour in relation. While this middle/passage reading might suggest looking at black and Indigenous histories in terms of their similarities or sameness, I argue that they must also be read more productively in terms of co-constitutive differences. This micro-level reading of the middle/passage offers conceptual space that the Atlantic, as a macro configuration, does not, despite its expansions. A middle/passage reading reclaims and mobilizes movements that might be internal and recursive, rather than singularly outward and accumulative.

Passage as Method

I read for Conversion as part of a middle/passage mechanism for understanding Indigenous forced labour prior to black chattel enslavement, analyzing this labour both as *and* as not a type of Atlantic or middle/passage history of bound labour in order to articulate a concept of passage, or crossing, as method. I argue that Indigenous enslavement and forced movements in the Caribbean Sea and Atlantic compel a rethinking of what, when, and where the middle/passage is and what it does. By contextualizing this argument within more contemporary works on Indigenous enslavement in the Americas, on a "red Atlantic" or "reverse middle passage," I propose a view of Indigenous enslavement that is a detour away from the routes dominating understandings of Atlantic slavery, and a return to a concept of the middle/passage that is both break and articulation. I suggest that the history of the so-called modern or post-conquest Americas is generated out of neither the unidirectionality of European crossing nor the dominance of triangular, chattel enslavement.

Instead, that history emerged from pre-conquest Indigenous movements (which I do not detail here), preconquest Indigenous labour, and Indigenous Peoples' forced crossings and movements. These processes signal the conversion of Indigenous Peoples and their labour to work (prior to and even current with their position in the dialectic as failed or unproductive labour), and are broadly impactful for our entire understanding of the Middle Passage, slavery, and the Atlantic. Moreover, these collective movements demonstrate alternate origins and outcomes for regional labour history. In the previous chapter, I used Las Casas's *A Short History* to demonstrate the concept of Conversion. I return briefly to that text to identify instances of Indigenous bound labour prior to the introduction of enslaved blacks in the Americas. Read through the optic of their conversion, Las Casas's discussion of Indigenous bound labour exemplifies an earlier starting point for regional labour history, describing the region's *first* middle/passage (as a value conversion of peoples).

A Short History records Indigenous slavery throughout the Americas and the Caribbean islands. Critical here are Las Casas's descriptions of slavery in the spaces that will become culturally Caribbean and/or Latin American, and of enslaved Indigenous Peoples' transportation between mainland and island territories. Recounting the "slaughter" of Indigenous Peoples on Hispaniola, he notes that it "began with the Europeans taking native women and children both as servants and to satisfy their own base appetites."[53] He also records slavery as punishment for failed extermination, writing that Hispaniola's new governor ordered the Indigenous Peoples of the kingdom of Xaraguá (home of the famed Anacaona) massacred; those who fled were "condemned to slavery."[54] Las Casas documents Indigenous labour in mining and farming (plantation work), during which they were starved and subjected to "floggings, beatings, thrashings, punches, curses," and "branding."[55] Writing of Nicaragua, Las Casas reveals not only an intensive process of slave procurement, but also Indigenous Peoples' transport aboard "slaving vessels" for sale in Panama and Peru.[56] He also chronicles enslaved Indigenous Peoples' "transport" to the slave markets of Cuba and Hispaniola.[57] Indigenous Peoples were also shipped as slaves from the Bahamas to Hispaniola, "kidnapped" from Venezuela, and transported to the islands of Hispaniola and Puerto Rico.[58] Moreover, in this removal, "at least a third of the poor wretches perish during the voyage and are thrown overboard."[59]

While Caribbean labour histories fixate on and repeat what we can call the pessimistic reading of Indigenous survival (i.e., the extermination in Las Casas's work that allows them to be absented from history), *A Short History* clearly supports two elements critical for understanding both labour history and the middle/passage's origin. First, the archipelagic Caribbean in Las Casas's work is always knitted together with the history of mainland territories by the crossings of Indigenous Peoples. Thus, the linguistic boundedness and cultural segregation of what becomes the (Anglophone) Caribbean from Latin America (which Atlantic studies has reinforced) is prefaced by an intraregional yoking where Indigenous Peoples' pre-conquest, volitional regional movements are deferred by their post-conquest, forced movements between island and mainland territories. Second, despite Las Casas's overriding extinction narrative (the texts' pessimism) due to Indigenous bodily weakness, he continually claims that forced labour caused this weakness. Las Casas's "gentle lambs" die by the hundreds not because they are weak, but because they are forced into brutal slavery and sexual exploitation. They die because they are both enslaved as "beasts of burden" *and* deliberately starved when their labour for themselves is cut off and they are forced to do extractive work for Europeans. Moreover, they experience the bodily disciplines characteristic of chattel enslavement, from corporeal punishment to branding. While Afropessimism would argue that this is not the reduction of bodies to flesh nor to the forms of porosity characterizing blackness as an object position, they nonetheless occur through the temporal mutuality of Indigenous dispossession and exploitation.[60]

To read Las Casas's writings *for* Indigenous work (and their sovereign labour) rather than for their work's causal result (extermination) and its alignment with Las Casas's religious motives, is a perspectival shift. With this shift, Indigenous extinction or extermination becomes a way of charting the failed conversion of Indigenous Peoples to value. Because they are forced to work and die, rather than are hearty enough (in Las Casas's eyes) to be forced to work and live, their bodies are not converted into value for accumulation, and Las Casas chooses to record this failure, rather than their labour for themselves, as that which is carried out and sacrificed under colonization. Moreover, because he emphasizes the literal consumption of their bodies in this process, *consumption* becomes the actual object of (their) labour, while for blacks it is *production*, which labour history records. For Indigenous Peoples at this sixteenth-century moment, only their deaths accumulate and can be recorded because the bodily labours in those deaths cannot even be salvaged as ecclesiastical labour for God. In contrast, as we saw in chapter 1, the deaths of enslaved blacks facilitate their conversion to value. In short, black Death allows for black transformation to value (to nearly permanent commodity status in chattel slavery), while Indigenous death becomes value itself by leaving *land open* for acquisition (or ownership) and development. Additionally, when Indigenous Peoples are enslaved for fleeing extermination, essentially rejecting the productive form of their deaths (their work for Europeans), enslavement becomes the *success* of the middle/passage transformation of their bodily actions to the accumulative structures of work (recall their transportation in the region for labour).

Thus, Indigenous Peoples have only two (economic) options after conquest: die and be productive in this manner, together with living and *working* as enslaved people, or labour in perpetuity for the well-being of the European soul, which is literally a political phenomenon. In tying Indigenous Peoples to the religious imperative, Las Casas seemingly effects their Conversion to non-value, or away from value. However, he must first ignore how their deaths actually function as a mechanism *for* accumulation and the fact that the spiritual labours to which they are condemned by Conversion are the product of an accumulative structure. Indigenous labour, though positionally on the other side of the dialectic, becomes an analogue of surplus *value* (of course not fully realized outside the formal structures of capital accumulation) through Conversion. This surplus, though anterior to capitalism proper, reflects the kind of phantasmic excess (above reproductive labour) that ultimately produces surplus values in capital. It is an anterior form of surplus value because it will exist *in excess of* productive, unwaged black labour.

This relationship between black and Indigenous Peoples is intrinsic, collectively, to the commodity's evolution. Moreover, occurring on the other side of the dialectic, the production of Indigenous labour as a ghostly surplus is a "vampire-like" product of accumulative work, and thus an early demonstration of the capitalist's consumption of the worker's labour, which we can rename *wétiko* consumption, and which characterizes capital as "dead labor" for Marx.[61] The transformation of living labour into dead objects (the commodity) not only is based on black and Indigenous Death/death through the middle/passages of Conversion that institute the dialectic as an accumulative structure, but also depends on the *concealment* of those deaths just as the commodity itself is the concealment, deferral, or eclipse of the labour that has gone into its production. What we see as an essentially spiritual or ecclesiastical process makes this possible, demonstrating the autophagia of both capitalism and its poetic or descriptive structures. Thus, while Marx describes surplus value as specific to capitalism, surplus value itself encapsulates and transforms an earlier process of surplus required to produce the initial values that can move economies from consumptive modes to productive and accumulative ones.

This reading of indigeneity in Las Casas *for* Caribbean labour history sits squarely within research on Indigenous Peoples' bound labour that does not engage the Atlantic as its primary analytic nor seeks a strictly additive model to address that labour. I primarily engage Andrés Reséndez's *The Other Slavery*, alongside a few other works, particularly Wendy Warren's *New England Bound*. These works seek to change not only how we read slavery, but also what bound labour is and its relationship to black enslavement and settler colonialism. They demonstrate that the Atlantic's displacement facilitates a redefinition and rediscovery of slavery, work, and labour for both black and Indigenous historical modernity. There is a robust history of Indigenous enslavement, particularly within Latin American studies.[62] However, although Indigenous Peoples circulated as both free and captive throughout the region, Indigenous slavery is still viewed largely as a Latin American rather than Caribbean phenomenon, with the exception of more recent work like Andrés Reséndez's and Erin Woodruff Stone's *Captives of Conquest*. In Barbados, for example, not only had Indigenous Peoples been transported from Dutch Guiana and enslaved since 1627, but their enslavement also overlapped with that of blacks. A 1676 act prevented further importation of enslaved native peoples to reduce the possibility of rebellion by black *and* Indigenous enslaved people. Barbados demonstrates a shared history and temporality of enslavement, legal mechanisms to control slave labour, and, more importantly, the same concerns over rebellion of blacks and Indigenous Peoples.[63] Moreover, the English used enslavement in Caribbean islands as punishment for "rebellious" natives with whom they were at war in North America.[64]

Rather than offer a study of Indigenous slavery in the Caribbean, however, I am interested in shifting and expanding the framing narratives of enslavement in order to suggest alternate ways of looking at blacks and Indigenous peoples as historical actors. I elucidate the significance of Reséndez's and Warren's texts, showing how their work helps mobilize the middle/passage (or middle/passages), rather than the Atlantic, as a method of recovering shared antagonistic (rebellious) and lost labour histories. In one of the most sweeping accounts of Indigenous enslavement in the colonial Americas, Andrés Reséndez demonstrates its *longue durée*, arguing not only that it is *another* kind of enslavement but that its failed terminuses constitute "the other emancipation."[65] For the purposes of this argument, critical is his desire to have readers understand this as a *kind* of enslavement that, prior to the New Laws of 1542, which protect Indigenous Peoples, may have been more akin to chattel enslavement. Moreover, after these laws passed, decidedly (though not definitively) bracketing off Indigenous Peoples from blacks, Indigenous enslavement still continued under different names and different terms.[66] In demonstrating this parallel to chattel enslavement, Reséndez makes several key arguments about Indigenous slavery relevant to this book, recovers Indigenous labour from its conversion, and allows us to rethink the middle/passage as a space of black origin and ultimately what becomes creole indigeneities.

First, he argues that Indian slavery has been obscured not just by the textual overrepresentation of African enslavement but also by attempts to categorize it (or work with its dominant colonial organization) under the encomienda and repartimiento systems that are always "distinguished from outright enslavement."[67] Thus, Las Casas's own conversion(s), its resultant Conversion of Indigenous Peoples into vassals as the antithesis of value (the 1542 laws), and their *ability to be converted* into a different category of sovereign being (vassalage) change the context in which their labour/work can be observed or made visible. Second, and of particular importance for the temporal grammar organizing black and native regional histories, Reséndez argues that throughout the Americas we need to "understand the reality of Indian slavery not as a residue of colonial wars or a transitional phase until African slaves arrived in the New World in sufficient numbers, but as an established network."[68] Third, he holds that Indigenous enslavement commenced *with* the Columbian error. Not only was it essential in the early colonial period, but from Columbus' *first* return voyage to the late nineteenth century, "between 2.5 and 5 million" Indigenous Peoples were in fact in some kind of bondage.[69] Further, he notes that not only was their population decline *statistically* greater than that of continental Africans, but while the Thirteenth Amendment to the US Constitution freed blacks, it did not free Indigenous Peoples who remained in forms of bondage including "convict leasing" and "debt peonage."[70]

While Reséndez ignores blacks' subjection in the United States to debt peonage and convict leasing (by which they were also not fully free), he ably chronicles a history of Indigenous enslavement beginning with Columbus, who he argues should be understood as nothing less than a slaver who established a "reverse middle passage" by sending 550 enslaved Indians to Europe in 1495.[71] Moreover, he distinctly links Columbus's slaving efforts to the influence of the early Portuguese castle and trading post São Jorge da Mina (Elmina), which Columbus visited prior to his New World voyage.[72] This reframing of Columbus as a slaver is essential to Reséndez's argument that while Indigenous Peoples' decline is often attributed to disease, it is in fact more likely that "between 1492 and 1550, a nexus of slavery, overwork, and famine killed more Indians in the Caribbean than smallpox, influenza, and malaria. And among these human factors, slavery has emerged as a major killer."[73]

Not only does he directly challenge arguments about inherent Indigenous bodily weakness by foregrounding slavery, but the accounts of Columbus as a slaver allow for another argument that directly challenges how we understand the separation of blacks and Indigenous Peoples around land and labour. While we differentiate so-called discoverers like Columbus and conquistadors from *later* enslavers and settlers, Columbus's slaving goal means that the figures of the conquistador, master, and settler are never separate but collapsed (as I discuss in chapter 6). Our dominant approaches to history disarticulate them artificially. Moreover, returning to chapter 1's discussion of primitive accumulation, we can argue that at its inception, the a priori of Indigenous enslavement *is not* land dispossession (the kind of eliminatory removal that places them under the purview of the *settler* and makes the land productive by positioning them on one side of the land-labour divide), but rather the kind of removal that places them under the purview of the proto-*master*, which correlates to the remaking of blacks as enslaved peoples. Put differently, it is premised on the removal from the land that would make their *bodies*, rather than the land, productive. Though this becomes foreclosed by Bartolomean docility and its required Conversion of Indigenous bodies away from value, it nonetheless exists, and thus Indigenous Peoples share this component of *Death* with blacks.

Moreover, this relationship to labour and forms of primitive accumulation is parallel to and concurrent with their land dispossession, especially if we consider that they also endured forms of enslavement through the nineteenth century. Reséndez's portrayal of Columbus's slaving goal definitively reveals just how much the first conversion of Indigenous Peoples actually concerns their bodies' productivity rather than their lands. Their supposed bodily weakness (read here Las Casas's own conversion) is what eventually separates them from blacks. This account of slavery's commencement in the Americas and the Caribbean with Columbus also means that Reséndez charts what will become the Atlantic slave trade as that which is actually inaugurated by New World Indigenous Peoples in (at this moment) their very *difference* from those of Africa's south and west coasts. That difference, which is their Conversion, will be pre-figured into the Atlantic trade so that Indigenous African dispossession will be read only through enslaved black labour exploitation as the trade and the methods we use to study it eventually valorize the first form of dispossession (labour exploitation) that Indigenous Peoples endured.

I want to outline in greater detail just how much the first conversion of Indigenous Peoples is a bodily one under the conquistador *as* master. The economic conversion depends on the fact that this inaugural slave trade in the Americas extracted value from the very Indigenous body that Las Casas saw as too weak to work. In complete contrast to Bartolomean docility, Reséndez writes that Columbus valued Indigenous Peoples as worth "more" than even enslaved black people when he wrote to the Spanish monarchs, enthusing, "May you also believe that one of them would be worth more than three black slaves from Guinea in strength and ingenuity, as you will gather from those I am shipping out now."[74] Reséndez adds that "Columbus's optimistic appraisal of the Indian slaves had a clear intention": "Ten days later, he wrote again to the Catholic monarchs, explaining that his stores of wine and wheat were running low. Requesting more caravels loaded with provisions, he proposed, 'We could pay for all of that with slaves from among these cannibals, a people very savage and suitable for the purpose, and well made, and of very good intelligence.'"[75] Reséndez's work reveals that while Columbus could not recognize Indigenous labour in the "abundance" of food/goods they possessed, he did recognize it in their "well made" bodies as value only where this labour could be productive and valuable for Europe. Thus, I argue that Columbus's statement (quoted again in Reséndez), that "the Indians of Española were and are the greatest wealth of the island, because they are the ones who dig, and harvest, and collect the bread and other supplies, and gather the gold from the mines, and do all the work of men and beasts alike," shows Indigenous Peoples' labour for themselves, which Columbus translates or converts to potential *work* of value to Europeans.[76] At this discursive moment, Indigenous Peoples' labour for themselves to produce their super abundance is fully converted—as work—into wealth for Europeans. *This* is the Conversion that both blacks and Indigenous Peoples have in common: that of their own subsistence labour, occurring within the specificity of their cosmogonic systems, to the European discursive and sociopolitical economy, as the expression of the latter's own Christian cosmogony.[77]

Reséndez does not challenge the extinction thesis, particularly for islands such as Hispaniola and the Bahamas, which saw the intensive decline of their respective Taino and Lucayo populations. Rather, he suggests that its true cause was forced labour as slavery itself prevented the Indigenous population from recovering from decimation.[78] He uses Las Casas and other contemporaneous corroborating sources to paint a picture of a vast network of Indian enslavement that commenced (though it was very distinct from later European forms of enslavement) with Indigenous enslavement of each other prior to conquest, and which "coexisted" with chattel enslavement through black emancipation.[79] Europeans traded in Indigenous enslaved people between islands and mainland territories, across the Atlantic, within the Caribbean Sea, and within and between mainland Latin American territories, as Las Casas described, and North America, as Warren's and Reséndez's works demonstrate. In that system, Indigenous Peoples eventually gained legal status based on the 1542 law that rendered their enslavement unjust except within a strict set of circumstances, and they could even seek legal representation to challenge their enslavement, particularly in Europe. However, while Reséndez recognizes that Indian legal status makes them decidedly fundamentally different from blacks (whose status was that of property), he reinforces that this vassalage did not stop Indigenous enslavement. Thus, Indigenous Peoples experienced the horrors of both chattel and post-chattel slavery, without the status. Like blacks, they underwent capture, the hold of the slave ship, the "wake" of the ship where their dead were thrown overboard, land transport, family separation, and forms of emancipation in which, like enslaved blacks with postslavery apprenticeship in the Caribbean, they were "still . . . required to work" for their own supposed good.[80] More importantly, they resisted.

We could argue that the wake, as an ocean-sea reality and critical black studies hermeneutic, is not just the concomitant of black enslavement but, in the Americas, is also its antecedent, having commenced with and extended from Indigenous enslavement. The wake, through Sharpe's multipronged engagement, is thus a shared context for Death/death that continues to shape black and Indigenous lives. In other words, the wake is not just the rear temporality of the ship within which blacks are caught, but also an antecedent structure of native slave making within which black lives are remade. When we do not read these (black and native) wakes as epiphenomena to each other, we in fact read blackness (and Indigeneity) out of rather than through their relational time. The difference of Indigenous enslavement is thus the context for black enslavement, which develops out of the former. It is delinked from it because of the legal differences between chattel enslavement and continuing forms of slavery under Indigenous vassalage, as well as the specific processes of being "black-ened" that enslaved Africans undergo.[81] It is also delinked because, as Weaver shows, the Atlantic sustains both movement and roots for Indigenous Peoples through their prior relationships to land in the Americas, which blacks do not share and within which they can only newly root through entanglement with settler dispossession. Reséndez's efforts sit with those of Stuart B. Schwartz, who prefaces his study of Indigenous Peoples' plantation work in Brazil by saying that "the attempt to use Indians as a coerced labour force . . . cannot be simply dismissed as a 'false start.'"[82] Schwartz corroborates Reséndez, confirming that Indigenous enslavement not only persisted in other forms after it had been deemed illegal, but also existed alongside black chattel enslavement through the nineteenth century. He further claims that black chattel enslavement grew out of extant slaving.

The early failure of efforts to protect Indigenous Peoples from the consequences of forced labour that led to Las Casas's first conversion, and the admittance of Indigenous Peoples to a higher degree of humanity, is thus the *second* Conversion of Indigenous Peoples. It obscures the first (their bodily conversion within the labour-work dialectic), which links up with black enslavement and is the reason that blacks *and* Indigenous Peoples *must* remain (i.e., are "produced" as) a global underclass today. The second Conversion is primarily seen as religious. It is based on the idea of Indigenous docility, and in the Caribbean it led to the erasure of Indigenous Peoples' work from labour history. Although anti-blackness continues to produce African-descended peoples as the zero sum of humanity, both conversions demonstrate that Indigenous Peoples and blacks (as uprooted Indigenes) are in a dialectic rather than a tiered/gradated system with regard to their mutual humanity/infrahumanity. Through that dialectic, whose mechanics I have articulated in *Creole Indigeneity*, their social-historical identities and material realities in settler states throughout the Western Hemisphere are continually produced as positive and negative outcomes of each other.[83] The overidentification of chattel slavery with blacks has led Caribbean labour history studies to ignore the evidence of Indigenous slavery and resistance as a starting point for a broader regional labour history.

Like Reséndez, in *New England Bound*, Wendy Warren changes our understanding of slavery racially and geographically by underscoring what I refer to as Indigenous Peoples' first, pre-Bartolomean Conversion. Focusing on slavery in the New England colonies, she writes that "before there was any large-scale English settlement in the region, there was already enslavement of Indians by English."[84] She directly compares black and Indian slavery by identifying African enslavement as "the mirror process of Indian removal."[85] Corroborating Reséndez, she notes that between two and three million Indigenous Peoples were enslaved in the Americas between the sixteenth and nineteenth centuries.[86] Warren adds that at one point, the same number of black and Indigenous Peoples were enslaved in the colonies, and like blacks, Indigenous Peoples were also sold into slavery in other colonies, including Caribbean ones.[87] Emergent slave codes in New England, she writes, "predate and formed the basis for similar laws in . . . New York, Virginia, and South Carolina."[88] Like Reséndez, Warren suggests that black and Indigenous slavery were similar in kind if not degree and that both Indigenous enslavement and colonization were concomitant with and mutually constitutive of black Atlantic slavery. Her work also indicates that although we generally think of slave codes as applicable to black bodies, they were always *already* conceived with bound American Indigenous labour in mind.

In other words, as disciplinary mechanisms, the slave codes were first designed to control Indigenous bodies and *then* evolved to control the indigeneity that must be *antecedent* to black(ness), so that enslaved black bodies could be productive. The codes are thus, more broadly, mechanisms for converting indigeneity into its productive, or accumulative, form. Warren critically links New England markets, bound labour, and the West Indian plantation economies by noting that New Englanders who traded with the West Indies often owned property there. Not only were these economies linked, but that tie was critical to the eventual transition from mercantilism to capitalism. According to Warren, "As early as 1636, the governor of Barbados declared, 'Negroes and Indians, that came here to be sold, should serve for Life, unless a Contract was made before to the contrary.'"[89] Later, she says, "Alongside imported Africans, many of the first labourers on Barbados were Indians, at least some of whom were brought from the colony of Guiana."[90] This also includes the shipment of Algonquians from North America to Jamaica for labour.[91]

Not only does Warren chronicle an economic, juridical, and forced labour connection between and among New England's colonies and the

West Indies, but at every step she demonstrates that Indigenous Peoples were present as enslaved labour. She also debunks Bartolomean docility and the idea that enslaved Africans were brought in to labour because Indigenous Peoples perished. In keeping with Bushnell's observations, she instead writes that the organization of Indigenous societies—or, more aptly, their continued labour for themselves—was one of the greatest impediments to their large-scale incorporation into forced labour economies.[92]. Her work indicates how Indigenous Peoples' labour contributed to the triangular trade by the very nature of their concurrent labour with blacks (e.g., in Barbados). More crucially, although the later parts of her book center on enslaved blacks, Warren links slavery and (settler) colonization, the disparate realms of blacks (Death) and Indigenous Peoples (death), respectively. She squarely locates Indian labour within the transformation of plantation societies and economies, complicating arguments that black enslaved labour alone aided the transition from mercantilism to capitalism.

In addition to chronicling Indian enslavement and shipment, especially to the Caribbean, Warren forces us to read the "extractive" labour of slavery *with* the settler colonial goal of attaining land. Her and Reséndez's work, I argue, suggest that we must consider the now former colonies of extraction as *proto*-settler ones since they both rest not strictly on Indigenous land but on the process of converting Indigenous Peoples in order to make their lands *and* bodies productive. Moreover, they realize the conquistador's *master function* (see chapter 6) in advance of the *settler function*. Warren writes: "Without a general practice of removing Indians by killing them, exporting them as slaves, and pushing many of the rest west or north or south or simply away, African enslavement would have had no room to grow in any American colony, an unpleasant example of Archimedean displacement."[93]

Warren's work underscores my argument that the only choice given to Indigenous Peoples for full existence within the European system of production was between death, enslavement, or ecclesiastical labour as an extension of their subordination. She suggests that such a choice is the fundamental link between Indigenous Peoples (land) and Blacks (labour). It is the outcome of the process of Conversion that was already operational from the first moment of slaving contact. The choice—singular, false, and misread—is to remain on only one side of the labour-work dialectic. Indigenous People can be productive as slaves or through the productive, space-clearing outcome of their deaths. Except where they can resist, retain their own social structures, and remain rooted, they must, like blacks, be productive in some form. This means that the labour side of the dialectic is not just about unproductive native labour. It actually also contains their first conversion to productive work, which, because of the extinction thesis and Bartolomean docility, is eclipsed by the overall function of this position to mark failed rather than successful labour. Indigenous Peoples thus, like blacks, share not just the history of slavery, but also the specific processes of being transformed to or from something, via both a middle/passage *and* Conversion as a recuperative process for productive labours lost.

With this in mind, a return to Reséndez helps identify particular issues around the conversion of the Indigenous body. Reséndez first draws attention to the complexities surrounding the Indigenous body by writing that in his first letter, Columbus saw Indigenous Peoples as physically suited for slave labour though not for "hard" labour. Later, describing how enslaved Indigenous Peoples from other islands came to Hispaniola, Reséndez highlights Spanish practices and reasoning. In one revealing example of the Bahamas' early Indian population where the land was felt to have few resources, Reséndez writes that Hispaniola's Spaniards agreed that "the Lucayos had to be removed from a place where there was nothing of value and transported to other islands where their work was badly needed."[94] Earlier, Reséndez concludes that before contact, Indigenous Peoples on Hispaniola "enjoyed a seemingly carefree lifestyle."[95] This and Columbus's observation reveal one essential thing: that Indigenous Peoples' labours for themselves could only be approached as value where they were transported or removed from lands in order to work elsewhere. This removal of Indigenous Peoples needs to be read *alongside* Warren's recourse to a red Atlantic formulation precisely because she discusses not Indigenous labour per se, but Indigenous peoples' removal and detention so that they would not be a threat to colonists. If, therefore, we are to talk about a red Atlantic, we must acknowledge that it is constituted by at least *two* early conditions of Indigenous Peoples' removal or forced movement: for *work* and to prohibit their labour for themselves that was always threatening to early colonists, either through direct attacks on settlements or by the continuing occupation of lands that settlers saw as devoid of useful (for them) work. This removal is the productive form of Indigenous labour, its Conversion to value.

These early Indigenous removals are both linked with and delinked from what blacks experienced when entering the slave trade. Blacks were removed from Africa, where their labour had no value for masters and settlers in the Americas; but the black Atlantic, at its inception, lacked this particular parallel of labour conversion because the hold and dungeon made black Elimination absolute.[96] In addition, value (for work) was always thought to adhere exclusively in the already removed black body, while for Indigenous Peoples it was *both* in the body (when they were seen as fit for work) and outside the body (i.e., useless labour) when it was seen as unfit and bound with unproductive land. This is the strategic difference between black Death and Indigenous extermination. The removal of blacks and Indigenous peoples in the Americas for work, and that of the latter for the threat of their subsistence labour, constitutes the first alienation in the capture of their bodies (read: Conversion) as products of their labour for themselves. Yet the twin motive for Indigenous removal in the Americas continues to delink blacks and Indigenous peoples because one attaches to sovereignty (from which, with important exceptions, diasporic blacks remain cut off), while the other does not.[97]

By highlighting the multiple forms of native removal (including slavery), or Indigenous conversion, Warren commands us to read Death and Elimination together as mutually and internally constitutive projects, not as linear processes where the emptying of land followed its population and transformation through productive work. She too underscores this by recalling the origin of the word "plantation" as "a synonym for colony."[98] For Warren, Indigenous Peoples both are constitutive of modern slavery and the laws used to govern largely black bodies, and are always implicated by and in land uses, having already suffered displacements and losses of homelands, at times similar to blacks transported across the Atlantic. In describing the hardships Natick Indians suffered in Deer Island in Boston Harbor, Warren turns to Jace Weaver, Paul Gilroy, Paul Cohen, and others to position the "red Atlantic" as a "corollary, just as tragic and coerced, to the more familiar black Atlantic."[99]

Finally, Warren's text clarifies the fundamental difference between black and Indigenous labour resulting from the labour-work divide, which needs to remain as a limit for studies seeking to add Indigenous Peoples into Atlantic frameworks. She asserts that blacks are as deeply implicated in the settler colonial project as Indigenous Peoples are in the project of (black) slavery. She writes that the forced labour of blacks "incidentally killed trees, thus clearing forests and making land available for English settlement," which "underlines how the[ir] work . . . was also the labor of a settler colonist" even when "the clearing of the forests for settlement" was "incidental."[100] By noting that it was incidental, Warren points directly to the provisional grounds upon which blacks later functioned, as I argue elsewhere, as involuntary settlers.[101] This incidental work of settler colonialism reinforces how, as discussed in the introduction to this book, the enslaved person doubles and defers the settler-master's body. However, since this doubling occurs within slavery, its fundamental condition (as Afropessimists remind us) is that enslaved people are socially and politically dead. Thus, we must foreground the delinking of labour and right during this period, which is the condition of the enslaved person even where their labour is the settler's work.

In the Caribbean, when blacks assert political right to (colonial) land, slavery's incidental settler labour begins to be elaborated within the prepositional grammar, taking on an epistemic, self-verifying status. Thus, black labour can only be apprehended as necessarily affected upon land that was always in need of clearing in order to be productive. The labour episteme allows blacks to reach back to claim a prior time tied to a specific transformation of the land through the plantation's productive socioeconomic machine, within which their labour accrues teleological value. As illustrated in *Creole Indigeneity*, Black plantation labour—the temporal origin of home/colony/nation—becomes the new time of belonging, displacing the prior and continuous time of Indigenous Peoples' presence and non-plantation subsistence labours, rendering Indigenous Peoples failed national subjects and market identities, and reproducing the opposition between productive work and unproductive or failed labour (see chapter 3).

Warren's work, therefore, includes a crucial, perhaps unbridgeable gap between thinking the red Atlantic as and in terms of the black Atlantic (with the labour that preceded the former and where it could be seen/captured) and the labour and systems (capitalism, etc.) that came out of both. Black labour thus is articulated with and for the settler/state in a way that Indigenous Peoples' labour cannot, even where and when they are enslaved and forced to work for the master. This remains the fundamental antagonism of sovereignty and Independence that additive Atlantic studies models do not address. The black versus red Atlantic thus captures a divergence of their actual labours within which black labour lies in its futurity (as work), while the Indigenous labour/work Conversion is always an inalienable priorness or origin haunting the plantation, its economies, and societies. This divergence is also complexly noted in Schwartz's work on Indigenous Peoples' modes of sustainability prior to European arrival, which influenced their eventual role as workers for Europeans and European markets. Schwartz examines Jesuits' repeated attempts to turn

Indigenous Peoples into a "Peasantry" and, where they failed, to use them as "contract labour."[102] Describing one of the better-known groups the Portuguese encountered in Brazil, Schwartz writes that at contact,

> [The Tupinamba] lived in villages of four to eight hundred individuals organized into large family units which shared some four to eight long houses. Patrilineal kinship was central to their societal organization, but divisions of sex and age also defined responsibility and privilege.... Their hunting and gathering economy tended to produce lower population densities, a simple material culture, and a nomadic existence.... If the Indian economy was essentially communal and subsistent, it was autoconsumptive as well. Each village produced what it needed and depended very little on trade in foodstuffs.... This relatively secure food supply also made it quite easy for the Portuguese in Bahia to obtain manioc flour (fannha) and other food by trade in the period of early contact.[103]

I quote extensively because Schwartz details not simply Indigenous social structure or organization, but Indigenous labour (outside the dialectic) as an expression of that structure, as "autoconsumptively" both base and superstructure. Moreover, it expresses their labour for themselves, resisting the very Conversion it undergoes. The labour (acceptable spiritual work) of Indigenous Peoples that went into mission construction, as indicated by Las Casas, is never wholly described as the work of settler colonialism, as black labour is in Warren's work. Even where, as Schwartz indicates, that labour resulted in goods (e.g., manioc flour) for the Portuguese, it remained connected to its pre-contact, precolonial labour form as difference, remaining at odds with post-contact settlement. This is the same difference I noted in chapter 1 about the gold produced by and for Indigenous Peoples that *then* had to be traded as goods (i.e., as a product of work).

English and Africana studies scholar Jodi Melamed has claimed that black enslavement was about production, while Indigenous enslavement in the Americas prior to black enslavement was necessarily about consumption, that is, the ability of explorers and others from Columbus on to survive.[104] While my work suggests that Indigenous labour always had both dimensions at different points, Melamed's claim shows how the productive ends of Indigenous peoples' labour disappeared into the later subordination of reproduction (as potentially the site of both material and ontological difference) to production within capital, as iterated by Arendt.[105] African and American Indigenous labour, through which these collective native peoples literally *reproduced* themselves, was fundamentally always opposed to the productive mechanisms that would generate capitalism as a world system. The productive ends of Indigenous labour that Columbus anticipated when he sought to use Indigenous bodies to find gold and other goods never materialized. Following Melamed, this was not because of Indigenous weakness but because that labour was still deeply imbedded in its extractive or consumptive phase (not to be confused with Schwartz's autoconsumption), a kind of *wétiko* consumption (after Jack D. Forbes, Powhatan-Renapé and Delaware-Lenápe activist, native studies scholar, and writer), through the end of the fifteenth century and into the early sixteenth century.[106]

The consumptive or *wétiko* phase had to do with the survival of Europeans and meeting their own basic subsistence needs. It was therefore always both a pre-contact form of labour and a labour that literally could not accumulate. However, it has an essential role in the eventual appearance of the dialectic, the productive mechanism of proto-capital accumulation. Indigenous labour (as a pre-contact phenomenon) was literally consumed before even its Conversion, which was actually a way to incorporate their labour into western economies and *make* it productive, which Bartolomean docility facilitated rather than impeded. Thus, the designation of Indigenous labour for consumption and black labour for production is accurate only up to a point: their entrance into and entanglement in the dialectic. Where Indigenous labour's productive (rather than consumptive) ends materialized (e.g., with their enslavement, because that labour is still always linked with its precolonial [resistant] *and* early colonial [*wétiko*] consumptive forms), it is left out of regional Caribbean labour histories because of its seeming failure to be productive, although its ongoing Conversion is intrinsic to accumulation. The imposition of the dialectic as a structure of accumulation means that regardless of which side of the dialectic blacks and Indigenous Peoples are placed on, both are caught in the outcome of *productive labour*. Productive slave labour is given primacy in contributing to mercantilism's demise and capital's rise, which led to a new accumulation, a new surplus of bodies for economic transformation. In other words, first there was an excess of raw materials and now there is an excess of bodies (of potential but not concrete value), hence the contemporary relegation of both black and Indigenous Peoples to poverty and state-sponsored death.

Sylvia Wynter's claim that "niggers" and "non-whites" must be "produced" as poor is critical in reinterpreting the ends of productive and consumptive labour for both blacks and Indigenous Peoples. By reading it materially rather than ontologically, we can suggest that both black and Indigenous bodies have now entered into a new consumptive process that links them. It is consumptive or *wétiko* rather than productive (because it occurs within late capitalism); their poverty (and structural death) is the new sustainability, the new subsistence for settler states in the Americas. This is not an ironic nor contrary outcome of the dialectic, but a resuscitation of one of its mechanisms for sustaining the conversion of bodies to forms of value for exchange or use. The productive labour process (read: manufacturing) has largely shifted to the East, particularly China, onto nonwhite bodies there. In contrast, in the Americas, free-trade zones and forms of service labour where blacks and Indigenous Peoples are employed enable the North's consumptive revolutions (diet, tech, housing). Black and native bodies are still producing, but the consumption of the North, and the displacement of production onto other racialized bodies outside the hemisphere, outstrips the products of that labour, rendering it largely invisible, just as native labour (again both in Africa and the Americas) was first made invisible where it was not seen as productive.[107]

We can argue that Black and Indigenous work/labour in the global and internal Souths have collectively now arrived at the same place despite their centuries of disarticulation in our regional histories and political-economic narratives. They are back at the original starting point for Indigenous labour in the Americas (consumption) as a collective terminus for black and Indigenous bodies, a reality that Atlantic frameworks fail to capture along with the specificity of Indigenous difference that inaugurates the slave trade *from* the Americas, rather than from Africa.[108] Black and native peoples arrive at the same point because the real force or direction of the middle/passage was the process of conversion itself. Thus, I propose that if the middle/passage is interminable for blacks as scholars suggest, it is also interminable for Indigenous Peoples and is the perpetual conversion and entanglement of both groups. The passage must literally become the method for our approaches to (labour) history as that which can mobilize the seeming breaks between our labours (and their outcomes) as the very point of their perpetual entanglement. Moreover, it allows us to read for where not only our converted *and* resistant labours are tied, but our freedoms as well.

Conceptual understandings and deployments of the Middle Passage as a method for organizing history have been premised on the prior exclusion of Indigenous Peoples, the same vertical limit of Atlantic studies. If, however, the Middle Passage has been the quintessential space for thinking black, chattel labour in the Americas, Indigenous Peoples factor into that passage both as the displaced inhabitants of the lands that passage culminated in and, where it is both real (ships) and conceptual, as originators of the passage itself whose own forced movements are situated within the context of their prior and continuous volitional ones (recall Weaver's red Atlantic). This middle/passage is therefore not strictly a movement from one point to the next but consists, collectively, of transformation and removal. Reading for this passage and the still ongoing conversions it facilitates is a method that can be taken into Caribbean labour history as a way of literally recovering the sea (Caribbean) that was lost to the ocean (Atlantic) and to understand and retain the revolutions of one, in and at the edge of the other. In particular, it allows us to see the more complex processes by which black and Indigenous labours are transformed, and where they resist in ways that cannot strictly be labeled as anti-capitalist. To think in terms of the epiphenomenal temporalities of the middle/passage or middle/passages, rather than the Atlantic's fixity/fullness, allows for a particular way of identifying and reading against the labour-work dialectic as it operates in Caribbean labour history.

According to Fred Moten, who discusses the middle/passage while explaining consent in *Black and Blur*, "The term consent doesn't merely defy but rather unravels a set of normative discourses on agency that are either denied to or unsuccessfully salvaged for those who remain in middle passage which is, as Cedric Robinson and Ruth Wilson Gilmore have said, eternal."[109] With this in mind, if we deploy the middle/passage as an ongoing structure of relation, then Indigenous and black labour (as elaborated within that passage) is perpetually dialogic rather than antagonistic. Therefore, we can both recover Indigenous labour/work history and capture the Zeleza's productive antimony, which rejects the closures of an Atlantic formulation that cannot elaborate the movements of both blacks (a post-contact marker of continental African descent) and diverse *Indigenous* African peoples, who have moved globally while still within their own cosmogonic systems and modes of identification. What Zeleza's diaspora captures that Gilroy's Atlantic cannot is that indigeneity shapes diaspora both where it can and cannot be converted. More than just recovering indigeneity for diaspora, his work reflects a middle/passage operation that engages blackness and indigeneity in terms of their relational processes and times. Reframing and even setting aside the Atlantic not only allow us to see *other* Atlantics that cannot be read through the strict analytics of race, but also bring into view other ocean-seas in which the "Atlantic" may, for instance, be outside its more normative constitution.

Conclusion

In a stanza of the poem "My Black Triangle," Caribbean writer Grace Nichols upends the dominant, phallic reproductive view of the Atlantic and Atlantic history brought about by the slave or triangular trade. Gone is Benítez-Rojo's inseminating bull and a passively receptive, racialized vagina. Instead, an imagistic, tonal slippage displaces the reproductive organs themselves:

> My black triangle
> is so rich
> that it flows over
> on to the dry crotch
> of the world[110]

Nichols's black triangle simultaneously recalls and resists dominant concepts of the Atlantic triangular trade by emphasizing re-productive labour and rejecting the feminine as passivity. It captures this chapter's reading against the grain of Atlantic origins that emerge from a singularly constituted Middle Passage by suggesting that the time, space, and function of our middle/passages have been misunderstood. Not only do we need to understand it better; we need new methods and new representations of the passage itself.

This chapter began by elaborating the limits of Atlantic historiography for approaching the past and present fracture of black and native labour through the world-historical function of the labour-work dialectic. Despite considerable attempts to expand the Atlantic's temporality and spatiality, studies could not avoid the hierarchies structuring Atlantic readings. These include the constant positing of the Atlantic as an always already world-historical entity; the fact that the field is both a direct beneficiary of and is generated out of the racism that subordinated those it designates or elides as actors; additive models limiting the base terms upon which nonwhite, racialized actors could be included; the consistent positioning of Indigenous Peoples as either outside the Atlantic proper or within only through acts of translation that liken them to extant Old World historical actors; and the fact that even in works that push against the Atlantic's sui generis nature to posit its emergence within native time and cosmogonies, no sustained attempt has been made to understand black and native labours' relationality *together with* their critical differences.

The limit of Atlantic studies is its very supersession of the (Atlantic to the Caribbean) sea, its knitting together of land masses, and its coercive organization of time into beginnings and endings. The chapter explored newer work addressing Indian slavery in relation to black enslavement (whether as coequal or parallel), noting that we pursue such readings of similitude, of a red-black Atlantic corollary, only up to a point. While Indigenous Peoples' forced labour diasporization is the *first* Atlantic, this book insists on refusing the Atlantic as a macro, epistemological tool arising to capture the modes of productive work it sees as generating the Atlantic itself. Instead, this chapter focused on the routes, passages, and crossings within the Caribbean Sea and South Atlantic that strategically undo the Atlantic's telos and geography. It foregrounded the continuing entanglement of black and native conversion in a prior middle/passage generated out of the crossing of Indigenous Peoples, compelling us to understand that not only are black and Indigenous labours entangled historically, but they are now in a recursive relation.

In place of the Atlantic, I offered the micro-formation of a middle/passage that emerges not out of any singular sea or ocean but in their relationality. This middle/passage, imagistically rendered through the geologic formation of the Anegada Passage, literally drowns the limit point of the Atlantic Ocean and Caribbean Sea as either separate spheres of influence or the dominant locations of only certain historical actors. I suggest that by focusing on the repeated act of drowning, entanglement, conversion, and its forms of death/ Death, we can read black and Indian labour productively together in terms of continuity and change (Elliot), different geographies and temporalities (Zeleza), and social and economic concurrrents (Bushnell and Schwartz) to the Atlantic as an economic unit, for which only black labour had been considered productive. More importantly, we can reject the ways in which oceanic frameworks largely read land-based transformations and formations as outcomes, by focusing instead on the function of crossing for black and native bodies. Such historical work already exists and includes *Saltwater Slavery*, in which Stephanie Smallwood refuses the Middle Passage as a master hermeneutic to instead focus on processes of commodification and black self-making. Thus, despite its titular reference, it represents a key shift in allowing black Atlantic crossings to potentially articulate with Indigenous movements rather than exclude or oppose them.

However, we must continue to actively and explicitly read how such works reformulate passages and resist incorporating them back into received frameworks. My examination of the Atlantic through the optic of Conversion and other movements that are not tied to the knitting together of an extant whole led to a rejection of Atlantic-based studies and dominant readings of the Middle Passage as constitutive, readings that largely capture only black work or articulate Indigenous labour/work in singular relation to black labour. In order to use passage as method, the chapter suggested resituating and better understanding those crossings as the conceptual entanglement of black and native peoples, of anti-blackness and anti-indigeneity, rather than their definitive break.

This reengagement and rearticulation of the middle/passage is key for the next part of this book, on openings to indigeneity within the black radical tradition, which identifies where the radical tradition meets and engages histories of Indigenous work and labour. Chapter 3 uses the concept of passage as method elaborated here to begin offering a new reading of black political economy. Focused on Cedric Robinson's work, chapter 3 begins a tripartite reading of that tradition (continued in chapters 4 and 5) for how it can be productively reoriented around what I find to be persistent openings of blackness and indigeneity to each other that reject the closures of the interface between land and labour/work that delinks the bodily labours of blacks and Indigenous Peoples.

PART II

Natively Rethinking *the* Caribbean Radical Tradition

3. LEFT LIMITS AND BLACK POSSIBILITIES

Working on Water

This is the first of three chapters to read against the grain of closures to indigenous labour in the Caribbean's radical tradition and apply a middle/ passage reading to elucidate what I see as its persistent openings to indigeneity. The shared point of departure for this chapter are two representations of pre-conquest Indigenous Peoples and post-conquest enslaved black peoples acting to manage the flow of water onto lands for habitation and agriculture. The first is from historian Amy Turner Bushnell's "Indigenous America and the Limits of the Atlantic World, 1493–1825"; the second is from Walter Rodney's *A History of the Guyanese Working People, 1881–1905*.

> Deep inside the continent, Amazonian societies had achieved high levels of population density and organization. Long before the Europeans arrived, the Arawakan chiefdoms of the Llanos de Moxos had addressed their region's flood-drought problem with massive earthworks, mounds, causeways, reservoirs, and 50,000 acres of raised, ridged fields.[1]

> Each square mile of cane cultivation involved the provision of forty-nine miles of drainage canals and ditches and sixteen miles of the higher level of waterways used for transportation and irrigation.... This meant that slaves moved 100 million tons of heavy, water-logged

clay with shovel in hand, while enduring conditions of perpetual mud and water. Working people continued to make a tremendous contribution to the humanization of the Guyanese coastal environment.[2]

In the first quoted excerpt, Bushnell, who details how Indigenous Peoples actively resisted enslavement, describes the work of pre-contact native inhabitants in modern-day Bolivia (in western-central South America). The enormous labour of the Indigenous Peoples of the Llanos de Moxos, the plains or savannah region of northern Bolivia, happens, presumptively, not just on the physical land, but within the *terra*/terrain of their belief systems and modes of being and acting on the land. That labour also happens within the greater context of the region's shared Indigenous space, where Indigenous Peoples interacted with each other rather than with conquistadors or settlers.

In contrast, the labour Rodney describes occurs during slavery in upper Amazonia through the doubling and deferral of the settler body (and its actions) in the figure of the enslaved person tasked with realizing the settler-/franchise-colonist/master's desires (see chapter 6) or goals for the land. Striking in both texts is the position of labour and land, which we can read through the labour-work dialectic. The first includes a kind of ownership: "*their* region's flood-drought problem," which is realized by the fact that the land is *occurring* simultaneously *with* or *through* the Arawakan peoples' labour on it. In other words, as the result of a reciprocal interaction with nature (recall the discussion of primitive accumulation in chapter 1), the land is neither static nor fixed, but action itself. Sovereignty is the simultaneity of its occurrence with Indigenous labour. In the second, however, the land does *not* occur at the same time as the enslaved's labour on it; it is not the product of reciprocal or sovereign interaction with nature. The land in this case is *work's* antecedent and a "problem" that has already been resolved by the so-called preference for inland locations of Indigenous Peoples, whose "shifting agriculture" was not self-sustaining.[3] Rodney echoes the oft-noted fact that Indigenous Peoples in Guyana never inhabited the coastal areas that eventually housed the plantations and became the center for colonial and postcolonial political life, and the assumption that any habitation there was impermanent, as exemplified by their lack of a fixed agricultural system. Worked by the enslaved, the land in Rodney's text is therefore reclaimed not from Indigenous Peoples but from nature as the result of their neglect. In foregrounding "shifting agriculture" and lack of permanent settlement in lands they would have traversed, Rodney essentially applies the Lockean "hunter-gatherer/agriculturalist dichotomy" in order not to privilege European discovery and right but to allow it to function as the basis for black agriculture as possession.[4]

The land is, therefore, *terra nullius*, with sovereignty tied to its futurity (thus neither antecedent nor occurring with black labour) under mechanisms of accumulation like the plantation. Although Indigenous Peoples circulated in, through, around, and out of Guyana's coastal region, made decisions about where to go and where to live, and hence related to the *entire* region from their own sovereignties, this is not elaborated. Instead, the assertion of the always already empty land within black left labour history becomes the gesture of clearing necessary for *terra* to become settler/settled land.[5] To be productive, the land requires an antecedent time to work, which clearing imposes. Thus, although Rodney's and other works in the radical tradition insist on the antagonism between sovereign black (being) and capitalism, they engage and redeploy normative categories of political-economic analysis defined for white (settler-master) humanism. Thus, Rodney bears out Film and African American Studies scholar Jared Sexton's point about a problem in black studies that "the general critique of the proper gives rise to the desire for propriety (in the fullest sense of the term)."[6] And, I would add, propriety as a relationship to possession: to the possessing, pre-positional subject as a necessary element for securing coherence in discourse. Black work here is thus a possessive structure, although blackness is defined by the literal inability to possess even oneself, or rather one as a self, and the possession is both deferred (until independence) and incomplete because of the anti-blackness of capitalist political economy.

In Rodney's text, enslaved, unwaged blacks are "working people" on land that is already emptied and unproductive, and we are left to assume that Indigenous Peoples either remain literally buried in the land or inhabit other lands unproductive for global capital, *outside* the labour problem. In *How Europe Underdeveloped Africa*, he employs the extinction thesis *as* the pre-position required to demarcate enslaved work within accumulation regimes, writing that "when European capitalism came into contact with the indigenous hunting societies of America and the Caribbean, the latter were virtually exterminated."[7] In his work we see the function of the pre-position to institute the dialectic by reinforcing the Conversion of Indigenous labours and the accumulative function of black labours. For Rodney, black work *against* nature—the removal of water and the erecting of structures to keep ocean waters at bay in a country whose coastal, arable land is precariously close to sea level—imbues the land with life. In contrast, the Arawakan people's labour occurs with(in) nature itself.

Therefore, essentially the same action by the Llanos' inhabitants and enslaved blacks of working *on* water, working to control it, is read only through this break around work as life and land as inhuman nature, death, or nonexistence. It is not simply that the delinking of black and Indigenous Peoples occurs through what are articulated as the separate labour aims of franchise colonialism and the land aims of settler colonialism, both of which are "structural."[8] It occurs through the positioning of the Llanos' inhabitants' actions on the land as unproductive (i.e., *only* reproductive) *labour* and enslaved black labour as a kind of (productive) *work*. In short, we understand these labours through the aftermath of the imposition of the labour-work dialectic, which fixes Llanos inhabitants' labour outside the radical tradition and enslaved labour firmly within it. However, if we read these seemingly same labours together, we are confronted with their different times and methods of representation. In the descriptive terms for capital accumulation, Indigenous peoples' precolonial labour is usually represented as subsistence by contrast to blacks' (and indentured peoples') presumably more fully incorporated labour, of which only a portion is subsistence. However, it should be remembered that blacks' entire material reproduction not only is for the master's profit (and thus not for themselves) but is also its own existential threat because blacks must reproduce themselves as commodities rather than humans. Since the radical tradition takes up the work of blacks, this impasse of indigeneity and blackness around land and labour, around economies of subsistence and economies of (capitalist) development and accumulation, is woven into its various dimensions and its routing in and through the terrains of 1434 (the Portuguese voyages around Cape Bojador), 1492 (the Columbian error), and 1516 (Bartolomean docility cum chattel slave making).[9]

For Rodney, enslaved blacks' work is both black dispossession and exploitation. It is temporally opposed to labour, which will not be alienated for Indigenous Peoples until their later dispossession. By "later" I mean simply the order in which dispossession and exploitation occur in relation to death/Death for both groups. We can thus make two observations: (1) the pre-position that places blacks *after* Indigenous Peoples and into opposing temporalities cannot recognize where they do essentially the same physical action on the land, and (2) it cannot account for the temporal order I identify: the dispossession of First Peoples in the Americas occurs *after* black dispossession and their own indigeneity become a postscript to black beginning. In other words, Indigenous dispossession is not a condition of this act of working on water, although for blacks it is. Exploitation is concurrent with Indigenous dispossession, while for blacks their dispossession is prior to their exploitation, their enslavement. My reading of black radical texts *for* and *against* the pre-position is therefore also meant to work against the progressive logics of (proto)capitalism because an emphasis on racialism and slave-making demonstrates how anti-blackness as a nonprogressive structure is both the possibility (i.e., the production of the commodity) and impossibility of this temporality.

In its implicit retention of the distinction between labour and work, the labour category in political-economic analyses obscures the fact that there are two modes of black labour in the Americas: one is tied to the plantation and later captured by the postslavery and postcolonial state, and the other dovetails to some extent with marronage and the "slave plot." Even where black left studies seek to capture blacks' plantation *and* nonplantation labour, however, they still valorize this as work and cannot address the fact that the second mode of labour (nonplantation) does not *originate* with an exit from enslaved plantation work. Instead, it continues an alternate, Indigenous mode of existence in the Americas that is divergent from the eighteenth- and early nineteenth-centuries' emerging capitalist globality.[10] The labour category in normative political-economic analysis not only eclipsed black bound and unwaged labour and South Asian indentured labour, which Rodney seeks to restore. It is also constructed on what is not considered to be productive work and is thus in tension with indigeneity and Indigenous labour, which it recovers only via marronage as an afterward to and then parallel of plantation labour, making Indigenous death just as central to the category's intelligence as black Death. Moreover, because black exploitation occurs *after* black Death (see chapter 1), by valorizing black work as the terrain of its fulfillment, Rodney and others essentially further negate the structure of black Death in the category itself. He retains or rather repeats the break between black Death and black exploitation as the very condition of possibility for representation within labour history. *Such representation is still keenly tied to the ontological closure of Death, which the labour category forcibly renews in its continued deployment, further reinforcing black Death as both a diachronic* (longue durée) *and synchronic (a syncopation at any given moment of repetition) structure of the labour category itself, deferring black labours, that is, black sovereignties, in perpetuity.* Echoing Arendt, political theory and Black studies scholar Franco Barchiesi illuminates this constraint, writing, "Despite its epistemological broadening, labour history still reflects the dilemmas of political economy, since it bestows ontological prominence on work as the terrain from which something globally essential, not just situationally contingent, can be enunciated about the meaning of freedom, indeed on the very definition of the human."[11]

The problem, then, for Rodney and black left studies in general, is three-fold: first, as Arendt notes, the category of work that it takes up is universally restricted to labours that end in the production of the objects, systems, and structures that emerge in the process of capital formation. Second, the category's foundational nature of anti-blackness captures blackness only through or after Death, which must always be brought forward. Moreover, this intrinsic anti-blackness is also the fundamental nature of its anti-indigeneity, even though the latter appears to be evolutionarily distinct. Third, the desire to represent black labour within extant categories means that in its adaptation and critique of political economy, black left labour history reinstitutes capital's global function, which is also (see the discussion of Sylvia Wynter in the introduction) the limit of Marxist critique. In other words, in taking up a labour category that already distinguishes labour from work without questioning how this distinction produces the onto- and sociogenic human same, black left studies continues to inscribe the subordination of Europe's human others as the condition of black representation and liberation.[12]

If the history of capital accumulation is the history of settler colonialism and black racialization's institution, and if the mode of production, as Wynter argues, sustains the mode of being human (where fully human status is determined by holding the consumptive position in the dialectic of conscience as a doubling of the social position of master/middle-class consumer), then the labour category in political economic analysis—including Marxism—is always already meant to track this mode of being fully human as a break within the human. Therefore, woven into the category of labour itself, for analysis, is the internal, onto-epistemological break between labour and work through which anti-indigeneity and anti-blackness literally maintain both blacks and Indigenous Peoples as boundary markers for both the human and its articulation within the "master discipline" of economics. The split between labour and work is how the category of analysis (labour) supports the function of capital that, to recall, Marx missed. Consequently, the affirmation of black work over native labour in the radical tradition is the moment of the reproduction of the labour-work division and the relegation of Indigenous Peoples to land/labour. Thus, both anti-blackness and anti-indigeneity in their universality remain problems for black political economy because it emerges out of a perspectival labour history.

Afropessimism has forcefully grappled with the anti-blackness of the categories of labour representation, and whether or not they can ever be useful for blacks. Frank Wilderson writes that even revolutionary approaches to labour struggle, such as Antonio Gramsci's, saw civil society as the "terrain" of labour struggle, an impossibility for blacks, for whom state-sponsored violence forecloses representation (recall the parameters of social death).[13] The black body makes possible all representative subject positions within the state because it is essential to the transition of *homo politicus* to *homo economicus*; the latter is a category of representation within the state that is possible for blacks only *after* their Death (or their foreclosure within the first term), and hence invalid. As many thinkers have argued, black Death is "foundational" to civil society and its categories of representation and analytic reflection, and, as Wilderson notes, it is also the possibility for "the worker's potential."[14] In short, the worker's position in labour history and even radical political economy is the very foreclosure of representation for blacks. Thus, all "the hegemonic advances within civil society by the Left hold out no more possibility for black life than the coercive backlash of political society."[15]

However, while Wilderson addresses the anti-blackness of the labour category, and here as in *Red, White and Black* he does a citational trace of arguments from Orlando Patterson to Saidiya Hartman to show that there is absolutely no symmetry between the enslaved person and the worker, he does not sufficiently address the orientation of the labour category toward work.[16] Thus, he reinscribes a recurring problem within black left critique—anti-indigeneity—despite his overall arguments that both the enslaved person (the black) and the Indian (the "Savage") are subject to "ontological death."[17] The problem congeals around the unavoidable temporalities in Wilderson's essay; he writes that "Capital was kick-started by the rape of the African continent. This phenomenon is central to neither Gramsci nor Marx."[18] Additionally, he argues that while Indigenous Peoples "have analogues within the nation's structuring narrative," the black subject's "experience is without analogue."[19] Even while stating that the categories for labour representation do not work for blacks, Wilderson relies first on a temporality that necessarily fixes blacks in terms of the time of capital accumulation. They are *before* accumulation because the theft of black bodies from Africa drives capital's formation.

Here Wilderson echoes *Capitalism and Slavery*, still one of the most compelling arguments for how black slave labour contributed to the rise of global capitalism and mercantilism's decline, in which Eric Williams argues that slavery was not a racial phenomenon but a "solution" to the problems posed by free labour.[20] Williams's argument stems from the role of black labour as only one of the experimental methods used to control the working population in the Americas. As Patrick Wolfe reminds us, however, labour depends on the clearing of land. Thus, Wilderson accepts the temporal logic of primitive accumulation, which reduces it to labour in works like Williams's. Although blacks are represented as outside civil society, they are temporally situated within the teleology of capital accumulation's mechanisms, on which representation depends. This anachronism of sorts demonstrates how blacks are always pulled into times and their representative frames even where they are in fact foreclosed.

Wilderson's argument raises another temporal issue by suggesting that Indigenous Peoples can be (not that they are) represented within the state. Thus, he locates them *after* capitalist state formation, a position in time that blacks do not have, ignoring both their ante- and anti-capitalist labour, and their own coerced labour. Indigenous Peoples become subject to the same anachronism as blacks, just in a different way. Wilderson still valorizes black *work* as distinct from Indigenous *labour*. Both *before* (blackness) and *after* (indigeneity) are other ways of reconfiguring the labour-work division and reinscribing the limits of capital's subject-making function. As a critique of the anti-blackness of labour analysis, Wilderson's discussion of Gramsci iterates the accumulative settler grammar of the pre-positionality of blackness and indigeneity that haunts black left critique.

This part focuses on how and where the radical tradition and black left studies can go beyond work's reinscription and political economy's structural anti-blackness *and* anti-indigeneity. The first step is to resituate that labour of blacks moving "100 million tons of heavy, water-logged clay" in terms of the "50,000 acres of raised, ridged fields" that the Indigenous inhabitants of the Llanos de Moxos created. In other words, I reposition enslaved work within Indigenous Peoples' sovereign labour in terms of the latter's future exploitation and dispossession, which blacks share. I choose to locate enslaved labour within Indigenous labour rather than in terms of settler desire, which forces Rodney to represent it as the humanization of land by blacks, and thereby affirm work over labour in the particular grafting of unwaged, black labour struggle onto the categories of waged labour struggle. I want to read against the ways of seeing the labour of the Llanos' inhabitants as occurring to make the land more habitable, and the labour of blacks as occurring to make the land more productive *as* its habitability.

To do this, we literally need to drown the limit of the labour-work dialectic. We need to resituate black and native labour in terms of this collective or shared work *on* water, on points of contact rather than deferral and antagonism. The specific antagonism here is the way that water disarticulates black and native lives. Water is *also* land for Indigenous Peoples (it is literally bound up with the soil), but not for blacks, for whom the act of reclaiming land from water does not provide a home. Moreover, through the Middle Passage crossing, water is the fundamental element of black dispossession whenever they encounter it.[21] While, however, the radical tradition is preoccupied with black exploitation, it misses this element of black dispossession from land (i.e., from their own labour and how it transformed continental African lands into occurrences) that has been the terrain of philosophy and poetics (e.g., Langston Hughes's "House in the World"). This prior labour is shared with Indigenous Peoples as is the middle/passage dispossession from this labour (read: land), regardless of their differing times, just as exploitation is also shared. Such an understanding would mean a reinterpretation of that lack of cartography/land for blacks that Wilderson claimed, to focus instead on the cartographic failure as the loss of a sovereign *labour* relationship to the land.

This study shifts the parameters of labour with which black left studies works in an effort to delink its consolidation with the outcome of work through continued reinscriptions of the labour-work dialectic. The middle/passage—as a method that pushes back against the grain of historical materialism, though in no way rejecting it entirely—becomes a way of recognizing that both groups experience conversions within the terrain of capital. Indigenous people experience the conversion *to* "analogues" of extinction (for Wilderson they are "even the most massacred subjects"), while blacks experience the conversion *to* analogues of "structural adjustment" (through violent suture and the forms of quotidian and spectacular death they require, or structural impossibility as we saw with Gramsci).[22] In short, blacks and Indigenous Peoples are both analogues of Conversion.

This project rejects the valorization of work and, by extension, accumulation in the radical tradition, but not by moving around or beyond it. Instead, it reads *for* the middle/passages within the tradition that link black and native labour before and after their Conversion. It reads for the ways that—despite the positioning of Indigenous Peoples outside the labour problem and radical tradition—they are firmly within it. Moreover, their inclusion is not based on an additive model for political economy in which

Indigenous labour and modes of social organization are grafted onto extant modes. Instead, Indigenous Peoples' position inside the radical tradition forces a reconfiguration of the labour problem, not singularly as one of scarcity (recall chapter 1) or exploitation (recall chapter 2) but of the tradition's origins and orientation.

In the preceding part, reading for the shared processes of Conversion and middle/passage entanglements emerged as a way to reconfigure black-native relationships so that black work in the Americas is interpreted not always as superseding Indigenous labour but as a relation to it. This chapter argues that black labour actually exists as a continuation of *Indigenous* precontact labours, and that it opens backward rather than forward. I apply a middle/passage method (a reading for points of entanglement) to political scientist and black studies professor Cedric Robinson's *Black Marxism*, originally published in 1983, and reissued in 2000. As a signal work in the black radical tradition, Robinson's text engages the writings of several others, including Eric Williams, C. L. R. James, Richard Wright, and W. E. B. Du Bois. I focus this chapter on a close reading of moments in Robinson's text because Robinson first pulled these diasporic works together to argue that they constitute a recognizable black Marxist tradition oriented around shared approaches to blackness, labour, and resistance as phenomenological and, in Moten's terms, (para) ontological. The tradition, Robinson suggests, was even unaware of itself as such despite the various pan-African conferences his subjects attended, and because of the fissures of culture, geography, and colonialism that intervene and prevent the tradition from emerging thusly.

Not only does Robinson articulate the tradition to and for itself, but I argue that in doing so, he effects two middle/passage openings to (black) indigeneity around our understanding of Elimination and Time and Marronage. Through these openings in his work we can return to and reread other crucial texts in the black radical tradition for the same purpose. Robinson challenged capitalism's universalism by positing its racialism. He also affirmed black life, through his focus on culture and historicity, as what survived Death—or the indigeneity that could not be fully erased and survived through its perpetual re-creation. It is indeed culture, a point reinforced in *The Futures of Black Radicalism*, that shapes black resistance to subordination *over* the paths to restricted forms of liberation from within racial capitalism.[23] Robinson thus addresses the eclipse of blackness from the labour category in a way that, I argue, does not have to reinscribe anti-indigeneity. He makes labour categories significant for blackness by working back in the structuring antagonism of work and labour as an essential racialism. Below, I begin by framing Robinson's approach to what he terms "racial capital" as a critical reorientation to and elaboration of the racialism that drives capital formation, and the anti-Indigenous limits of his critique. I then identify and elaborate a rupture and the two "openings" to indigeneity in Robinson's text that can be read back into the tradition more broadly. Robinson's work allows me to argue that the radical tradition is composed of two strands: one affirming black labour's critique of capital, and another opening toward indigeneity and parallel forms of labour that are routed not *only* through this critique.

The chapters in this part are concerned with rereading the textual tradition of black labour *against the grain* of its affirmation of black work over Indigenous labour. They therefore constitute a collective rereading of the radical tradition in and for the Caribbean, so that after the elaboration of a method for representing their historical labours, Indigenous Peoples can be centrally and complexly figured. I seek a "delinking," after Walter Mignolo, proceeding from reframing key texts in the black radical tradition from the point at which they open up to or become closed off to indigeneity and the possibility of Indigenous labour.[24] By rethinking black political economy, this chapter moves beyond the impasse surrounding black and Indigenous identity with regard to post-contact labour. I deconstruct the narratively instituted, structurally elaborated breach of blackness and indigeneity around work and labour. Without both the consistent development of such deconstructive readings *and* reading for and extending these ruptures where they exist textually, black labour history in the Americas will always reduce Indigenous labour (pre) history to its conversion within the global political economy.

Rupture and Racial Capital

Robinson's *Black Marxism* is one of a slew of texts within black left studies to specifically tackle the structural relationship among race, capital, and class formation.[25] In his introduction to the edition published in 2000, social movements historian Robin D. G. Kelley neatly frames *Black Marxism's* project as a critique of "western" Marxism, a recentering of the colonial "periphery" as constitutive of black radical thought, and an alternative account of the evolution of race (whiteness and blackness) and racism. He reminds us that for Robinson, the latter not only emerges as a product of capitalism, but has precapitalist origins that continue long after the rise of capital. Most importantly, Kelley reminds us that in his rethinking of *Black Marxism* as more than and never equal to a variant of white/western Marxism, what becomes central for Robinson is African origins—culture, labour, and society. These suggest that what is affirmed as black radical thought around labour and possibly black labour itself on plantations was always informed by a different relation to labour that was precolonial and culturally specific, that is, neither black nor even African per se, but fundamentally Indigenous.

Robinson goes so far as to suggest that black culture(s), not race, are in fact the "contradiction" within capital.[26] Moreover, he argues not only that black radical thinkers realized the role anti-blackness played in capital accumulation, but that by seeking to address both racism's role in capital formation and black ante- and anti-colonial resistance to it, they also developed a more accurate account of capitalism's evolution and anti-capitalist resistance that exceeds traditional political economy. For the purposes of this study, Robinson makes two fundamental points about capitalism as a social formation and how we study it. First, racism is not a contradiction nor outcome of capital, but an essential preexisting element that facilitates its structures of accumulation. Second, radical Caribbean thinkers such as C. L. R. James and James Padmore not only realized the role of anti-blackness in capital accumulation. By seeking to address both racism's role in capital formation and black ante- and anti-colonial resistance to it, they developed in the radical tradition a robust account of capitalism and resistance that exceeds traditional accounts of political economy. A black Marxism, as a *left* of *left* practice, is in many ways its own productive pessimism.[27]

For Robinson, "racial capitalism" refers to the central place race holds in capital's development. Race, as an evolving structure of first internal and external demarcations of difference, is a rationalizing structure intrinsic to its development. In elaborating the structuring element of race in the entirety of capital's history, Robinson suggests that we stop thinking of race/racialism as either mere ideology or as a pseudo-scientific strain of thought that emerged in the nineteenth century. Indeed, political economy fails when it does not articulate race as an anterior, structuring element of capitalist accumulation regimes. Moreover, it is race that always makes explanatory tools such as traditional Marxism "inadequate," blind to the reality of the mechanisms of capitalist reproduction and exploitation. Political-economic critique is, in short, always in need of the "stretching" Frantz Fanon suggests in *The Wretched of the Earth*.[28]

The significance of Robinson's work, however, is not limited to his articulation of the role race and culture play in black subordination and resistance. William David Hart writes that Robinson "may be the first person to explicitly construe the relationship between capitalism and antiblackness as an ontological question."[29] Moreover, this anti-blackness as a "structuring reality" of "western metaphysics" that precedes and articulates outside *and* through capital formation (i.e., "exceeds the logic of capital and labor" but is fundamental to it) is not acknowledged by traditional Marxism, making its categories of analysis inadequate for accounts of blackness and labour.[30] For Hart, this excess leads Robinson and his interlocutors in *Black Marxism* to offer a "critical dialectic" with Marxism. An analytic of and for racial capital requires a *black* Marxism that is both a stretching and completion of the Marxist project. It is also a perpetually open-ended working through of the antagonism between black object (chattel) status and capital's descriptive language, which is meant to capture objects with no prior "sentient" life, as well as the relations between human actors that objects enable, from which blacks are cut off.[31] It requires an attention to the roles that both racialization and anti-blackness play in capital's formation. Anti-blackness (a process of slave making) is a specific form of racialization intrinsic to accumulation and commodity production, through which only a subset of humans are transformed into objects in order to mark accumulation (wealth) as the terrain of more fully human subjects. Fred Moten, too, reinforces this excess that blackness represents as a critical negation necessary for the specificity of a black radical tradition not only to emerge but to be understood against how a radical tradition in Europe has been articulated. He writes that in Robinson's and C. L. R. James's work, the tradition "has a complex origin of rupture and collision that moves across a range of negations of Europe."[32]

Rather than elaborate the arguments that develop out of Robinson's work, I want to focus on *Black Marxism* itself. In his prefaces to both the 2000 and 1983 editions, Robinson deliberately addresses where and how black (enslaved) labour exceeds dominant accounts of historical materialism. He suggests that "race" was "the organizing structure" of coercive labour and, in the first part of the book, argues that both race and nationalism form the "non-objective character" of capitalist development.[33] However, he makes two additional claims that I pursue as divergent lines of inquiry. Robinson establishes that the "Black Radical Tradition was an accretion over generations, of collective intelligence gathered from struggle."[34] Prior to this, he notes, this tradition is "historically and immediately linked to social bases predominantly made up of peasants and farmers in the West Indies, sharecroppers and peons in North America, or forced labourers on colonial plantations in Africa."[35] Yet Robinson also says that "the first organized revolts in the slave castles in Africa, and on board slave ships, were generally communal in the terms of their Old World kinships. . . . These rebellions sought return to African homelands and a repair of the discontinuity produced by enslavement and transportation."[36] He gestures to the similarities of such culturally based rebellions with those of Maroon communities, "newly transplanted 'outlaw' Africans and creole Blacks, and sometimes Native Americans and European slaves."[37] In fact, African natives, *before* transport, are linked with rebellion rather than work in Robinson's text.

Thus, the black radical tradition begins to emerge from the first attempt to transport blacks, bridges the old world and the Americas, and is composed of (or has its origins in) two strands: one of modern workers (labour routed through the plantation), and another that we can read as both prior labour (resistance to capture and transport on lands that *occur* for Indigenous African peoples) and *post*work, which is a *return* to labour (rebellion and marronage). For Robinson, these strands become constitutive of a tradition that, while it cannot be captured fully by Marxism as articulated by European writers, is nonetheless a kind of countercurrent or parallel. This becomes a point of closure in which black labour and resistance are concretized in a tradition that still does not engage Indigenous labour, or does so only tangentially. Yet I suggest that through a rupture in Robinson's work, we can return to the tradition as syncretic rather than singularly one of "accretion," and establish another way of reading black radicalism and black labour that opens onto and links up with that of Indigenous Peoples. Below, I do this by first looking at Robinson's motive for the work's more capacious orientation.

In *Black Marxism*, Robinson is mainly interested in exploring Europe's "native racialism"[38] and the broad set of financial and other motives that shaped the rise of the creation of the negro. This focus leads him to periodically mention Indigenous labour in the Americas without discussing it substantially. Robinson eventually reiterates the extinction thesis, writing that African enslaved peoples were brought to the Americas to work because the native population perished: "With the massive demands for labour that sugar production engendered, the appetite of colonial production for labour increasingly outpaced supply. Having already decimated those aboriginal populations they had encountered in the West Indies, the English mercantile and planter bourgeoisie found it necessary and expedient to expand their Irish (and homeland) strategy to West Africa. As they did so, the scale of their enterprise grew beyond anything seen in English history."[39] Robinson establishes the temporal, pre-positional relationship between blacks and Indigenous Peoples that, I argue, is the structural imposition of the labour-work division. Moreover, he drives home the extinction thesis by sourcing writings on the decimation in the Spanish territories that is epistemologically structured on Bartolomean docility. Robinson explains that "'diseases, wars, relocations, and the ecological changes wrought by Spanish settlement and control' *and (it should be added)* slave labour had reduced the number of indigenous inhabitants to an estimated 1,075,000."[40] The extinction thesis becomes even more complicated when he tries to link Indigenous Peoples and black peoples by saying that both were understood under the already existing racialist logic that had been applied to the Irish as "savages." Indigenous Peoples are "the native savage," and blacks are "the imported one."[41]

Here, Robinson relies on the extant racialization of whiteness in Europe to indicate how savagery functions as a transfer of an internal racialism onto external Others. He seems to want to think and write about blacks' and Indigenous Peoples' shared situations and conditions of domination, but it proves ineffectual. While blacks essentially escape the condition of abstract/ed slavery to become "the negro," Indigenous Peoples never actually escape a sort of mummifying savagery. The "native savage" was for Robinson "incapable of resistance," leading them to be "transformed and trivialized, becoming the romantic residue of an archaic past, living in museum pieces."[42] In contrast, "the Negro" moves forward into history because of the need for African labour through the nineteenth century. "As a consequence," he writes in Hegelian cum (anti-black) Arendtian fashion (see chapter 1), "the political, social, and cultural significance of the African was more enduring."[43] Thus, while savagery seems to be the place where Indigenous and black subordination intersect, it has a mummifying, monumentalizing effect on one population, and a mobilizing one on the other.

The extinction thesis and its attendant assumptions would, on its face, be a point of disarticulation or aporia for thinking black and Indigenous labour together. Indigenous labour within black political economy has no forward motion, no potential to be captured by dialectics of struggle, be they material or ideological. However, within *Black Marxism*, I suggest, this and other moments of foreclosure include a rupture and an opening we can pursue. First, it is important to note that Robinson's claims are still part of the book's (however circumscriptive) effort to account *for* (American) indigeneity within a black political economy, though this is limited to an overall comparative approach to racialized labour in the Americas and the collective decline of other sources of labour. For example, in noting the supposed disappearance of Indigenous labour, Robinson also identifies the disappearance of European labour (in a section titled "Reds, Whites, and Blacks"). Moreover, even in 1983, he teases out what Andrés Reséndez, discussed in the preceding chapter, would later dedicate an entire book to—the fact that Indigenous Peoples also died from the ways in which the colonizing Europeans exploited them as a labour source so that their deaths are also the result of "slave labor."[44]

While Robinson cannot fully account for Indigenous slavery because it is still subordinated within the linguistic structure of Bartolomean docility as a boundary for what is representable within political economy and, for him, exists in the past of black labour, this small insertion of the *conjunction* "and" within the deployment of the extinction thesis reflects a generalized impetus to account for racialized—rather than Indigenous—labour that does not stem from a deliberate effort to excise the latter. Moreover, Robinson insists that while nonwhites make up the "majority" of subjugated "workers," *all* racialized labour, including some white and native labour, must be subordinate within capital.[45] This larger goal of his work, which requires a conjunction rather than just the temporal pre-position, suggests that there is a way to read the black radical tradition beyond the point of closure.

I argue that because his albeit brief mention of Indigenous "slave labor" occurs within an overall attempt to make Marxism account for both its constitute strands and internal limit (the role race plays in subordination) as either a universally applicable explanatory tool for economic formation or as a tool of liberation, this inclusion represents a kind of rupture within and for black political economy. It is the moment when Indigenous labour (in the Americas) haunts and *inhabits* black labour formation at one point in its early development, and it is thus present for black political economy in the same manner that, as Robinson demonstrates, race (racialism) is present for capital formation.

This rupture that I identify, and for which I suggest we read Robinson's work, is, however, also accompanied by an even more capacious element.

The rupture is situated alongside an understanding of blackness and its difference that exceeds the very racialized tradition in which it emerged to justify enslavement through the production of blacks as infrahumans. What emerges in Robinson is that while European modes of being determined slavery's evolution, "black" "being" (its nativity and evolution) rather than slavery actually determines resistance and what blacks will in fact become. It is a contradiction and antagonism that is not solely structured in response to anti-blackness. Indeed, he writes, "The Black radical tradition cast doubt on the extent to which capitalism penetrated and re-formed social life and on its ability to create entirely new categories of human experience stripped bare of the historical consciousness embedded in culture."[46] Thus, while blacks were property, they opposed chattel status not singularly from within its constraints or its limited modes of being human, but with an attempt to preserve who they were outside slavery, their "ontological totality" as "African people."[47] For Robinson, slavery could "alter" but not singularly redirect black "being."[48] Thus, his attempt to tease out these radical differences or excess of blackness, I suggest, consistently produces openings to indigeneity.

By foregrounding its difference and even antagonism to modes of being dictated by capital, blackness emerges as that which is not overdetermined by the teleology of capitalist development. Therefore, a labour solution or a solution to the labour problem cannot be the single orientation of a critical black political economy, even if it had been the focus of black labour historiography. This "anti-logic" consistently produces the limits of political economy, which Robinson sees as the radical element in black historiography from Dubois to James. Thus, while consistently demonstrating how black bodies and labour were instrumental to capital's rise, Robinson is careful to show that capital formation does not overdetermine blackness, which is like the conjunction—implicit, excessive, and disruptive. This insistence on the excess of blackness to anti-blackness, where blackness exceeds the simple positionality of a linear resistance to exploitation, frames what I see as two persistent openings that resist what political scientist George Ciccariello-Maher would see as the easy dialectical closures of the dominant history, in this case, of capital.[49] These separately elaborated openings allow the labour-work dialectic to operate within the black radical tradition as both an unavoidable structure *and* site of rupture out of which a new methodological direction for black political economy can be elaborated.

Openings

The first opening of blackness and black labour history to indigeneity in the Americas occurs around what I read as Robinson's encounter with Elimination in his elaboration of the creation of the figure of the negro. To reiterate, one of the ways in which settler colonialism is often seen as distinct from franchise colonialism is that the former rests on the so-called structural element of Indigenous genocide in order to acquire land, while the latter rests on black labour. The Death that the enslaved black native undergoes in order to make that body productive is not theorized as *an* elimination. The result is that Death and Elimination, the respective undergirding mechanisms of franchise and settler colonialism, house the difference between blacks and Indigenous Peoples within critical thought, maintaining blacks in a continuum between the land and the person who settles the land. However, Robinson's work, as I demonstrate, provides an opening for rethinking Elimination to better understand it as a point of black and Indigenous relationality in the ongoing, violent attempts to remake non-settler sovereignties. This relationality is key in moving beyond the way in which settler and franchise colonialism, and the histories of labour and land they support, prevent an account of native labour histories from both their difference and relation to blackness.

The possibility for this new reading of Elimination as a shared middle/passage point of connection occurs in Robinson's discussion of the West's "construct" of the "Negro," which evolved to manage blacks as enslaved labour. Robinson writes,

> The "Negro," that is the color black, was both a negation of African and a unity of opposition to white. The construct of Negro, unlike the terms "African," "Moor," or "Ethiope" suggested no situatedness in time, that is history, or space, that is ethno- or politico-geography. The Negro had no civilization, no cultures, no religions, no history, no place, and finally no humanity that might command consideration. Like his eastern, central, and western European prototypes, in their time, and the French peasants, the Slavs, the Celtic peoples, and more recently the American "Indians," the Negro constituted a marginally human group, a collection of things of convenience for use and/or eradication. This was, of course, no idle exercise in racial and moral schemata since it directly related to a most sizable quantum of labor disciplined and applied in a most extraordinary way.[50]

Despite the likening of the concept to anterior racialized groups in Europe and the overarching claim that the negro is a mechanism of control for black labour, Robinson's elaboration of the negro is in fact an understanding of the construct in relation to indigeneity, not simply mechanisms of accumulative work. To the extent that, as Robinson writes, the negro was meant to have "no civilization, no cultures, no religions, no history, no place," the negro functions as the invention of an idea of blacks that can be voided of indigeneity as a threat and managed as simulation much like Minnesota Chippewa writer and Indigenous and American Studies professor Gerald Vizenor describes Indian identity in *Manifest Manners*. The Indian, particularly depictions of Indigenous Peoples in settler colonial writing, is a simulation through which Indian identity can be managed. The simulation is thus an active form of Elimination. Viewed in this manner, the invention of the negro and black flesh as the usurpation of land and cosmogony that I have previously gestured to becomes the moment of "elimination," after Patrick Wolfe, to which Indigenous Africans became subject, and which informs black identity in the Americas.

Moreover, this Elimination can be studied contextually as a structural element in the production of the negro and the disciplining of the enslaved person. In other words, it was essential to black slave making and it is also not confined to a specific time. What Saidiya Hartman and Afropessimists read as Death might explain the lack of "ontological resistance" for blacks. However, we must recognize that this Death is actually structurally premised on a practice or habit of Elimination, which is neither static nor confined to the prior time of the Indigenous African subject. It is instead the repeated Elimination of the black native to the extent that it is the culture of the native—as the resistant element of black being—that must be excised.[51] In other words, Death works similarly as Elimination does in Wolfe. I am not challenging the structural element of Death that makes the black body productive. I am, however, suggesting that by foregrounding (Death) to the exclusion of Elimination, because Death is required for accumulation, we repeat the western logic and structures we criticize. The opposition of black Death to native Elimination institutes the break between exploitation and dispossession that Robert Nichols (see chapter 1) suggests are actually *both* essential to primitive accumulation. Thus, the elaboration of black Death in Afropessimism relies on the institution of the labour-work dialectic and ignores the Elimination that settler colonialism requires of all natives, even when they are removed for work rather than to simply clear land. Settler states that employed enslaved labour in fact rely on two kinds of native death in perpetuity: the death of the black *as* native and the death of the native occupant of the land.

This perpetual death (as opposed to the initiative Death in the dungeon/hold designed to consolidate the black body's removal from the land and its stars) is eliminatory and is the bridge between settler and franchise colonialisms. Black Death is *not* Elimination by itself (composed as it is of two parts outlined in chapter 1, and in which the master's right to property takes the place of the native black's sovereign relation to land), but Elimination is a crucial component of Death because it is the moment of dispossession (the removal of the body from cosmogonically charted nature and the labours that transformed it into land). Elimination and Death are not the singularly distinct spheres of indigeneity and blackness, respectively, but must be understood in terms of exchange and continuity between initiative and punitive forms of Death/death for sustaining anti-indigeneity and anti-blackness as capital's accumulative structures.

The second death that must be undergone by blacks and Indigenous Peoples, as I suggested in chapter 1, is actually the punitive form required by settler political and social structures. Death is the clearing of the land from black bodies (removal from African homelands through the hold), after which and in tandem with their exploitation, blacks also undergo the second and repeated clearing of the body from their land (think the establishment of sharecropping and then its sabotage, which led to the decades-long mass migration north in the United States) so that their labours cannot be reentrenched, that is, Elimination. Blacks and Indigenous Peoples experience dispossession and exploitation as shared phenomena in their reproduction inside settler sovereignties. For Indigenous Peoples, exploitation is prefaced on prior dispossession, while for Blacks, dispossession is premised on prior exploitation. Citizenship and political representation are the production of analogue status (as per Wilderson) for *both* blacks and Indigenous Peoples, which brings forward the primary accumulative gestures or mechanisms of early capital formation.

This argument engages with Patrick Wolfe's concept of the Elimination of Indigenous populations as a key feature of settler colonialism. While it has appeared in a number of his works, Wolfe provides a cohesive statement of elimination in a 2008 chapter titled "Structure and Event." He argues that because settler colonialism requires land, it must first clear that land of Indigenous Peoples through various eliminatory strategies ranging from outright extermination to cultural, political, and even racial assimilation. Elimination is thus not equivalent to genocide. Partly for this reason, separate forms of racialization adhere to blacks and natives, as each become subject to biopolitical strategies of representation designed to augment and secure the enslaved population and clear the land of the Indigenous population.

While Wolfe's concept has been a tremendously useful explanatory tool, its reiteration of settler logics and its disappearing of African natives has been criticized, so I want to complicate my use of it. In a 2016 American Studies Association panel in honor of his most recent book *Traces of History*, White Earth Band of Ojibwe historian Jean M. O'Brien faulted Wolfe for the fact that the concept of elimination neither expresses nor makes visible Indigenous "agency." Considering "how to think about Indigenous resistance and sovereignty," she writes in the panel's published proceedings:

> Embedded in the logic of elimination is the possibility of slippage between the intent of settler colonialism and its tangible outcomes, which carry the implication of extinction.... While Wolfe is likely theorizing within the rubric of the logic of elimination, I see such a perspective as writing Indians out of existence through denying them modernity. Through such an approach, Wolfe leaves no room for Indigenous agency and resistance on the part of those who opted to remain behind, and thus by implication, the reader is free to conclude that these Choctaws were no longer Choctaws.[52]

The problem O'Brien identifies with Wolfe's work is in part the larger methodological and situational difference between settler colonial and Indigenous studies. As much as it is meant as a kind of intervention, settler colonial studies is still a critical apparatus that comes out of the western intellectual tradition that has always marginalized, rather than centered, Indigenous Peoples' knowledges and lives. This conceptual framework thus unwittingly repeats the logic and motive of settler colonialism for which extinction or elimination is the logical outcome. It thus extends and enacts the very settler logic it seeks to elucidate.

In his response to Wolfe's work at the same ASA panel, Robin D. G. Kelley used the opportunity to place into interlocution his work and Cedric Robinson's, which Kelley had urged Wolfe to consider prior to the publication of *Traces of History*, to no avail. Kelley holds that this lack of interlocution with Robinson "impoverished much of" Wolfe's work.[53] Although Wolfe attempted to think race as instrumental to settler colonialism, Kelley faults him for ignoring Africa, continental indigeneities, and the modes of settler colonialism that took root in southern Africa. Kelley writes that Wolfe's work

> presumes that indigenous people exist only in the Americas and Aus-
> tralasia. African indigeneity is erased in this formulation because,
> through linguistic sleight of hand, Africans are turned into Black
> Americans. The Atlantic Slave Trade rips Africans from their home-
> land and deposits them in territories undergoing settlement and dis-
> possession, but renaming severs any relationship to their land and
> indigenous communities. Limited by a thoroughly materialist frame-
> work, Wolfe misrecognized, and unwittingly contributed to, what
> was clearly a process of elimination: eliminate the culture, identity,
> and consciousness while preserving the body for labor.[54]

It is the same problem O'Brien notes: the repeated performance of eliminating the native, in this case African natives. Wolfe's work necessarily reinscribes elimination as part of his method. Kelley charges Wolfe with repeating essentially the same error as Marx, who ignored that blacks brought their cultures with them to the Americas.[55] He suggests that Wolfe not only disappears the process of settler colonialism in Africa, but "also eliminates the settler from African history."[56] Thus, Wolfe cannot think complexly about how, as Kelley demonstrates, settler colonialism in Africa was never singularly eliminatory, but cleared blacks off land and reintroduced them as enslaved and later proletarianized masses. Kelley states, "The complete elimination of the native was hardly the objective. Yes, the expropriation of the native from the land was a fundamental objective, but so was prole-tarianization. They wanted the land and the labor, but not the people—that is to say, they sought to eliminate stable communities and their cultures of resistance." In contrast, he writes, "Robinson identified this process as the destruction of the African and 'the invention of the Negro.'"[57] Kelley concludes that "*Traces of History* not only fails to account for labor regimes in which the native is simultaneously 'eliminated' and exploited; it forecloses a discussion of what it means to *decolonize* settler societies."[58]

While Kelley finds other weaknesses in Wolfe's work, I want to dwell on the dimensions of Elimination that Wolfe missed. Not only does Robinson capture blacks' cultural retention and hence indigeneity, but in doing so he also elaborates how dimensions of Elimination actually adhered in the taking of land from blacks (i.e., the Belgian Congo) and in the very production of the negro. This latter continuous eliminatory gesture (rather than one fixed in the past) allows us to read the negro as a concomitant of the Indian (the production of what Wilderson would call the "Savage" in the Americas), to the extent that this figuration is possible only through Elimination. We need to think about post-slave black cultures in the Americas in terms of their own enduring and evolutionary indigeneity (not the teleologically nationalist practices of becoming native that, as I outlined in *Creole Indigeneity*, are anti-Indigenous) and, consequently, in terms of the processes of Elimination to which blacks remain subject. In other words, blacks are subject to state-sponsored violence today not because of racialization alone (anti-blackness) but also because of the very cultural, *indigenous* difference that adheres in their racialization. Thus, my goal is to open up the black radical tradition to Indigenous labour and simultaneously open up indigeneity to blackness and recover what Wolfe and others miss.

In *Black Marxism*, Robinson foregrounds specific moments in which Elimination adhered in the production of blacks as capital. In his work, both slavery and Elimination are structural elements in the disciplining of racialized labour, and both seem to have no terminus. Elimination, in Robinson, is clearly part of the disciplining of blackness within the very stage of primitive accumulation so essential to the rise of capital (franchise colonialism) and settler colonialism. While Elimination is a space-clearing gesture in white settler society, it is a disciplinary mechanism in the colony of exploitation. Robinson's account of Haiti prior to the revolution is one significant place where Elimination adheres in the transformation of black bodies into capital, in blackness's productive capacity. He cites the well-known fact that most of the half million enslaved peoples in Haiti during the revolution were directly from Africa because "Haiti's slave population . . . was not self-reproducing" and died from overwork before they could reproduce.[59] While this constant infusion of bodies supports Robinson's claims that African cultures in the Americas were continuously renewed throughout slavery, it also points to another phenomenon—the continued operation of two kinds of Elimination in the Americas: through the death (not Death) of the cultivating body, and through assimilation (becoming Creole). This *inability* of blacks to reproduce, which needs to be looked at in terms of black maternal and infant mortality today, is a feature of (native) Elimination, not anti-blackness.[60] In contrast, slavery's reproduction of black bodies through the amniotic *sea*, in which black children took on the enslaved status of the mother, is the deployment of anti-blackness.[61] Moreover, while the Haitian Revolution is captured within a historical narrative of blacks' forward motion in the Americas, Elimination as a still underlying element means that to read black evolution only as dialectical is as much a problem as denying Indigenous Peoples' dialectical positions.

Another related moment for reading Elimination in *Black Marxism* occurs when Robinson cites Philip Curtain's framing of the enslaved population in "the Caribbean and South America . . . as 'a naturally decreasing slave population.'"[62] Rejecting black slave reproduction as the singular biologizing of enslaved peoples, Robinson necessarily interprets it as one of many reasons that the transport of peoples from Africa continued to grow: enslaved people literally could not reproduce themselves, in direct contradiction of the assumption that blacks were somehow just better suited to slavery in the Americas than Indigenous Peoples. "Many slaves," he notes, "never survived their initial acclimatization and training."[63] Indigenous Africans' persistent death in the process of being remade as hardy negroes might on its face not seem to be Elimination for land (space clearing). However, it does clear the land of those black occupants who cannot perform the work required for franchise colonialism. It also clears the land, as a sovereign occurrence, from the black body itself. It should thus be read as the type of Elimination that is specific to colonies of exploitation and that was also endured by Indigenous Peoples who perished in forced mining and other forms of compelled work. Thus, some of the Indigenous death chronicled by Las Casas should be read as the death or eliminatory gesture that is crucial to *franchise* colonialism, not only settler colonialism. Therefore, Elimination is a mechanism that moves across both colonialisms and is specific to or acts on the focus of both, the productive body and the potentially productive land. Patrick Wolfe also gestures to this possibility of reading Death and Elimination together in later periods by noting:

> On emancipation, Blacks became surplus to some requirements and, to that extent, more like Indians. Thus, it is highly significant that the barbarities of lynching and the Jim Crow reign of racial terror should be a postemancipation phenomenon. As valuable commodities, slaves had only been destroyed *in extremis*. Even after slavery, Black people continued to have value as a source of super-cheap labor (providing an incitement to poor Whites), so their dispensability was tempered. Today in the US, the blatant racial zoning of large cities and the penal system suggests that, once a colonized people outlives its utility, settler societies can fall back on the repertoire of strategies (in this case, spatial sequestration) whereby they have also dealt with the native surplus.[64]

Although Wolfe figures Indigenous labour as surplus, ignores or literally eliminates Indigenous Africans, as Kelley observed, and recognizes only post-emancipation violence, he essentially argues that racial terror and black death become, in the post-slavery period, strategies of space-clearing Elimination. Therefore, we cannot read these strategies singularly as the Death that produces blacks as socially dead and not full political subjects. Blacks, like native peoples, must now be removed from the land to make it newly productive because their own indigeneities of the flesh—of the terra that is flesh rather than soil—persist and continuously place them at odds with the political systems that sustain capital accumulation.

The transformations of blacks into negros and Indians into post Indians are read separately because one is understood as nonbeing (becoming negro fixes one in a subdialectical zone), while becoming Indian is not thought to be the complete lack of humanity, ontological resilience, or the capacity for political representation. Thus, the master-slave dialectic is supposed to operate on fundamentally different terms than the settler-native dialectic. Robinson's attention to the role of negation (recall "the black has no . . .") in the transformation of enslaved people into negros should not distract us from the fact that this latter becoming is meant to be the redemptive Conversion of blacks, and thus the invention of both the negro and the Indian share middle/passage transformations and the process of Conversion, just at different times.

Robinson's emphasis on what I read as blacks' entrance (via the creation of the negro) into a process of *failed* Conversion as and *as not* Indigenous Peoples (associated with successful Conversion) in a work ostensibly concerned with labour, value, and the emergence of capitalism suggests that we should continue to read it as a central point of difference and connection. The Conversion of blacks to negros is failed because their middle/passage transformation excluded vassalage as a pre-political subject position.[65] Moreover, for blacks as it was for Indigenous Peoples, this conversion is meant to manage what is seen as a lack of bodily productivity, especially after slavery as Wolfe suggests. If we remain nominally focused on the outcomes of these collective Conversions, we read them through the teleological ends of materialist dialectics and disaggregate them through the Middle Passage, which leaves us stuck in the zero-sum argument or so-called oppression Olympics. If, however, we can look at the relation between Death and Elimination and approach both not as terminological but as processes, we can foreground the Conversions or becomings themselves as non-teleological. By suggesting that these racialist structures and conversions are intrinsic to and exceed capital formation, Robinson critically pushes back against the tendency to read them as *only* structural and thus as mutually exclusive.

TIME AND MARRONAGE

The second opening in Robinson's work occurs in his temporal extension of the black radical tradition by positing a concept of marronage in which black resistance *exceeds* the immediate conditions of enslavement. This historical excess both links up with indigeneity and, I argue, forces us to read for a new point of entanglement of blackness and indigeneity in the Americas, in which the middle/passage is configured as exchange or relation. In laying the groundwork for his reconceptualization of the time of blackness and hence of black labour/work, Robinson first reveals the constraints historical materialism places on understanding black social evolution. According to Robinson, western approaches to black radicalism failed to understand that there was an extant tradition and instead "reconstructed social and ideological movements among Blacks to conform to the exigencies of specific locales and of immediate social causes."[66] Robinson's challenge is not only whether Black radicalism's origins should be understood outside and prior to the encounter with the modern west. It is also "a negation of Western civilization, but not in the direct sense of a simple dialectical negation."[67]

I therefore argue that for Robinson, the black radical tradition is composed of two strands: one of modern workers (labour routed through the plantation) and another that we can read as both *prior* to modern work (black Indigenous labour resisting capture and transport) and *after* work (marronage). These strands constitute a tradition that cannot be captured fully by Marxism as articulated by European writers, yet is nonetheless presented as a kind of countercurrent or parallel only up to a point. This break in black radicalism's origin narrative is critical for repositioning the time of black labour before European encounter, and black work after it. Moreover, if we read the tradition(s) as syncretic, which is what I think Robinson wants to do, rather than as just one of "accretion," we can read black radicalism and black labours that link up with that of Indigenous Peoples.[68] Below, I argue that the restoration of black *labour* as the prior context for black resistance to capture and enslavement provides the opening.

I further argue that Robinson's desire to move beyond a biologized idea of blackness or a "black-ened" subject acted on by history as a false explanatory tool for black resistance moves him to recover black labour (a sovereign, cosmogonically ordered interaction with nature) before and as the context for black work. He rejects the thesis that black social movements originate from "a general racial order shared by most blacks," positing instead "a historical or political consciousness or social tradition among [them]" that is precolonial, and Indigenous in origin.[69] Here we have an opening onto that parallel mode of labour (and resistance) by blacks that is both precolonial and precapitalist. The work of blacks on plantations and their resistance to it are thus not *only* dialectical, not only a response or a position. From the outset of *Black Marxism*, Robinson underscores that black cultural difference or African identity is the limit of historical materialism for understanding slavery. What Marx missed, for Robinson, is "the historical and social consciousness" that crossed the Atlantic and limits his categories of analysis.[70] This consciousness, he says, adheres in the creation of seventeenth-century quilombos, the free societies created by enslaved peoples who fled (i.e., resisted) plantation work in Brazil.[71] Writing of one chief, he says that "in his accession to authority, it is possible to recognize what Ramos and others have described as the 'Bantu origins' of Palmares. The perception of authentic authority as identical with secured social integrity was characteristically Central African."[72] On its face, Robinson here merely reiterates the findings of those who foreground cultural retention rather than loss as a significant force of Creole and Maroon identities in the Americas.[73]

However, this emphasis on a strand of black resistance or marronage whose origins lie outside the plantation's time or space leads Robinson to reject the narrow periodization within political economy that confines blackness to stages of European development. Following European Marxism's own dissident strands, he uses Leon Trotsky's rejection of the idea that human life is only epochal, suggesting that the "limited utility" of "periods of time . . . is often abused when we turn from the *ordering* of things, that is chronological sequencings, to the *order* of things, that is the arrangement of their significances, meanings, and relations."[74] Robinson's refusal of epochal time allows him to delink the black radical tradition from the singular time of capitalist development and suggest that that time is incorrectly understood. Through this delinking, Robinson approaches figures of the black middle class and its intellectual elites not in terms of the plotted time of their achievements, but from an attention to the intersection between their lived realities and those of their subjects. Thus, while he readily admits that C. L. R. James, James Padmore, Eric Williams, W. E. B. Du Bois, and Richard Wright—the subjects of his analysis—shared a proximity to the black "petit bourgeoisie," he argues that they could never singularly be understood as members of that class. Instead, what drove the radical elements of their work was the "people."[75] Moreover, the time of the people, rather than that of the black middle class, propels the dynamism of their work. The "people" thus remain anachronistically inside and outside time, inside and outside a singular class status. Later in Robinson's analysis, this dissonance of the people is instrumental in allowing him to claim a continuous link with and prioritization of culture over class formation.

Robinson's rejection of historical materialism's periodization undoes the one-to-one relationship between black colonial labour's performance and its repetition by cultural thinkers (which I discussed in *Creole Indigeneity*). It also crucially tries to approach black labour prior to its point of conversion as or to work. Thus, not only does the already Dead (black) body resist, but also it is one that is imbued with labour/life/land, and which now sits anachronistically *inside the negro* in Robinson's work as an analogy (up to a point) of the post Indian. Black enslaved labour is thus not positioned singularly with regard to the time of capital's evolution or black labour history (see Williams). These perspectives are not invalid. Instead, Robinson proves them to be partial. In short, Robinson achieves the kind of backward (looking back) reconfiguration of black labour history, arresting its forward motion in ways that foreground how it both articulates with African indigeneities and might articulate with American indigeneities. Thus, I argue that in *Black Marxism*, Conversion and its concomitant installation of the labour-work dialectic is at least partially rejected as the ordering principle of black identity and any notion of black material progress. Instead, Robinson privileges what I read as modes of middle/passage relation or entanglement within which collective Indigenous labours can function as the point of departure for black work. With this in mind, I turn to how this rethinking of blackness' time away from the epochal also leads Robinson to situate marronage, as we saw with the quilombos, through entanglement with indigeneity, rather than as a singular response to enslavement. It is not limited to nor occurring only within the time of pre-capital formation within political economy.

Robinson's desire to expose Europe's "native racialism" and restore the more immediate contexts for black identities prior to European involvement, such as pre-fifteenth-century Islamic influence, compels him to make strategic distinctions among African peoples that are either read out of labour histories or not sustained within them.[76] For example, he significantly breaks Africans into at least three groups that contributed to the world system economy: extant Indigenous continental Africans (those who, for instance, would remain to face Leopold II and the "scramble for Africa"), the negro (the product of the plantation system's ideological, political, and economic demands), and the maroons or runaways. Despite his iteration of the extinction thesis, Robinson introduces a dynamic difference into blackness that links up with indigeneity in its pre- and post-contact dimensions, where it is not overdetermined by European social and historical forces. Thus, he writes that in fleeing plantation work, blacks actually "followed" Indigenous Peoples. Robinson cites Joshua Giddings as saying that in resisting enslavement in Florida, "Indians soon began to make their escape from service to the Indian country. This example was soon followed by the African slaves, who also fled to Indian country."[77]

Marronage is imagined here not as a form of freedom that is singularly an outcome of *black* plantation work, despite being shaped by it, but as having its origins outside and within the shared forced labour and pre-contact cultures of formerly Indigenous Africans and Indigenous peoples in the Americas. Moreover, indigeneity is imagined as having some routes *through* the plantation, through enslavement, rather than existing as either prior to or even singularly parallel to it. Thus, Marronage in Robinson is both determined by slavery and a cultural phenomenon that necessarily precedes and exceeds it.[78] This is particularly true when he uses historical evidence to suggest that marronage developed as a practice *prior* to the emergence of a strong slave economy in Brazil, and that slave revolts had their cultural origins on the continent of Africa in, for instance, the "wars of religion" that shaped the continent *prior* to the rise of the slave trade.[79] In another example situating black resistance to forced labour with American indigeneities, he cites an account of marronage in Virginia and Maryland, where blacks tried to mobilize resistance on the grounds that an Indigenous Peoples' revolt against whites was imminent.[80] What emerges in Robinson is a "citational practice" that deliberately frames or reframes blackness in terms of where and how it exceeds capital formation.[81] In these moments of excess, blackness is in fact linked with indigeneity as a global condition adhering to practices not just of resistance but of refusal.

Robinson's new timeline also significantly links Indigenous black resistance to continental colonial incursion with black resistance to slavery in the Americas, suggesting that both are part of the same history of resistance. They are thus situated in terms of each other, rather than European action. In particular, he writes that "in Southern Africa, the Xhosas' Hundred Years War (1779–1880) with the white colonists . . . would take its people as deeply into the historical tradition as any Black people, even the Haitians, had dared."[82] For Robinson, resistance to European colonialism is an "integrating experience" that produces "the peoples of Africa and the African diaspora."[83] Nowhere in his work is he comfortable with the idea of an organic concept of the people defined from without rather than through self-making.[84] Whether blacks were capital or would-be capital, he argues that the material tradition of the West has its limits, and the limit is very literally where it seeks to engulf blackness.

For Robinson, blackness is ontological and historically tied to a revolutionary consciousness of self that exists outside slavery. In noting the small number of whites who died during revolts, he writes that blacks in fact turned violence "inward": "This violence was not inspired by an external object, it was not understood as a part of an attack on a system, or an engagement with an abstraction of oppressive structures and relations."[85] Instead, he frames it as "the renunciation of actual being for historical being; the preservation of the ontological totality granted by a metaphysical system that had never allowed for property in either the physical, philosophical, temporal, legal, social, or psychic sense."[86] Blacks are who they are for Robinson because of resistance, but that resistance was always launched not singularly against capital, but to "preserve" what in fact preceded it: "the collective being, the ontological totality."[87] Black resistance and refusal are therefore both ante and anticapitalist, as is indigeneity. Marronage, as both a historical phenomenon and a phenomenon internal to blackness' formation, emerges as the fugitive acts of self-making that always attach to blackness and never make it solely a function of capital. The practice of marronage houses the time of black indigeneity, bringing it forward where it does not need to be enacted only as a countercurrent within and in excess of capital's racialism. His work is a generative source for a middle/passage method that can work from this reengagement with indigeneities. Moreover, such readings make it possible to reject additive models for political economy that gesture to Indigenous modes of social and economic relation in an effort to include them rather than rethink the history of labour (work) and thus political economy from the ground (or water) up.

Conclusion

In *From Class to Race*, political philosopher Charles Mills argues that white supremacy needs to be understood as a structure on the same level as class, race, and gender, rather than simply be subsumed within any of them. In "colonial settler states inhabited by an aboriginal and slave population," he writes, "White supremacy is . . . established as a system in which one's identity as a settler, a member of the *Herrenvolk*, generally overrides one's identity as a worker."[88] Consequently, he states that "in the 'New World,' one has to speak almost from the beginning of a white-supremacist capitalism, the capitalism of white-ruled colonies and white settler states," rather than in terms of capitalism's "abstract" universalism. His immediate goal is to task "black philosophers" with accounting for "global white supremacy."[89] Mills's emphasis on global white supremacy offers a way of productively rereading Wilderson's critique of Gramsci (above) such that the critique can move beyond the point of temporal closure to indigeneity through its reinstitution of the labour-work dialectic.

Wilderson suggested that the worker cannot function as a figure of full representation for blacks because as a normative and norming (i.e., the production of the human same) category of political-economic analysis, it is made possible by black Death. However, if we read his critique through Mills, it is not strictly black Death that makes the category one of exclusion. It is the fact that for settler colonies—and here I would add franchise colonies where the master's fundamental function is to displace his settler labour in the body of the enslaved person—the worker is the settler. In restoring this fact of the worker—ignored in Marxist analysis, black political economy, and their critiques both of capital's master narrative and of Marxist modes of liberation—Mills allows us to think of the worker as the category that functions within political economy to displace both blacks *and* Indigenous Peoples. This category rests on both forms of Death/death. The worker's representation is the function of the labour-work division, but it takes up that division in terms of how *work* reproduces the worker *as* the settler. Mills forces us to rethink the worker from the linkage of the settler/franchise and colonist/master rather than from their break into closed, categorical formations.

Moreover, Mill's concept of white supremacy should be read as an articulation *with* Aileen Moreton-Robinson's concept of white "possessive logics" and how they should be understood to structurally re/produce the nation as property. Mills states that "the *Herrenvolk* Lockeanism of white-supremacist American capitalism restructures property rights along color-coded lines, with 'whiteness' itself then becoming property, and with full self-ownership restricted according to racially demarcated persons and denied to those humanoid entities characterized, on the basis of their phenotype, first as chattel and later as subordinate citizens."[90] Although Mills focuses on the way that racialization distributes conditions of *bodily* ownership, particularly for blacks, he offers a broader articulation of ownership's function within not only capitalism, but the very terms of articulating subject positions in relation to it, that is, the worker, and therefore resistance. In this significant moment of redress within black political economy, ownership is configured in terms of both exploitation and dispossession. Moreton-Robinson writes of the failure of African American cultural and literary criticisms of whiteness to address the fact that "The existence of white supremacy as hegemony, ideology, epistemology, and ontology, requires the possession of Indigenous lands as its proprietary anchors within capitalist economies such as the United States."[91]

On its face, Mills retains this disavowal of land in favor of labour, but he actually clarifies whiteness's broader possessive logic within which the black body is possessed as part of a common condition of ownership under capitalism. This recognition of the logic and structure of possession can be read through both Moreton-Robinson and Mills as a shared recognition of the role of possession in Death and Elimination to the extent that both are mechanisms for capital accumulation. It is a recognition of racialization as a mode of delimiting relationships to ownership for blacks and Indigenous Peoples. Further, if we read white supremacy as a settler logic (as Fanon asks us to do) rather than just a racial logic extended from non-settler European societies, it becomes a point of recovery for understanding the processes of Elimination adhering in black Death. Therefore, I suggest that Mills offers not only one point of rejecting the labour-work division (such that it is affirmed in a manner that forces labour history to reinstitute the divide between settler and franchise colonialism). Instead, by showing the fundamental problem work poses for political economy as the expression of the settler function of capital accumulation, his text can be read *for* those ruptures and openings within black political and economic thought, which need to be sustained in future approaches to labour history and political economy.

This reading of Mills through a middle/passage method underscores the main claim of this chapter: although the radical tradition articulated by Cedric Robinson privileges black work on cleared lands, within it remain at least two persistent openings to indigeneity that move us beyond both the labour-work divide and the land-labour interface. These openings are made possible by Robinson's very construction or articulation of a radical tradition, of a black Marxism that exceeds the strictures of Marxism's dialectical method and teleological outcomes as a limit for black freedom. The first opening I elaborated—Elimination—allows us to work beyond the labour-land divide's supposed impasse by suggesting ways to read the structures of black Death and Indigenous Elimination together. The second opening, Time and Marronage, posits a different time for the radical tradition, one not limited to modern, enslaved, plantation, and post-plantation work or its outcomes. This time allows Robinson to configure Marronage for black political economy in general—not just in terms of black flight from the plantation and hence an afterward to plantation work that then becomes bound up with indigeneity, where fleeing blacks are culturally rooted apart from or with Indigenous Peoples. Instead, it must be understood in relation to and hence as articulating with multiple levels of indigeneity existing prior to, after, and through the plantation, linking black Indigenous labours of self-making and resistance with those of Indigenous Peoples in the Americas.

The chapter demonstrates that the black radical tradition can be viewed more expansively beyond the progression from unwaged and unfree to waged work and to the inhabiting of class positions that, as we saw in chapter 1, cannot be a starting point for black subjecthood. It argued that there is a kind of recovery of black labour in the radical tradition that constitutes a rupture and middle/passage relation to Indigenous labour, reconfiguring labour for black political economy more broadly. Blacks and Indigenous Peoples thus relate in material history in ways that are not exclusive or additive. The following chapter continues utilizing a relational method for labour to partially reread some classic labour histories of the Caribbean that have traditionally disappeared the history of Indigenous labour/work. It takes up these openings in Robinson, reading them into and with those emerging in the radical tradition in the Caribbean. Not only do I argue that it is possible to read them more expansively through the optic of the middle/passage and Conversion, but the chapter also suggests that we can change how we write and read Caribbean labour history outside the division that the Atlantic imposed on our labours.

4. AGAINST THE GRAIN

Resisting Inscription

I want to begin again with Walter Rodney. I was five years old and living with my family in South Ruimveldt, Guyana, when he died. I don't remember anything about the actual event, only that at some point, a shadow seemed to fall over us and the possibility for a more progressive government. Two years later, my brother, myself, and my mom, a librarian who would fulfill Rodney's requests for research materials at the University library, left Guyana.[1] A tireless labour historian and activist, Rodney unflaggingly rejected what he saw as the racialism of nationalistic party politics, the co-optation of the "bourgeoisified" working classes, and how his own bourgeois position (as part of the intellectual and cultural elite) functioned as an impediment to workers' freedom.[2] Additionally, he saw, like Fanon, that violence enacted by the masses would be a definitive component of resistance to capitalist political economy's neocolonialism.[3] For this, he was banned from Jamaica in 1968, forbidden to teach at the University of Guyana, banned from leaving the country, and ultimately murdered by the Forbes Burnham regime in 1980.[4]

Rodney represents a dissident, rooted strain of black political economy fundamentally antagonistic to the liberal structures that attain in postcolonial government, even when espousing and enacting socialist economic policies. He was acutely aware of how global capitalism's structural "contradictions" meant, in Wynterian fashion, that precisely developing countries, such as Guyana, were required to *be* and be reproduced as underdeveloped, and that a true socialism was a necessary, organic response to this material and ideological dependency.[5] Moreover, Rodney anticipated Cedric Robinson's *Black Marxism* by also identifying (as William David Hart argues about the latter) the ontological closures of blackness generated out of capitalism.[6] Rodney not only argued Césaire's position that capitalism institutes worker exploitation and anti-blackness as foundational to its development, but also that the "essence of white power is that it is exercised over black peoples" regardless of the location or social configuration of the societies where blacks live.[7] Capitalism is thus anti-blackness's generative mechanism, producing an anti-black world.

While Afropessimism might see work like Rodney's as insufficient to explain anti-black violence because that violence exceeds the forces of production and hence political economy's explanatory models, his and similar works achieve a critical recovery, making black labour visible within the historical record toward a practice of liberation.[8] As an even more radical account of black labour than Williams's *Capitalism and Slavery*, Rodney's writing is essential to the radical tradition's ongoing possibilities, and we should return to it precisely at this moment not only to understand black political economy but also to confront anti-blackness' political and economic mechanisms in postcolonial and settler states. However, we need to find a way to work beyond his and similar works' inscription of the labour-work dialectic within which Indigenous Peoples remain on one side in a persistent act of disappearing their labour and hence their sovereignty. Moreover, this reinscription of the division allows even these works in the radical tradition to remain available for both normative and even nationalistic accounts, the very ones Rodney resisted, of black struggle and rights. We must still counter and revise the tradition's own negative inscription of the logic of capital.

In the Caribbean, the black radical tradition has been used to support a version of history, postcolonial nationalism, liberation, and territorial rights, which continues to exclude Indigenous Peoples and limit their sovereignty by identifying formerly enslaved blacks, South Asians, and other indentured populations as workers to the exclusion of Indigenous Peoples. As I have demonstrated, the disappearance of Indigenous Peoples is the tradition's founding historical and hence ontological conceit. Thus, the histories reinforce and are made possible through a double space-clearing gesture straddling the colonial and postcolonial periods: the removal of the native onto interior, reservation lands that then become part of the teleology of capitalist development because of enslaved and indentured peoples' labour and historians' reiteration or inscription of that removal.

The discursive moment of these historians' works is not just a reliance on the pre-positional structure as history's underlying temporal mechanism. As I suggested in chapter 3 regarding Rodney's work, it must be understood as a formal space clearing for cultural nationalism, political economy, and labour's resistant futures, achieved through the repetition of Indigenous extinction. That space clearing is equally structural (supporting modes of governmentality that fully enfranchise Creoles by restricting Indigenous sovereignty) and, sadly, has no terminus yet. The Black radical tradition still needs to address how blacks' assertion of rights through labour can also be anti-Indigenous within the diaspora because it resuscitates the land-labour division central to both franchise and settler colonialism. I maintain that moving beyond the tradition's anti-indigeneity is also the point at which we move beyond its anti-blackness since these antagonisms were instituted as structurally necessary to each other.[9]

This chapter is the second of a tripartite reading of the black radical tradition (Caribbean Marxism) through a middle/passage methodology that looks for its persistent openings to indigeneity. Chapter 3 set the terms for this reading by identifying (narrative, analytic) strategies that resist the reinscription of political economic processes of Conversion at a key moment when the black radical tradition articulated itself as such (in terms of its visibility to itself). Its primary goal was to suggest that middle/passage strategies allow for a recovery of black *labour* and a reappraisal of black *work* that might allow it to be situated in terms of extant Indigenous labours. This chapter continues this interruptive reading of the radical tradition by focusing on the left tradition in Caribbean historiography. As I demonstrated with Cedric Robinson's work, there is another possible reading of the radical tradition, and, I argue, it is time for us to pursue it more broadly. This does not mean that we remain blind to these texts' closures to indigeneity, their exclusive representation of Creole workers, or the narrow versions of history and nation they support. However, we must begin to look at how they might open to Indigenous histories, labours, and ultimately sovereignties.

Rodney's work is a prime example of how possibility and limit—situated together—create a point of rupture that can be recovered. He is also the one who, in a 1976 interview, points in a rather Foucauldian way to the consequential nature of *how a thing is said* (its grammar) as an effect of its politico-economic alignment, suggesting that out of this reading, a new alignment can emerge. On the one hand, Rodney, leader of the Working People's Alliance (WPA), is invested in a normative concept of work and production that reinforces the primacy of accumulative *work* over *labour*. He writes of Guyana, "I do not think that our society is potentially any less productive, for its size and population, than any other part of the world that will be called upon to make a socialist revolution. Indeed I see our societies as far more productive than some parts of the world which are already wrestling with social transformation."[10] He therefore defines socialism as "the seizure of power by the working class, and the determination over affairs by the working people."[11] There is no socialism without the structures of accumulation that workers must resist, the working classes' consciousness of themselves as a class, and the kinds of action transforming the *mechanisms* of ownership, placing them in the hands of the working classes.

This position seemingly embraces capital's very teleology and accumulative mechanisms, where socialism is possible only after forms of incorporation. However, at two key moments, this articulation includes its own internal contradiction and possibility for an alternative reading. First, Rodney identifies the co-optation of a subordinate class not just in terms of its alignment with the interests of the petit bourgeois class but in terms of how the working class comes to articulate itself to and for itself. This is clear when he describes a sector of the working class in Guyana who "have been given new slogans to shout and it does amaze me how these slogans don't stick in their throats. It is not a matter of a small deflection here and there, the fellows actually have to turn their sentences around in exactly the opposite direction."[12] Here Rodney does not reductively single out ideology as that which is produced by the upper classes and works through a kind of veiling or mystification of the workers' real conditions of existence, through which they literally cannot see.[13] Nor does he interpret this struggle against the word in terms of the dialectical struggle of the Césarian slave cum interlocutor/intellectual (i.e., Caliban).

Instead, ideological speech is materially constructed in the worker's mouth with the potential to choke ("stick in their throats") unless the worker manages to "turn their sentences around in exactly the opposite direction." Ideology is a counter-revolutionary, transubstantiated force; even where it is antagonistic to the worker's material and cultural status, the worker themself actually still effects or forces it into position. Moreover, the worker has to literally work and struggle with ideology in order to manifest or express it discursively.[14] Discourse is thus also a site of struggle for the labourer, not just for the degreed activist, like Rodney. Thus, the working classes and their position and roles are overdetermined by neither ideology nor their real economic position. At this point, the worker as an abstract social and historical figure is actually exceeded by the fact of the worker as a concrete, historical actor.

Second, Rodney's socialism is not imagined as a singularly rational or rationalizing force. In the interview, he says that in Guyana "the call for socialism was one to which many workers responded, at least at an emotive level, and with which they could identify their immediate interests."[15] In contrast to this stands the fractious game of racial politics played by Guyana's political elites, out of which a nationalist, socialist policy emerges to divert and appropriate workers' self-interests. Here, race emerges for Rodney as a significant player; he suggests that "there was another level of rationalization which was racial, and Afro-Guyanese workers were really responding to that." On its face, the racialization of class interest here attracts and mystifies workers' conditions, but he adds that "at no time did these workers really forget their own class interest."[16] Against race's structural force, which rationalizes degrees of worker exploitation, Rodney posits emotion, which functions similarly to culture, to which Robinson pointed as the central contradiction to capital's racialism (see chapter 3). Thus, within the formation of the working classes and their self-aware, resistant consciousness sits the counter-hegemonic, unbounded force of emotion as an anti-structure that is thus open-ended with regard to social formations. Emotion is a non-dialectical force that drives opposition to capitalist structures of incorporation such as race. The worker is thus positioned not only abjectly in terms of anti-blackness (in the case of the African-descended worker) but in terms of their own extra-rational, extra-material response to oppression. In short, neither race nor capital determines what the worker will become or how the worker will resist. I read this as the point at which Rodney's socialism and the terms of his class analysis become more capacious, working beyond the constraints of normative political economy to effect overtures to indigeneity as similarly unbounded and unable to be fully represented within capitalist social formations or political economic accounts of their evolution.

In pursuing the possibility for a wider, regionally significant reading for these openings or overtures, this chapter centers texts by C. L. R. James and Rodney. While Robinson covers James's work, he does not consider Walter Rodney's writings, which Robin Kelley affirms he would "situate squarely within the Black Radical Tradition," as part of this beginning.[17] Additionally, despite what I identify as the openings to African and American indigeneities and labours in *Black Marxism*, Robinson of course does not read the works in the Caribbean radical tradition that he discusses *for* these areas. Thus, I look collectively at specific works by these authors through the lens of the critical intervention I sought to stake in Robinson. However, I do not track or recuperate all their individual records or intellectual trajectories for this project. This is not a detailed meditation on their works, nor an attempt to thickly represent their already well-known projects and political stances. Instead, like other chapters, this one offers a close reading of specific textual moments. I argue that in all three works, the openings identified in Robinson show us that we need to grapple with the unit of analysis: *work* (which often appears as time, land, and structure, i.e., the plantation), which is the anti-Indigenous element in these texts. Moreover, the same anti-Indigenous unit of analysis is, as Afropessimists reveal, decidedly anti-black. Thus, although these works address the latter while attempting to correct the material tradition, they never fully succeed because of the former.

James and Rodney have each been cited thousands of times and are synonymous with labour history and black political economy in the region. However, those *citations* also affirm and reproduce the overrepresentation of black (and Indian) labour through the disappearance of Indigenous Peoples and Indigenous labour in these texts. Instead of abandoning these works or reducing them to this single point of closure to indigeneity, this chapter reads them against the grain of the disappearance of New World Indigenous Peoples. It seeks an alternate reading of the radical tradition in the Caribbean to undo the pre-positional structure of historical materialism in Caribbean studies of labour history, which is possible precisely because of the black radical tradition's provisional relationship with Marxism. The chapter offers an original, recuperative reading of key texts in the historicist tradition *for* indigeneity. It uses well-known works by James and Rodney to think *through*, *with*, and *against* what I identify as the moment of closure toward indigeneity with which they are all constituted.

While intellectuals like Rodney could articulate the need for a purposefully antagonistic, self-reflexive critique, the limit of a socialist deconstruction of one's bourgeois class position is that socialism (and Marxist critique in the Caribbean) cannot recognize those continued sites of struggle that are their ground of possibility. These places elude political-economic critique because they function as the very ground of possibility for the material and ideological criticism of capital: that is, settled/settler land. Yet, within texts like his, the possibility exists for radically reading and recovering not just *work* for the *labour* of sovereignty, but even the world-historical category of the *worker* itself for black and native representation. The chapter uses James's work to illuminate the relationality of Death and Elimination, and Rodney's work to demonstrate how the problematic categories of human representation in political-economic analysis can be engaged for the representation of those to which they are antagonistic.

The chapter is also critically a refusal of Indigenous death (not a rejection of the fact of ontological death) or disappearance as the starting point or precondition for black political economy. It asks what happens if black political economy takes political Death as its starting point (despite the Afropessimist position that it does not or cannot). What happens to Afropessimist thought if it directly engages labour and phenomenological blackness? A provisional response to these questions begins precisely by finding a way to read against the grain statements in works by, for instance, James or Williams, which hold that Indigenous Peoples are not a significant part of regional labour history either because they perished or because their enslavement was "inefficient."[18] These problematic statements occur in a radical tradition that seeks to argue for black dignity and demonstrate that four hundred years of black enslavement continue to have a structural effect on capitalism's global development.

Blacks' and South Asians' involuntary settlerhood, which seeks to assert the nation as a patrimony that might mitigate against the ongoing disenfranchisement of and efforts to eliminate the descendants of former enslaved people, is part of this legacy. We cannot discard it even where it necessarily imposes a structural impasse for thinking black and Indigenous freedoms together. However, if we only see disavowal of indigeneity in these texts, do we also simultaneously close off or blind ourselves to dimensions of black being and humanity that intersect with indigeneity and are not routed through violent modes of being human? What would be restored to blackness and to indigeneity if we read for rather than against how the black radical tradition might actually point to ways around the impasse of blackness and indigeneity in the Americas that have always been there and exist as potential countercurrents within the tradition? What might be the possibilities for black-native alliances if we were able to do so? This chapter, "Against the Grain," probes these questions, suggesting that an overall change in how we see and cite the radical tradition can be effected. The tradition can begin to resist the inscriptions of capitalist logics against indigeneity, to articulate differently *with* rather than through similitudes (i.e., the inscription of the capitalist same).

Interventions: C. L. R. James and Walter Rodney

C. L. R. JAMES

In *Black Marxism*, Robinson dedicates an entire chapter to the Trinidadian Marxist, historian, reporter, fiction writer, and journalist Cyril Lionel Robert James. The chapter opens with an attempt to capture the Caribbean as an archipelagic tropicality of "African labor."[19] In Robinson's work, the Caribbean appears to be first black, as an enslaved cum peasant cum proletarian cum middle-class population, and also later a largely South Asian peasantry (having emerged thus from India) cum proletarian cum middle-class population. Robinson emphasizes each group's cultural retention, focusing on James as someone who has emerged from the colonial middle classes, a particular stage of capitalist and social and cultural evolution. Robinson charts the development of James's critique of capitalism and colonialism, and his labour activism. There are numerous books on James, so I won't recount details of his life here, but of central interest for Robinson is James's engagement with Marxism as a member of the Trotskyist movement (the Johnson-Forest Tendency).[20] He notes that "it was as a Trotskyist that James would author *The Black Jacobins*," being particularly committed to, among other tenets, "Trotsky's concept of permanent revolution."[21] James's writings, for Robinson, represent particular moments of ideological development shaped by the various anti-imperial, anti-colonial movements, and pro-workers struggles he was engaged in during his peripatetic life between Trinidad, Great Britain, and the United States.

For Robinson, the success of James's seminal work on the Haitian Revolution, *The Black Jacobins*, on which I focus, has to do with a particular moment in James's intellectual evolution, his confrontation with the way European imperialism dealt specifically with black peoples, black workers throughout the globe. Robinson argues that this led James to outstrip his commitment to European left politics, "the anti-Stalinist Left and Engels and Marx themselves" and recognize, years ahead of Césaire, that (as Robinson puts it) "the radical Black intelligentsia was now compelled to seek the liberation of their peoples by their own means."[22] However, Robinson writes that James would eventually return to a commitment to the European and American Left, and like so many others would never "come to terms with" the "theoretical error" of accepting the role of the "petit

bourgeoisie" as mediators of the relationship "between the mass movement and the representatives of imperialism."[23] The limit of James's left
critique was thus both the limit of left politics for black liberation and
precisely the role established within left politics for members of the petit
bourgeoisie (like himself) as an intellectual cultural elite functioning to
renew imperialism's ideological and economic mechanisms, a limit with
which Rodney also struggled. Nonetheless, *The Black Jacobins* stands, for
Robinson, as a particular expression of and commitment to the black radical tradition, challenging Marxism's orthodoxies and insisting on the role
of enslaved peoples and the later working classes—rather than any local
bourgeoisie—in shaping world history and capitalist development. Therefore, Robinson writes that *The Black Jacobins* "broke with the evolutionist
chain in, the closed dialectic of, historical materialism."[24] This break, however, is even bigger than Robinson suggests in ways that are consequential
for this project.

Robinson reads in James what for him is essential in understanding the
evolution of black resistance to colonialism: the culture of the masses, of
the enslaved. That culture, James suggests (rather than the French Revolution), propelled the Haitian revolution. I agree with Robinson, suggesting
further that this emphasis on culture opens up *The Black Jacobins* to both
African *and* American indigeneities despite its limits. In upending the
order of things, to echo Robinson, James places culture over time, thereby
accomplishing far more than Williams, for whom time is paramount to
culture and functions as a causality for labour forms.[25] There are moments,
for instance, when this is not the case, as with James's discussion of Toussaint within which, as Robinson suggests, we see James struggle to reject
the orthodoxies of Marxism, and his capitulation to them emerges.[26] However, this overwhelming focus on enslaved peoples' concerns and cultural
differences from the rest of the Haitian population informs his analysis.
Here, I argue, the radical tradition in the Caribbean might ably engage indigeneity and Indigenous labour, over and above the moments in which its
historiography closes it off. James's work shapes significant interventions
in our understandings of Elimination, the colonist (conquistador cum
settler-master), the land as a product of *labour* versus *work*, and the crucial
and hence nondeterministic relationship between modes of oppression
and modes of resistance that allow for a reading of the alignment of blacks
(as both Indigenes and Creoles) and Indigenous Peoples in the Americas.

Despite their vast differences, James's *The Black Jacobins* contains similar
arguments to Williams about slave labour's relationship to the development

of the world economic system. He even, in some places, exceeds Williams's claims about blacks' role in the rise of global capitalism and European societies. While Williams argues that black labour's material force helped to propel the Industrial Revolution, James (who through observations of cricket and fiction writing was as attentive to social and ideological forms as material ones) goes so far as to suggest that the French Revolution was made possible not by internal social economic forces, as is often argued, but by enslaved blacks. He surmises, "Long before 1789, the French bourgeoisie was the most powerful economic force in France, and the slave trade and the colonies were the basis of its wealth and power. The slave trade and slavery were the economic basis for the French Revolution."[27] In this powerfully astute observation, James encapsulates the French Revolution's ultimate failure to root out inequality in the fact that it was based not on some ideal of human freedom but on the reality of human bondage. Moreover, while peasant revolt was instrumental in the Revolution (as enslaved peoples are in the Haitian Revolution), in France it was not the peasants but the elite classes that made the constitutional changes. If one explores James's arguments alongside the principle of *raison d'état*, as found in Foucault, the colonial social formation, built on slavery, engenders the state as something that must be preserved against the kingdom as an inimical state form that inhibits capital's growth.[28]

However, James's arguments for blacks' greater role in the evolution of European continental social, political, and economic forms results in the disappearance of Indigenous Peoples within the text. Indigenous Peoples remain in the past of James's analysis of the Haitian Revolution in *The Black Jacobins*. He begins the prologue with Columbus's landing and the subsequent near extermination of the "Red Indians." These Indians, within the same paragraph, also seem to be repositioned as "Haitian Indians."[29] James cites the well-worn thesis that blacks who entered the Americas as enslaved people did so in large part because of Las Casas and the vassalage of Indigenous Peoples in exchange for the African slave labour force. Bartolomean docility thus both corroborates the Indigenous Population's near extinction and provides the raison d'être for the introduction of blacks. James positions slavery as a "drain from Africa" resulting from Indigenous bodies' drain from the Americas by forced labour and other Spanish abuses of Indigenous Peoples, particularly "the destruction of cultivation to starve the rebellious."[30] The disappearance is carried forward in labour history more generally and the radical tradition specifically as James's work, like

Rodney's, is used to support political-economic analyses of the region as built on the productive unit of the plantation.

The eclipse of Indigenous Peoples from James's narrative seems insurmountable. However, in looking at the texts in order to explore what possibilities arise for the plantation to not eclipse indigeneity and external modes of production, it is important to note that despite his seeming positioning of indigeneity in the *past* of enslaved peoples in the Americas, his work includes three key observations about the disappearance of the Indigenous population and unwitting parallels between the treatment of continental African and American natives. First, while suggesting that some form of weakness specific to Indigenous Peoples in the Americas led them not to withstand Spanish abuses, James notes both their enslavement and resistance as central causes for their population decline. Second, he uses the language of Europeans placing all natives in the past of "higher civilization."[31] While this seems to be specific to Indigenous Peoples in the Americas, it is not because African natives will fall under the same force. Moreover, James's concept of a higher civilization is not a negative assessment of non-European cultures, but is likely based on his extensive knowledge of European culture and interest in and possibly imitation of satire as a form of critique by European authors.[32] Finally, in elaborating the "drain" from Africa, James hits upon what I identified in chapter 4 as a crucial element in the making of blacks as enslaved people and the dispossession of Indigenous Peoples: Elimination.

Elimination in the text conforms with James's broader concept of time and the time of events as not singularly linear nor static. He writes, "Tribes had to supply slaves or be sold as slaves themselves. Violence and ferocity became the necessities for survival, and violence and ferocity survived. The *stockades of grinning skulls, the human sacrifices, the selling of their own children as slaves*, these horrors were the product of an intolerable pressure on the African peoples, which became fiercer through the centuries as the demands of industry increased and the methods of coercion were perfected."[33]

This is a clear example not of the Death that shapes blackness (the dungeon's and the hold's clearing of the land from black bodies) but of the specific element of *Elimination*, the "grinning skulls" that result from that clearing, which enables Death as a social and ontological closure for black representation in the so-called modern era. Another example of Elimination occurs in James's description of a market or shop for the sale of people to be enslaved that he says presented "a revolting picture of dead and dying thrown pell-mell into the filth."[34] The immense profits from slavery, such that "San Domingo supplied two-thirds of the overseas trade of France" in 1789, which led to the conditions that positioned the French bourgeoisie on the eve of the Revolution, often obscure how Elimination is a structural part of slave making.[35] Elimination is a decided element of the production of the 400,000–500,000 blacks in Haiti *as* enslaved people, the majority of which, he notes, were not Creoles.

Another significant example of Elimination recalls James's initial brief description of Indigenous Peoples in the Americas. That description, I want to argue more forcefully, suggests that even where they are delinked by the time of labour's development in the Americas, all natives are in fact similar in their encounter with European imperialism. Moreover, I argue, James quite clearly details the processes of Elimination inhering in the very (primitive) accumulation (i.e., bourgeois wealth) that supposedly separates disappearing natives from productive blacks. In particular, James's description of the "misery" that captured blacks endured, which was inherent to enslaved people's "seasoning" and disciplining throughout the epoch of slavery, suggests that misery in his text renders Elimination visible.[36]

His discussion of enslaved people's inability to reproduce themselves in Haiti, as argued in chapter 3, further supports a reading of Elimination: "But the slaves in San Domingo could not replenish their number by reproduction. After that dreaded Journey across the ocean a woman was usually sterile for two years."[37] While this infertility prompts greater numbers of enslaved peoples to be brought from Africa, it is also a clear measure of how Elimination adhered in the process of enslaving people either as a deliberate or as a consequential strategy. James reinforces the unnaturalness of this sterility by noting that those who escaped slavery, the maroons, "reproduced themselves."[38] Another clear contrast was the deliberate taking of life in Haiti in order to escape slavery. According to James, up to one-third of enslaved newborns perished from the "jaw-sickness,"[39] caused deliberately by "negro midwives" so the children would not follow the condition of their mothers.[40] On the one hand, these deaths result from slave making. However, in foregrounding them as a specific, strategic form of resistance to enslavement (together with, for instance, the fact that blacks were chained in the holds of ships to prevent resistance), James emphasizes two things for a population that is mostly (as must be recalled) directly from Africa. He underscores that resistance to slavery demonstrates how black cultural origins culminate in and shape modes of resistance to circumstances not of their making, together with the fact that the humanity of blacks precedes and exceeds the plantation, which is the appeal, I would say, for Robinson. James's recounting of Elimination and resistance aptly demonstrates Robinson's thesis that a black radical tradition ontologically rooted or charted in Indigenous African cultures existed prior to slavery and guided black resistance. More importantly for this project, not only do blacks share Elimination with Indigenous Peoples, but Elimination is the outcome of (read: response to) resistance. In other words, Elimination does not precede resistance, as Bartolomean docility would have us believe. This is evidenced, as James notes, both in how "artificial famine" was a response to native rebellion in the Americas *prior* to black enslavement and in how enslaved blacks' killing of newborns was a response to enslavement and the forms of both physical death and ontological Death for blacks. Elimination is thus not simply a space-clearing gesture. It is in fact a direct *response* by whites to resistance by African and American Indigenous Peoples in the processes of their remaking.

Together with Elimination, James significantly changes our understanding of where and how blacks are and are not aligned with the colonist's (conquistador cum settler-master's) aims, which may be productive for linking black and native struggles today. Throughout *Black Jacobins*, James uses the term "colonists" to describe the white French in San Domingue, and is always careful to distinguish them from mulattoes and blacks. He likens the latter category in particular to "revolutionary peasants everywhere" and a "modern proletariat."[41] These two terms even seem to carry greater weight as world-historical categories that are more agential and productive than colonists. Indeed, colonists are nothing without the wealth they earn from the bodies of enslaved peoples. They thus have no real historical force on their own. The term *colonist* loses traction, however, just prior to the revolution when mulattoes begin to assert their rights to full humanity, separately from the enslaved people, or in James's term "the property." This leads us to the broader complexities of settler coloniality in the Caribbean. I therefore suggest that while the terms "peasant" and "proletariat" may seem to be fundamentally within the orbit of capital and the terms of Marxian analysis, they are, in James's handling, the province of a kind of indigeneity. There is a way in which the terms are not limited to the parsing of bodily labours in the labour-work dialectic, even if they exist as standard categories with particular conditions of emergence in Marxian political economy. As such, they help us rethink settlers and settlement.

When, for James, "the San Domingo masses begin," their goal is freedom and an affirmation of that prior humanity revealing itself in the cultural links with Africa that inflect the revolution. Enslaved peoples who resist begin to destroy the economic basis of bourgeois (France) and proto-bourgeois (colonies) wealth at the start of the revolution. James writes, "The slaves destroyed tirelessly. Like the peasants in the Jacquerie or the Luddite wreckers, they were seeking their salvation in the most obvious way, the destruction of what they knew was the cause of their sufferings; and if they destroyed much it was because they had suffered much. They knew that as long as these plantations stood their lot would be to labour on them until they dropped. The only thing was to destroy them."[42] The first stage of the revolt is thus to destroy not necessarily life or land, but the basic economic unit of the plantation on which blacks can only ever be property. According to James, the resisting enslaved people never saw the plantation itself or land as property: "If they had had the slightest material interest in the plantations, they would not have destroyed so wantonly."[43] Thus, when they "gained territory" in the fight for freedom, it was not for productive purposes but for subsistence.[44] Therefore, the state that emerges as the outcome of the Haitian Revolution is not tied to the state that will emerge in Europe after formal breaks with monarchic rule (the French Revolution). Moreover, it is not simply tied to either capital evolution or the evolution of worker's consciousness as determined by that state.

In the 1962 preface to his study, James repositions the work in terms of Africa's imminent independence. Thus, while 1492 is the start within the original work, he revises it in terms of something that had not yet happened in 1938, but had certainly already begun in 1962. If we can take James at his word that this was indeed the context for the study, the time it signals powerfully undermines the organizing time of much of the work itself. That time clearly links the development of the capitalist mode of production to the formation of what would become nation-states, the most productive units for capital even as it outstrips and threatens to undermine them. There is a Marxian causality there, a kind of economic determinism that even James cannot reject.

However, his peasantry, the revolting enslaved people, deliberately work against this causality in their bid to be free. Their destruction of the plantations can be read as an attack on the capitalist system that their labour engenders. Additionally, it can be read as a rejection of the object(ive) relationship between them and the land, out of which they create a new relationship to land that is decidedly not one of ownership, possession, or abstract productivity. It is an attempt to relate to the land not necessarily in terms of a "patrimony" (as the object of *work* as it becomes as Césaire notes under Henri Christophe and therefore begins to take on new forms of alienation) but in terms of their *labour*, rather than their *work* as a mechanism of accumulation.[45] Liberated lands at the start of the revolution are important only to the extent that they can sustain the concept of freedom and the bodies seeking to produce it. Enslaved people reject the land as an object of their *work* (the plantation) in favor of a relationship to the land as in need of their *labour*, which here must first destroy (rather than harvest or build) to realize the latter relation. Thus, no telos surrounds James's workers.

In contrast, the mulattoes seek to usurp the colonists' place. In their relation to the enslaved at the beginning of the revolution, they are nothing less than settlers to the extent that the enslaved are not on productive lands but on lands from which they will need to be removed or eliminated (as revolting enslaved people) in order for it to be productive (returned *as* workers for the modern state and its various iterations). The colonists were settlers in relation to Indigenous peoples, while mulattoes become settlers in relation to the enslaved not singularly because the majority of the enslaved are in fact Indigenous Africans, but because they seek to affirm a mode of being human that is prior to and outside the concepts of capital, accumulation, and property through which they necessarily reject the prepositional temporal arrangement into which enslavement forces them. In his detailed account of the revolution, James draws our attention to the fact that Haiti (as a state) was not singularly or necessarily the outcome of black resistance. It became such possibly with Toussaint, but even he was initially motivated not by an idea of wealth or accumulation but by a concept of universal freedom.[46] Black liberation in the Caribbean is thus not causally linked to the postcolonial state nor overdetermined by its capture, and neither are the terms of our political-economic analysis.

If we read James in terms of *imminence* (that possibility of the not yet to which I gestured in chapter 1 and which we see in Robinson's deconstructive temporal opening in chapter 3), we can foreground how the postcolonial state, as an inheritance of the colonial state, has a parallel existence of *immanence* (inherence) or not yet becoming. This not yet becoming that is most prominent in the Haitian case nonetheless exists at the moment of independence when blacks across the region begin to leave the plantations and seek out modes of life that can sustain them outside its productive economy and forms of society. This is the same for the various village schemes in Guyana after emancipation, for instance.[47]

This immanence/imminence is the capture of indigeneity (as a mode of being in relation to one's bodily labours and cosmogonies) against the futurity of settler colonialism, and it allows us to see how Caribbean political economy contains units of being/existence that fundamentally reject capitalist teleology (rather than units of production). The clear link to indigeneity here is its direct but not overdetermined opposition to settler coloniality. I want to reinforce that this opposition is always already captured by the colonial/postcolonial state; another economy and thus another mode of thinking about productivity is possible. Here, indigeneity is productive for an extant mode of being human that relates to the land in terms of sustenance rather than profit (rather than how the labour-work divide privileges accumulation). This is a continuous *American* mode of being and production that is a parallel to the plantation mode of production and the states it effected. The slippage that James makes in reference to Indigenous Peoples as both Red and Haitian Indians is in a way the naming of that parallel. Not only is Haiti the island's Taíno name, but it signals that other mode of production out of which and in opposition to the first attempt to undermine Indigenous modes of being human it emerged. This slippage of Red/Haitian reflects a middle/passage method in James's work, which we can read as an act of recovering Indigenous (rather than just anticapitalist or anticolonial) labours for political economy.

Collectively, James narrates not only resistance to enslavement and anti-blackness ("so despised was the black skin that even a Mulatto slave felt himself superior to the free black man").[48] His delineation of various groups' economic and ideological aims at the start of the Revolution contains a break from normative Marxian political economic categories, allowing us to read *for* indigeneity as an even more dissident and divergent strain in the analysis. Moreover, I argue that we can bring this reading forward into contemporary political-economic analysis in the region in order to reject the prepositional arrangements and structural causalities that make independence sovereignty's antagonist. This reading not only places the radical in the radical tradition under even greater pressure, but is a place to sustain it. This, I argue, is the more profound break with "the closed dialectic of, historical materialism" that Robinson initially identified. The actors in the Haitian Revolution struck a powerful blow against the anti-indigeneity and anti-blackness of *work*. We must find a way to return to it and elaborate it in black political economy.

WALTER RODNEY

In prior work, I discussed how Rodney's *A History of the Guyanese Working People* actively disappears Indigenous People from labour history. The book is a study of Guyana's working classes' proto-evolution more than forty years after the end of slavery and during the period of late or later indenture. The book's constraint for acknowledging Indigenous Peoples' labour on the land was not necessarily the start of his history in 1881, but the geography of the study and what it privileges. I return to an expanded quotation from chapter 3 in order to continue to resituate black and native labours in relation and demonstrate the book's greater geographic limit. Rodney writes, "The first Indigenous Guyanese, in the persons of the Amerindians, displayed a preference for inland locations, where shifting agriculture was heavily supplemented by fishing and hunting. The upstream position of the early Dutch trading posts was mainly meant to facilitate exchange with the Amerindians, and Dutch agriculture was initially carried on within a belt that lay approximately thirty to one hundred miles upriver. However, the significant trend of the second half of the eighteenth century was that of coastal reclamation and settlement."[49] The plantation emerges here not as a unit of analysis on its own, but through a double deferral or disappearance of Indigenous Peoples and a teleological inscription of the land. Not only are Indigenous Peoples associated with unproductive lads outside the coastal area, but their presence is tied to the old settler-colonial master, the Dutch, and the spaces and economies (trade) that emerged as central within Dutch colonial rule.

The Dutch have been superseded by the British, and so has the land and the native by the enslaved and indentured. Guyana's relevant geography, the plantation, is rendered through the coloniality of progression. As I argue, the plantation as the core unit of analysis not just accomplishes the waged worker's prehistory, but simultaneously repositions indigeneity in the region. The plantation achieves the development of capital in the region and the evolution of the enslaved-worker-proletariat. It also Indigenizes. Coastal development or "humanization" by enslaved blacks repositions indigeneity such that it can be superseded in both space and time. Not only is the time of the plantation not the time of the original native, but its space is not that of the prior native; it is the space of the *new* native. Indigenous Peoples are acknowledged as a "first" people, but that time is simultaneously rendered as being outside the *space-time* of the unit of analysis for any study concerned with capitalist, class development, and worker consciousness. When Indigenous Peoples—in this case Africans—do substantively matter for Rodney, they are located elsewhere and in the past, as in his *A History of the Upper Guinea Coast.*

For Rodney, a history of workers—in which he carefully delineates the distinctions among wage workers, peasants, and others, and the methods used to control labour—is also simultaneously a history of the region's development. The worker's development, consciousness, actions as a class, and the economy's development are bound together in this analysis. Moreover, in outlining the state of worker struggles in the 1970s, Rodney says that in

> the Working People's Alliance, our contention is that, first, what is going on can only be interpreted as one stage in the development of the nationalist revolution, and this must be completely separated from the idea of a socialist revolution. Secondly, the transformation towards socialism must come through the deepening of working-class power and the defence of this class against all others who seek to continue its exploitation either overtly or covertly, and who seek to deprive that class of political hegemony. So that our policy is that of *critical exposure* rather than support.[50]

Rodney here outlines the WPA's goals, consisting of four extant groups, two of which he identifies as Marxist.[51] Although he distinguishes nationalist or false forms of socialism in Guyana from worker-determined ones, he is committed to progression toward socialism by workers who are narrowly defined in his writings. This progression toward a socialism of the workers rather than the political elites is part of his commitment to hemispheric socialism as both possible and necessary for the Americas.[52] Rodney strongly rejected race and its appropriation by the elite as a false organizing principle for workers and saw workers in Guyana and elsewhere in terms of a broader dialectical struggle against capitalist formations. "We have tended," he says, "through force or circumstance, to become involved in what we may broadly call the international revolution, or Pan-Africanism, or something that seeks to hasten the total dialectical change from a capitalist, eurocentric society to one in which our peoples as a whole—whether as working peoples, as African peoples or Third World peoples—will participate more fully."[53] Regardless of *how* populations are organized in anti-capitalist struggle, that itself is always the struggle's organizing principle, which essentially and dialectically incorporates those resisting capital accumulation *as* workers.

On the one hand, Rodney's anti-racialist commitment to a true socialism has become central to the realization of more inclusive and, I would add, more conceptually radical groups, such as the Red Thread Women's Development Programme.[54] However, on another level, the work still supports dominant national narratives of economic development by positioning blacks and Indians as the principles who need to be liberated (from capital) through evolutionary forms of socialism as part of an international workers' struggle. Moreover, to recall Wilderson and Coulthard, the worker's subject position is an antagonism for black workers because it evolves in the Americas and globally through the mechanisms of both anti-blackness (Death) and anti-indigeneity (death). Rodney thus inscribes the worker as an evolutionary figure for social change without challenging the worker's limitations as a figure of anticapitalist resistance and their fundamental limit as a category of the human and rights for nonwhites. While identifying History's anti-blackness, he does not identify the anti-blackness and anti-indigeneity of the worker category per se despite his recognition of the overarching structural antagonism of black, sovereign identity within capitalism. Moreover, the worker's "political hegemony" as a material echo of Fanon's natives' entry into the master's quarters does not address the fact that workers' struggle is not waged elsewhere, but on colonial cum postcolonial lands; should a true socialist state emerge, it will not resolve the problematic fact that this is settled/settler land.[55]

Despite this limitation, Rodney's work can be instrumental for a new methodology of Caribbean labour analysis. If we look not strictly at his economic analysis but at his approach to history as an overarching framework, we can see how history itself does not support the kinds of national or regional economic narratives into which it has been pulled, leaving more possibilities to emerge beyond that of the worker against capital (the latter interpretation is in fact reductive and ignorant of Rodney's larger position). This is only possible, however, when we carry forward Rodney's rejection of anti-blackness over and above any form of (capitalist) racialism, which helps foreground what I see as a singular *possibility* in Rodney's writing: the actual redefining of the "worker" as a historical figure and category of representation. I do not deny the limitations of Rodney's work, but they do not have to be engaged as absolute, and they still contain greater possibilities for the black left. Rodney's 1968 lecture at the Congress of Black Writers in Montreal, Canada, is of strategic importance here. It facilitates a rethinking of his work for potential openings to both a more expansive concept of labour and an indigeneity that is not always already overdetermined by the plantation as a political economic unit that elides or eclipses it. Entitled "African History in the Service of Black Liberation," this lecture is ostensibly Rodney's argument about history's role in the black struggle against colonial domination. However, the lecture does much more because before Rodney can center "history" as an object, he sets out to deal with its inherent "contradiction," the concept of civilization. In seeking to evacuate history of civilization's historical weight, Rodney signals to readers that his work should always be read in terms of a radical open-endedness.

The lecture begins with two framing assertions, or "rules," as Rodney terms them: that blackness is overdetermined by the idea that blacks lack humanity *and* that Africa's history "must be seen as intimately linked to the contemporary struggle of black people."[56] He identifies the idea of black infrahumanity as a contradiction haunting any approach to black history, which is tied to a European concept of civilization that can only reinforce black backwardness. That concept, he says, enables a recognition of African societies that conform to it. To earn such recognition, groups had "to be living in this large political conglomeration, you had to be writing, ... and you had to be engaged in a political and administrative process which is rather similar to that, let's say, of the modern United States. In other words, the greatest expression of human progress is in terms of the size of the state ... [and] the armies that the fellows can send against each other to kill each other out and the like."[57] Rodney outlines the conditions by which Europe may identify African societies as civilized and historically significant. However, what he stresses over and above everything else—particularly through the example of Egypt as being *in* but not *of* Africa when this definition of civilization is applied—is that by looking at African societies through this European concept we do no more than "play the game of proving to white society" that blacks have humanity.[58] For Rodney, humanity, by comparison, is a contradiction that must first be applied in order to be superseded, so blacks are always without humanity until proven, and humanity, when confirmed, is always accorded by whites and/or white concepts of civilization. For him, civilization operates in a dialectical system where black negation (as what is, in Kantian fashion, a categorical imperative of native negation) is an a priori: "we use it as a prop so that we can advance our thoughts and at a certain stage it will abolish itself, as it were."[59]

Rejecting the term "game," and the inherent contradiction entirely, Rodney argues that civilization should be understood as an "arbitrary" concept. Moreover, black engagement with it can happen only after such philosophical repositioning. He writes that "that is a definition which we as black people cannot accept at all. And once we throw [it] aside . . . we have to start working with other things. We have to . . . determine what is meaningful in social relations and what . . . features of African social relations . . . were most meaningful."[60] Thus, having excavated the term, Rodney applies it to pre-contact African societies, suggesting that their modes of "hospitality," forms of law, methods of policing, and "principle of gerontocracy" (implying that pre-contact economies were not organized around surplus accumulation) all constitute not the "so-called principles of civilization" as externally determined, but internally determined "principles of human activity."[61] Moreover, socialism as a mode of organization is actually, in Africa (particularly under his example of Julius Nyerere in Tanzania), a modern expression of the principles of human activity. Thus, Rodney returns to the concept of dialectics to suggest a particular relation between the past (not directed through the contradiction) and the present, which propels toward a revolution that for him is always imminent and not, in 1968, connected to the singular achievement of any post-independence or postcolonial status: "It's not just going back and taking out, harum-scarum. It has to be a dialectical [sic], you have to see what still exists in the contemporary situation that comes from the traditional roots. And, in that sense, the analysis of culture-history is extremely relevant to the present revolution."[62]

Rodney exceeds Marxian critique because—in Wynterian fashion—he questions the assumptive, unarticulated terms of the analysis: society and civilization. He thus rejects not only the concept of civilization, but the mode of the state form it engenders, which he suggests is essentially barbaric in the European case. The valorization of African societies only to the extent that they conformed to European concepts of civilization, for Rodney, necessarily leads to the unsustainable assumption that "human development can only be expressed in its highest form in that type of structure which Europeans call a state and within the terms that they consider civilized."[63] Yet, he says, "For an actual political purpose related to the revolution, we have to indicate that this cultural basis existed quite independent of states because, if not, there are certain types of contradictions into which we fall."[64] African history thus has a revolutionary potential precisely because it exceeds the dialectic of history that, for Hegel, produces the state as the highest expression of a kind of rationality.

This is the same emphasis on precolonial and precapitalist forms of culture that Robinson saw as the critical difference for black struggle. Moreover, like Robinson, Rodney does not engage that cultural element as unidirectional or even as its own causality, thus affirming both African cultural differences and those of blacks in the Americas as related though evolutionarily distinct. For example, while Rodney says the Caribbean cannot use African history in the same way as revolutionary struggles in the continent, he affirms that we can "do more with our own history, the history of black people in the New World, as a basis for working out what is a revolutionary strategy in the New World and what will be revolutionary in the new situation."[65] What we find in Rodney is, I suggest, both a place of radical opening and persistent yet not absolute closure. While he seems to suggest that it is blacks who would effect revolution in the "New World" (a term he does not rescue from its contradiction, thereby disappearing extant indigenous modes of existence), he does not necessarily put in their place the new (or even post) indigenes of his study—blacks—as moving toward a kind of history or social formation—the state—that is antithetical to indigeneity broadly. While Kelley would frame Rodney's work as decisively engaging the black radical tradition, his work also grounds humanity in "principles of human activity" that are Indigenous, ante-capitalist, anti-state, and "anti-anti-blackness," and bound to a dialectical movement that, far from closed or fixed, remains open-ended, revolutionary.[66]

I argue that Rodney's philosophical questioning of the perspectival categories of existence (civilization and society) means that his analysis of the working people does not move singularly toward the history of the Guyanese state that it is ostensibly used to shore up. This is his work's radical potential, where we can suggest that in Caribbean history, another approach can emerge for thinking and talking about labour that is open toward indigeneity. In Rodney, it is already there and it is our job to tease it out. We can read blackness and black labour in terms of the rejection of the contradiction and absolute categories that are antithetical to indigeneity. Moreover, Rodney's working people are engaged in a kind of labour (struggle) that for Rodney necessarily rejects the capitalist state, the form that is always antithetical to black being. This challenge to the state is even *exceeded* by the worker's extant culture. This is his work's persistent and radical opening, the ground for a new method of labour analysis. In such analysis, *work* itself is redefined away from political economy's absolute categories of analysis, and its only capture is the indeterminacy of revolution, not stages of capitalist development. It is not enough to say that Rodney was socialist or anticapitalist; it is more important to understand exactly how and what possibilities these positions hold for a new labour history of the region, and that the philosophical base of the categories he employed is antecedent to the outcome of the plantation mode of production.

Below, I return to the ontological dimensions of blacks' physical inability to reproduce under slavery in order to achieve a new reading of the category of the worker in *A History of the Guyanese Working People*. Rodney, I argue, gives us two critical interventions for political economic analysis: the above emphasis on cultural difference and a way of rethinking the worker for black representation *after* social Death. It is a way of moving around or through the limit of the worker as a human category of representation (i.e., anti-black and anti-indigenous) in which the worker's conditions of exploitation are rendered in terms of an enslavement that defers and makes invisible the real conditions of enslavement experienced by black and Indigenous Peoples.[67] To tease out this possibility, I work through what I argue is a pause in Sylvia Wynter's work between the reproduction of the black as worker and the re/production of black ontologies.

In his study of "the Caribbean plantation complex" as the basis for social structure and nationalism in the region, Franklin Knight notes that enslaved blacks' inability to reproduce themselves was inimical to the plantation's function: "Nowhere throughout the plantation Caribbean did enslaved social units procreate and maintain their demographic viability as other social units did in Africa, Europe, and within the indigenous American communities. As a rule, the Caribbean plantation society demonstrated some . . . contrived traits: predominately male, predominately adult, predominantly unfree, and relentlessly coerced."[68] Knight suggests that this inability to reproduce was thus not an anomaly but is intrinsic to the plantation, as James also demonstrated. As I have argued, this inability, apart from the *just* deaths experienced under slave conditions (recall, from chapter 1, that since blacks could be enslaved, their deaths under slavery are already just), is eliminatory. While we can look at blacks' physical deaths, this Elimination, as one function of the mechanisms of Death, must be understood as a site of ontological rupture.

In Sylvia Wynter's essay "Beyond Miranda's Meanings," to which I return in chapter 5, this inability to reproduce takes on an ontological function in the birthing and maintenance of the European versions of the human arising after the Columbian error. Wynter argues that Caliban in Shakespeare's play has no "physiognomically complementary mate." This lack is a function, she says, of the new "global order" that will emerge out of the

European discoveries, "integrating behaviour-regulatory system of meanings and 'semantic closure principle.'"[69] In short, the lack of a reproductive mate in the play is meant to reflect the fact that blacks are not meant to reproduce themselves and their difference *as* hu/man. Wynter illuminates the very condition of blackness in the Americas, the inability to re-produce the black as different *and* human, rather than as "mimetic" (of whiteness as rationality) and as, therefore, lack. She outlines in Shakespeare's early seventeenth-century text the governing logic of the plantation economy: the disciplining of the body. The seasoning that made blacks physically unable to procreate in *The Black Jacobins* is not meant to make the body singularly unproductive, since the ability of enslaved people *as* objects to produce more objects or enslaved people is a mechanism of accumulation. However, it is meant to reinforce the ontological negation of blackness in its socially symbolic closures.

Wynter's essay introduces a pause in thinking about how blacks in the Americas and the Caribbean reproduced themselves, with consequences for what it means for them to inhabit the category of the worker as a world-historical structure, and for how Afropessimism engages the material tradition of the black left. This is not an argument about how much African culture blacks retained, transformed, and transmitted in the Americas. The ontological pause elaborated in Wynter's work is usually ignored in attempts to show how enslaved blacks retained their culture. For instance, arguments about cultural retention privilege this over ontological negation. Blacks reproduce their cultural selves, and culture is elaborated as the site of ontology.[70] Reading Césaire via the Francophone writer Maryse Condé, Wynter foregrounds how culture cannot be ontological reproduction because the latter is foreclosed for blacks in order for whiteness to produce itself as the human same.

Robinson's work seems to hit up against the pause, but also to skip over or work around it. For him, black cultural retention in the Caribbean, especially the ways enslaved peoples organized their lives, evinces their resistance to colonialism as part of an extant, pre-contact radical tradition that affirms a pre-contact experience of being that is carried forward. In Robinson, these two things are linked, leading to a reproduction of black selves in difference. In other words, despite blacks' inability to reproduce themselves during forced, captive breeding, they always (re) produce a (cultural) version of themselves *without* physical re-production as a strictly biological phenomenon. In short, they reproduce themselves culturally (and even at least partially libidinally) outside and against the disciplining of their physical reproduction as the site at which the mechanisms of anti-blackness (the whip, etc.) work to foreclose black ontology.[71] This is the pause or contradiction that Robinson does not probe, and what it would mean for black political economy to begin with black Death. Since there is no pause (the rupture is not sustained), for Robinson, enslaved blacks, despite their difference, ultimately attain a dialectical, world-historical position as workers, as proletarian. However, if, for instance, blacks have an ontological difference (which is absolute negation and not the types of differentiation within the category of the human), then how are they the same as workers everywhere?[72] Does this make liberation abstract or concrete and rooted in the specificity of the difference of individual sets of workers?

As a result, the radical tradition contains within it two sets of limits: one for black ontologies and another for native representation where blacks, when they do inhabit the category of the worker, move through particular stages of transformation that New World Indigenous Peoples seemingly do not. While the ability to reproduce without physical reproduction has specific possibilities and limitations for thinking about gender in the region (in Wynter, both the physical and (non)mimetic reproduction are heterosexual), I argue that the tension it produces for political economic analyses, which are forced to prioritize one reproduction over the other, is still useful and should be maintained for Caribbean labour history. It is an essential element in reading labour history in terms of its alternative possibilities rather than in the ways in which our historiography fails to singularly capture the concrete social identities produced through stages of social development (such as the worker as an outgrowth of the plantation system) even where it concretizes the abstract category of the worker.

With the pause in mind, I return to Rodney's history. If we read it in these terms, we can reclaim the category of the worker for the region, not just for those whose labour was routed through the plantation. Additionally, we can reclaim it in such a way that its anti-blackness and anti-indigeneity are an antagonism to the category as a whole rather than an articulating structure that sustains it. The category is thus read not only materially but ontologically and, more importantly, in terms of the time of both. Rodney's writings mark a shift in Caribbean historiography from both Eric Williams and Franklin Knight. Though a critical tool in the argument for self-government in the region, the former sought to strictly reconcile enslaved black labour to the world-historical function of work. In other words, they sought mainly to account for the role of blacks in the production of the world-system economy. Both are thus teleologically oriented, unlike

Rodney's *History*. While Knight and Williams ostensibly focus on the plantation, in Rodney's work the plantation is actually parsed into three categories or classes of labour: labour on the plantation for the planter class, labour on the plantation for the self, and labour off the plantation, also for the self. These categories of labour are not only where Rodney resolves the universal in favor of the particular. This more expansive picture of labour relies on and simultaneously rejects the labour-work dialectic and singular notions of productive work that derive from it.

Earlier, I discussed the plantation's geographic limit as an optic for Creole labour as the imposition of a temporal (read: pre-positional) structure in Rodney's work. The plantation compels a type of productive *work*; Rodney's history rejects exploitation but not compulsion, which is historically necessary for the evolution of the worker. However, here we encounter the real marginalization of Indigenous Peoples and might discover their potential reentry into Rodney's picture of labour. At the outset, Rodney focuses us away from Indigenous subsistence labour to the demands of black, coastal plantation labour. Notably, the plantation is limited by the extent to which it can be kept free of sea water. Rodney details the flooding and the attempts to rescue the polder that forms the base of the plantations. He identifies this, together with the planter class and the power it held in the legislature, as the two main constraints of working people (the third is the world market for sugar and other crops).

The attempt to keep the water at bay as the defining factor in the colony's labour actually turns Rodney's subjects into workers. In other words, the term "working people" that emerges early in the text is less about just work on the plantation, and more about a broader kind of work required for the plantation to emerge and be sustained. Thus, we see two parallel economies, even though Rodney presents a number of workers (free blacks, a quasi-peasant class of blacks, largely Indian indentured and non-indentured workers, etc.). In the first economy, after emancipation, blacks organized themselves into skilled work gangs and hired themselves out to plantations. This economy also includes indentured labourers on the plantations (including those whose terms expired). In the second economy, labour is not directed to the plantation. Rodney notes, "Only the cultivation of sugar cane was considered industrious by the planters, while peasant production of provisions was said to have been a waste of time and resources. This attitude strongly influenced planter decisions on most of the questions connected with sea defense, drainage, and irrigation."[73] Thus, subsistence economy is deemed unproductive. Moreover, as Rodney argues, this distinction is not a simple matter of separating the classes of workers because many work gangs lived in villages where subsistence was dominant, so there was actually a thorough imbrication of subsistence and task work for the plantation.

Despite this overlap, Rodney ably charts a distinction between peasant labour for itself and that of the proletariat who through efforts to control their labour (such as striking, etc.) evolve into such within, he says, three years of the end of slavery.[74] This group produced the "first recorded strike in the history of the Guyanese working class."[75] Moreover, earlier he noted that the Guyanese people emerge nominally as such through their efforts to resist domination by the planter class.[76] In contrast to the achievement of the strike in pushing workers forward into proletarian status, slavery has no such effect. He is keen to note that slavery ended not because of resistance, which is a larger factor in Robinson, but, in keeping with Williams, because of unprofitability.[77] A critical dimension in Rodney's argument is that he essentially credits blacks with achieving this first strike that is necessary to the evolution of the worker and worker consciousness. However, the limit of Rodney's work is that when he writes of black proletarianization, the other dimensions of labour and resistance—by blacks, South Asians, and Indigenous peoples—must recede into the background. He ultimately sacrifices the complexity of his categories of workers to the world-historical logic and its abstract, biologically based, rather than ontologically determined, categories. When he returns to his categories, we find overlap between free and indentured labour where in one moment he notes the former often "substituted" for the latter and a mortality rate that haunts both plantation and non-plantation workers. Additionally, we find a decided rejection of the time of the plantation and how that time organized work when Rodney reinforces workers' concrete realities and cultures over that of the plantation. He writes, "Their own garden plots, their minor subsistence endeavors and their estimate of necessary relaxation came before the time and motion of the plantation. . . . [P]lanters and African villagers had conflicting appraisals of what constituted a 'decent' living wage—a concept that must be based on minimum objective standards of physiological subsistence but which in the final analysis is socially, culturally, and historically determined."[78] Rodney also outlines a more complex picture in which it was not only South Asians, Chinese, and other indentured peoples who replaced black plantation labour, but Africans and other islander Creoles after emancipation.[79]

Reading Rodney's categories in terms of their nuances makes it possible to talk about two overarching possibilities for labour: labour that is compelled (*work*) and *labour* that is resistance. "Compelled labor" appears in an 1889 document by the colony's governor and in a petition by Creole workers.[80] The use of the terms is instructive because of the stark difference between coercion, which is more likely applied to labour during slavery, and compel, which suggests a dynamic of pressure and resistance. Moreover, this optic brings into focus the "eras[ure]" of the distinction between them, and hence the antagonism between blacks and Indigenous Peoples whose labour is necessarily closer together, rather than the conflict between forms of post-slavery "bound" and free labour.[81] The larger categories of compulsion and resistance allow us to return to an earlier point in Rodney and recognize Indigenous labour. I juxtapose two earlier-quoted sentences from Rodney to show how this possibility emerges:

> The first Indigenous Guyanese, in the persons of the Amerindians, displayed a preference for inland locations, where shifting agriculture was heavily supplemented by fishing and hunting. The upstream position of the early Dutch trading posts was mainly meant to facilitate exchange with the Amerindians, and Dutch agriculture was initially carried on within a belt that lay approximately thirty to one hundred miles upriver.[82]

The first sentence provides evidence of an Indigenous labour system that is not compelled but *ante-* or *before* resistance. In the second sentence, we have an economy that is coming in greater contact with that in which labour is compelled, but even that contact is not occurring under any single, universal term or field of understanding because trade resolves into the separate economies of the Indigenous and the planter class. The former subsistence economy remains and intersects with the plantation under indigenous peoples and with indentured and emancipated peoples. All engage in these two economies, and while it would be possible to break enslaved labour into these two (as Robinson does by essentially noting the distinction between subsistence labour, marronage, and the like), it would be a mistake because coercion is an intrinsic factor of enslavement that cannot simply be superseded.

Looking at it this way, I suggest that the "first" strike is not postslavery but is *prior* to it, and that strikes (less strictly defined through European political economy) are a key part of resistant labour more broadly. I am not disputing Rodney's categories nor his concept of when workers become proletarians. However, I suggest that if we look there alone, we leave his work trapped in both a teleology and epistemology that it significantly undercuts at times. My question is, What if we read Rodney's work in terms of where it undercuts rather than where it is reconciled to the world-historical/abstract? Reading this way helps explain Rodney's statement at the outset of the work that he believes that the 1881 census underestimated the number of Indigenous Peoples in the colony. We have to wonder how, in their labours for themselves (which falls more broadly into the category of resistant labour), they have in fact resisted Elimination so much that Rodney *had* to note their presence. This resistance to Elimination that surfaces in Rodney can be reread in terms of a continuous strike by Indigenous Peoples against the conversion of their *labour* to *work*. By contrast, blacks' strikes shortly after slavery meant to recover their *labour* from *work*. The strike here is thus conceptually and temporally expanded, allowing us to recognize Conversion rather than capital as its larger organizing force. We can then recover the strike itself from its own Conversion as a tool *of the* worker, as a restrictive world-historical formation of (resistance to) capital and anti-blackness and anti-indigeneity.

Rodney allows us to break workers' labour into at least two kinds. I argue not only that we need to bring forward both labours within political economy, but that we can actually rethink and redeploy the category of the worker not as an outcome of the evolution of capital formation or simply a mechanism for measuring a particular relationship to it. Instead, by focusing on their actions, the workers, in producing both *labour* and *work*, and in reproducing both their physical and ontological selves (both the affirmation and the negation of existence), can be articulated as an aporetic category that can represent labours that are not fully determined or defined by capital. The particular rather than universal expression of the category of the worker is not just through a localization of world-historical struggle against the forces of capital. It is also the specific way in which this dissident elaboration of the category of the worker ruptures the category and forces it to work against itself. If there is a break between ontological and physical reproduction for blacks (recall Wynter's pause) that we can sustain as a point of pressure in left analysis, then we can sustain the category of the worker as that which both does and does not reproduce causally determined identities, anti-blackness, and anti-indigeneity. Thus, the recovery of (Indigenous) labour is the general recovery of *labour* (not *work*) for the category of the worker and a way of reinscribing the representational possibility that arises from the break between ontological and physical, or material, reproductions of the self. The worker, as an abstract, world-historical figure, is made specific in terms of its possibilities for representing blacks after Death (there is no black before Death, only Indigenous Africans) and Indigenous Peoples before and after death, Elimination. By retaining Indigenous/black cultures as essential to the formation of the category of the worker, together with the category's management of the *ruptures* of ontological, cultural, and physical reproduction for blacks against the human same, we can resist the inscription of accumulation in the term, and appropriate it for black and native *labour* struggles *as* struggles for forms of sovereignty that might converge.

Conclusion

This chapter offered a reading against the grain of anti-indigeneity within the black radical tradition in the Caribbean. Developing out of the discussion of Cedric Robinson's work in chapter 3, it argued that a counter reading of the radical tradition is possible despite its seeming closures to indigeneity. The chapter looked at the work of two giants of labour studies in the region—C. L. R. James and Walter Rodney—to argue that in works by each, it is possible to find a countercurrent allowing Indigenous labour histories to be articulated within the tradition. In rejecting the function of the "single-country" or single story of capital formation to eclipse the fact that "racial violence and domination" function to "reproduce capitalist relations of production," Nikhil Pal Singh underscores why a racial account of capital is required.[83] As I read it, in his focus on race as a structure intrinsic to capital development, Singh challenges the pastness of "primitive accumulation" because, at least in one sense, its racial structures are enduring in continued forms of exploitation and dispossession and in the persistent "cheapness of black life" under capital.[84] Singh also suggests that the Afropessimist position that black "social death" cannot be understood through the available concepts explaining "workers' exploitation" is insufficient.[85]

We are left with two persistent questions: What would happen if black political economy takes as its starting point political Death (because the Afropessimist position is that it does not)? Also, what happens to Afropessimist thought if it directly engages labour and phenomenological blackness? Though not a direct answer to either question, this chapter suggests that reading for openings and ruptures that take the radical tradition beyond the single story, to echo Singh, of work over labour, such that Indigenous forms of labour can be made visible in the tradition, is a position we can take to pursue answers. Where the radical tradition affirms black proletarian actors, even as it seeks to attend to the ontological excess that is blackness, it still needs to grapple with the fundamental anti-blackness of *work* itself, its categories, and its forward motion in history. It also needs to grapple with the categories' anti-indigeneity for understanding labour exploitation and how the category separates labour exploitation from land dispossession, as though labour somehow exists without land. The next chapter concludes this reading of the radical tradition for indigeneity by looking at Sylvia Wynter's work, which, it argues, has the potential to renew the radical tradition in this direction. The chapter also looks at the limits of this recovery of labour and the reenvisioning of the categories of labour representation in the face of the emergence of new, epochal considerations of capital and exploitation in the last twenty years in the academy.

5. "MARXIAN AND NOT MARXIAN"

Centering Sylvia Wynter in the Radical Tradition

Un/Disciplined

Throughout *Beyond Constraint*, the weaver Sylvia Wynter's writings have been used strategically to illuminate critical turns in my intervention in understanding black/native relationality. In the introduction to this book, I showed how Wynter helped illuminate Marxism's emancipatory limits for both blacks and Indigenous Peoples. In chapter 1, her work helped clarify the problem of the biopolitical figure in Hannah Arendt's critique of Marxism and illuminate the more general limits of the biopolitical as a critical mode for understanding blackness and indigeneity. It also served as a point of departure for my interpretation of Conversion as an *economic* phenomenon and its role in the disappearance of native labour by outlining how black, enslaved labour could be considered *just* against nominally free native labour. In chapter 4, Wynter's work was useful to delimit the problem of the category of the worker as a human category of representation and reread Walter Rodney's worker as a potentially representative structure not overdetermined by anti-blackness and anti-indigeneity as it is in traditional political-economic analysis. Finally, in chapter 6, I will use Wynter's work to point to the desire that I suggests underpins the emergence of the labour-work dialectic. Collectively, these brief engagements stem from the breadth of Wynter's critique of the figure of *economic* man whose emergence she tracks across her work. They also reveal her anticipation of many of our contemporary avenues of criticism from biopolitics to Afropessimism.

Although preceding chapters in this part explored extant texts in the radical tradition to suggest how they can be stretched to think Indigenous labour within the tradition itself, the most capacious reading for rethinking labour, however, is not in these works but in Wynter's. Her work has broadly been labeled a humanist project focused on mythocultural poesis, on the larger systems of meaning (language or the symbolic) regulating human behaviors within all cultures, a designation that has in many ways left her out of the radical tradition. Although her illumination of capital's ontopoetics *coincides* with the twentieth-century emergence of the black radical tradition's historicist and Marxist-oriented writings, her work has been neglected there, much like that of many women writers and activists, such as the Trinidadian American communist Claudia Jones (1915–1964) and Guyanese historian of slavery Elsa Goveia (1925–1980). Moreover, except for her unpublished work *Black Metamorphosis* where, for instance, she directly addresses enslaved blacks' commodity status, Wynter does not appear to do the types of *strict* labour history or political-economic analysis that we find in Williams's and Rodney's works. Moreover, her creative writing has not drawn robust literary and cultural analysis, so the elements that link her work to those of, for instance, the Marxist-influenced Haitian writer and activist Jacques Roumain have not been significantly explored.

Over a decade ago, I was told that Wynter has no material analysis because she is essentially an idealist philosopher, which undermines her work entirely. Although Caribbean sociologist Paget Henry recognizes Wynter's critique of Marxism and liberatory projects tied to it as limited because they maintain epistemic, sociopolitical categories of lack and liminality, he argues that her emphasis on "the categorical" and the "autopoetics of founding schemas" would ultimately mean "replacing" Marxism as an explanatory model for economic domination.[1] Henry criticizes Wynter for ignoring the relative "autonomy" of market forces in favor of emphasizing knowledge production, meaning making, and language, writing that "Wynter has not been able to control the discursive tendencies toward overrepresenting founding categories."[2] She is thus somehow guilty of the same gesture of overrepresentation she finds at the heart of western culture's establishment of the figure of the hu/Man. Moreover, to the extent that she suggests that "Caribbean people make a radical break with the *episteme* of material redemption," she is not attuned to the acuteness of Caribbean economic underdevelopment.[3] Although he sees her work as a "bridge" between the two dominant strands he identifies in contemporary

Caribbean philosophical thought—the historicists and the poeticists—Henry ultimately places her in the latter, along with figures like Guyanese writer and essayist Wilson Harris.

However, we must remember that Wynter's life (b. 1927) and work coincide (i.e., share the conditions of self-awareness under colonization, segregation, apartheid, anticolonial resistance, civil rights struggle, African and Caribbean postcolonial independence, etc.) with the output of so many black radical thinkers, activists, and labour historians with whom she was either a contemporary and/or directly influenced by, and in some cases, like James, likely influenced. These include C. L. R. James (1901–1989), Eric Williams (1911–1981), Frantz Fanon (1925–1961), Richard Wright (1908–1960), Walter Rodney (1942–1980), Manning Marable (1950–2011), Cedric Robinson (1940–2016), Charles Mills (1951–2021), and others. Across her work she either engages, anticipates, or shares perspectives with these writers. Additionally, through her anticolonial activism, she worked with Marxists like Guyana's former president Cheddi Jagan.[4] The "bridge" Henry identifies between her work and those constitutive of the historicist strand—and within it a more dominant Marxist rather than pan-Africanist approach to liberation—*is* Wynter's deliberate, sustained engagement with political economy across all her work, and her original contribution to the radical tradition.

Wynter consistently offers an *un/disciplined* critique of capitalist political economy.[5] Though *not* Marxist in its totality, her anticapitalist critique emerges from her previous experience and practical engagement in anticolonial, Marxist politics.[6] Moreover, her anticapitalism is wedged within a broader critique of our academic disciplines and fields—from economics to literary studies—as the spaces of the elaboration of the human, or (capitalist) economic man, that are fundamentally antagonistic to black and native being. She deploys these criticisms precisely from what is labeled her *humanist* perspective, although she works literally at humanism's limits and calls for displacing its subject entirely. Moreover, she reveals how political-economic categories work as both objects of knowledge and the mechanisms for enacting social policy aimed at markets and populations. Through this critique, she unearths what she critically defines as "*native* labour," a colonial mode of extractive work applied to those *already* broken off from the human categories that track the worker and the modes of productive work they identify and represent.[7] Wynter thus distinguishes what she calls "the normal proletariat" from those whose representation in the category of the worker would be an adjustment and misrepresentation. At the risk, therefore, of limiting her work, I suggest that centering Wynter in the radical tradition in the Caribbean, and particularly her attempt to elaborate this *other* labour, moves us most significantly beyond the unthinkability of Indigenous labour within it. More importantly, her use of "the categorical" as a decentering refusal (rather than outside engagement) of Marxism makes this indeed possible, so it must be respected as *part* of her anticapitalist critique.[8]

It is precisely her desire for a scientifically based—and hence self-correcting—humanism that does not yet exist, to think (black) indigeneity, and her elaboration of a closure around the figure of the black woman in feminist studies that have led her to critique the radical tradition from the standpoint of its poetics rather than singularly in terms of its objects and outcomes or terms of analysis. Moreover, this effort leads her to account for native (black and Indigenous American) labour *within* Caribbean labour history, making her work a critical starting point for labour history and political economy in the region. Indigenous labour is a fundamental element of Caribbean labour history rather than an adjunct of her approach to political economy. For Wynter, Marxism seems to have a profoundly revelatory rather than prescriptive (liberatory telos) function, so her analysis does not just break from it, but extends it. Wynter's criticism of capitalist political economy *and* Marxist critique is focused on foundations, antecedents, and unarticulated yet constitutive processes of race making and capital formation. Her analysis does not rest on the always already of the break between black and native labours, but simultaneously points to critical misreadings of historical materialism that limit our ability to understand black and native labours together, revealing the assumptive logics of liberal humanism undergirding Marxist critique. Moreover, I argue that her political and economic criticism is grounded in a robust understanding of how scarcity operates in political economy, a broader consideration of the relationship between land and labour in stages of primitive accumulation, and a different account of labour resistance and black death/Death.

What follows is not a definitive or comprehensive reading of Wynterian political economy, but simply an effort to begin illuminating it as such and to respect the limits of trying to map it within the dominant strands of Marxism/Leninism/Trotskyism for Caribbean black radical thinkers. I could not consider all of Wynter's essays, nor her unpublished *Black Metamorphosis*, which is where her most cohesive articulation and sustained discussion of labour history lies, and where she most directly works with a range of texts on capitalist political economy.[9] Thus, this is not a full outline of her political-economic critique, which might trace her influences and outline links with other writers and ideological positions in the tradition. That is a different project. Moreover, while *Black Metamorphosis* may further cement Wynter in the radical tradition, it may potentially be read similarly to other texts, without attention to indigeneity—either blacks' or First Peoples'—as constitutive elements of labour history and political economic analysis.

Black and native indigeneity in their relationality is the key to both Wynter's material critique and her orientation toward a humanism that as yet does not exist. I therefore suggest that when we read for her critique of capitalist political economy and labour exploitation, we do not ignore how it attends to the *anti-blackness* and *anti-indigeneity* of both the processes of exploitation and the languages we use to apprehend them. Nor should we ignore Wynter's deliberate engagement with what lies *beyond* representation in narrow political-economic terms, which is a major part of current anticapitalist critiques in black and Indigenous studies. Finally, this reading of Wynter runs partially against the grain of her use by Afropessimists. It sees her anticapitalist critique as part of a larger project of revealing Man's constitution and constitutive structures as having its own mode of optimism. That optimism is precisely her ability to work at the edge or impossibility of representation and reconfigure the subject of capitalist political economy in terms of its own provisional conditions of possibility. It is also her recovery of dimensions and figures lost to political economic critique without overdetermining either their forms of disclosure or their roots to freedom, as well as an account of black Death embedded within *native* resistance.

This chapter begins by primarily tracing Wynter's political-economic critique in three of her essays: "Beyond Miranda's Meanings," the two-part "New Seville and the Conversion Experience," and "Jonkonnu in Jamaica." I argue that through these essays, we can clearly see Wynter's criticism of capitalist political economy and renew its promise by formally foregrounding it and centering her in the radical tradition. The chapter's second section proceeds from a kind of caution. It recognizes that this collective recuperation of the radical tradition *for* indigeneity, for which Wynter is central, is situated alongside the epochal shift within the last twenty years in our thinking about capital and labour: the Anthropocene-Capitalocene debate. This debate reiterates Arendt's planetary concerns, discussed in chapter 1, while heralding new closures of capital formation and capital's poetics. In short, the debate threatens to reinscribe the big time of capital for all dissident, radical, and still emergent strains of political economy. It also imperils the misreading of this recovery of Indigenous labour as though it were *for* capital and the sui generis evolutionary struggles against it. In other words, it repositions critique as a new inscription. The chapter thus looks at these epochal ways of imagining capital's terminus and opposes them to the refusal of (Fanonian) *skins* as a new way to ground this alternative, radically open reading of the tradition. I consider what the rejection of a politics of Recognition means as a shared point of entanglement for black and Indigenous freedoms and as a break between blackness and indigeneity.

While the preceding chapters have suggested that we consider the relationality of Death/death, and this chapter continues to push black left studies past this point, I also tackle their delinking around Recognition. While both Afropessimist and black optimist traditions refuse Recognition as an ontological position for blacks, critical borrowings from black philosophical thought, such as Glen Coulthard's use of Frantz Fanon, actually subordinate this ontological refusal in favor of more urgent phenomenological needs. Coulthard utilizes Fanon's rejection of structures of recognition to situate refusal as a political stance with regard to Indigenous Peoples' land claims. However, it becomes a moment in which the land is both phenomenological *and* an ontological force—thus its potential to continuously *occur* for Indigenous Peoples—becomes situated *against* the ontological closures that refusal poses for blackness. Therefore, in contrast to the preceding chapter's examination of how black *labour* could be recovered from black *work* and resituated within the terms and fact of Indigenous labours and resistance, this chapter looks at where Indigenous articulations of struggle need to be slightly tweaked in order to reach out to black *labour* and labour struggle. Where Indigenous forms of resistance and refusal do not do this is their own moment of inscribing anti-blackness. This chapter thus returns to Frank Wilderson's question, What it would look like if coalitional politics between blacks and nonblacks started from the point of black Death rather than from its refusal, in order to work within the openings created by black struggle.[10] It also links openings within the radical tradition to Indigenous attempts at modes of relationality around anticapitalist critique.

An Un/Gendered Critique of Scarcity in Capitalist Political Economy

Sylvia Wynter's critique of capitalist political economy hinges on gender, although hers is not what we can label a (Marxist) feminist analysis of women's economic subordination or labour exploitation. It is also not the kind of race and gender-based class analysis that would position her with someone like Claudia Jones, who illuminated both the concealment of black women's labour in capitalist political economy and the foreclosure of black women's representation within class-based structures of redress. Wynter's critique stems from the black woman's figurative expulsion from the symbolic order, elaborated in "Beyond Miranda's Meanings." The essay first appeared in *The Black Feminist Reader* in 2000, and marks the nonintegrative (i.e., demonic) difference with (white) feminism that black women's articulations represent. It approaches black women's voicing of their subordination and resistance without the always already of its reconciliation with or co-optation by the larger feminist project as its sphere of intelligibility and possibility. Scholars have used this essay to identify Wynter as a black feminist and simultaneously—almost contradictorily—to support Afropessimist understandings of blackness, where (with Hortense Spillers) Wynter is seen as suggesting that black women constitute another sex entirely, excluded from the normative category woman on both biological and cultural grounds, thereby cementing the argument about black ontological death.[11] However, this essay can also be read another way because her critique of capitalist political economy's constitutive mechanisms emerges precisely from this point of difference and lack around black women's un/gendering, prompting her to theorize race's role in political economic analysis. Moreover, because she has to account for gender and race as nonequivalent structures of difference, Wynter firmly theorizes the *native* within political economy as literally the limit point of the liberal humanism haunting Marxist critique. She weds this native figure to an original account of scarcity's emergence as a political-economic index or descriptive marker of the point of exhaustion of *human* needs, and as a critical element of capitalist political economy.

In "Beyond Miranda's Meanings," Wynter reads William Shakespeare's character Miranda in *The Tempest* as reflecting a fundamental shift in what it means to be human that occurs in tandem with, and is hence motivated by *and* motivates, the development of capitalist political economy. It is a shift, she says, from a primarily anatomical (biological sex tied to social gender) understanding of human difference to a physiognomic one (skin color, bodily features), which hinges on the production of the figure of the native as the secular other to (western) man. Miranda represents the production of a rational (rather than primarily religious) human subject (who will become white) against the figure of the black/native represented by Caliban, the now irrational other who will be fundamentally "dys-elected" by the evidential function of race.[12] Miranda, though subordinate to Prospero as a form of gendered property, is now fully consolidated as human *with* Prospero as his interlocutor, so Wynter emphasizes Miranda's literal speech (capacity for reason) in the text. Consequently, Miranda's human status, its intelligibility, emerges *against* Caliban's infrahuman status and his absent "woman" who are both, across Wynter's text, "American-Indians" *and* the black enslaved person as the "native/nigger."[13] Plainly put, Miranda speaks, and therefore reasons, because Caliban cannot speak (except, as Aimé Césaire notes, to "jabber" in response to commands), thereby reinforcing his incapacity for reasoned speech and his instrumentalization as a labour machine.

As Wynter explains, this evolution of man into an eventual racial category in which whites, blacks, and natives are biologically different—with biology being the fixed expression of either intellectual inferiority or superiority—begins to be effected from the fifteenth century with the Portuguese and then Columbian discoveries, which functioned to shift the then dominant religious view of the earth and man. In that view, outlined in both the Miranda essay and "Columbus and the Poetics of the *Propter Nos*," the subordinate placement of the torrid, lower hemisphere below Cape Bojador (presumably underwater and/or uninhabitable), in contrast to Europe's habitable, raised, temperate realms, is coextensive with the earth's overall subordinate place to the lighter heavens, and within that earth a laity is securely in place as subordinate to the clergy and monarchy.[14] The discoveries, however, literally (raising earth), together with Copernican heliocentrism, also simultaneously shifted (lay) man out of place since the earth's geography and its relation to the heavens no longer supported the hierarchical, totemic structure that secured the social order. With the "discovery" of thriving non-Arab and non-Moorish/Muslim peoples in Africa below the equator and later Indigenous Peoples in the Americas, their deviance from natural law becomes primary—the negro emerges as a category of color distinct from religion, while the structure of Indigenous belief systems prevents Indigenous Peoples from being easily categorized as infidels. It allows both to be grouped, eventually, as secular, irrational subjects whose deviance is self-verifying through visible, *physiognomic* difference, in contrast to now rational and also secular Europeans whose superior status will eventually be visibly self-verifying through its physiognomic coding as white. In short, the temperate/torrid division of Christian and non-Christian peoples, respectively, will be attached to and *read on* the bodies that will function as lighter firmament (white) and fixed/fallen earth (black and native).

The Miranda essay clearly critiques the problem feminism poses for nonwhites, demonstrating that black women in fact not only are broken off from the social category of womanhood, but constitute a different anatomic sex, which is sealed in their blackness. It has also been read in the long-standing discussion of whether Caliban is native or not, and in terms of the mode of racialization and secular otherness initiated with early modern discoveries. Wynter's theorization of what *race* means within the category of gender is not seen as a material analysis because race serves a troping function for her. However, she *pre-echoes* Robinson in *Black Marxism*. For Wynter, race is *not* a contradiction in the category of woman, nor for capitalist political economy, because it is formative for the creation of the category of the native as a "labor machine," of which she says the "nigger," the enslaved person, is the "most primal form." Miranda's other, Caliban, is not only an irrational other incapable of reason/speech; he is also positioned against Miranda as a central figure to Prospero's ability to recover his wealth and accumulate. In addition, he is what Wynter describes as a figure of material "lack." Importantly, race becomes the organizing principle of accumulation, symbolically creating the figures of lack and consumption, and then literally producing those bodies. The emergence of physiognomic racial difference is also tied to nature's emergence as that which now causally determines bodily difference in relation to lack and accumulation.

The absence of a mimetic mate for Caliban (his woman) forces Wynter to take the analysis further. It is, she says, an "ontological" absence.[15] It is also to be understood as a political and economic absence because the economic expression of his physiognomic difference from Miranda is tied to "global expansion" and the "marginalization of all the Other population-groups of the globe."[16] These Others, she says in "Columbus and the Poetics of the *Propter Nos*," must be produced literally as the physiognomic category of global lack. Caliban's mate, here both the native woman and the black woman, is thus a figure identified in terms of an inexhaustible, unreadable moment of production. The black/native woman thus sustains both the figures of the white woman/western man and the black, male enslaved person. White middle-class feminist critiques of political economy reject only women's "chaos" function, not the black woman's *human* function, or role in delimiting what can be human and recovered from chaos.[17]

This helps us to rethink, for instance, the depth of what Claudia Jones reads as black women's superexploitation. Jones has argued not only that black women's labour exploitation is a mode of surplus tied to their blackness but that their exploitation is also tied to their lack of representation within structures (i.e., unions) where nonblack female workers can seek visibility and redress.[18] While Jones elaborates then-contemporary twentieth-century exploitation, it stems from the a priori surplus of black women's non/re-productive labour (which, as we saw with James, can be *eliminatory* even as it reproduces blacks as dead things) that Wynter outlines. Jones's critique in many ways anticipates the Afropessimist criticism of the worker category, pointing precisely to the black woman's liminality that Wynter elaborates. What has been ignored in some left analysis, and which is therefore the starting point for Wynterian political economy, is black women's reproductive labour, which is meant to sustain the loss of what Fanon calls the negro's "metaphysics," the reproduction of ontological negation, and the physical production of these figures of lack. It is both a totemic and symbolic production, and the material substrate of (the condition of possibility for) bourgeois accumulation.

More importantly, Wynter's articulation of this phenomenon directly engages and critiques the concept of scarcity, of finite resources—literally those of an island in *The Tempest*—against captive but disobedient labour (i.e., which requires coercion). She writes, "The 'mimetic model' or totemic operator . . . which legitimates these relations in now *purely secular* terms, as relations ostensibly pre-ordained by the extra-human ends [was] set . . . firstly, in the narrative schema/story of the monarchical discourse of civic humanism (as enacted in *The Tempest*) by an allegedly universally applicable 'natural law,' and later in the Malthusian-Darwinian-Haeckelian narrative schema of a monist discourse of "social naturalism" or "biological idealism," by, allegedly, evolutionary biology."[19] In her conversations with black feminist geographer Katherine McKittrick, Wynter elaborates "the ruling-class bourgeoisie as *the naturally selected (eugenic) master of Malthusian natural scarcity*."[20] Since the human is now based on the biological understanding of man and man's others that she outlines, that biologized figure rests at the base of Malthusian (economics) and feminist critique. And not just any biologized figure, but the bourgeois subject whose condition of possibility is this seventeenth-century shift in the underpinning of the sociopolitical order that Wynter tracks. Thus, the a priori condition of political economic critique is a physiognomic cum biologized subject that is already the product of an operation that produces man as an outcome of the distinction between wo/man (Miranda) and the native (Caliban/worker, "as both the Arawak and African 'forced' labour needed by the mutation in the land/labour ratio which followed"), a point to which I return later.

For Wynter, existing ways of interpreting gender are fundamentally limited by this break between man and the native, which produces man/human as a distinct figure who is not only already broken off within accumulation mechanisms and from the true figures of lack, but also is the *perspective* of the political economist whose elaboration of scarcity is capital's poiesis. Here and in the earlier cited passage, nature undergirds scarcity and is tied to the racial order's emergence/production. Wynter thus outlines the conditions of possibility not just for black/native subordination and labour exploitation but also for accumulation *and* the language of political economic elaboration and critique. She writes,

> since this order/field is transformative, generated from our present purely secular definition of the human on the model of a natural organism, with, in consequence, this organism's "ends" therefore being ostensibly set extra-humanly, by "nature," i.e., Haeckel's monism, neoclassical economics' Natural Scarcity, Marx's "materialist" imperative of the "mode of production," Feminism's bio-anatomical "universal" identity, we shall need to move beyond this founding definition, not merely to *another* alternative one, non-consciously put in place as our present definition, but rather to a frame of reference which parallels the "demonic models" posited by physicists who seek to conceive of a vantage point outside the space-time orientation of the homuncular observer.[21]

If we return to the arguments from chapter 1 on the late fifteenth and early sixteenth centuries' break between abundance and scarcity (not yet *the* category in capitalist political economy) that distinguishes blacks from Indigenous peoples, then here we can read scarcity as a dialectical category emerging to manage the labour of the black-native and essentially corral it into its singularly productive (accumulative) ends. Wynter deliberately cites English economist Thomas Robert Malthus here with Darwin and Marx, in what we can read as a broad critique of the scarcity concept.

Malthus, of course, has been criticized for his position on the poor in developed countries. In *An Essay on the Principle of Population*, though arguing that wages are kept artificially low and workers are not paid because of ameliorative measures like England's parish laws, he blames the poor for their condition, suggesting they are irresponsible (for starting families they cannot afford) and fundamentally wasteful. While this position is abhorrent, we have not left the Malthusian perspective behind. He argues that social support mechanisms make people less likely to work, and greater purchasing power will drive up prices and lead to inflation: arguments of blame directed at contemporary, impoverished populations of color.[22] By linking Malthus with Darwin, who not only cites Malthus in *The Descent of Man* but relies on his concept of population (drawing a line to Marx), Wynter instructs us to read for something in Malthus that exceeds his political economy, impacting all modes of capitalist political economy and critique; she asks us to rethink scarcity.

Malthus repeatedly refers to "laws of nature" governing what he refers to as the "population." Arguing that the population cannot exceed its "subsistence" level without natural checks and consequences as necessary control mechanisms—misery, vice, famine, and so on—Malthus clearly evinces a kind of biological determinism here, despite and maybe through his belief in some grand design (Being).[23] However, if we read him in terms of Wynter's suggestion of a break between man and the *savage*, we can see that the population in Malthus is biopolitical and meant to refer only to certain groups, peoples, and nations. Malthus's empiricism (e.g., "What can we reason but from what we know?"), as Wynter's homuncular observer, is based on the idea of a "law of necessity which prevents population from increasing in any country beyond the food which it can either produce or acquire."[24] This law of necessity is tied to a concept of nature as a regulatory force applicable only to "civilized" society.

Wynter's recourse to Malthus supports an emerging distinction between *nature* and *the biological*, as that which expresses but *transcends* nature. The black-native woman not only produces in a way that cannot be read; her position correlates to that of nature as extra-human, making her different even from Caliban as one form of infrahuman. She is not a biological organism but a *natural* one. She is thus the figure that totemically codes *against* human difference, that cannot be captured by the now liminal (and hence still part of) marker of humanity, woman. Moreover, in this civilized society/population, Miranda is inscribed in Malthus's formulation of scarcity: "women live longer upon an average than men, and although I would not . . . say that their intellectual faculties are inferior, yet, I think, it must be allowed that, from their different education, there are not so many women as men, who are excited to vigorous mental exertion."[25] This opposition between nature and the biological is the general and irreconcilable opposition between the figures of lack—the black and the native—and wo/man. Malthus, who necessarily presumes but cannot theorize women's reproductive function to produce the populations beyond the "passions," articulates the place of women (not those in "savage societies") as rational subjects who are part of this biopolitical unit of the population. It is Darwin's "civilized populations" against his "savages."[26] This is not a straightforward matter of reading Malthus in Darwin, or David Hume in Malthus. However, Malthus refers to the "savage" as inhabiting "the rudest state of mankind," including in this category Indigenous Peoples of both North America and Southern Africa.[27] Later, returning to the Americas, he not only suggests that native peoples have an unnatural (in Wynterian terms, *purely natural*) population growth. Demonstrating his theory of the relationship between subsistence and growth, he refers only to the populations of cities after colonization.[28]

Critically, the "population" in Malthus (who enthusiastically reads Adam Smith) is literally evolutionarily distinct from the savage. Thus, when he talks about the worker, this category can only emerge from the population, which is fundamentally broken off from the native/savage who can be near the population but are *not* the population. The scarcity of the commodity that arises from the artificial supplementing of the worker's wages is then specific only to the "population" that follows the extra-human laws of nature that keeps it in check.[29] Malthusian scarcity is thus intrinsic to what we understand as the commodity; Wynter wants us to understand that the native has been cleaved from this political economy of the human. Moreover, Wynter also asks us to understand that scarcity thus depends on a biological concept of the population that is *separate* from that of lack. The production she signals of the global, racialized poor is not because of scarcity that applies to the homuncular population, but is the production of the category of lack of those who cannot be part of the population or who will eventually be integrated only through the adjustment of scarcity. If we recall the dialectic of scarcity and abundance (see chapter 1), the latter category pertained to Europeans, and it will evolve into scarcity within political economy while the former category will come to signal forms of labour exhaustion and disposability.

Here we can reread this sentence in Wynter's "Columbus and the Poetics of the *Propter Nos*": "Because these *jobless/underdeveloped* categories/areas serve as 'mobile classificatory labels' of the genetically dysselected boundary figures, outside the limits of evolutionary Grace (as the jobholding/developed categories areas are supposed to exist, as the ostensibly *genetically* selected or *redeemed inside* the limits of the same Grace), they must be socio-institutionally *produced* as the embodiment of the legitimately impoverishable; so too *Zanj* had been made to embody the category of the legitimately enslavable, and the *idolator*, the category of those whose lands as *terra nullius*, were legitimately expropriable."[30] Wynter refers to the global, racialized poor that geographically begin at or near the equator, occupying the globe's lower portion. Important here is the assertion that they are "legitimately impoverishable." For Malthus, poverty is a natural condition produced by scarcity (a market feature) and limits of subsistence (nature). Wynter outlines not poverty, but something that is always unnatural and excessive (just like its original cognate abundance): the kind of condition that will lead, for instance, to the consequences of Hurricane Katrina and forms of disposability that are not and cannot be seen as a correction of the market/population.[31] Her critique of scarcity illuminates not just the anti-blackness and anti-indigeneity of political, economic categories and the foreclosure of our representation as infrahuman subjects. Black and native representation is foreclosed within political economy's normative categories precisely *because* economic scarcity never applied to the black or native. Hence, our own overrepresentation in categories of statistical (percentage) lack—such as unemployment and poverty (Wynter's homeless and jobless), which express our surplus function and the way we statistically accumulate in these categories—is the abundance that is *already* broken off from scarcity. The native/black figure helps secure scarcity as the infinite field of unmet needs that can never be satisfied, so markets correct always for signs of abundance. More importantly, if we work back through Columbus and such early texts depicting native abundance, what we actually see is how native peoples in the Americas are first broken off from those who become the antecedent receptors of capitalist political-economic scarcity, a cleavage from which the collective disposability of blacks and Indigenous Peoples stems. Not only do Indigenous Peoples initiate the category of scarcity in its difference from abundance, but Death and Elimination make abundance (excess or what will become unruly nature) available *for* scarcity as a commensurate measure of economic need. Wynter thus elaborates the constitutive forces of racial capital *and* settler colonization for capitalist political economy.

For Wynter, despite the evolution of political and economic theory and the emergence of a robust anticapitalist critique, nothing displaces the "homuncular observer" (the political theorist) and their conditions of possibility as coextensive with the categories of analysis in the literature. In other words, capitalist political-economic theory (Smith, Malthus, etc.) does not work or make sense without the inscription of the behavior-regulating (and economic) break between these human groups, or without this conception of the population as a bio/political entity subject to (natural) causes that act as market forces. Therefore, the critic (including Marx) must always represent this foundational relation rather than illuminate or challenge it. This critique is ahead of the biopolitical turn, and is more extensive than Wynter's assertion of Marx's failure to question the function of ownership. Nor is it equal to her criticism that "The middle-class model of *Man* is represented as if it were isomorphic with the well-being of all humanity."[32] Both positions are regarded as pivot points for her break with material critique, but they also allow her to rethink political economic categories in her evaluation of man as an autopoetic biological figure who tautologically invents scarcity in order to secure needs as the terrain of the human.

Thus, Marxist analysis is useful only up to a point ("Marxian and not Marxian," as Wynter says in the Miranda essay). The dominant critique of reproduction in women's and gender studies is still wedded to an anatomical model that cannot be extended to black women as a literally unthinkable gender in *The Tempest*. Thus, black/native women's unthinkable genders and alternative sex (because they are positioned literally *after* sex) are in effect the ground for Wynter's un/gendered critique of political economy as a field that cannot escape the function of its own categories to secure the now "purely secular" biological man at the base of its criticism: that organism who can experience scarcity against the organism who must experience lack. The unthought black/native woman ("gender and not gender") is the condition of possibility for Marxian political economic critique. Mainstream feminism's criticism of Marx's lack of consideration of women's reproductive labour is thus secured by the black woman's *not gender* just as Marxist political economy is secured by gender, the reproductive function of women, *and* the *not gender* of women who produce lack and secure the function of scarcity. For Wynter, however, it is more than the categories that we have gotten wrong. It is also not simply a matter of the problem of our collective reinvention as proletarian classes (see the introduction to this book). Instead, accumulation is based on the native cum slave. Even where we need to revise the analysis of slave labour's role in the industrial revolution, we still have to account for the slave-native's larger systemic function to effect that revolution and the role of lack necessary to its evolution.

By reinscribing the category of the worker, political economic critique relies on the worker's position to now capture all others (former lay people) against those who must be left out of the category (Europe's infrahumans and homunculi). Moreover, the call to see blacks and others as proletarian is a moment of conscription into the category where they can underscore its human function. Wynter's material critique is therefore an ontological critique and vice versa. She also asks us to read in Darwin the conditions of capitalist, political-economic critique, and to read in Smith, Malthus, and Marx a kind of Darwinism at the heart of political economy, even emancipatory projects tethered to a Marxist critique. Science not only completes the philosophical project, as Denise Da Silva has argued, but also consolidates the biologized human figure *for* political economy. Wynter is no less aware of normative political economic categories' limits for thinking about black labour than are James, Rodney, and Williams. Her "Marxian and not-Marxian" and "gender, and not-gender" descriptor in this essay is the provisional engagement and negation we find across these texts.[33] However, instead of centering that negation on the black as others do, Wynter centers it on the native. Caliban/native as "pure sensory nature" is a labour figure out of which the "degodded" black evolves; the *native* as a flexible figure of accumulation (because of the geomorphological shift from Indigenous African to Arawak to the indigenizing black and the native's ability to signal both land and bodily labour) grounds Wynter's political economic critique, making it simultaneously incomprehensible within, yet ultimately necessary to, the radical tradition.[34] Not only does Wynter's critique of scarcity refuse historical determinism by not situating the black/native in a trajectory that exists for the human. She also illuminates the fundamental problem with Marxism: it is indeed a humanism (*for* man), and not a non self-correcting one.

Indigeneity as Labour Resistance: The Wynterian Critique of Land-labour

In addition to her critique of scarcity, Wynter's critique of the land-labour relation results in a different account of primitive accumulation. It does not focus on productive labour, but hinges instead on the reproductive labours of self-making that are not singularly labour resistance. Here she locates black resistance to enslavement as both inside and outside chattel slave making. In so doing, she shares the same emphasis on black culture and cultural difference (not race)—as a contradiction within capitalist political economy and slave making—as Cedric Robinson. Moreover, Wynter centers Indigenous Peoples as the beginning of Caribbean labour history. Reading for this centering requires first a confrontation with the places where Wynter repeats the extinction thesis—the point at which we inscribe material lack and historical failure as a condition of freedom—and where the black enslaved person necessarily eclipses the native in her work. I begin by outlining the implications of her first conjoining and later disaggregating the native and black.

For Wynter, Caliban indexed native *and* black identities, representing compelled Arawakan and African labour.[35] Her note on this point reads: "Europe's expropriation of the lands of the Americas initiated a land/labour ratio of a new and unprecedented extent. Both the encomienda and hacienda and the plantation institution were the answer to this vast 'enclosure system' by which the category of 'native labor' and 'native being' came into existence."[36] While foregrounding Indigenous American labour here, Wynter eventually repeats the extinction thesis for native peoples in the Caribbean that surfaces throughout texts in the radical tradition, writing that "with the rapid decimation of the indigenous Arawaks of the Caribbean Islands, Africans bought and sold as 'trade goods' were now made to fill the same slot in the behaviour-regulatory schema, as they were made to fill a parallel slot in the system of forced labor."[37] However, of critical importance is her identification of the encomienda as the structure that emerges to produce the figure of the native as productive. It is, therefore, not the black but the native who *first* functions as a labour machine. Moreover, this labour reflects a new relation to land that is not singularly native death or Elimination, but the transformation of land together *with* native bodies into productive units.

The mutation in the "land-labour ratio" that Wynter outlines *is* her account of primitive accumulation, which we can argue forces us to read *against* the eventually imposed opposition between land and labour. In other words, the split theorized in chapter 1 between productive work and unproductive labour that, I argue, attaches to black and native bodies is both provisionally enacted by Wynter through the extinction thesis but also simultaneously disavowed when she sees the encomienda (and its suture of native land and labour) as the origin of accumulative labour in the Caribbean. In her two-part essay on Las Casas (referenced in chapter 1 as my point of departure for reformulating Conversion as an economic rather than strictly religious phenomenon), Wynter accomplishes several things that make her contribution to the radical tradition around primitive accumulation important. The essay focuses primarily on how Las Casas came to realize all peoples' *"culturally relative forms of rationality,"* which led him to argue that Indigenous Peoples in the Americas were *not* irrational (and therefore could not be justly enslaved), but simply displayed an "'error' of natural reason."[38]

In deploying this argument, however, Wynter must first outline Las Casas's social and economic position as an encomendero. She theorizes Indigenous bodies and labour not strictly in terms of Conversion's outcome—their position as failed labour in the labour-work dialectic. First, explaining what she terms Las Casas's "societally-coded motivation" to *not* initially see any problem with Indigenous enslavement, she explains the political and economic forces that led to the exploitation of land and labour in the Americas.[39] The Reconquista and "the religio-military machine consisting of the great nobles, the military orders and the higher dignitaries of the Church" were essential in effecting not only the reconquest of lands, but imperial Spain's economic and political expansion to the Americas.[40] In the Reconquista, the "aristocracy" became significant by acquiring recaptured Moorish lands, simultaneously creating "a de facto form of enclosure system in which *landlessness* for a growing stratum of the dispossessed . . . became a fact of life."[41] "And since ownership of land was the basis of wealth and the symbol of power in the *hidalguía* complex," she adds, "the opening up of *new world lands* to Spanish settlers and the opportunity to become *landed* in the context of the new frontier provided a powerful psychoeconomic motivation to emigration and settlement."[42] As a secular priest, Las Casas is thus part of the hidalgo class for whom wealth and land acquisition are interwoven with the monarchy's larger spiritual mission.

The grand Conversion imperative therefore expresses *class* interests, not just socially coded behavior. What Wynter describes as this class's "settler-psyche" or "normative settler mode of perception" is a political and economic phenomenon, not simply an ideologically motivated behavior.[43] Wynter accounts for class interest tied to the settler's evolution in the Americas, suggesting essentially that the aristocracy is to the encomienda as the bourgeoisie is to capital. In other words, she outlines how the encomienda *extends* extant forms of landlessness for masses in Europe that evolved from a shift in power triggered by the Reconquista. Moreover, she restores the settler figure to class analysis, as we saw with Charles Mills in chapter 3, when he forces us to read for white supremacy and the worker's evolution as/from the settler. Las Casas, whom she dubs a "settler/priest," is thus carefully located here within a political economic system, and his conversion is both religious and political as he literally rebels against his class and helps effect the confrontation of settler colonialism and black racialization (via enslavement) as structures that must be understood together in capitalist political economy.

Second, in identifying Las Casas's class position and the extension of Old World social, economic, and political structures into the Americas, Wynter's account of Indigenous labour is more aligned with the texts discussed in chapter 2 that explore the history of native labour. She notes Indigenous Arawaks' transportation for work on different islands like their export from Jamaica, which, I suggested, should be read as an inauguration of the middle/passage through Ron Welburn's text (see chapter 1).[44] However, Wynter connects native peoples to Caribbean and global political economy more directly by detailing how they produced for this class and tracing the wider economic forces that saw their exploitation as profitable. She notes that although enslaved Indigenous Peoples had been used for mining in some places, "Indian slaves had at first been used for sugar" because of the early sugar plantations and sugar mill in 1506 in Cuba, then Española.[45] Indigenous Peoples thus undergo a shift from working on one type of commodity to another: from the appearance of sugar in the Caribbean with Columbus's second voyage in 1494 to its evolution through and after 1510, as she notes the "rising price of sugar on the emerging world market."[46] According to Wynter, fifty sugar mills operated on Española in 1520, just two years after the first four thousand black enslaved people (who would eventually be valued against Indigenous Peoples four to one) were sent to the Americas.[47]

Consequently, she outlines Indigenous labour's centrality to the development of the global sugar market, a central feature of Caribbean political economy left out of dominant narratives that begin with enslaved peoples. Moreover, when the proposal to enslave blacks on a wider scale came along, the trade allied with extant interest and Flemish capital that had already been invested in the slave trade from Africa.[48] Wynter differentiates this "agro-business" and "settler economy" from native Arawakan economy, which she describes as a "leisure civilization" because of the high starch yield of cultivated yucca.[49] Scarcity (and the commodity) are thus not natural because they do not exist in Arawakan society. This leisure is *not* the abundance I theorize in chapter 1, which emerges in *relation* to scarcity and needs only after European arrival. Wynter thus describes a fundamentally different approach to nature and the laws of nature that allow Arawakan society to thrive, and which must be understood *outside* the dialectic of abundance and scarcity or the symbolic economy.

Notably, with these arguments Wynter relies on Immanuel Wallerstein (and Eric Williams) to theorize the captive relationship between Europe and America, writing that "between 1494 and 1560" and "1494 and 1670" Europe came to control "half of the population in the western hemisphere" and a "land-mass area" that reached 7 million kilometers.[50] Through Wallerstein and Williams, she reads this shift in the "land-labour ratio" as the condition of possibility for the mercantile system, and of course the eventual rise of the bourgeois class. The collective condition of possibility is a mode of primitive accumulation that initially depends on native land *and* labour, and more aptly described by Marx, as Rob Nichols suggests, as "exploitation and dispossession" as intertwined or relational features (see chapter 1). In short, Wynter elaborates the centrality of black and Indigenous Peoples to primitive accumulation, which can be read as a relation between Death and Elimination.

In Wynter's work, Indigenous Peoples establish the world-historical function of captive and coerced labour in the Americas, initiating the market transformation with which enslaved blacks will later be credited. Moreover, it is not possible to talk about primitive accumulation in terms of labour alone (as narratives overemphasizing black slave labour do) without the particular transformation of labour relationships with nature through the encomienda structure as an appropriative system of native lands *and* native labour, modeled on extant European land enclosure systems. Wynter's work as an investment in understanding and articulating the evolution of the humanist project and blacks' role in it reveals her deliberate attempt to account for that project in terms of Europe's capitalist political economy during its evolution. Both efforts lead her to locate Indigenous labour firmly within Caribbean labour history and offer a different account of primitive accumulation. Moreover, the commodities that begin to revolutionize European markets—gold from Caribbean mines, sugar, and so on—are first produced through a form of labour that (though non-chattel) initiates the structures of accumulation that will come to characterize black enslavement. Wynter's more expansive account of the origins of Caribbean labour history also leads to a different, more expansive account of labour resistance, black indigeneity, and black death/Death.

In her essay on the Jamaican folk dance Jonkonnu, Wynter theorizes black "indigenization" in the Caribbean, that process of black self-making which I suggest be read as a new relation to *labour* rather than strictly culture. Unlike the need to theorize slave revolts as an originary mode of labour struggle in the Caribbean as she will do in *Black Metamorphosis*, the dance exceeds labour struggle and is preserved alongside it. Wynter demonstrates how black cultural resistance to colonial domination in the Americas is not simply "reactionary" or derivative, but is in fact an Indigenous mode of resistance.[51] Previously, I have discussed black self-making in these essays.[52] Here, I want to strictly focus on how Wynter articulates this resistance as a labour resistance, with the caveat that a fuller consideration of her *Black Metamorphosis* will extend this criticism further. Moreover, although the black will literally be broken off within and from the category of the native in Wynter's work, we find here the same thinking together of black and native resistance that appears in Robinson's work when he writes that blacks *followed* natives off the plantations.

In her Jonkonnu essays, Wynter uses the work of economic historian and political economist Karl Polanyi, who is central to her thinking on class and market forces, to elaborate a relation to labour and land in which blacks and native peoples are not on opposite sides of the land-labour interface. In what we can read as a Marxian concept of nature as explained by Nichols, she writes that "nature *became* land; and land, if it were to be exploited, needed no *men* essentially, but so many units of labour power."[53] The opposition Wynter sees is between nature and the productive forces needed to develop it, rather than between land and labour or natives and blacks. Moreover, black slave resistance is an indigenizing process because enslaved peoples entered into a relationship with *nature* that was not extractive or devaluing, although for the planters "they represented both *labour and capital*," a convergence literally only possible in machines. She writes: "Out of this relation, in which the land was always the Earth, the centre of a core of belief and attitudes, would come the central pattern which held together the social order. In this aspect of the relation, the African slave represented an opposing process to that of the Europeans, who achieved great technical progress based on the primary accumulation of capital which came from the dehumanization of Man and Nature."[54] Later, she writes, "To the African the Earth is not property or land."[55] It therefore becomes critically important that through indigenization, a process that exceeds both resistance to domination and creolization, a relationship to land is maintained. This is similar to, or can be read alongside, James's observations that the enslaved people destroyed tirelessly. There, enslaved peoples resist *land* as a mode or source for accumulation, and Wynter foregrounds this difference of black labour even to the exclusion of productive work for accumulation. Moreover, this is a native labour not just because it is black rerooting but also because it retains an antecedent relationship to land *as* nature, that is, land that is the embodiment or expression of culturally specific modes of engagement with it.

The antecedent relationship to nature that Wynter charts also causes her to break off indigenization from creolization and offer an alternative account of black Death, as well as what we can read as a critique of biopolitics. Jonkonnu as folklore, as a "cultural guerilla resistance against the Market economy," is "not only the relation of Man to Nature but of Man to himself."[56] While Wynter cites this as resistance against market forces that dominate black labour, she simultaneously charts nonaccumulative labours of self-making. Wynter does see Africans as engaging in that same "rehumanizing" with which Rodney credited enslaved people to the exclusion of Indigenous Peoples in *A History of the Guyanese Working People*. However, Wynter starts from the position that indigeneity is a process that exceeds the making of both native and slave subjects, noting, like Robinson, that both American natives and blacks (also as natives) "ran away to avoid forced labour."[57] Wynter seems to hold Williams's thesis that the Industrial Revolution hinged on black enslaved labour. However, not only is her account more complex, but she represents Williams's black workers in terms of both their productive labour power and their reproductive cultural and Indigenous selves. Throughout, Wynter's critique of capitalist political economy is thus an account of two forces with regard to labour: the native and the cultural processes of indigeneity that at various points she breaks off from creolization. She does this because throughout the essay, she tracks the retention and transformation of African *religious* practices in ceremonies like Jonkonnu. This emphasis on that which makes such folk practices not just creolization (which she regards as a more secular process) also accomplishes something else as "the more secretive process by which the dominated culture survives" and has clear ties to African religious cultural elements.[58] These ties importantly offer another perspective on social death.

In describing the Jonkonnu dance, Wynter, a former dancer, writes: "RHYTHM is the universal life force. On donning the mask the dancer enters into this force, the god possesses him, and in a modern Jamaican cult term informed by the same meaning, the dancer '*delivers*' himself by patterning the steps of the god, or ancestral spirit. Rhythm is part of the dance, and the dance is a part of the rhythm. The theme is set by the drum controlled by the sacred rattler which determines different beats."[59] Elsewhere, she outlines the important role of black death in the retention of African religious practices, saying, "As the Slave Laws show, the planters came to learn that 'negro-dances' were the occasion for the planning of revolt."[60] These are the same revolts that she earlier indicates are marked by religious acts.[61] However, she adds that since the dances were forbidden, enslaved peoples had to find other ways to meet, plan, and resist, and for this funerals were essential: "For a long time therefore the slaves' largest areas of freedom for assembly was at funerals. The mortality rate of slaves was high. Funerals, always central to the African world view took on an added significance. The very rate of death, which occasioned the funerals and therefore frequent meetings at the graves of their dead, would have increased their instinct for revolt." Finally, she states, "It was the custom, too, at funerals to dance war dances."[62] Here, I suggest, Wynter accomplishes (1) an alternative account of black labour, (2) an alternative account of black death that is tied to that labour, and (3) a black labour critique of biopolitics.

First, the account of black labour. Here and later in the essay, Wynter spends significant time on dancing, from early ritual, adaption, and revivals to reggae. At one point she notes that "revivalists through spiritual 'labour' and 'work' deny brute facts of everyday existence by their transcendence. . . . They establish in dance 'a putative society[,' i]n which they are the elect. . . . Dance turns [the] world upside-down, liberating participants."[63] Her use of labour and work is not specific to the political economic distinction I track in chapter 1, for which Arendt and Mbembe have criticized Marx. However, I want to read it as part of the dance's two levels of performance. First, the dance above is a process of embodiment and transmittal whereby the god moves through the dancer. The act of putting on the mask (also a product of labour) initiates a type of labour within which the god works through the performer's body. Moreover, even in its transmutation in revivalist religious cultures, the dance is still a possession capable of literally changing or transcending reality. The labour of performance is fundamentally productive as the material world of man's work is subordinate to his spiritual labour. The dance "for" the god thus has two types of labour: the labour of resistance *and* that of self-making. Moreover, the dance as a spatially ordered phenomenon is a *labour* relationship to land that does not depend on ownership.

Second, Wynter complicates understandings of black death by noting, like James, enslaved people's high mortality rate and, consequently, funerals' function as spaces of resistance. The legal prohibition against certain types of gatherings, particularly dances, restricts black labour's unfolding outside the plantation's narrow political economy. This leads to the performative function of black death itself: the literal, regular rhythm of black death creates or occasions the dance again. Moreover, the dance as spirit possession, as Wynter indicates early on, shows a specific African relation to death and spirit. Here Wynter thus has two forms of death: black death that is a political-economic product of market forces (the eliminatory death in James) and black death as a generative labour for resistance and self-making. The enslaved person's social death is also simultaneously the dancer's and the conspirator's life/labour. Moreover, "as a spirit," the dead "does not cease to play his part in the life of the others. The relation of Man to his ancestral spirits is a historical and an actual living relation. The ancestral spirits are numerous and extended aspects of the life force."[64] Here, death is a point of renewing an extant relationship with Earth not as exploited nature; death is a fundamentally generative, life-giving process. Wynter does not ignore the real deaths of enslaved peoples. She shows how those deaths are embedded in a generative system of meaning making, self-making, and how they reflect a nonaccumulative relationship to the earth. Black labour, she suggests, like black death, must be read in terms of its relationship to political economy and structures like racialization that produce the enslaved person *and* also for the places where it exceeds any type of political economic analysis. Black death, as for Fred Moten, is the source of a mode of optimism through resistance as both a self-making or poesis and an oppositional force, but more importantly, it is a source of nonaccumulative labour.

My final point concerning Wynter's analysis is about the possession of the performer's body. The practice or act of possession, I argue, is part of Wynter's account of the inadequacy of biopolitical categories of analysis for blacks. Earlier, I discussed the problems with Marxist critique like Arendt's as based on what Wynter (and Moten) argue is liberal humanism's purely biologized subject. The subject of such criticism, if we follow Wynter's sex/gender critique of political economy, coheres as such only because it is already broken off from native-black peoples. Thus, to track the black as worker, as singularly proletarian, always already reinforces black-native ontological lack. I argue, however, that Wynter's discussion of indigeneity critiques the biopolitical category of political economy's subject. The producing or labouring subject that Wynter tracks while accounting for black indigeneity does not emerge *after* biology. The dancer involved in that literal process of world making through negation is both flesh and spirit. This means that the "labour machine" produces for (markets) and reproduces a subject that is not biopolitical or can never be biopolitical because it is based on a relation to earth, rhythm, and mask that is wholly outside biopolitics.

Indigenization produces black subjects between life and death (between dancer and spirit) in a manner that exceeds the native as a political economic and biological global figure of material lack. Wynter not only contrasts black performers' disavowed and disciplined reproductive labour to accumulative labour or any labour that is singularly directed at destroying the mode of accumulation. She also suggests that it is an *alternative* to biopolitics. Despite how Wynter is read for Afropessimism, and indeed preechoes or anticipates its problems with Marxism and Marxist categories of representation, her account of black life does not correspond with and therefore cannot be theorized from that split between productive work and unproductive labour that is internal to the category of the native and which separates blacks from Indigenous peoples within political and economic analysis. We can take Wynter seriously as having within her theory of black indigenization a labour analysis that shows us how to recover lost labours: those lost within political economy, and those that remain outside.

Of Skins and "Cenes": Relationality and the Epoch

The recovery of labour and sovereignty for political economy broadly and the black radical tradition is not without its limits. Specifically, what are the consequences of contemporary planetary thinking regarding capital for recovering forms of bodily action that have become lost in the endless conversion of our labours in the labour-work dialectic? What are the risks of recovering *labour* from its antagonism to *work* and the attempt to locate in that recovery, in that middle/passage, spaces of action and representation that are not anti-black or anti-Indigenous? In short, the limit of this recovery of labours lost is precisely the attempts to redeploy larger, more encompassing political economic analysis which only allow us to position ourselves *against* capital rather than in terms of the myriad ways in which left politics for black and Indigenous Peoples have other origins and directions. Anticapitalist critique is still hugely relevant, but not at the cost of reinscribing the structural limits of representation for those subject to modes of Elimination and Death, what Wynter would see as the autopoiesis of subject making in capitalist political economy. It is not enough to recover this labour. We also need to find ways to carry forward its attendant methods and orientations, without having them simply read back into dominant analyses of capital formation and anticapitalist struggle. We need to continue, as stated at the beginning of chapter 4, to resist inscription.

Attempts to insist on a name for our present epoch is one way in which capital's autopoietic master narrative reasserts itself over and at times against other conversations about being in difference and being in struggle, such as ongoing theorizations of racial capital and the methods of "grounded relationality" (as both place-based Indigenous philosophical and critical thought *and* a mode of conceptualizing Indigenous lives and futures relationally with, in this instance, black lives and outside the logics of possession, accumulation, and even redress as a state-mediated action).[65] I begin by discussing the limitations of the autopoiesis of epochal time. I then consider black and Indigenous criticisms of capitalist violence, framed through the concepts of *skins* and *grounded relationality*, or methods and sovereignties of refusal. "Skins" is the term I use to signal the elaboration of a Robinsonian "racial capitalism" that I outlined in terms of its *engagement* with indigeneity. In other words, it is a collective term for stretching this "activist hermeneutic" that I envision as a necessary part of its continued application.[66] "Grounded relationality" is the term that the editors of a special issue of *Social Text* ("Economies of Dispossession") use to articulate a critical position putting place-based Indigenous thought and critiques of capital in relation to other histories of racialization, colonization, and exploitation. "By *grounded*," they write, "we mean quite literally situated in relation to and from the land but without precluding movement, multiplicity, multidirectionality, transversals, and other elementary or material currents of water and air." They understand this "relationality grounded both in place and in movement, which simultaneously addresses Black geographies, dispossessions, and other racialized proprietary violences as incommensurate to yet not apart from Indigenous land and sovereignty."[67] Thus the term conceptually parallels the rereading of the radical tradition that I term "skins," framing positions like "grounded normativity" that I consider below. Both methods are conceived in terms of an internal relation to each other, rather than as a response to external forces or methods.

I focus on the concept of skins to index and reframe projects on racial capital that engage with indigeneity through the anticolonial perspectives of Fanon, Césaire, and particularly the Barbadian writer George Lamming's literary meditation *In the Castle of My Skin*.[68] In Fanon, black flesh is produced through revulsion and disavowal "by a racial epidermal schema" reflecting a paraontological (Moten) condition predicated on phobia rather than conflict, in which the body as a whole is deferred for blacks by objectification. For Fanon, this becoming flesh is an "amputation."[69] In Lamming's work, the flesh is a product of a narratively enacted dimensional split where the skin exists between the first and third person in the interstices of narrative capacity and those of the horizontal and vertical organization of the physical village (and larger society) that displaces and unhouses black flesh.[70] Additionally, the skin in the novel is a composite of the material and psychic, the concrete and abstract, knowledge and flesh, a secret being between the human and animal ("creature" status) and between Death and memory, blacks' prohibited desire for subjectivity, and the desire for the black body to function as a repository for the illicit or prohibited. More important is the literal condition of the being of skins on the land as always already unhoused in a Hughesian way.[71] These perspectives sit in conversation with the theorizing of black skin/flesh in African American literature and theory, particularly black feminist theory such as Hortense Spillers's work. In her essay "Mama's Baby, Papa's Maybe," Spillers distinguishes skin or "flesh" from the "body," arguing that the latter corporeality (and mode of ontological coherence) is reserved for human subjects, while the former is essentially the black body's anatomizing through the forms of violence that turned black embodied selves into enslaved people.[72]

Skins thus represent the dilemma of sovereignty for blacks and the absolute lack that cannot be made whole within meaning-making systems tied to human status. I therefore use the term both as a rubric for a collective position of refusal represented by black anticapitalist critique and to delimit a position of ontological risk that is always present in the face of critical discourses that rely on strategies of representation tied to the human. Together, *skins* and *grounded relationality*, I argue, should be the broader context for this recovery of *labour* in the record of the black radical tradition, and function as the bridge for understanding critiques of racial capital, going forward, in terms of both refusal and sovereignty, rather than degrees of independence and rights within the capitalist state.

There has been vigorous debate about what to call this epochal moment of geological time. I summarize the relevant positions below before making my arguments. The first concept to gain purchase was the Anthropocene, broached in the 1980s and outlined in a *Global Change Newsletter* by Paul Crutzen and Eugene Stoermer (2000).[73] Theorization of this term has seen a fair amount of criticism for rearticulating an arrogant ontoepistemology that reinforces the us/them divide both of the global poor and the racialized and of nature and man.[74] In contrast, the term "Capitalocene" has gained increasing popularity. Advanced by economic historian Jason W. Moore, the Capitalocene is meant to address the Anthropocene's false divisions. Moore rejects the organizing idea of the Anthropos, the divide between man and nature, explaining that "the Capitalocene signifies capitalism as a way of organizing nature—as a multispecies, situated, capitalist world-ecology."[75] He writes that "capitalism appropriates human activity just as it does the rest of nature."[76] Critical to Moore's elaboration of the Capitalocene is a rejection of the Industrial Revolution (central to the Anthropocene's conceptualizing of *our* epoch) as the origin of our planetary crisis. Thus, he offers a different account of capital's emergence that tracks back to European colonialism, stretching from the mid-fifteenth through the first half of the seventeenth century.[77] Moore's account of capital's rise is more robust and far-reaching, taking into account both enslavement and Indigenous genocide and treating both Old and New World colonialisms as fundamental to the development of capital's mechanism of extraction and accumulation. Thus, in Moore's assessment, capitalism emerges as a fundamentally integrative machine that captures not only paid work but also the "unpaid work of human and extra human others" and "unpaid work/energy from manifold natures."[78]

Despite the reach of Moore's analysis, however, three other, conceptually interrelated terms have emerged to push back against the Anthropocene's limitations: the Chthulucene, the Necrocene, and the Plantationocene. The work that the Plantationocene tries to accomplish is tied to a broader rejection of a kind of innocence in the critical narratives of the Anthropocene and Capitalocene, which, as Françoise Vergès suggests, fail to foreground the racialization of their negative outcomes. Vergès argues that the Anthropocene's grand, color-blind, "apocalyptic narrative is an ideological strategy that blames out-of-control forces rather than structures of power."[79] Vergès suggests the Anthropocene would be better understood as the "racial Capitalocene" in which "human praxis as labor and the global use of a color line in the division of labor" are responsible for current environmental and human catastrophe, "*not* a 'human' death drive."[80] The "racial Capitalocene" (over the Capitalocene proper) and the Plantationocene also, more pointedly, reject what Kathryn Yusoff refers to as the Anthropocene's "white geology" in *A Billion Black Anthropocenes or None*. Yusoff argues that the Anthropocene is based on the elaboration of geology as a racializing material practice that works by inscribing a material distinction between human and "inhuman matter." Moreover, despite its belated engagement with global capital's destructive force on nature, the Anthropocene rests on a white possessive (recall Moreton-Robinson) concept of geology. Yusoff analyzes geology's "modes of inscription and circulation as a doubling of the notion of property."[81] Not only does the Anthropocene, therefore, rest on actual geologic transformations wrought by the institution of capitalist regimes of accumulation, but its "grammar," which Yusoff tracks, is also "the work of *geology* in the world," and as such the reinscription of capital's accumulative and possessive functions.[82]

Vergès and Yusoff reflect a position shared by Axelle Karera, who argues that broad anthropogenic narratives erase "racial antagonisms" by putting forward an ethics of grievability based on a concept of political relationality for human subjects predicated on anti-black violence as essential to the very realization of the human as a subject of rights.[83] To recall Sylvia Wynter's critique of Marx (see the introduction to this book), the Anthropocene names the problem of the erosion of nature but not its *function*: us. Thus, the Anthropocene, as elaborated in Yusoff's critique, is not necessarily an awakening to human suffering, but yet another neo-Darwinian mechanism extending the differences of the human same and the infra/human other, and relying on the labour-work dialectic and its Conversion processes to function.[84] Geology itself, if we accept Yusoff's arguments about its function to make distinctions among and to reposition matter, cannot emerge without the actual process of Conversion that facilitates the remaking of blacks and Indigenous Peoples into *kinds* of matter. Moreover, it threatens to overwrite or incorporate dissident forms of critique like Yusoff's and to reincorporate the parallel of *labour* that I recover from *work*.

Collectively, each of the subsequent ways of naming the epoch—Capitalocene, Plantationocene, Necrocene, and Chthulucene—seeks to make an intervention, all suggesting that what is at stake is not only the earth itself, but how we talk about what is happening to it, so all seek to reorient us epistemologically. However, each is founded in one kind of narcissism: that of man (Capitalocene and Plantationocene) or of man's things (Necrocene and Chthulucene). I refer to it as narcissism because all are object-oriented, whether that object is a system, 75 million acres, or a way of thinking. Even where the Chthulucene seeks to have us know ourselves differently in relation to the earth, as "compost," for instance, its narcissism remains global, structured by man's way of apprehending the earth without announcing the conceit of its genre-specific mode of knowledge production, and these terms, within that genre, emerge from the most privileged man of all: western, First World man.[85] Thus, while these approaches reject the Anthropocene, they are still elaborated through its central, homuncular narcissisms.

Second, all in some way rely on Indigenous extinction and on slavery's extinction. Each references native death without noting native repopulation or land claims. Extinction thus works as the denial of sovereignty on an imminently apocalyptic, deterritorialized earth where no sovereignties exist other than that of man's things. With regard to slavery, extinction is indexed together with native genocide in a kind of pastness. Although Donna J. Haraway's Chthulucene seeks a positive (rather than eliminatory) account of indigeneity as "continuing" in the Chthulucene (in a footnote), Indigenous Peoples are indexed early in her essay together with blacks in a reference to "plantations, indigenous genocide, and slavery."[86] Haraway thus reads and inscribes the Conversion of Indigenous Peoples and Blacks as a *condition of possibility* for the Chthulucene to emerge as a kind of recovery of their lost lives and labours. Death and Elimination, slave making and "savage" making, are anterior events for Haraway, so the Chthulucene does not have to grapple with the always *now* of anti-black and anti-native violence and death as the collective condition of possibility for what Karera sees as an ignorant vitalism.[87]

The Capitalocene, in particular, remains integrative of *all* bodily actions in their Conversion in Moore's elaboration of "unpaid work" as a critical part of the "four cheaps" that for him comprise capital as the "web of life": labour power, food, energy, and raw materials. The Capitalocene thus iterates the collapse of work and labour. The Plantationocene does try to capture what is left out of nature's white Anthropogenic account, but it mobilizes race in terms of capital, rather than anti-blackness and anti-indigeneity as the actual forces behind the plantation. Anti-blackness and anti-indigeneity as central processes to both capital and the production of the human are thus literally capitalized (i.e., a delayed or deferred expense of capital's emergence), reduced to structures they exceed. Race as structure—rather than ontology—becomes the optic for capital's emergence, and the plantation resurfaces again, embedded within the history of capital's development as a machine of accumulation and difference. Even the "counter-plantation" necessarily indexes the former as a way of knowing the planetary.

Finally, all remain committed to statistical and hence bounded representations of time and space as they reinforce the accumulation of wealth. All remain epochal ways of knowing that conflict with what I see as a counter way of apprehending the earth in smaller units of knowing and being: the relationality of both sovereign earth and skins as states that move across black and native experiences. Haraway's plea to "make kin not babies" is a solution from the *outside* perspective to Indigenous, Maroon, and other non-western ways of already existing populations that have undergone Death/death and extinction and face low life expectancies, as well as modes of dispossession that make possible Haraway's own middle-class turn to kinship as a *post*-biological concept.[88] It is also fundamentally from an perspective outside black existence, especially when blacks' infant mortality rate is reportedly higher now than at the end of slavery.[89] In essentially, as Jenny Turner intimates, recovering extinction as a planetary good, it is thus not "*outside*" the Anthropocene's "order-specific mode of rationality," as Sylvia Wynter would posit.[90] Moreover, it seeks to reinscribe what might constitute true outside perspectives as its internal own in another extension of the Anthropocene's white possessive logics. In short, the Anthropocene and its elaborations are structurally premised, and hence must bring forward, black and native Death/death because they are still modes of human inscription.

In contrast to the epochal approach of periodized "cenes" and epistemological objects, another body of work centers indigeneity in anticapitalist critique, resisting incorporation by the grand narrative of capital and by the left, and is in dialogue with the openings to indigeneity that I sketch in the radical tradition. One of the most important is Glen Coulthard's rethinking of primitive accumulation for anticolonial, Indigenous left politics. Coulthard emphasizes "indigenous land-based direct action" situated within a broader anticapitalist, political orientation for native struggle determined not by pure capitalist critique but by (settler) colonialism, and the fact that violent and strategic forms of "primitive accumulation" are still ongoing for Indigenous Peoples in Indigenous land dispossession.[91] Coulthard shifts the emphasis in primitive accumulation from black bodies to Indigenous lands, suggesting that the dispossession of Indigenous bodies from lands is foundational. Primitive accumulation is ongoing because it is the only way the land can function as a sovereign space for the settler. The settler thus has to enact sovereignty through native dispossession as a condition of possessive being in relation to the land via the state's legal and military apparatus. Coulthard says in a *Jacobin* interview,

> I ... reconstruct primitive accumulation in a way that I think is actually true to its original form, ... see[ing] dispossession as an ongoing constitutive feature of the social relations of capital but also, in our

case, of colonialism, particularly in settler-colonial states like Canada. . . . I . . . elevate dispossession . . . as an ongoing feature of the reproduction of colonial and capitalist social relations in our present. If we base our understanding of originary dispossession from an indigenous standpoint, it's the theft not only of the material of land itself, but also a destruction of the social relationships that existed prior to capitalism violently sedimenting itself on indigenous territories.[92]

I want to return to primitive accumulation (chapter 1) and Elimination (chapters 3 and 4) to read Coulthard's engagement with the former and suggest that he provides a way of approaching black and Indigenous struggle together, up to a point. Moreover, while this point may seem to delink black and native struggle, we can use it to think together racial capital (iterated here as skins) and grounded normativity, as a partial mode of left practice.

As I do in this book, Coulthard foregrounds colonial dispossession not simply as land theft, but critically as a disruption of an ongoing *labour* relationship. The "social relationships" he sees as disrupted by dispossession are actually labour relationships, in which nature is transformed into engaged land (not in an objective sense under proto-capitalism) through native peoples' cosmogonically charted actions. He also critically repositions the time of primitive accumulation as an original moment and continuing practice that are both violent and thus keenly effected through forms of Elimination. For instance, in the *Jacobin* interview, he says that he wished he had made "clearer" that Indigenous dispossession or primitive accumulation is still in fact violent, even where it seems to be enacted at the level of ameliorative legal and economic systems.[93]

However, I want to suggest that, to the extent that violent Elimination is an ongoing practice of primitive accumulation that disturbs extant land relationships, it still happens not singularly for Indigenous peoples but also for blacks. Blacks, often associated with primitive accumulation as coerced labour in the past, are still subject to forms of violent *dispossession* that seek to prevent their rerooting in ways that are radically different from state-sanctioned modes of settler rooting. Here we can consider water (Hurricanes Katrina, Harvey, Irma, Maria, etc.), lack of wealth accumulation, state-sponsored violence, and worse health outcomes across generations, together with blacks' greater statistical deaths in the COVID-19 pandemic.[94] Thus, the anticolonial orientation of Coulthard's anticapitalism is a bridge to black left's anticapitalist critique, which emerged together with anticolonial struggle, although that struggle has engaged indigeneity only at certain moments. The limit, however, of Coulthard's work is precisely where his anticapitalist reading leads to a Fanonian rejection of Recognition, understood as a colonial extension of primitive accumulation by the settler state.[95]

In refusing *political* Recognition as the horizon of native sovereignty, Coulthard puts in place "grounded normativity," which comes out of a critical placedness serving as the locus of belonging and resistance. In a cowritten response to the 2015 American Studies Association (ASA) presidential address by David Roediger, Coulthard and Leanne Betasamosake Simpson outline grounded normativity as "the ethical frameworks provided by these Indigenous place-based practices and associated forms of knowledge." "Our relationship to the land itself," they add, "generates the processes, practices, and knowledges that inform our political systems, and through which we practice solidarity."[96] Here and in *Red Skins, White Masks*, Coulthard reaffirms a commitment to "Indigenous claims to self-determination *grounded* and informed by our attachments to land and sovereignty."[97] "The biopolitics of settler-colonial recognition" will always result in implicit recognition of the settler state's power. This is the problem Coulthard finds with claims for land recognition, particularly where recognition is the state's strategy to essentially "co-opt" native struggles.[98] He sees grounded normativity as a position in line with Fanonian refusal of colonial recognition, agreeing with Fanon that the colonizer's recognition of the colonized is inherently limited. He writes that for Fanon, "Recognition is not posited as a source of freedom and dignity for the colonized, but rather as the field of power through which colonial relations are produced and maintained." He summarizes "Fanon's critique of colonial recognition politics" thus: "when delegated exchanges of recognition occur in real world contexts of domination the terms of accommodation usually end up being determined by and in the interests of the hegemonic partner in the relationship. This is the structural problem of colonial recognition identified by Fanon in *Black Skin, White Masks*."[99] The limits of Fanon for Coulthard are the fact that Fanon's stretching of Marx does not fully apply to his method, where he still sees a stilted materialist dialectic privileging the evolution of class and class consciousness through a rejection or superseding of the past.[100] Fanon, for Coulthard, is still too heavily invested in capitalist, class struggle (over culture as praxis) as the agent of social change.

Coulthard rejects the anti-indigeneity of such dialectical progression, where it seems the native must be transcended by the worker or *as a* worker engaged in class struggle. Instead, in *Red Skins, White Masks* he argues for a "place-based foundation of Indigenous decolonial thought."[101] This grounded normativity, rooted in past and ongoing relationships and ways of being that should not be transcended but reenchanted, is a kind of critical, epistemological placedness that Coulthard sees as opposed to forms of state-sponsored "recognition" that undercut Indigenous sovereignty.[102] More crucially, Coulthard essentially suggests that we cannot simply translate Indigenous anticapitalism or see it in terms of extant left or socialist strands because they disappear the native. On the one hand, we can see this as Coulthard's rejection of the category of the worker as an abstract, world-historical figure (premised on anti-blackness and here anti-indigeneity). On the other, as with the discussion of Rodney, we can see this as a rupture of the category itself in order to make it represent indigeneity as that which, because of the praxis of grounded normativity, will always exceed the worker.

For Coulthard, Fanon grounds a way of refusing colonial modes of recognition precisely because black racialization forces Fanon to engage with the category of the worker on different terms (stretching). Even where Fanon mobilizes a materialist dialectic that is anti-Indigenous, his confrontation with anti-blackness itself—by elaborating the politics of refusal and recognition and the need for self-recognition—makes his work useful for Coulthard. Reading Fanon via Jean-Paul Sartre, Coulthard affirms where Fanon sees Indigenous cultural elements as essential to decolonial struggle, but—and this is where Fanon's materialism limits him—writes that "he was decidedly less willing to explore the role that these forms and practices might play in the construction of *alternatives* to the oppressive social relations that produce colonized subjects in the first place."[103] He sees Fanon in his "early" work as subscribing to the Sartrean idea that "the moment when the black consciousness comes to fruition and affirms its work as such, it must immediately seek to abolish itself as a form of individual/collective identifications."[104] Material class struggle must here triumph over any racialism or racial identification, which, as an essentialism, can only be a stage. Moreover, any racialism is an overdetermining of colonized subjects. This is a particular limitation of Fanon, for whom this racial essentialism of self-recognition must always be in the past: "by the time we reach Fanon's conclusion in *Black Skin, White Masks*," Coulthard writes, "it is clear that the cluster of practices associated with self-recognition are valuable only insofar as they reestablish the colonized as historical protagonists oriented toward a change in the colonial social structure."[105] He adds that Fanon's "work tends to treat 'the cultural' in a manner inappropriately similar to how Marxists treat the category of 'class': as a transitional form of identification that subaltern groups must struggle to overcome as soon as they become conscious of its existence as a distinct category of identification."[106] In contrast, while he utilizes Fanon to point out the trap of recognition as a form of sociogenic masking or Elimination of indigeneity, Coulthard finds Fanon useful only up to a point in his attempt to situate Indigenous forms of refusal in terms of resurgence rather than rejection of culture.

I quote extensively from Coulthard because the ontological relationship in Fanon substitutes for the political relationship in Coulthard. I am not saying that there is no such relation. My point is that Coulthard articulates the zone of "non-being"—that "native declivity" that is ontostructural to blackness as "nothingness" (in the Afropessimist reading of Fanon)—to explain why political recognition is a dead end for Indigenous Peoples, for whom the land is not *only* the flesh (recall my earlier reference to skin as land for blacks). Coulthard reads Fanon, in other words, in terms of *a conversion for* Indigenous struggle, rather than in the terms of the specificity of the Fanonian critique. Coulthard foregrounds the phenomenological as structural, but it is the ontological that is the structural closure in Fanon, or which makes material structures foreclose black representation. The phenomenological world is the structural expressions of anti-blackness.

Fanon is keenly aware that the native exists in tension with the negro. On the one hand, the negro is not the native (in Algeria), but in Fanon, the native (in the Caribbean) is the negro, and both these identities are held in tension across his theorization of ontological lack for blacks and natives in the colonial Francophone world. They are held in tension in such a way that, although they seem to reinstitute the break between the ontological (as lack in *Black Skin, White Masks*) and the material (as landedness in *The Wretched of the Earth*, or as cartography for Wilderson), they are relationally understood, especially in Algeria where anti-blackness was driven both by French colonialism *and* by native, Algerian identity as not black. While the native seeks political recognition first and foremost for land and well-being on land, blacks (in the context of the larger Algerian Revolution) did not seek liberation alone, but also an ontological affirmation that would move them from nothingness to maybe a kind of resonant "thingliness."[107] Moreover, that liberation in the form of the nation-states that blacks fought for in the Algerian context is a native state, but Fanon's is also a generalized attempt to think the condition of blackness under coloniality, so it extends to *all* colonized blacks, be they natives or Creoles, whether they can fight for rights only within (such as civil rights) the settler/settled state as the United States or Canada, or for rights outright, as in postcolonial Algeria and independent African and Caribbean countries. Moreover, to the extent that Fanon articulates the ontological foreclosures for all blacks, he is acutely aware that the black functions as the Elimination of the native. What Coulthard reads as a rejection of culture is, rather, a representation of this antagonism for blackness.

Coulthard is right that Indigenous Peoples' anticolonial struggles are most often disappeared in the anticolonial tradition, which is more readily identified with black left, anticolonial thinkers. This, of course, is the very problem in the radical tradition that *Beyond Constraint* addresses more broadly. What Coulthard misses, however, in seeking to correct this elision, is the very condition of Fanonian "skins" and the function of black flesh to signal terra in its absence, and that ontological/cosmogonic grounding that is not lost in the exchange of skin for land. As I have argued in *Creole Indigeneity*, our skin, because of slavery and racialization, is the land to which we belong and which is constantly being written over, negotiated through, and fought for against the settler state. Fanon's native, as black, is both housed and unhoused. Not only does Fanon recognize this, but his confrontation with it is precisely what leads him to culture as the limit point for liberation. This is also the invigoration of the Wynterian pause as critique. The native as black for Fanon is always subject to reinvention that cannot singularly be housed in the land and past practices. However, in rejecting Fanon's seeming break with culture as the ontological limit for blackness, as the limit of Indigenous place-based refusal, Coulthard sets aside the very core of Fanonian critique and his engagement with black Death. Thus, Coulthard inadvertently resurrects anti-blackness as the ground for Indigenous engagement with black anticolonial thought precisely because he needs to oppose land to skins and read Fanon, as he does at the end of *Black Skin, White Masks*, as dialectical in a particularly narrow Hegelian cum Sartrean way, when in fact Fanon may be proposing a grammar of negation built around the repetition of "I am" and "I am not" at the end of the text.

This is Fanon's confrontation with the lack of "ontological resistance" and his recognition of ontology as structure. It is also the *grounding* of black struggle in the recognition of the Death of blacks, which must be accounted for in any praxis of liberation. It is Fanon's extension of the dialectical method (which also undergirds Robinson's work) in the service of black freedom. Moreover, while this freedom might have concrete material moments (as in the outcomes of struggle in *The Wretched of the Earth*), it is also this endless push and exercise of negation and affirmation. What Coulthard also closes off for blacks is a painful reality that Fanon on some level anticipates and that remains an opening to indigeneity across Fanon's works: for blacks to truly respect Indigenous sovereignty, we would need to give up those lands on which settler colonialism's "incidental" work has left us, and return *only* to the land of our skins and sovereignties hewn and won there. Thus, blacks must undergo two kinds of refusal, ontological and material, the latter being the refusal of land as a product of *work*. This double refusal remains at stake and is our possibility for engagement with each other. When blacks position Indigenous Peoples in the past of their forward motion as the Other/worker, and Indigenous Peoples rescript black flesh for recovery of past and landed sovereignties without acknowledging that time and place are always the limit of black freedom and at the same time that this is the only possibility for "black sovereignty" (see below), we both accept the epistemological structures of anti-blackness and anti-indigeneity.

Despite the limitation of Coulthard's work, however, to truly acknowledge how Death mediates refusal in Fanon, both his and Fanon's work present the alternative terrains of place/dness and skins, respectively, as smaller units of relation to earth, space, and time for which neither the Anthropocene nor its criticisms account. None of the critiques foregrounds or articulates sovereignty or the disalienation (refusal) necessary for achieving these sovereignties. Moreover, Coulthard's routing of Indigenous refusal through the terrain of black flesh, of unhoused skins, profoundly links black and Indigenous struggles, pointing to how both sovereignties can be affirmed with each other. I suggest that we need to stretch both Fanon *and* Coulthard into greater relation in order to effect a collective terrain of refusal, rather than pit land-based claims against claims that are literally unbound and unhoused, except reflexively. We need to find ways to situate skins as a true middle/passage encounter rather than just another moment where our meeting and divergence are overdetermined by the logics of anti-blackness and anti-indigeneity.

At present, the black radical tradition in its extension under racial capital newly insists on Fanonian skins, linking up with discussions on flesh and fleshliness as they are captured by the meter/measure of race. This is evident in Afropessimism and engagements with it that foreground black bodies' plasticity, particularly by Tiffany Lethabo King, Kathryn Yusoff, and Zakiyyah Iman Jackson. We can argue that racial capital and the insistence on the body are collectively the praxis of Fanonian skins. My concern here is what it means for this critique to become newly situated under epochal approaches to capital/man/things, or to be translated for other struggles. What does it mean for these discourses of skins and grounded relationality to be entangled with concepts of the earth as either *man*made or *man* thought? What foreclosures renew around concepts of labour? The skins that constitute racial capital represent a tense, problematic, nearly untenable relation to capital. On the one hand, skins suggest the need for a new accountability, but precisely because of those skins' difference, any kind of representation/reparations that hinges on capital is the limit for blacks in their infra-representation as nothing in the Afropessimist articulation (see chapter 1). As both Afropessimists and black optimists remind us, true political subjecthood is foreclosed for blacks by the very history of capitalist development, which positions black bodies on the extractive side of capital's accumulative regimes.

Futures of Black Radicalism, the work dedicated to extending Cedric Robinson's anticapitalist critique, has the potential, as I see it, to create more openings, to foreground skins in the radical tradition over the closures of structure without losing sight of anticapitalist critique as also an *ante-capitalist* one, as Robinson's emphasis on culture demands. The essays pursue "abolitionism" and "freedom," but not as some kind of terminus (time) or space (place).[108] Instead, through a refusal that actually links up with the Wynterian critique of Marxism that we consistently leave out of the radical tradition, they seek to bear out Robinson's conviction that one critical difference between black Marxism and Marxism proper is that the former "is about a kind of resistance that does not promise triumph or victory at the end, only liberation."[109] For the editors, it is precisely Robinson's "dialectical thinking" that allows him to suggest that the black radical tradition's orientation is an open-ended struggle *as* freedom, as the possibility for what Robinson seeks recourse to DuBois for: "black sovereignty."[110]

However, in this quest, we still need to radically reject the time of capital that creeps back into our analysis, overdetermining its orientation. For example, in Françoise Vergès's challenge to the Anthropocene, what is a critical, effective redress nonetheless accepts the premise of the Anthropogenic narrative: "to unpack the different levels of racialized environment we need to go back [to] the long sixteenth century, the era of western 'discoveries,' of the first colonial empires, of genocides, of the slave trade and slavery, the modern world mobilized the work of commodified human beings and uncommodified extra-human nature in order to advance labour productivity within commodity production."[111] Here, Jason Moore's dating of the Capitalocene is accepted for dating the racial Capitalocene as a corrective to the Anthropocene. While the racialized mode of production within capitalist society has indeed produced environmental catastrophe, this starting point reinforces the labour-work divide as a structure of anticapitalist critique, reinstituting the land-labour division ("work of commodified human beings" vs. "extra-human nature").

However, Robinson's work says that we should start not here, but with what literally exceeds these "cenes": culture and relationships to nature, which are in fact *labour* relationships, not *work*. The liberation of skins and place that the black radical tradition and grounded relationality seek are not epochal ways of knowing and being. They must work to continuously resist the epoch and its modes of reinforcing anti-blackness and anti-indigeneity *as* our absolute difference. Whether we elaborate skins' sovereignty (as a future past in a present labour) in terms of a Fanonian or Robinsonian dialectical method, or Rodney's socialism, in terms of ontology's limit or the possibility of culture and action, they are like grounded relationality in both their ante- and anticapitalist orientation, and this must be sustained in order to *resist* the reinscription of black left critique as singularly anticapitalist, and therefore as fully anticipated within and satisfied by material struggle. We need to sustain the critical practice and being of unbounded, resistant, or supervened skins (blacks) as a kind of grounded relation, and to sustain the latter as the praxis of *occurring* or grounded labour (Indigenous Peoples) without losing sight of how these groundings are phenomenologically different. To do this, we need not only to work to elaborate our own individual subordinations but to imagine ways in which our struggles are open to each other.

Conclusion

In its general argument that Wynter should be included in the radical tradition, this chapter has focused on her explorations of scarcity, the land-labour dialectic and primitive accumulation, and black resistance. First, I argued that she has an original account of scarcity's emergence as a political-economic category. Second, I demonstrated that her account of primitive accumulation resists the split between black labour and native land and centers native labour. Third, I argued that her account of black resistance forces a rethinking of black Death. Collectively, Wynter's critique of capitalist political economy makes hers a singular voice in the black radical tradition because she goes beyond just emphasizing the "categorical" and "liminal," and actually restores key formulations to the tradition of Marxist critique and the radical tradition in the Caribbean. Most important is her centering of indigeneity as a relation between black and native peoples that she restores to an account of labour history in the region, while simultaneously accounting for those very labours of self-making that Cedric Robinson suggests are so important to the tradition. Despite Wynter's understanding of the critical ways in which the material substrate impacts the sociocultural and political, her belief that "the superstructure was not automatically determined by the mode of production" and that material social change is thus not singularly dependent on bread, rather than culture or spirit, means that not only does she not singularly subordinate the material to the ontological/cultural, but she also understands the latter as an elaboration or expression of the former.[112] It is also a Fanonian perspective (see the introduction to this book), which actually gets to the heart of why Marxism cannot be the main framework for liberation. We miss this dimension of her work when we see her as singularly concerned with discourse or poetics, rather than material analysis. The chapter then argued that scholarship that has focused (since the early 2000s) on periodizing the epoch risks foreclosing these alternate readings by inscribing them again within the big time of humanism of capital, of man and man's things, that they were initially meant to both intervene in (as alternative accounts of bound labour's role in global, capitalist development) and from which they always represent a difference. The chapter argued that the very ways in which the black and Indigenous radical traditions remain methodologically open to each other are precisely those in which we collectively resist the reinscription of the big time of capital's master narrative in all of its real and discursively seductive forms.

I close by returning to the place I began, looking at how gender for Wynter informs a larger critique of capitalist formation because this is where she foregrounds labour and a mode of nondeterministic liberation tied to black-native self-making. In the Jonkonnu essay, she notes, "The guilds of Africa now became the tribal groups in Jamaica. Later on they came to represent crafts and trades. The common features are there: The animal masks, the male and female Connus, respond to the Egungun claim that in performing the Egungun play they have the power to metamorphose themselves into animals and to change their sex."[113] She never returns to this small point in the essay. She instead details the kinds of masks and how they link creolization to indigenizing practices. However, in this point about the masks, we glimpse an elaboration of native identity (as a relation to but still not Creole identity) that is noncartographic (i.e., indexes not land but only a geography that is the labour of the space of the dance) and a relationship to the animal that is not dependent on a concept of the nonhuman or infrahuman. The animal *as* mask or sign and the body as animal but *not* sign exist outside black infrahuman status.

Moreover, the black woman's unthought gender that becomes her hypersex (Spillers) and the black man's hypermasculinity that becomes his animality are distinct from this performance of animal, which provides the ability to change sex. This sex change is thus not from male to female or female to male in a physiognomic sense; it is not based on the western anatomical model. I suggest that this is the possibility (and threat) of nonaccumulative black labours. There is something in black indigeneity, in black *labour* that not only troubles cartography (as a break between black and native identities in Afropessimism) through its insistence on labour, but that can also literally change us and our sex: move us away from sex/gender and race as the limit of our representation. Thus, I suggest we also reread black radical critiques of black women's labour as essential to critiques of capital. If, for instance, we return to Claudia Jones through Wynter, we can reread her explanation of the labour exploitation of black women domestic workers.

Domestic work is fundamentally based on the presumption of normative sex-gender reproduction and whites' ability to attain middle-class status. Thus, Jones illuminates black women's work to ensure the stable reproduction not just of middle-class domesticity but of the very system of sex/gender that marks the human as distinct from the black/native. However, the nonrepresentative quality or invisibility of black women's labour that Jones tracks is in fact where that *labour* refuses and exceeds the sex/gender system and feminist critique, the capitalist class system and Marxian modes of critique and resistance that cannot move beyond the consolidation of the black woman as the outside or liminal marker for inclusion, nor be reconciled with it. Black labour has this endless capacity to mask and reroot in a space and time/rhythm that is not that of the slave driver or task master. This capacity is preserved in and through black Death as the excess that cannot be reconciled in the Conversion process to the mechanisms of artificial scarcity. In her account of black *work* in terms of its immediate and antecedent world-historical conditions and structures, Wynter preserves native and indigenizing *labours* as those that need to be reconciled with the extant account of labour in the radical tradition. She also demonstrates that narrow material readings always need to be invigorated by attention to both poesies and poetics, which are not automatically inattentive to material structures.

Finally, in locating a practice of resistance in and through black Death, Wynter offers a parallel of Death: the immanence of black and indigenous labours that we saw preserved with C. L. R. James. In this refusal of sex/gender and recovery of a native mode of resistance that is also the work of death we can locate not Wynter's pessimism, but the *optimism* of her anticapitalist critique. Possibility and optimism emerge from those like her working in the tradition of Fanonian skins, demonstrating how nature, the geological, and the animal are based on the specific way in which the human/nonhuman is produced and sustained—not, I argue, in their exclusion, but in their relation. This chapter both relied on and at moments refused Afropessimism by suggesting that "relation" is indeed possible between blacks and Indigenous peoples.[114] Moreover, what threatens our understanding of this relation is precisely that new ways of epochal thinking reinscribe the labour-work dialectic on which our divisions are premised.

In critiquing the Anthropocene's conceptual limits, Yusoff quotes Césaire's spectacular, well-known line about blacks being "walking compost" to underscore her point about geology's racialization.[115] I recall it here to foreground how an urgent emphasis on skins forces us to reframe it. It is not only walking compost (recall Nikhil Pal Singh's cheap blackness, discussed in chapter 4) but walking houses (Fanonian skins). It is the skin as blacks' housing (and unhousing) that we can recover, and more ethically locate and articulate the material place of these skins on Indigenous lands, recognizing the latter's own urgent practices of grounded *normativity* or sovereign labour. To this the radical tradition must remain open going forward as it works through capital's material *and* ontological violences. *Beyond Constraint*'s next and final part shifts away from the material and historicist tradition to address representation and desire as scenes or modes of control informing the material.

PART III

Rights *and* Representations

6. WORK AS METAPHOR, LABOUR AS METONYMY

Resisting Hieroglyphs

The preceding part reread the black radical tradition for openings to indigeneity, suggesting that while we could begin to recover Indigenous labour from its conversion in the labour-work dialectic (see part I), we also needed to "stretch" existing historiography. This stretching opens the radical tradition to new readings linking blacks' labour with that of Indigenous Peoples in ways that renew the tradition's anti- and ante-colonial, as well as anticapitalist, dimensions. While parts I and II have, respectively, diagnosed a terminological and hence methodological limit within labour analysis and elaborated and applied a method for reading labour history in the radical tradition against the closures to indigeneity, this part, "Rights and Representations," shifts the focus to address *re-presentation* more formally as both the possibility of and limitation for strategies of including Indigenous labour in the radical tradition.

Across all chapters, *Beyond Constraint* deals with representation: the preposition and the labour-work dialectic are at base processes or strategies that use representation to control sovereign labours that threaten settler and involuntary settler forms of independence. Conversion, as a strategy of control and dominance, is a method of establishing relationships of kind and time where there are none. It allows for the deployment of metaphor or similitude as the scene of control of potentially sovereign labour. While representation may seem to be, literally, an immaterial process, it is a strategic way of preventing or circumventing the sovereign *occurrence* of Indigenous labour. If we recall that labour is the *occurrence* of sovereignty (see chapter 3), Conversion deploys similitude as a tactic of representation that restricts Indigenous sovereignty by converting Indigenous labour in the dialectic and changing the time of the occurrence of those labours so they happen not epiphenomenally for Indigenous Peoples, but within settler control *for* settler sovereignty.

Metaphoric simulation is essential for transforming Indigenous sovereignty *into* rights that the postcolonial state can grant or withhold. In the postcolonial state, the *legal* and the *constitutional* are positioned, respectively, as the terrain of *labour* and the terrain of *work* that together reinvigorate the dialectic to manage indigeneity's translation into rights that the postcolonial state can manage. This difference is exemplified in Guyana's legal and constitutional documents. The following examples are from the 2006 Amerindian Act and from Guyana's Constitution:

> An ACT to provide for the recognition and protection of the collective rights of Amerindian Villages and Communities, the granting of land to Amerindian Villages and Communities and the promotion of good governance within Amerindian Villages and Communities.[1]

> Sovereignty belongs to the people, who exercise it through their representatives and the democratic organs established by or under this Constitution.[2]

The Act exists *distinctly* from Guyana's Constitution, which in fact authorizes the Act, existing as a provisional granting of power that the Act cannot supersede. It effectively *reproduces* Indigenous sovereignty within or through forms of postcolonial right that can therefore manage it. The Act is an integrative mechanism that maintains Indigenous labour in its difference (and hence comparison to) from work and through its failure to produce sovereignties based on accumulation but instead based on protection where the latter is literally the failure of native labour. Thus, in the Act, Indigenous sovereignty is the surplus of work rather than what it really is: work's negation and hence the negation of Independence derived out of the condition of coloniality. The Constitution, in contrast, allows for "democratic" representation to supersede "protection." As the mechanism of full enfranchisement for Creole citizens, the Constitution codifies accumulative work as a sovereign patrimony. The law, in these examples, translates the terms of pre-contact Indigenous sovereignties into those of post-contact, rights-based postcolonial governmentality. It is also the specific way in which the state uses biopolitics to control Indigenous labour as that which makes their sovereignty in the land *occur* for them. The law is then the point at which representation or simulation allows for the control and management of Indigenous labour as an ongoing threat to the moment of Independence (and hence conquest) on which the postcolonial state is based.

Documents like the Act effectively suture the gap between Indigenous bodies and lands as threat or excess to the state, recognizing indigeneity as *ante*-colonial and cosmogonically charted while simultaneously representing Indigenous Peoples in terms of a post-contact, secular, biological life that can be governed as a state-defined, politico-juridical body. It is the legal substitution of a space of excess at the limit of postcolonial state sovereignty for a space that can be governed, and thus erodes the real *truth* of a territory and people who presumably do not have their origin in the colonial state and the Atlantic crossings that helped generate it as such.[3] In re-presenting Indigenous Peoples as governable bodies and thus controlling Indigenous lives, the Act reflects how the state makes all lives—and all death—manageable, revealing that the management of Indigenous life necessarily includes the management of Indigenous death.

The Act is part of a broader structure of governmentality—biopolitics— that achieves the management of Indigenous Peoples. Just as state constitutions regulate the actual *lives* of their subject populations, so does the Act. It reproduces Indigenous space as *always within* the state's bounds. As a mechanism or "how" of power, the Act constitutes a point of symbolic and material application that is Indigenous lands and in effect achieves a "where" of power. In other words, the Act does not merely define Indigenous peoples and territory in order to govern them, but legally simulates or reproduces territory as a terrain that facilitates such governance. The Act, however, is insufficient by itself to achieve the governance of Indigenous Peoples; first, indigeneity, or the Indigenous body, had to be created as an *object* of power—the "what" of governance (i.e., that which can be governed)—within and for the postcolonial (rather than colonial) state. In short, since its point of application is both Indigenous bodies and lands, the Act defines who Indigenous peoples are in order to govern them, reproducing Indigenous space *as* governable. This objective reproduction of indigeneity for and inside the law, which enacts control of Indigenous Peoples spatially and materially, is precisely the point where the occurrence of Indigenous labour (as an expression and reinforcement of sovereignties that predate and coexist with and within the postcolonial state) is managed through processes of simulation. The law is thus not about controlling Indigenous sovereignty in the abstract, but concretely controlling Indigenous labour as its enactment. The law's biopolitics essentially makes Indigenous sovereignties available for the forms of recognition that Glen Coulthard refuses (see the introduction and chapter 5). Additionally, it is the absolute limit point of the middle/passage strategies of reading that I suggest need to be enacted, out of which new sovereignties can be supported beyond the antagonistic relation of anti-blackness and anti-indigeneity.

To achieve inscription in the postcolonial polis despite the structural deferral of being, blacks and later South Asians reimagined their bare life not as an internal exception, what I call an intimate or proximate exception, but as an external one in the Indigenous body. In other words, not only did they need to represent Indigenous lands as potentially colonizable to meet the demands of capitalist economic conscription/mimicry and labour's teleological ends. They also needed both to make the Indigenous body governable and representable within state law *and* to position that body as humanity's new limit/threshold within the state. Moreover, that body becomes the space/place of a disciplinary mode of regulation both necessary to and exceptional within the postcolonial state. Thus, it became necessary to initiate a new discursive relationship to the Indigenous by managing Indigenous culture *as* sign, like the transformation of Indigenous petroglyphs at Timehri, Guyana, into painted hieroglyphs gracing the nation's entrance at the airport, for instance. The substitution and erasure performed by the symbols *as* hieroglyphs function as a writing in which the non-biological, cosmogonically charted Indigenous body is inscribed within the realm of the political and their own bare life, of which the now transcended but recursive petroglyphs become a sign and can be both captured and excluded. Biopolitics as applied to Indigenous Peoples allows their bodies to be read via the logics of state citizenship, which means that as state citizens, their lands can be held in reserve for the state and their lives (tied to those lands) are subject to market needs. Moreover, attempts to develop their lands within the logic of the larger postcolonial state are a form of assimilation that, after Patrick Wolfe, we must view suspiciously as part of the logic of elimination. While I have previously argued that elimination cannot be the singular goal of this type of postcolonial state, it nonetheless manifests at particular moments to facilitate governance and the Creole population's well-being.

The hieroglyphic recasting of Indigenous pre-contact cultures and cultural symbols is a form of simulacrum that facilitates biopolitical modes of governing indigeneity in the postcolonial state. They are the literal mechanisms of Conversion necessary to conscript Indigenous labour within the law both for global capital and against its sovereign occurrence as a threat to the nation-state. When we see simulation (cultural appropriation and representation), we actually see the mechanisms of the labour-work dialectic. Reading for simulation is therefore a way of reading for (and against) the ongoing conversion of our labours. The remaking of Indigenous pre-contact symbols is the deployment of *metaphor* in a critical moment of biopolitical governance at work. It is the re-production of indigeneity, which facilitates the legal mechanisms of control (the Act) that recast Indigenous Peoples as the "bare life" of the Creole, postcolonial subject. It is a form of bare life that manages the particular way that racialized groups, even postcolonial ones, haunt the threshold of humanity as conceived by the West, demonstrating the continuing structural relationship of anti-blackness and anti-indigeneity. What I mark as the legal and the constitutional in the postcolonial state function together to enable the constant Conversions of indigeneity and blackness to their overall accumulative function in the dialectic. They thus sustain the antagonism of anti-blackness and anti-indigeneity as a feature of postcolonial governmentality, revealing how biopolitics—as the mode of governmentality under which the modern state operates—is in fact a general conscription of our human freedom to our racial subordination.

To produce more capacious radical labour histories or represent sovereignty at the end of Conversion, we must recognize and move away from the fundamentally conscriptive languages of our dominant discourses and reject simulation as the terrain of right. This chapter therefore asks: How can Indigenous labour be re-presented without reducing it to the forms of similitude (i.e., Conversion) produced by the labour-work dialectic and the interpretive strategies for reading it within capitalist political economy? How can we work from the point of Indigenous labour's absolute difference, as, for instance, Wilderson says we must work from the absolute difference of blackness as the compulsion of black Death, rather than from where we translate Indigenous sovereignties *for* our struggles? In approaching these questions, this chapter elaborates simulation (legal, cultural) as a larger semantic, unconscious drive or libidinal structure of incorporation essential to the institution of the labour-work dialectic and the grammatical and epistemological mechanisms of its deployment.[4] It explores how we might begin to approach Indigenous labour not just from the point of its over- and mis-representation within the symbolic, but from that at which its enactment and re-production resists its hieroglyphic simulation.

In *Creole Indigeneity* and elsewhere, I suggested that literature by Caribbean anti- and postcolonial writers (such as Rooplal Monar's short story "Bahadur") "doubled" the work of their enslaved and indentured ancestors.[5] This doubling works as a poetic unconscious in the literature, elaborating a labour episteme where brought-forward (i.e., discursively repeated) modern, colonial labour secures the postcolonial nation-state and its enfranchised, citizen-subject identities. The initial labour of the enslaved and indentured needed to first be deferred in time, then recaptured and hence brought forward, in order to function as the new time of Creole belonging. Thus, the region's literary and historical tradition is articulated by Caribbean writers who consolidate the necessary repetition of enslaved and indentured labour for Caribbean nationalisms. This doubling strategy, however, is at odds with how Indigenous pre-contact labour unfolds and extends geographically and temporally across the region. Thus, when this labour aesthetic is used to interpret Indigenous labour, it deliberately misreads it. Indigenous labour neither repeats nor relies on the writers' symbolic doubling of enslaved and indentured labour. Nonetheless, the constraint of doubling remains.

Both cultural discourse and the law use what can be identified as strategies of metaphor in order to make indigeneity re-presentable and affectable. Thus, the law as a terrain of the simulation of right is a structure of misrepresentation of Indigenous labour and sovereignty. Metaphor is not an individuated form of representation or appropriation, but part of an assemblage or dyad with metonymy. Together, metaphor and metonymy are the structures of labour's incorporation and conversion within political economy. They are the legal, political, cultural, and discursive strategies of incorporation that continuously renew the initial transformation or conversions of sovereign labours into their accumulative forms. However, although they function within capitalist political economy to renew the labour-work dialectic, they are structures generated *not* from within political economy itself but from a specific kind of unconscious drive or desire that the dialectic actually emerges to satisfy. In other words, they manage the desire that produces the master-settler political and economic orders in which we live. Moreover, as that which precedes and exceeds political economy, that desire is the externally validating element of capitalist political economy. Thus, I discuss them in this chapter in terms of both political economy and psychoanalysis.

Although metaphor and metonymy work *together* to achieve the acts of translation and re-presentation that make black labours and Indigenous sovereignties accessible for the postcolonial state, I posit metonymy not as the singular terrain for the conscription of labour but as the opposite of work. I use metaphor to designate forms of representation that allow for the kind of appropriations and transformations of right captured by documents like the Amerindian Act, which are tied to work and regimes of accumulation. In contrast, I use metonymy to indicate political-economic forms of representation for labour practices that can still contain native labour's fundamental irrepresentability within the labour-work dialectic. Metaphor designates a literal replacement or substitution of labours within the terrain of accumulation, while metonymy is a point of incomplete translation and excess of both bodily action and meaning. It is thus both a term of Conversion *and* a point at which a middle/passage reading for rupture can also be deployed.

Indigenous labour, if we are to represent it within analysis—being aware that such representation is already outside Indigenous Peoples' social and political structures—would better be elaborated or approached not from its full Conversion within the dialectic, but in terms of the points of contact or metonymy that also do the hard work of resistance. Relying on the poststructuralist elaboration of the difference between metaphor and metonymy, I read the latter as the point of sovereign Indigenous labour's difficult, resistant, incomplete incorporation into the labour-work dialectic. Metonymy is thus a point of partial, not absolute, control or management of Indigenous labour. In other words, although it works together with metaphor to manage the Conversion or incorporation of Indigenous labour for accumulation regimes, metonymy is also the only point of pressure and refusal available to us. By understanding how metonymy works to incorporate Indigenous labour precisely at its points of resistance, we can turn to it for the possibility of recovery. Thus, reading for it emerges as a middle/passage strategy of reading in which black work's excess (as we saw in part II) can be articulated *with* Indigenous labour's excess. This chapter is therefore not about simulacra as the ground of metaphor required to restrict Sovereignty, but about the coextensive practices of metonymy, difference, and contiguity that sustain it.

To elaborate both the unique and sovereign form of doubling that some contemporary Indigenous labour performs *and* how that labour is always already converted as a condition of our encounter with it, I begin by outlining one example of how Indigenous Peoples double their own sovereign labours. I discuss Indigenous use of technologies to map their lands, as well as the conscription of that labour (its Conversion or simulation) in the global environmental prize system. With specific emphasis on the Wapichan (or Wapishana) in Guyana, I articulate how mapping, as a *labour practice*, sits at odds with its forms of recognition within global, humanitarian efforts. Later, I elaborate the significance of misreading this work within global conservation or humanitarian efforts in terms of the poststructuralist distinction between metaphor and metonymy as a way of both seeing representation's limits and sustaining an unincorporated or nonsimulated view of Indigenous labour.

I explore the labour-work dialectic as a semiotic practice of desire that brings forward what I refer to throughout *Beyond Constraint* as the *conquistadorial habit*, a desire for the human that the dialectic originally emerged to satisfy. This desire emerged roughly in the mid-fifteenth century for a new mode of defining political subjectivity and social status that could not be characterized strictly by lineage (nobility) or redemption (clergy).[6] Its roots in earthly gain are apparent in Gomes Eanes de Azurara's *The Chronicle of the Discovery and Conquest of Guinea*, where they are tied to the acquisition of bodies (rather than nonhuman matter such as wealth and spices) when he notes that the sight of "houses ... full to overflowing of male and female slaves" prompted requests for licenses to obtain "Moorish captives" in the 1430s, the first from a squire seeking "honour and profit for himself."[7] Later, this habit is exemplified by Columbus's desire to receive a title for newly discovered lands and crystalized in his attempts to extract wealth from those lands and their inhabitants.

The conquistador is, of course, considered historically as a later figure than Columbus, commencing in the sixteenth century with soldiers cum explorers like Hernán Cortés. However, Columbus exemplifies the brutality and plunder characterizing conquistadors, which led to the institution of structures like the encomienda and (chattel) slavery that facilitated wealth extraction and early modes of accumulation that gave rise to European economies and social classes that Columbus and other lay peoples sought. This desire is shared by Las Casas who, while serving as a secular priest, was also an encomendero, and later, after entering the Dominican Order, owned enslaved blacks.[8] Columbus is in effect an *evolutionary* stage of the conquistador, and the desire initiated with him exists— until we can find a way to overcome it—as a literal *habit* in our political economic critique that will continuously repeat, reflect, and reinforce the division of labour structuring black and native lives and possibilities for both political sovereignties, and sovereignties of relation to each other.

Moreover, that desire is first for "native" bodies in Africa post-discovery and secondarily, by Columbus's time, for mineral and other nonhuman matter. In other words, while capitalist political economic critique focuses on the relationship between human exploitation and nonhuman matter, its accumulative structures are at least partially generated—even prior to chattel slavery—not from the conversion of "slaves . . . into gold," as Yusoff noted, but from the conversion of the native (constituted in Azurara's text through the slippage between negro and Moor—or infidel) into matter that will serve as the abstract form of wealth's potentiality.[9]

This consideration of the dialectic as a semiotic practice leads again to grammar (see the introduction to this book). By looking at the dialectic as the outcome of a form of conquistadorial desire that the language of political economy expresses and enacts, and which continually seeks to conscript Indigenous labour, as we saw with Rodney's work in chapter 3, we can understand the grammatical and temporal *pre-position* as both a conscious and unconscious practice. Moreover, since the dialectic as a mechanism of bodily conversion to matter and value is actually the product of this desire, the languages of critique for capital also simultaneously redeploy the epistemology of this desire that often remains unconscious in our work. This chapter thus uses poststructuralism and psychoanalysis to elaborate how this originary desire generates the oppositions that constrain Indigenous and black bodily actions and modes of representation.

I use psychoanalysis not to study race or identity but to uncover the forms of desire that force us to affirm simulation and accumulation in our work over and against incomplete, resistant forms of representation. If we understand how this impulse informs our representative languages for labour and the mechanisms of their active conscription or conversion of difference to its useful forms, we can develop strategies that resist simulation and its inherent refusal of sovereignty. We can also better approach Indigenous labour from the point at which it fails to be fully incorporated into, and hence partially refuses, the language of contemporary political economy.

Saving Latitudes

In 2017, the University of the West Indies at St. Augustine, Trinidad and Tobago, convened a conference titled "Indigenous Geographies and Caribbean Feminisms: Common Struggles against Global Capitalism." The conference, which brought together scholars and Indigenous and Maroon leaders and activists in the region, was critical in centering women's scholarship and organizing explicitly not just in the face of global capitalism, the singular legacy of franchise colonialism, or some world-historical category of feminism/feminist, but in terms of settler colonialism and different, perspectival relationships to it. Such a platform allowed for a reconciliation between Cristina Coc, Q'eqchi Maya co-spokesperson for the Maya Leaders Alliance, and the Garifuna women at the conference (see the introduction to this book), after decades of a painful antagonism of Maya and Garifuna struggles for sovereignty in Central America.[10]

In her presentation at the conference, Jean La Rose, Arawak/Lokono head of the Amerindian Peoples Association in Guyana and 2002 winner of the Goldman Environmental Prize, repeatedly told J. Sharon Atkinson, the Association's former president (Lokono), to "stand up," in recognition of the land tenure assessment and mapping work that was being done for an Indigenous mapping project in Guyana.[11] Atkinson's standing was striking both for her shy compliance and because she was called on to do so not by the conference organizers but by the head of this Indigenous-led and Indigenous-run advocacy organization. This and other moments at the 2017 conference, I argue, allow us to see where Indigenous representations, or reproductions, of their own actions exceed black political economic critique (chapter 3), the autopoiesis of the Anthropocene narrative (chapter 5), and the forms of postcolonial, nation-state appropriation of Indigenous culture. Specifically, it allows us to see the re-presentation of Indigenous labour, I suggest, on its own terms because La Rose's asking Atkinson to rise made visible at least three dimensions of Indigenous labour that exceed its Conversion for accumulation. First, as noted above, Atkinson represented her work at the conference not for the participants per se, but within Indigenous political structures of land rights advocacy. Second, Atkinson's standing can be understood as the doubling or re-presentation of her own, prior labour. Finally and most critically, Atkinson was asked to stand up for a mapping project that retraced and documented prior and continuous Indigenous land use.

To the extent that contemporary mapping projects are digital or symbolic doublings of the land, Atkinson's standing was the deferral and doubling of a doubling, the repetition of the symbolic as sovereign. Therefore, I argue that Indigenous Peoples' digital mapping work is actually the *doubling* of their *pre*-contact sovereign labours. This is true no matter where or how it is captured by development discourse, the global environmental prize system (which reflects a *return* to labour from within political economy rather than from Indigenous prior sovereignty), conferences, or any other means. It is thus a representation of Indigenous labour *outside* its Conversion in the labour-work dialectic, even though the language of development seeks to incorporate it and we can only read it *after* the imposition of the dialectic: after its Conversion to unproductive status as a renewal of the pre-positional relationship between native peoples and Creoles.

Indigenous mapping is thus a key site where extant political-economy (i.e., its representative language) breaks down because that language is based on a valorization of the division between productive/accumulative and unproductive/nonaccumulative actions, and Indigenous Peoples' labour in this instance exceeds its Conversion. Although mapping is the doubling of Indigenous labour within the sovereign (not postcolonial) terms of that labour, we translate the latter falsehood and ignore the former truth. Thus, any new method for political economy must consider where labour reaches a point of exhaustion, like the category of the worker under Rodney (chapter 4). This chapter thus explores Indigenous mapping as a sovereign *labour practice* that resists and breaks open labour representation at the very point of its conscription. Contemporary Indigenous mapping practices reveal the multilayered ways in which Indigenous labour in the Caribbean straddles (and supersedes) the labour-work divide and the land-labour divide, simultaneously resisting and renewing the radical tradition.

Scholars have critiqued geography as a colonial endeavor and located Indigenous mapping as a critical practice not confined to the visual map itself.[12] Discussing Indigenous cartography, Citizen Potawatomi cartographer Margaret Wickens Pearce and Hawaiian cartographer Renee Pualani Louis write that although digital mapping practices have been used since the 1970s to support "Indigenous self-determination," their basis in "Western cartographic language" often means that "Indigenous cultural knowledge" is "distorted, suppressed, and assimilated into the conventional Western map" because "cartographic language" is not objective but reflects perspectival, "ontological assumptions."[13] They argue, however, that while these problematic methods often eclipse Indigenous groups' "diverse" mapping practices, Indigenous Peoples can effectively use them to represent "traditional Indigenous cultural geographies."[14] Pearce and Louis's attention to mapping as both useful for and antagonistic to Indigenous practice makes their work important for situating a reading of Indigenous labour *for* its difference.

This chapter explores mapping as a site of redoubled Indigenous labour that reveals where it exceeds its antagonism to work and hence the possibility for singular representation in political economy. It posits that

Indigenous mapping practices are not the benevolent suture of the ancient and the modern, nor simply the outcome of how capitalist economies (through digital technology) based on the valorization of work meet and overdetermine Indigenous labour. Instead, mapping is the repetition of Indigenous Peoples' sovereign labour even where they do not yet possess land title. This is what the radical tradition needs to take as its starting point of engagement with Indigenous labour: its absolute *difference* from its Conversion.

The use of mapping technology by the Wapichan peoples of the (South and South Central) Rupununi–Region 9 in Guyana sits alongside a host of similar global efforts by other Indigenous and Maroon groups.[15] Other examples within the last decade from the Upper Amazonia (region of the Guiana Shield) and the Amazon River basin in South America include several Maroon groups in Suriname, and the Trio, Wyana, Suruí, and Cofán peoples. Popular discussions of mapping in South America share an overriding salvific narrative, in which technology has the predominant, agential function of working to "save" the environment and/or Indigenous Peoples. In 2016, a *National Geographic* blog by Mireya Mayor, an anthropologist and primatologist working with the Amazon Conservation Team reinvigorated the conquistadorial perspective for the First World observer on the "virtually unexplored jungles of Guyana," addressing some limitations of "the cutting-edge technology" that is "empowering local tribesmen to protect their forests."[16]

Collectively, such articles are object-oriented toward outcomes organized within a perspectival framework that sees these technologies as benevolent products of developed nations.[17] With an emphasis on benevolent outcomes, nowhere is there mention of mapping as a settler colonial technology used to first restrict and usurp Indigenous sovereign space (think Meriwether Lewis, William Clark, or Robert Schomburgk). Nor is there mention that increasing technologizing is an outcome and intensification of uneven wealth distribution in a global class system, nor how these technologies function in other ways to police and discipline populations, such as Israel's use of drones to surveil and attack Palestinians, their use by the United States to surveil protestors, or their use to surveil Haitians near the border with the Dominican Republic.[18] The technology not only has a redemptive function when it moves from the First to the Third World, but that move is its *own* redemption and delinking from the forms of militarism and capital accumulation that contextualize its production in the first place. This discrepancy between the overdeveloped North and underdeveloped South is a structuring element of the global, environmental prize system that rewards Indigenous efforts, including the Wapichan's, to "save" their communities and the environment more generally. These include international, regional, and country-specific prizes. The first category includes the Equator Prize (on which I focus), as well as the Goldman Environmental Prize, the prizes awarded by the UN Environment Programme, and the World Conservation Award, among many others.[19]

In 2015, the Equator Prize was awarded to nearly two dozen groups, including the South Central People's Development Association (SCPDA), a federation of Guyana's Wapichan communities. Awarded since 2002, the Prize is given by the Equator Initiative, a network comprising the "United Nations, governments, civil society, businesses and grassroots organizations" that is heavily supported by the government of Norway. Its stated goal is to "recognize" and support Indigenous sustainability efforts across the globe through a three-pronged strategy that includes the Prize.[20] In many ways, the Initiative responds to the environmental challenges faced by Indigenous communities and is a way for those communities to liaise with non-Indigenous governmental, legal, and policy "actors."[21] On the Equator Initiative website, one can click on an interactive Google Earth map showing prize winners' locations, which straddle, above and below, the 0 degree latitude line of the equator (see figure 6.1).[22] The Initiative also specifies which countries' geolocation makes them "eligible" to be considered for the prize.

The prize, both nominally and in terms of the spatiality of its awardees, brings home the equator's significance as a global position in both degree and time. Of significance is explorers'—including Columbus's—use of latitude (before the eighteenth-century development of accurate longitudinal measures) to navigate untraveled seas, map lands new to them, and understand newly encountered human populations.[23] While Columbus, for instance, used dead reckoning rather than celestial latitudinal navigation, his voyage was based on latitudinal calculation or speculation in order to travel westward around the globe to the same latitude as the "Indies."[24] The equator and the lands straddling it thus have a long speculative and conquistadorial history from Columbus to Mark Twain, Robert Louis Stevenson, Joseph Conrad, and books that focus on its role (and replicating the function of that role) in European exploration such as *Latitude Zero*.[25] As the line marking off the temperate from the torrid zones and thus the absolute difference of Europe's southern Others, the equator—as a navigational element and narrative structure—is critical in the evolution of race,

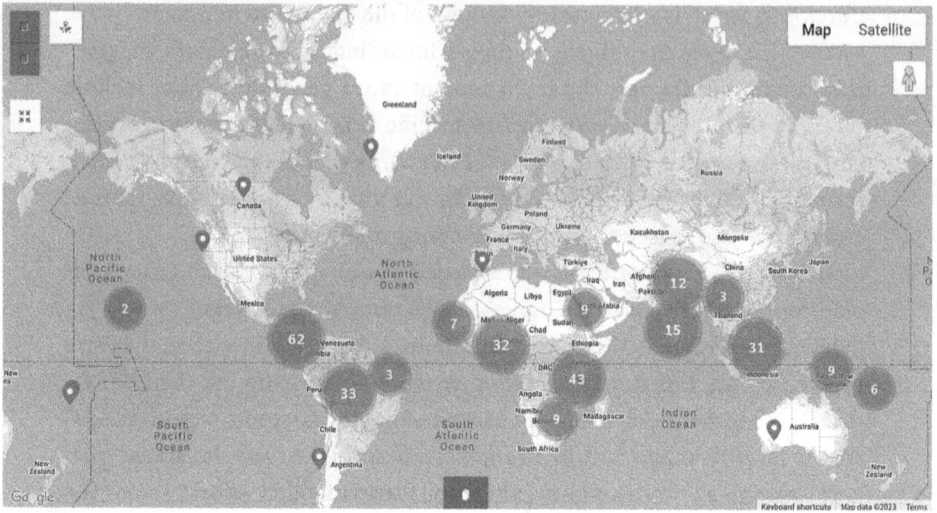

FIGURE 6.1: Map of the Equator Prize winners.

racial categories, and racial subordination.[26] Without it, the narratives that came out of the discoveries from the fifteenth century onward do not make sense. As a fictive line dividing the earth, the equator is literally concretized through narrative strategies cementing the difference of the populations above and below it. Thus, the global prize-giving system essentially converts what had functioned as latitudes of mis/recognition and conquest into latitudes of resistance as the latter is partly an outcome of the first. It is not unlike the reinvention of empires' heirs as humanitarians and of former colonies of exploitation as political partners.[27]

The awarding of the Equator Prize by First World actors to Third World indigenes means that this particular latitude reflects the collapse or layering of temporalities of domination and resistance. The zero-degree latitude reflects Indigenous labour pre- and post-Conversion, both prior to and after the institution of the labour-work dialectic, where their sovereign labours are now object-oriented under capitalism's unequal wealth distribution. The prize and the *environment* (not nature), as that which is enfolded within and exceeds Indigenous sovereignties, are the new orientation for nonaccumulative labours. To the extent that the environmental prizes create both a new narrative context for Indigenous sovereignty and, as with the Equator Prize, allow the redistribution of corporate wealth, leaving its real (goods) and fictive (stocks, futures) accumulation structures intact, they represent one form of capital's autopoiesis. Within this process the environment becomes the object not necessarily of *sustainable* funding sources for conservation, but intermittent economic support depending on the market success of capital accumulation. The prizes thus reflect a redeployment of the dialectic, a mechanism for its integration of those labours that are collectively opposed to the accumulative structures of work regimes. They thus convert Indigenous labour again to its accumulative *function* for capitalism.

Although it is not clear who the stakeholders or investors were in 2015, the 2019 awards ceremony for the Equator Prize was supported by a broad range of groups including Conservation International, Fordham University, the United States Agency for International Development (USAID), the World Wildlife Fund (WWF), Regnskosfondent (Rainforest Foundation, Norway), and Estée Lauder Companies. While one may analyze the limits of a human rights approach to Indigenous issues, the corporatization of sustainability and knowledge, the use of the term "liaise" to describe relationships among unequal actors, the overidentification of Indigenous Peoples with animal and nonanimal nature, the reliance on Indigenous Peoples to respond to climate change outside clearly marked anti-settler colonial frameworks, or the unholy partnerships of Hollywood actors, corporations, higher education, and governments, these are not the focus of this chapter. Instead, I look closely at the Wapichan win and the significance of their mapping project to illustrate the Conversion of Indigenous labour and how it exceeds it. The case study describing the win contains three maps: a replica of the Equator Initiative website's map showing awardees across the globe, another highlighting Guyana in relation to other countries in upper Amazonia, and a shaded map that enlarges Guyana and some of Venezuela.[28] The project is framed by a description accompanying the prize map highlighting how the Initiative supports Indigenous efforts to "secure" land rights, address poverty, create sustainability, and "strengthen resilience in the face of climate change."[29]

The Wapichan are heavily focused on protecting Wapichan lands from mining, logging, and other incursions, as well as addressing climate change that has led to "persistent drought," making vulnerable "the savannah and forest" near the Kanuku Mountain range (also referred to as the Kanukus) in the Upper Takatu–Upper Essequibo (Rupununi) Region.[30] According to the Project Summary, the Wapichan federation of communities that won the prize (SCPDA) "developed an innovative land use plan and a 'living digital map' of their traditional lands to promote secure land rights and socioecological resilience."[31]

The mapping work over a period of seventeen years, according to the study, has been broadly impactful for the Wapichan communities, the Indigenous Peoples of Guyana more broadly, and the Guyana government. The maps they created have been approved for land rights negotiation with the Guyana government, impacted the 2006 revision of the Amerindian Act, contributed to the government's Low Carbon Development Strategy (which I discuss as a strategy to control Indigenous right; see the introduction to this book), and facilitated land-use agreements among Wapichan groups.[32] The Wapichan use of digital technology is cited as a direct response to contemporary threats to their communities; the case study presented as part of the Prize selection and win articulates it as a *response* to a challenge by the Guyana government to demonstrate the validity of their land claims.[33] In describing the Wapichan lands, the study holds that "The political history of the Rupununi began with colonial dispossession and has since led to unfulfilled land claims and the deliberate misinterpretation of understood customary land uses."[34] Land rights in the document seem to be the most urgent issue for the Wapichan, from earlier struggles under British colonial rule to current efforts in independent Guyana. The land issue is particularly complicated as the document describes the well-known "condition of independence" in which the British recommended awarding Indigenous Peoples with rights to lands they had traditionally claimed.[35] The case study cites the failure to fully grant the lands, noting that by the early 1990s, "Guyana's Indigenous peoples had re-gained less than one third of the land area that the Amerindian Lands Commission had recommended."[36]

The legacy of colonialism and slavery in the region means that the central change agents in the Wapichan struggle for rights are both the post-independence government and climate change. The postcolonial government has failed to honor the wishes of the colonial government with regard to land titling, and climate change has significantly impacted sustainable farming and agriculture, putting the Wapichan at risk of poverty and starvation. When the document argues that the Wapichan's "political" life began with their resistance to colonial incursion, it offers a particular date or temporality for Wapichan actions on the land. However, by citing mapping as a direct *response* to governmental prompts to prove that they in fact need and use the land, it suggests another, contemporary postcolonial start date of Wapichan resistance. Thus, while the Wapichan act to protect land use and occupation of precolonial origins, they are understood only in terms of their postcoloniality.

Although the study goes on to discuss impact and outcomes, I focus here on what the Wapichan have done, similar to other Indigenous nations, with regard to the *labour* they put into mapping. The Wapichan case study lists the "impacts" of the mapping work as the "collection" of 40,000 GPS points and the creation of "dozens of log books," the training and equipping of "community monitors" in the seventeen Wapichan communities, and the collective work of the Wapichan villages, SCPDA, and the South Central and South Rupununi District Toshaos Council (DTC) "to develop an innovative programme using smart phones, field visits, and drones to watch over local lands and document illegal resource use."[37] Prior to winning the prize, in a 2012 article by the human rights organization Forest Peoples Programme, the Wapichan describe their development and production of the land use map in greater detail. Patrick Gomes, then Wapichan Toshao (Indigenous leader) of Morora Naawa village and chair of the South Rupununi DTC, contextualized the need for the map: "We have sought recognition of our land rights since the time of the British. After independence, our leaders submitted applications seeking recognition of our lands to the Amerindian Lands Commission (ALC) in 1967, yet we still did not achieve full recognition. In 2000 we started to map our lands in order to show how we use them and how we are attached to them."[38]

In the same piece, Angelbert Johnny, Sawari Wa'o Village Toshao, described the mapping work in the early 2000s: "It was based on working with our elders, land users and knowledgeable people in our villages. They guided our mapping.... Trips could sometimes last up to three weeks in the forest. It was hard work. Land use was carefully recorded by hand, as well as by GPS, in field log books which came in handy to cross-check information. Draft maps were validated and corrected among our communities in a painstaking process from 2006–2011."[39] Although Toshao Gomes underscored Wapichan use of mapping to demand and secure rights since British incursion, that incursion was not the main context for the mapping, which he says was done to demonstrate *extant* use of lands. Wapichan land use thus exceeds the time of the challenge to land rights to which it is delimited by the Equator Initiative case study.

After the win, then president of the SCPDA Cedric Buckley reportedly claimed that while "the sustainable use of forest was not documented by their fore-parents ... it was handed to them in oral language and practical use. Since then, he says, they have been using, managing and protecting the forest."[40] Describing the win and its contexts, Nicholas Fredericks, the head of Shulinab village, reportedly said that "the territory used by the Wapichan people is consistent with what was developed prior to independence by the British Government which had formed the Amerindian Lands Commission."[41] Fredericks, Buckley, and Johnny pointedly debunk the idea that contemporary digital mapping is the singular result or outcome of the challenge to codify land use by government actors or the pressures of postcolonial government. That mapping work is situated within the context of extant land use and its oral (read: symbolic) representation.

Wapichan use of technology to support rights claims, defend against encroachment, document biodiversity, and promote sustainability is in keeping with what other Indigenous Peoples have done in South America. Moreover, although I do not use it as an interpretive lens here, Pearce and Louis's elaboration of a "depth of place" reading of Hawaiian mapping practices better explains how different cultural practices (oral and material) effectively produce the digital map for Indigenous communities, rather than the map being superimposed on the communities. Within depth of place mapping, the physical and metaphysical, the cultural and the spiritual are brought together within the cartographic space. The space is therefore mapped not objectively, but from within the Indigenous groups' multidimensional, perspectival relation to it. This is what I see as the sovereign practice of labour undergirding the mapping. In 2012, the Kogi in Columbia "began a partnership to acquire and manage their most endangered coastal sacred sites," which led to the return of roughly 400 acres to Kogi control.[42] With the technology the Kogi use, "Cultural data can be collected in multiple dimensions, enabling the generation of records on ancestral roads, archaeological sites, and petroglyphs and permitting younger members of the Kogi survey team to record oral histories regarding the importance of the sites for transmission to future generations."[43] Here, what seems like a conservation effort on the Kogi's part is a sovereign practice that *leads to recognition* of sovereignty through conferral of land rights. The Kogi mapping is thus both *occurring* and *reoccurring*, the latter translating the former into the accumulative language of conservation as right. Indigenous land conservation is done within the purview of their sovereignty and through their own labour on lands as a sovereign act. In the Wapichan case study, for example, the seventeen Wapichan communities "developed a common Land Use Plan between 2007 and 2012," based on which they decided to "establish a Wapichan Conserved Forest that would encompass over 1.4 million hectares of rainforest."[44] Conservation thus is not an outcome of a general human, ethical need to protect the environment, but is specific to Wapichan land use and reflects their sovereign labour practice.

In other examples of Indigenous labour around mapping, the Wayana and Trio in Suriname use a combination of GPS and physical paper logging to track "natural resources like the Tasi palm used to thatch traditional roofs, environmental threats like leafcutter ants and signs of gold mining activity, and village infrastructure like water taps and buildings."[45] The writer concludes that the technology Indigenous Peoples use "helps" them "gather information they have long sought to demonstrate to the world their special understanding of their local environments and their special competence in managing these lands."[46] This "special understanding" reductively assesses Indigenous knowledge as a product of their labour. The *Pacific Standard* article about the Cofán efforts to map their lands in Ecuador reveals how sovereignty and the preservation of sacred sites go hand in hand, only briefly recognizing map use by "people in power" (presumably governments) for militaristic purposes. The Cofán's aim "is to use this map to demonstrate their ancestral connection with the land, and to establish standing to apply for an official land title. Such a document," the piece continues, "would finally allow the Cofán to have autonomy over their territory after years of fighting for land rights, and trying to fend off miners, poachers, and illegal loggers on their own."[47] This mapping will involve, the writer notes, "trekking through 55,000 hectares of mountainous, roadless terrain in the Amazon rainforest in the northeast of Ecuador."[48]

I quote extensively above to underscore how a western perspective organizes our view of Indigenous labour, to represent how the enormous amount of labour (and sovereign exercise of that labour) is subordinated under conservation. The object or goal orientation that the prize system and development discourse impose on the actions of the Wapichan, Cofán, and others is undergirded by *several* forms of Indigenous labour required for the mapping. This is an absolute difference of human action precisely because it is outside the political, economic, and environmental languages seeking to capture it. These labours include training on GPS equipment (including drone manipulation), the arduous task of coordinating and walking over tens of millions of acres, entry of physical (paper) data, reviewing collected data, reconciling field data with the cultural record, and collecting and using "cultural data" that may exist as oral histories that have to be recorded, likely transcribed, and re-presented or documented as points on a map. Thus, the points on the map in figure 6.1 awarded by the global prize system displace and double several layers of embedded labour over both the period of data collection and that of the historical labour on the land that becomes recorded, like the places where Tasi palm was traditionally collected. In particular, when the Wapichan note that "Land use was carefully recorded by hand, as well as by GPS, in field log books which came in handy to cross-check information," we see that the technology of recording by hand is no less central to the project than GPS.[49] Oral histories in and of themselves are also a *technology* that the Wapichan used to record their own labour practices.

Mapping is thus a specific kind of doubling and redoubling of Indigenous labour, suggesting that rather than congeal in objects, that labour congeals in repetitive or repeating practices. Recursive rather than progressive, Indigenous labour has a relationship to contemporary mapping technology that is antecedent to digital mapping. In other words, contemporary mapping technologies are modern and progressive only *outside* Indigenous use, and provincial and redundant *within* it. Moreover, I want to elaborate that recursive structure of Indigenous labour (recall Atkinson's standing) as Indigenous sovereignty's terrain or occurrence, contrasting with the terms of the prize system that converts it within the labour-work divide through the affirmation of latitudinal distinction as a substantive break among human groups. Indigenous labour defies metaphor's repetitive structures and metonymy's integrating function. The prize map is a simulation of Indigenous labour that relies on metaphoric and metonymic structures that force that labour to be productive for processes of accumulation even as the environmental prize system, as an *outcome* of global, capitalist markets, ideologically opposes that sovereign labour. The map of the Equator Prize winners (figure 6.1) includes points of fixed location that are the metaphoric simulation or recreation of actual sovereign labour practices. In contrast, the actual land-use map(s) produced by the Wapichan themselves (and literally subordinated or made secondary on the website) are based on contemporary labour practices that double prior and continuous ones that, with those very maps, are substituted for the practices themselves, which are metonymically always adjunct to or in excess of both maps. Because the actual mapping practices themselves (again substituted in and by the prize map) cannot fully be incorporated, we can see how its metaphoric conscription to and for the function of accumulation abuts a contiguous practice that is an active point of failure of full Conversion. Therefore, in reading Indigenous labour, we must identify how it effectively negotiates or is negotiated between these practices of outright, productive assimilation (metaphor) and partial or failed incorporation (metonymy).

In addition to the surfacing of the salvific narrative, these accounts of mapping suggest that mapping by Indigenous People is an outcome (an after) of the introduction of western technologies. Mapping as a practice also emerges as a *new* approach to sovereignty, which must support or affirm occupation, customary land use, and traditional knowledge about lands. As I have suggested, however, none of this is new. It is a continuation not only of Indigenous occupation and stewardship but of pre-contact and colonial-era Indigenous labour practices. Mapping, in effect, traces and thus doubles sovereign Indigenous labour. Its reading *as* new, however, occurs because of the always prior Conversion of Indigenous labour, which does not allow us to see it outside the language generated by the dialectic's accumulative structure and its re-presentation as unproductive or nonaccumulative labour. We therefore see the labour of mapping *after* its translation or simulation. Thus, we need to recover this labour for the radical tradition (not white, capitalist political economy), but not necessarily from before this moment of its replication. It would be false to suggest that we can deploy a reading practice that is somehow prior to the Conversion of our bodily actions. Instead, we can recover Indigenous labour through a middle/passage reading for the apparatus of simulation, in this case metaphor and metonymy, and their constitutive action to manage translation. However, as I stated at the outset, although these terms work for and from within political economy, they do not originate with it. Instead, the apparatus of simulation and Conversion, this dyad of metaphor and metonymy, works as a structure *to manage and sustain conquistadorial desire across time* as what is *necessary* for capitalist political economy. Such attention helps us understand why metonymy is a point of failure or incomplete incorporation, and hence a useful point of engagement.

For this shift to the a priori desire behind accumulation's structures and methods, I begin with a basic working definition of the terms. A metaphor is a figure of speech creating an analogy between objects or structures where one becomes related to or *means (takes on meaning)* through comparison with another. In contrast, metonymy is a figure of speech substituting a thing's portion, attribute, or name for the whole.[50] I suggest that this distinction, like the labour-work split, is one of strategic relation indicating two different, but intermingled practices of representation and reading that go beyond simple linguistic equivalence or synecdoche. These practices capture the actual physical labour of blacks and Indigenous Peoples to not only divergent but conflicting end, and are, in effect, an operation of a historical desire that is brought forward. Moreover, these practices of reading and re-presenting consolidate and perpetuate the labour-work divide such that Indigenous labour cannot be included within the radical tradition unless it is translated and doubled in a specific way. To simplify the distinction between these forms of representation, the Creole writer's doubling (read: simulation) of the labour of the enslaved and indentured, mentioned earlier, should be understood as metaphoric, while Sharon Atkinson's standing, the redoubling of her own labour together with the actual work of mapping Indigenous lands, should be understood as metonymic or partial. This is a particular divergence of black and Indigenous labours not strictly as they are performed, but as they are represented or doubled within political economy. I unpack the distinction between them by using poststructuralist theory, arguing that once we understand key differences in the articulation of these labours, we can begin to decolonize left reading practices that are unwittingly anti-Indigenous.

Looking at metaphor and metonymy helps us move around one false division between black and native labours. First, if labour is how the land occurs or is made sovereign for Indigenous Peoples, then native labour (prior to the imposition of the labour-work dialectic) is not simply pre-political, but outside the political. Yet, to reiterate, Wilderson argues that native peoples have the capacity for representation within the terms of the settler political system because they have land that the settler wants. Blacks, in contrast, are political subjects only after Death, and (as I demonstrated in the introduction and chapter 1) because they are cut off from the land's sovereign occurrence (their indigeneities) and from the settler-master's subject position, they must belatedly convert economic right into political right. However, both blacks and Indigenous peoples are cut off from the political (in different ways), and both gain representation, however partial, through what I see as necrotic practices of simulation, be they constitutional or legal (recall the distinction between Guyana's constitution and the Amerindian Act). Metaphor is in many ways the scene of both black and Indigenous Death/death within political economy, although it must necessarily be employed to support the transformation of right for Creoles that maintains the delinking of Independence from Sovereignty.

As a tool that supports the representation of black labour from within the terrain/terms of its position in the dialectic, metaphor is a necropolitical, rather than benign, mechanism for converting Indigenous sovereignty because it seeks to disrupt and replace Indigenous Peoples' (and blacks', as those who have been cut off from their indigeneity) prior relation to labour, which did not rely on the delinking of the political and the economic. Metaphor, as an intrinsic and first unconscious structure of representation, is in essence pre-political. Thus, to the extent that Elimination is the first move of the conquistador and only later the settler, Indigenous Peoples are, like blacks, trapped in a system of representation based on their *outside*, disavowed position with regard to politics. Although Achille Mbembe outlines precise conditions for necropower's enactment and is primarily concerned with militaristic forms of violent death, if a sovereign labour relation is replaced with one that allows for the kind of "vertical sovereignty" made possible by the global division of labour and work, then even without intensive forms of surveillance and mechanisms of death, that abrogation of right is necessarily necrotic because, as I suggested in the introduction, it is based on the imposition of life-death as the axis for all bodily action.[51] At stake here is the affirmation of labour as the terrain of sovereignty for Indigenous Peoples and the understanding that this labour is fundamentally opposed to biopolitics, or politics routed through the labour-work dialectic and the limitations it places on subjectivity. Also at stake is black labour itself and its recovery from work's accumulative structures. Below, I elaborate the un/conscious desire that informs and limits our reading (and writing) of labour.

Stemming in large part from work like Valentin Voloshinov's early attempt to apply and use Ferdinand de Saussure's structural analysis of language to understand the role among material structures, ideology, and consciousness, or more simply between base and superstructure, a long tradition within Marxist thought approaches it in terms of semiotics, and also psychoanalysis. Within it, both fields are seen as essential to understanding the relationship between material structures, and our social, political, and psychic selves by studying the following: how subjects are constructed, the mechanisms by which ideology works as a practice of signification to produce social subjects, the semiotics of cultural value in the production and maintenance of social and material class (i.e., how classes reproduce through structures and the individuals who belong to those classes), and class as an internal structure of consciousness.[52] Although not directly engaged with the Marxian elaboration (or critique) of semiotics and psychoanalysis, theorist and art historian Kaja Silverman's discussion of psychoanalysis as a semiotic practice, particularly her underscoring of the sociocultural nature of consciousness, in keeping with what the Marxist tradition finds essential in Saussure and Freud, is instructive for this project. Through her work, I reframe the labour-work dialectic as a "symbolic order," suggesting that rather than a strictly material practice, we are seeking to recover labour as a form of meaning and representation.

Silverman's main goal in *The Subject of Semiotics* is not only to demonstrate how the structuring elements within discursive practice produce subjects but also to uncover the patriarchal system of signification that governs subjectivity and to suggest strategies of signification through which female subjectivity can be recovered for itself.[53] My use of Silverman may be dismissed as a problematic recourse to post/structuralism as an explanatory tool for labours that I suggest are in some ways outside and resistant. Nor am I interested in a gender analysis here. However, Silverman's discussion of semiotics is useful for demonstrating that while the Conversions Indigenous Peoples and blacks underwent facilitate the appropriation of their bodies' productive capacity, enabling the material functions of capital accumulation, it also institutes a system of meaning making for those bodies within political economy and cultural discourse. Silverman's work allows us to understand or approach the semiotic structure of that system. Moreover, as Hortense Spillers has identified, that system is not specific to either blacks or Indigenous Peoples, although the semantic closures around our flesh are different, but they apply to both "African and indigenous peoples." She further bears this out by, for instance, discussing the former enslaved person and abolitionist Olaudah Equiano through the very ways in which blacks are "culturally unmade" as Indigenous Peoples.

The use of psychoanalysis, however, is also troubled within Afropessimism. Wilderson has argued not only that psychoanalysis cannot represent black dispossession but that it remains "parasitic" on it. In his critique of Jacques Lacan, via Fanon, Wilderson writes that as a "discursive, or signifying process of becoming," subjectivity depends on "alienation" as a grammar "underwriting all manner of relationality." These signification practices that govern subjectivity are, however, fundamentally predicated on the violence of the division between the Human as capable of being "positioned by the symbolic order" and the black/enslaved person as fundamentally governed by the "absence" of all forms of "relationality."[54] Wilderson discusses Silverman's work and similar feminist discourses for what he sees as the libidinal economy of our cultural discourses (e.g., film), claiming that the subjective violence between white men and white women is still only "contingent" rather than strictly antagonistic as is the "gratuitous" violence that closes off blacks from these forms of becoming.[55] This is because white men and white women still have available to them "signifying practices" from which the violence of slave making or "blackening" permanently excludes blacks.[56] Spillers contends that the body that is literally separated from the flesh through the forms of physical, kin, and psychic ruptures that attend in slave making means the "severing of the captive body from its motive will, its active desire." While she tracks what this means for black men and women who are, as enslaved people, expelled from gender (or into sex as pathological after gender—to recall the reading of Wynter in chapter 5), what is important is the fact that the kinds of sovereign desire that psychoanalysis elaborates are not that of blacks.[57]

Thus, precisely because Silverman elaborates what we can argue are the unconscious impulses that attain for normative (white, western) subjects within heteropatriarchy, I find her work useful for tracking the conquistadorial desire that brings political and economic structures into being. My goal is to move beyond not just the antagonism of the desire for blackness, as that which literally forces blackness into being, but to also show how black humanity is in fact always undercut by the ways in which we sustain portions of the desire as that which leaves partially open human subject positions (e.g. the settler) for our enfranchisement. If, as Spillers argues, our slave making is predicated on the inability to desire ourselves, then one of the most insidious, destructive ways in which we are systemically reproduced as Wilderson's enduring slaves is through the substitution of conquistadorial desire as our very own. That desire is therefore the unconscious scene of our displacement. It reflects our *will* to be human not in terms of our own making since the unconscious reflects a double negation for us: *acceptable* representations for us are, as Fanon and Spillers make clear, only as phobic objects, only after we accept our fall into degraded flesh. Consequently, the *undesirable* and illicit wishes are for blacks to be human outside the material and symbolic life of anti-blackness.

In elaborating Sigmund Freud's structure of the unconscious ("impulse" and "taboo") and pre/conscious ("cultural norms"), Silverman makes plain Freud's intent to have them understood as modes of signification that are fundamentally necessary for the subject's emergence as both a product of signification and "a signifying complex."[58] Moreover, if we understand subjectivity (for normative subjects) as the outcome of unconscious and preconscious meaning-making practices, then these practices have primary and secondary processes, which are in constant relation and symbolic negotiation between what is desired, the "displacement" of "unacceptable" desire, and the signifying operations allowing the subject to manage and release that desire in culturally acceptable, accessible terms to them.[59] Silverman probes "three sets" of essential "signifying strategies" in managing the relationship between the signifier and signified in what she identifies as the "primary and secondary systems" involved in the production of meaning and subjectivity as fundamentally "social" processes despite their seeming individuation in the subject: condensation and displacement, metaphor and metonymy, and paradigm and syntagm.[60] Of critical importance is her explanation of condensation and displacement in Freudian psychoanalysis as structuring elements of dreams that "create *acceptable* representations for *unacceptable* wishes."[61]

These processes or operations, as different ways of placing things in relation, manage desire. The first half of each set "derive[s] from the perception of similarity," while the second terms "are all seen as involving the principle of contiguity."[62] She describes metaphor and metonymy as basically intermediary processes between the first sets as primary and secondary ways of managing desire. While displacement may seem to be about difference and deferral, Silverman notes that "relationships of similarity" are more central to it.[63] In describing the secondary processes of paradigm and syntagm, Silverman notes that the former are based on resemblances, however forceful or diminished, while the latter are based on "formal contiguity" where the essential "difference" between terms is maintained as necessary "to the operations of meaning."[64] Describing the operation of the primary and secondary processes, she writes that difference in the latter is not absolute, but is the mechanism through which objects remain "present in their absence" even though the secondary process functions to maintain the differences between signifiers and signifieds (discontinuity), while the primary functions not only to "blur" but to have the signified function as though it were the signifier.[65]

Metaphor ("conceptual similarity") and metonymy ("conceptual contiguity") stand in the middle of these processes, which she argues are central in the "expression of nonlinguistic relationships" among *things*, rather than words.[66] It is a kind of privileged operation that mediates between the first and secondary processes and "between the two elements which they conjoin."[67] She notes: "Sometimes metaphor and metonymy are used by literary and cinematic texts to sustain the absence of a given term indefinitely (allegory, for instance, is often defined as an extended metaphor, one which never dissolves). On other occasions metaphor and metonymy are employed to create a dialectic of absence and presence; here the missing term always re-emerges after a time."[68] Elaborating the semantic operation in *Swann's Way*, the first part of Marcel Proust's *In Search of Lost Time*, she notes that a portion of it "renders equally transparent the metaphors and metonymies which constitute the history of desire, the displacement of affect away from one term onto another which either resembles or adjoins it, and which it thereafter represents."[69] Finally, according to Silverman, what may seem as "minor displacements" in the operation of the association of the signifier and signified do not in fact "diminish" desire, but "increase" the appeal of the desired object.[70]

Silverman's work helps illuminate how the labour-work dialectic—not as strictly material—functions as a symbolic practice to continuously make different or divergent labours representable within the system of capital and its poetics in works by Adam Smith, Karl Marx, and others. Her work allows us to read the imposition of the dialectic in the Americas as clearly an operation of desire. It results from a conquistadorial desire that helps effect the emergence of a new political-economic system that can sustain it. Moreover, because the conquistador is the desiring subject whose desire works *against* the extant religious orientation of the Christian social-political order (i.e., against its conditions of emergence), the imposition of the dialectic must ultimately lead to the overcoming of the conquistador through their transformation *into* or *as* the settler and the master as figures, respectively, of power's *continuity* and *contiguity* (of the Old World order), rather than an absolute break from monarchic rule. Thus, when Foucault elaborates the seventeenth and eighteenth centuries' shift to modern forms of power, the conquistador and the dialectic are key figures and prestructural elements, respectively, in that power's emergence as a new mode of managing and/or "disciplining" the specific desire for a new way of being human emerging outside the religious, monarchic, social and political order.[71] Columbus's return to the Old World in chains after serving as governor of Hispaniola was not therefore simply because of his despotism. It was because he failed his own Conversion to proto-settler, which meant that the *unacceptable* form of his desire (i.e., the challenge to the monarchic system) outstripped its *acceptable* limits (i.e., the Conversion and extension of monarchic power).

In her essay "Columbus and the Poetics of the *Propter Nos*," Wynter elaborates the conceptual shift effected by the Columbian-era discoveries as the philosophical question became, Why must the earth exist for God rather than for man (*propter nos*)? Wynter argues that Columbus's desire to find new lands was an "apocalyptic millenarian" challenge to the social order based on geographic division as the underpinning of the Christian or "theocentric" order that legitimated the redeemed status of the king, clergy, and nobility and the fallen status of lay peoples, including Columbus himself (see chapter 5).[72] Columbus's voyage and desire to accumulate wealth (and titles) are thus the material realization or expression of a philosophical-psychic desire to exist in a fundamentally different way within the real and symbolic world, so that the theocentric re-presentation or duplication of the real world does not continue to restrict meaning and the production of subjectivity (and citizenship) through its very processes of relation or continuity and discontinuity.[73]

This desire expresses itself in terms of its own contradictions, for example, in Hernán Cortés's letters about his explorations and conquest of the Americas. The first letter (initially referring to Cortés in the third person) holds that no one is better suited than Cortés to take possession of and govern certain lands "because, besides being a most suitable person, he is moreover very zealous in the service of Your Majesties." The text continues: "Having done as stated, and, being all assembled in our Council Chamber, we agreed to write Your Majesties, and to send you, in addition to the one-fifth part which belongs to your rents, according to Your Royal prescriptions, all the gold, and silver, and valuables which we have obtained in this country . . . and above which we keep nothing for ourselves. We place this at the disposition of Your Royal Highnesses, as a proof of our very good will for your service."[74] Here we see Cortés's desire to possess wealth and land expressed *as* a higher good for the sovereigns (Queen Doña Juan and Emperor Charles V). The gifting of additional sums or quantiles of gold above what is required does not simply pacify the sovereign. It is the moment when the possession of excessive accumulation has to be made acceptable, so that the acquisition of property and wealth does not threaten the monarchy. Such threat is plainly outlined in the letter when Cortés must assume the position he does because one of the king's subjects (Cuba's first governor Diego Velázquez de Cuéllar) has—clearly out of pure and unacceptable "cupidity"—usurped land and wealth not for the king but for himself.[75]

Wynter's elaboration of this lay or Columbian/conquistadorial desire shows that it is composed of two parts: a primary plane of expression—that which is acceptable within the social structure (discovery as a real and philosophical gesture)—and a secondary one—that which is unacceptable even to the conscious knowledge of Columbus and Enlightenment humanists: the outright rejection of the social order. Thus, this desire is structured, in some ways, like the unconscious (following Silverman's reading of Freud). This matters not only because the libidinal leads to the transformation of matter, to that of black (and native) bodies to and from value, into things and commodities.[76] The desire's representative strategies manage its productive and problematic halves.

As I discussed in the introduction, the settler allows for the continuation of empire's political power/right. As essentially an evolutionary conquistador leaving behind a contingent of men in the Caribbean before his return voyage, Columbus initiates the settler function of extending political right to the sovereign's land. Indeed, he is supposed to transition into a proto-settler. Although historians separate voyages of discovery from conquistador voyages, by the time of Cortés's arrival in the Americas (1504, only two years after Columbus's fourth voyage), we can see clearly that the goal to "colonise" and settle is key for the conquistador.[77] However, because the desire to climb the sociopolitical order of late fifteenth-century Spain cannot be singularly satisfied with a title or extension of royal power, the unacceptable part of Columbus's desire—the *propter nos*—seeks fulfillment in the master function. Columbus, in other words, becomes a proto-master, which is the usurpation and transformation of sovereign power over the lay body. The proto-master position he sought manages the *unacceptable* part of the desire for a new social order, while the proto-settler position he also failed to effect manages the *acceptable* form of the desire for a new social order as a no less tautological extension of imperial power.

The master position reinstitutes a kind of bondage (although that is what lay people try to escape), allowing for a more complete break with the old system because the master assumes sovereign power in a new form. This requirement of bondage for freedom—the fact that some class of the human has to be "produced" (Wynter) as subordinate for another to achieve their relative freedom—has its robust articulation in the master-slave dialectic, where the management and transformation of sovereign power occurs. It is a dangerous, unacceptable form of the conversion of sovereign power, but also one that could be constrained by the proto-settler position. Moreover, when the settler splits his labour between himself (in the function of the master) and the enslaved person, he not only causes a precarious condition as the enslaved person actually works on the settler's *propter nos* freedom in true Hegelian fashion. He also effects the movement between the political and economic, whose eventual dissolution into each other will of course characterize the biopolitical under capitalism. This, then, is what black and native labours resist at the very point of their conscription, and why they are fundamentally dangerous.

The labour-work dialectic is therefore a mediating structure managing the disavowed relationship between these levels of desire. The labour-work divide is the essential semantic mechanism effecting this *propter nos* shift; hence, Silverman's elaboration of psychoanalysis as a semiotic process is essential to identifying this as a desire connected to subjectivity. It is based on the desire of the conquistador cum master cum settler, and is the base desire for settler sovereignties. In effect, we live the political order of conquistadorial desire. In this particular anachronism, the settler is made possible only through the rejection of more constraining modes of being human under Christian monarchic rule, which is reinstituted in terms of a psychic rather than primarily somatic desire, the latter of which will ultimately be realized through regimes of accumulation.

The greed of Columbus and others that Las Casas and fellow priests found so abhorrent (see chapter 1) was the unacceptable part of their desire that could only be managed by the Conversion of labour to work.[78] That greed could only be managed by regimes of accumulation. Thus, it is ultimately not Las Casas's own conversion that triumphs in the Americas because it is outstripped by the unacceptable needs and wants by those, like Columbus, seeking to shift the social order. This is true, although his conversion (Bartolomean docility), as I have argued, causes the disappearance of Indigenous labour in the historical record. Capital accumulation is thus the result of a desire (unacceptable portion) that creates new political-economic structures that ultimately allow for the transformation of the Old World order into new forms. Those new forms are a transformation of old forms of power into the biopolitical, which although not a terrain of representation for blacks, is still based on the precondition of black *and* native bodily transformation as the critical element of the economic and political orders of the settler state. Moreover, I argue that we should see this operation of acceptable versus unacceptable or latent desires in terms of metaphor and metonymy, and their very function to maintain the primary and secondary operations of managing desire through meaning.

As a structure of Conversion, the labour-work relation mediates between two very different economic systems in the late fifteenth century: the European and the Indigenous. Thus, the acts of translation of indigeneity through British labour history (see chapter 2) were so problematic. More importantly, the terms themselves are maintained in a particular relationship to each other in order to manage this difference. Returning to Silverman, they serve the function of condensation and displacement in the first system of meaning making to produce or create "acceptable" forms of representation for "unacceptable" desires. Recall that the stated goal of the discoveries is religious Conversion. Las Casas rebelled because the conquistadors acted not in a godly way, but like savages and brutes. Thus, Conversion manages the unacceptable desire of material gain by creating an acceptable break between the undesirable or rather (after Las Casas's appeal) the prohibited desire (labour) and the acceptable or desired outcome (work). Not only are labour and work still in relation; Las Casas essentially allows that relationship to function much in the way Silverman describes as, in the first instance, a substitution ("the displacement of affect away from one term onto another which either resembles or adjoins it, and which it thereafter represents").[79] In the second instance, it produces "a dialectic of absence and presence; here the missing term always re-emerges after a time."[80] The dialectic thus works semantically through two kinds of operations that arrange work as metaphor (i.e., the reduction to what is both known and desired) and labour as metonymy (i.e., the contiguity of the difference of Indigenous labour practices, inclusive of African and American native practices and those of the enslaved for their own well-being). The first operation establishes relation, and the second maintains difference so that one term—work—can continually be appropriated or represented in the semantic system through what it differs from and what it reinscribes (or reduces to elements of necrotic similitude).

To hold in place a deferral, the peculiarity of presence and absence, the labour-work dialectic successfully imposes meaning on very different actions and controls them. Moreover, the dialectic's function is not to singularly push aside difference but to continuously find ways to reduce or represent it through operations of similitude that retain difference as relation because, as Silverman notes of semantic systems by elaborating Saussure, "meaning emerges only through the play of difference within a closed system."[81] Through the constant elaboration of the dialectic, the settler's displaced desire onto the body of the enslaved is continuously renewed, leading to limiting outcomes for labour history and black political economy, as we saw with Rodney's reference to black labour as the "humanization" of the landscape, to which I referred as an expression of the settler-master's (conquistadorial) desire. Moreover, the desire is what Wynter (and Fanon; see the introduction) would call the external validating element for labour history and black political economy. Taking this analysis further, we could argue that the labour-work dialectic sustains settler desire across time in its material expression and its unconscious (libidinal and psychic) expression within social and economic structures, within the global class system, by delinking black and native identities as they are woven into our critical practices. Thus, our political economic analyses of labour (like the law) function as scenes of libidinal fulfillment when we strictly apply the terms of analysis, and are yet another place where we fail to desire ourselves or at least where the prohibition against such desire is continuously enacted.[82]

With the law, we see the metaphoric structures allowing Indigenous life and labour to be re-presented within the very postcolonial state that their sovereignties exceed. For example, the practice of referring to the Toshao in the law (not necessarily in practice) as similar to a constable is the exercise of similitude as translation and control. This is the use of metaphor as a form of power that is critical to biopolitics and the need to re-present all sovereignties as biopolitical so that modern, nation-state sovereignties can be extended and other sovereignties cannot threaten it. In many ways, the failure to threaten is the mode of extension. In this chapter, the global prize system—based on a concept of the environment sustained precisely through the functions of the global capitalist system to produce and maintain the difference of the human same from the human other—redeploys the labour-work dialectic.[83] This deployment works through the operation of metaphor as evidenced by the superimposition or substitution of prize points on a global map for the 40,000 GPS points of the Wapichan, for example. The global prize system in some part has to acknowledge the difference of Indigenous actions on the land and the changes they might affect (preservation, conservation, and sovereignty). However, the accounting for this difference is still partially defined by the forms of accumulative work that produce the global prize system in the first place. Indigeneity is thus still negotiated within capital's symbolic order and semantic mechanism, and the prize system must subordinate sovereignty, as an incomplete point of suture or extension, to the object-orientation provided by the environment and conservation as incorporative mechanisms. It thus functions unlike the law (the singular terrain of metaphor), precisely by managing the conflict between global capital's acceptable and disavowed desires. It is thus a site of both appropriation, or metaphor, and incomplete conscription, or metonymy.

The representations of Indigenous mapping practices discussed here present us with a particular problem. On the one hand, the prize system and postcolonial and settler governments reduce this doubled labour to its metaphoric function only insofar as it is defined with/through the metaphoric structure of incorporation, work as it is tied to, for instance, the gross domestic product. On the other, if Indigenous mapping is the repetition (i.e., simulation) of their prior labours (of prior "land use" as a sovereign interaction with nature), then we need to precisely work from the left hand of the labour-work divide, from the process of metonymy, to recover and resituate their labours first in terms of their contiguity, and then in those of what lies outside this relation and resists the ways that the operation of Conversion always tries to abolish where metonymy breaks down and cannot hold the outside as presence. Mapping is still constrained by the labour-work dialectic, but Atkinson's doubling and deferral (standing) of the first doubling (mapping) is, I argue, the point not only where similarity or metaphor fails but where we see metonymy, as a structure of conscription, representing indigeneity at its limit point. La Rose's invocation is a distinct kind of repetition that falls outside the discursive economy of the Creole writer, for instance, and the way in which that writing doubles or repeats the work of the slave cum proletarian in order to support both rights claims and Creole indigeneity. However, we can recognize it through metonymy as a relation that is a difference. In other words, we cannot approach the representation of Indigenous labour from within that perspective, so we are left with the moments of rupture provided by metonymy's failed incorporation. Moreover, this is how we must view the Wapichan use of technology.

Conclusion

At the 2015 Equator Prize ceremony, everyone, from actors such as Alec Baldwin to the renowned anthropologist and primatologist Jane Goodall, collectively framed the event as "honor[ing]" prize winners "for their remarkable achievements in tackling climate change using innovative measures to reduce poverty, protect nature and strengthen resilience."[84] Goodall, in the available excerpt from her speech, notes, "So many people in the developed world have lost the wisdom of the indigenous people where you make a decision only after considering how will this decision affect our people generations ahead." She adds, "I truly believe that we will only achieve our true human potential when head and heart work in harmony."[85] Despite her own advocacy, Goodall reinforces the general problem of capitalist overdevelopment and climate change, above Indigenous rights claims, land use, and sovereign relation. Moreover, she not only accords a salvific function to Indigenous Peoples' "wisdom," but that wisdom is oriented toward "nature" as an objective structure that is prior to sovereignty.

In contradistinction to this framing, when Indigenous actors talk about the environment and the threat to it by global climate change or big business, they deliberately do so in terms of their sovereignty, as for instance

La Rose does in her piece with Griffiths, "Searching for Justice and Land Security," noting that mining in the Upper Mazaruni region in Guyana causes the "*actual* destruction of *ancestral land* and therefore violation of the rights of the Upper Mazaruni indigenous peoples."[86] Nature is not abstract or prior to Indigenous sovereignty. The Wapichan project and the other descriptions of labour by Indigenous Peoples in the Americas to protect their lands underscore how that wisdom is a critical labour that is then doubled through the mapping projects for which Indigenous groups are honored. While "nature" for Goodall stands as that which must be protected, Indigenous wisdom is what has transformed nature into the terrain of their sovereignty (see chapter 1). The global prize system supports Indigenous efforts to secure and extend their land titles while managing to conceptually subordinate and integrate Indigenous sovereignty (and labour) into the global political economy.

The prize system's language expresses a mediated desire for the human to come into being *above* (i.e., as a transcendence) infrahumans and homunculi alike. It occurs within another general move toward the human (i.e., *propter nos*), but this human is effected upon the reinscription of expressions of Indigenous sovereignty in the labour-work dialectic. In it, the "developed" world is antagonistic to indigeneity; in reconciling this antagonism, a new relation of man to the environment emerges. Indigenous sovereignty is thus affirmed through a new objective status of perspectival man. Indigenous Peoples' labour is now conscripted in the service of man as the outcome of a desire that is brought forward in its unconscious structure where the desire for its realization negotiates with its necrotic or destructive political and economic basis in the capitalist class system. To return to language from chapter 5, the desire for man's things will always prevent the becoming of man outside of possessive structures. However, metonymic practices of reading and representing can begin to reject and correct this desire.

In these re-presentations of Indigenous labour, from the global prize system through the law, representation becomes an operation of simulation and desire. To resist it, we need to find a way to read at or for metonymy's edge in order to restore difference in and for itself. We need to work from the point of contiguity's failure rather than metaphor's erasure. Our goal is not to recover Indigenous labour *in* the labour-work dialectic, but to recover it precisely at the point of its partial engulfment and resistance to the operation of Conversion. In order for Indigenous labour to be represented within the radical tradition, the tradition must literally break open and reject the organizing force and symbolic operation of work to incorporate all outsides to the terms and terrain of capital. Moreover, we must actively work against the unconscious desire for translation and similitude as modes of conscription into the dialectic and its structures of meaning, and instead work from those places where we can see the desire's operation and the representations it fails to fully incorporate and foreclose. To echo Fred Moten, not only is the grammar of separation of blackness from indigeneity not ours, but neither is the desire out of which it emerges (see the introduction). The latter is in fact the precondition of our status as infrahumans and homunculi and as such is the limit point of our humanity.

Coda

The Ark of Black and Indigenous Labour

Stephanie Pruitt's poem "Mississippi Gardens" opens with its speaker re-peating an answer to a question. That answer is *"slaves,"* but we don't know the question until the end: *"Mama, what did they used to grow here?"* The ques-tion then has a double resonance: cotton and also slaves.[1] The poem reads:

> *slaves*, she answers, as I sink
> my fingers beneath the roots.
>
> the knees of that blue housedress are threadbare.
> she wears it on Tuesdays and Fridays when we tend the flowers.
>
> *pullin' weeds ain't a time for talk* she chides.
> I watch her uproot the creeping charlie.
>
> the fragrant blossoms we protect, hug our whole house.
> sweet peas were my choice.
>
> we rarely buy those things for sale in the garden aisle.
> *don't make sense to work the earth and not feel it.*
>
> I wanted those thick cotton gloves, but they stayed on the shelf.
> *you gotta learn the difference between dirt and soil.*
>
> sometime I notice how the ground changes.

denser, darker, moister, a little more red in some places.

in social studies class I learned about crop rotation

and how it keeps the land fertile.

Mama, what did they used to grow here?

Cotton as a natural, agricultural crop is made to seem unnatural here through its displacement by enslaved people as those who were reaped from the land. Chattel slavery turned blacks into crops that were reaped from Africa, transplanted to the Americas, and grown *as* enslaved people on plantations only with the ministration, love, and knowledge of the enslaved themselves. The tender care of the garden flowers by the speaker and the speaker's mother is the care of the black self that was necessary for generations of enslaved peoples to survive. This care leads the speaker to note that despite the desire for gloves that would create a barrier between the body and the earth, *"don't make sense to work the earth and not feel it"* because *"you gotta learn the difference between dirt and soil."* Moreover, this participatory, felt knowledge—material and affective—is opposed to the technical, alienated textual or institutional/structural knowledge of "crop rotation."

Pruitt's engagement with slavery here, in which care for the land is a material knowledge tied to care for the self, is a reflection of black *labour*. In the poem, slavery does not overdetermine blacks' relationships to land, but deeply informs it. Her poem indexes slavery, black *work* (for white humanity), *through* black labour, rejecting the productive, accumulative form of black enslaved work in favor of the black labour of generational care and self-making. This is not a denial of the work blacks did to build white, settler wealth, but a two-fold critical rejection of the desire sustaining white settler colonialism, and the representative, symbolic strategies of mimesis and metaphor that execute and fulfill that desire. Instead, the poem presents what I refer to as a working at and from the point of metonymy, destabilizing the natural relationship of similitude or substitution between crop and cotton through a form of displacement that is not reinserted into a system of meaning overdetermined by the fulfillment of settler desire. The poem rejects the economy of the word and the function of language to sustain and reinforce our political economy. Moreover, it shows us how our imaginative engagement with the word can both reflect and generate new languages for a black political economy and for being outside the forms of antagonism necessary for capitalism.

Pruitt's poem encapsulates what it would look like if land served as "the source of relation rather than the site of boundaries" to "define a politics under which Indigenous sovereignty and Black reparations movements can (re)build capacities for relationality."[2] Throughout *Beyond Constraint*, I have worked beyond and through the division of black and native lives around the land-labour split in political economy and economic/labour history, re-theorizing both labour and land "as a source of relation" in order, as the editors of the special issue of *Social Text* seek, to "shift the ground of racialized and embodied histories away from the territoriality of the state."[3] I have argued that black and native bodies are used to achieve a split between productive work and unproductive labour. This split is effected through the literal transformation of these bodies through Conversion and the Middle Passage into forms or degrees of value in order to initiate the settler-master function as a way to manage and sustain conquistadorial desire through the constant play of difference between, and management of, its acceptable and prohibited forms.

The delinking of blackness and indigeneity, of black independence(s) and native sovereignties, as a formative component of the new political and economic systems that begin to emerge from the late fifteenth century, is thus intrinsic to capital accumulation in perpetuity. Because this break between blackness and indigeneity (which is both internal to blackness and between blacks and natives in the Americas) is necessary for capital accumulation, the explanatory languages we use to describe it and its (productive) ends or outcomes sustain it. As Fred Moten writes, echoing Wynter, "one of the fundamental contradictions of capitalism is that it established conditions for its own critique." Even where the radical tradition supersedes this limit, however, as Moten suggests Cedric Robinson does, it still confronts another.[4] This is the limit of black radical material critique: where it is forced to repeat (read: simulate) and reinforce this break between blackness and indigeneity, and hence be complicit in extending settler-master desire and its manifestation as capitalist political economy.

The labour-work dialectic is an integrative mechanism that converts bodily and land-based sovereignties so they can be managed under settler colonialism. It compels black and native peoples into and *as* property relations based on lack so that we can be useful for accumulation without accumulating by ourselves, which is a threat to settler-master right. Because the dialectic is an accumulative structure, it conscripts the material and discursive alternatives that Indigenous and black peoples create. We are thus constantly being converted into positions of antagonism against each other, or of lack vis-à-vis the state and within global political economy. Thus, native sovereignty emerges in the postcolonial, involuntary settler state as the antithesis of Independence, which, as a vehicle for enfranchisement and right, is simultaneously a fetter on black freedom.

Exemplifying how the state continuously evolves its conscription methods, Charles R. Hale delineates the "entanglements" of the territorial claims of Indigenous and black communities in Central America with neoliberal development goals oriented around multiculturalism and greater economic production. Echoing some of the issues that surfaced in my discussion of Iwokrama (see the introduction), Hale outlines how even though Miskitu (Miskito) land claims, which govern their mapping projects, predate the formation of the Honduran nation-state, the eventual gains they make are ultimately a negotiation that, in many cases, serves neoliberal aims.[5] He argues that

> Even if large swaths of territory are excluded from the land market, regularization of land tenure pays off, both because the rest of the land becomes fair game for commoditization and because the existence of collectively owned property poses no direct challenge to the principle of private property or to the reign of market forces, but does achieve the key goal of replacing chaos and contention with an intelligible, predictable and market-friendly grid of property rights. These two principles together—special rights and reinforcement of a capitalist market for land and resources—converge to yield an especially compelling logic: states devolve authority to far-flung spaces, recognize the inhabitants' rights and let them govern themselves, ... constraining their political participation beyond the local level, especially in relation to broader structures of political-economic inequity.[6]

Indigenous land tenure ultimately serves the state and large international lending bodies like the World Bank and International Monetary Fund that "establish," as Hale argues, "clear rules by which all actors—whether individuals or communities—can turn their resources into commodities."[7] Indigenous land-based sovereignties, however negotiated or impinged on, are still critical, having both co-equivalences and parallels. Equivalences include, for example, Maroon land title and villages in Suriname, and the communal land titles and villages of the black-Indigenous Garifuna. Parallels include the post-emancipation Caribbean "village schemes" of freed peoples in Guyana, and the communally owned Barbuda, as examples of alternative forms of possession. US examples include collective endeavors like Soul Fire Farm in New York and the Black Family Land Trust in North Carolina.[8] Such initiatives are not mainly about forms of reparation based on accumulation and wealth redistribution. Instead, they seek nonaccumulative sovereignties out of our direct relationships with earth, dirt, and soil.

The COVID-19 pandemic, however, has forced us to confront the wide-scale consequences of a lack of any form of global reparation or restoration for blacks. Moreover, lack of historical, global wealth and the types of access it facilitates meant that blacks', Latinx People's, and native peoples' Death were literally the pandemic's systemic product, intrinsically tied to the forms of recovery and economic stimulus meant to bring wealthy nations out of forced recession. Structural poverty and colonialism's consequences in African, Caribbean, and Latin American states have been leading to forms of Death and uprooting as a way of life for black and brown peoples, alongside continuing attempts to either constrain or conscript Indigenous sovereignties, particularly in the Americas, even and especially where they are augmented by land title grants and exercised through protests against, for example, potentially disruptive pipelines (e.g., the Dakota Access Pipeline and the Coastal GasLink Pipeline), or attempts to simply close borders to prevent disease spread.

In the United States, we have also had to confront the harsh facts of chronic black impoverishment, under which "Today's black-white wealth gap is estimated to be $840,900 per household based on data from the Federal Reserve's 2019 Survey of Consumer Finances (SCF)."[9] Moreover, postslavery/post-Reconstruction black communities have been subject to forms of violent *Elimination*, such as in the Greenwood neighborhood in Tulsa, Oklahoma, and terrorism against black sharecroppers in the South that led to the murder of over eight hundred blacks seeking to organize their labour in Elaine, Arkansas. An immediate, comparative context for this contemporary mode of initiative Elimination to exterminate blacks *as* would-be native peoples, making their lands valuable (and hence convert their bodies to an accumulative function), is the genocidal assault on Indigenous Palestinians in Gaza by the Israeli government, beginning in October 2023. Blacks have also been subject to forms of settler *Removal*, such as during Hurricane Katrina, as a mechanism of uprooting through "disposability," the mass black migration north in the twentieth century (precipitated by violence and disenfranchisement), and the displacement of the African American settlement in Seneca Village in New York, all of which subtend contemporary state-sponsored Death as a quotidian, social mechanism of discipline.[10] This is conceptually part of the United States' ongoing, post-nineteenth-century expansion to overseas and what we can call *internal* territories not recognized through the index of reservations.[11] In the Seneca and Greenwood cases, these respective attempts at Removal and Elimination of blacks differ from that of Indigenous Peoples because they are punitive rather than initiative. They demonstrate that the presumably separate experiences of blacks and Indigenous Peoples confined to slavery and settler colonialism are actually ongoing strategies of anti-blackness and anti-indigeneity exercised in relation to each other (see chapter 3). Moreover, anti-blackness alone cannot explain, for instance, the violence in Tulsa, which eliminated black efforts to accumulate rather than remain as vectors of capital accumulation for the (white) human. The violence was also about preventing, as with Elaine, the labour that blacks use to reroot themselves as beings for whom the land *can* occur. These examples of Elimination and Removal (rather than strictly Death, or as the transformation of black Death) reinforce the urgent need for reparations, as many have argued.[12]

However, a twofold problem remains. First, no matter how urgently needed, reparations within settler states still require colonialism and possession of Indigenous lands for capital accumulation through the prior transformation of Indigenous and black bodies by processes of Conversion and the Middle Passage. The laudable efforts of the Caribbean Community (CARICOM) Reparations Commission to seek reparations from former colonizers, for instance, still largely seek justice for slavery, not Indigenous dispossession as perpetrated by former colonizers and postcolonial governments.[13] Second, we (blacks) cannot get back what has been stolen from us: the old sovereignties of our skins. We have been denied not just land and wealth, but political systems that were not rooted in accumulation. There is no way for us to achieve ontological sovereignty (a sovereignty that holds our flesh like earth) within regimes of capital accumulation. We have had our sovereignties forced onto our flesh and endured centuries of interdiction against their unfolding. Our conversion has been *from* our sovereignties with a fundamental prohibition against their return as either rights (e.g., new voter suppression bills across the South, targeting urban black populations) or lands.

Moreover, to the extent that reparations are based on money/land, they essentially do what Wynter claims of Marx's criticism (see the introduction): seek to redistribute the products of wealth accumulation on Indigenous lands without disrupting the function of ownership. In this case, the theft of black labour and sovereignty and that of Indigenous land and sovereignty are still validated in the effort to redistribute the settler state's ill-gotten wealth to blacks. Arguments for a new humanism whose primary goal is to address black material subordination are compelling. Political scientist Michael Hanchard argues, at the end of *Party/Politics*, for an "agenda for black activism" based on a "materially based humanism aimed specifically at the amelioration of conditions of poverty, homelessness, land evictions, and the provision of healthcare, in addition to the elimination of racisms."[14] In other words, of course we (black or other racially/ethnically modified activists) must advocate for an economically based humanism because our humanity is fundamentally and totally determined by relationships to capital. Within the logic of Hanchard's and similar projects, humanist agendas would only be useful if at the end of the day culture was the second rather than the first term. The problem is that such redemption-oriented projects seek to make the current political-economic order better for blacks rather than address how the remedy for the structural anti-blackness that produces our ill health and displacement might radically exceed the structures of amelioration.

The forms of Death *and* Elimination to which blacks are subject also demonstrate that even where the types of care, knowledge, and bodily actions Pruitt depicts are the unfolding of our flesh in earth, they are still structurally negated. We therefore need to insist on our flesh, on ourselves, and develop earth-based political systems from our flesh and its forms of exchange and interaction with earth that do not start from alienation, and hence from the quotient of needs and scarcity that required the transformation of black and native bodies in the first place. Here, *earth-based* would function as a parallel to *place-based* Indigenous sovereignties, as they emerged in Glen Coulthard and Leanne Betasamosake Simpson's writings, wherever we grow ourselves. By itself, however, even this is not enough. We must also first *choose* to give up not our labour, but its accumulative form, our work. We must develop new languages to talk about our labour not as work's antagonism, but outside the dialectic of accumulation. It is therefore about broadening these extant nonaccumulative relationships to black labour, establishing new languages to capture the political economy of sovereign relation, and resisting their conscription back into the master structures and disciplines that shore up unequal modes of being.[15]

Some of this possibility for embracing a political economy of our *labour* with adequate language for it exists in our art, where we encounter a new *ark*, rather than *arc*, as a curve of probability for black and Indigenous labour.[16] Pruitt's work offers one example, showing how the substitution of crops undoes the naturalness of the language of capitalist political economy. She resists both capital's conscripting language and the structure of the plantation machine that transforms blacks to value. Although similarly resistant, embodied descriptive language exists across African diaspora arts, I want to conclude by foregrounding it in the work of two artists representing black labour without affirming the post-fifteenth-century value of work and its requirement of black and native subordination and antagonism. This work offers us language we can position in the ruptures and openings around labour and the political economic language of the black left we saw in Robinson, James, Rodney, and Wynter (chapters 3–5).

In *displacing* art with ark, I highlight the strategic move of deferring labour's object or product (both material and in the language of political and economic critique) by visual production as a point of relationality that recovers black labours against the accumulative function of black work, allowing it to articulate with sovereign Indigenous labours. This turn to art is not frivolous, speculative, or antimaterialist. Instead, it indicates how we have already been articulating relationships to our labour both against and in excess of its conversion to the accumulative function of our work. To illustrate how the visual makes space for our labours to be in relation outside their conscription and conversion, I turn to the work of an Indigenous artist from Guyana and two black American artists.

In 2018, I visited Guyana's Castellani House: the National Gallery of Art.[17] The colonial building was designed by and named for Maltese architect Cesar Castellani as part of the 1877 plans to "establish a large public garden" (now the Botanical Gardens) by the Royal Agricultural and Commercial Society.[18] Although the building has had various functions over the years, when I was a child it was the residence of then Prime Minister Forbes Burnham. In the online tourist site "Explore Guyana," though nominally an art gallery, Castellani House is listed together with the country's museums, including the Walter Roth Museum of Anthropology in Guyana, which was created in the 1970s and honors the Indian Protector Walter Edmund Roth, who worked in Australia and Guyana.[19] Roth was also a collector, and seems to have been obsessively interested in a broad range of Indigenous culture from totems to menstruation.[20]

Its larger colonial context aside, Castellani House contains the work of the late teacher and Indigenous Macusi (Makushi) artist from the Nappi Village in the Rupununi, George Tancredo, and has also featured the work of Guy Fredericks, another Indigenous artist from the Nappi village who, like Tancredo, works with balata.[21] Tancredo uses balata to recreate, in miniature, Indigenous life in Guyana, where the balata export industry commenced in the 1860s, peaked in the early twentieth century, and began declining by the 1930s.[22] Harvested from the bullet tree in Guyana, the latex or milk from this species of rubber-producing tree was never, as Sarah Albuquerque demonstrates, as profitable economically as other dominant species of rubber plants. However, despite its lack of profitability, balata was a labour-intensive, environmentally unsustainable industry that was a twofold site of Indigenous subordination. Indigenous Peoples who worked balata had to pay the colonial government for access to the Crown land the trees were on, and the industry itself could not sustain Indigenous People, contributing to their impoverishment.[23] Moreover, Albuquerque writes that its pre-industry use by Indigenous Peoples was entirely different, centered on using the tree's latex sap as a drink to replace milk.[24]

In an autobiographical statement about his work from Castellani House, Tancredo says he was a "balata bleeder" like his father, and began making "figurines" out of unsold balata. His piece, titled *A Dream of My Ancestors and the Past*, is on permanent display at Castellani House ("donated" by businessman and collector Inderjeet Beharry).[25] In a brochure that Castellani House gave this author in December 2018 (which also contains an autobiographical statement), Tancredo describes the exhibition. He states that the work depicts Macusi village life scenes, including medicine people; the Kanaima as a mythical "assassin"; "creative activity" that includes "two women spinning and weaving cotton"; food preparation including a man cooking meat and the preparation process for cassava; "women returning from the bush" carrying "firewood"; and "Parishara dancers and humming-bird dancers" getting ready for a party or celebration. In an accompanying brochure situating Tancredo's work within the larger terms of reception for Indigenous art, Terry Roopnaraine (consultant in social development and poverty alleviation) claims that such *art* has been deliberately mis-understood as "craft" through the reinforcement of Indigenous Peoples' status as homunculi. Indeed, an article about an exhibition that included Fredericks's work at Castellani House refers to Fredericks and others as "craftsmen," discussing this kind of sculpture alongside "handbags," "baskets and ornaments, bracelets, necklaces and earrings," which are distinguished from "artwork" such as painting and sculptures.[26] Additionally, in the brief descriptions of Guyana's Indigenous groups, the Ministry of Indigenous Peoples Affairs reinforces their cultural labour as craft.[27] Roopnaraine thus makes a plea for reading Tancredo's work in terms of extant Indigenous artistic production, pointing to its fundamental misreading *outside* an Indigenous worldview. He also suggests that the balata art is both a product of economic forces ("the decline of the balata market") and an internal shift in Indigenous groups' representative strategies and aims. In the brochures, Tancredo writes that "Balata sculpture is not a 'traditional art form of Guyanese Amerindians; on the whole, three-dimensional sculptural art is a rarity among the Indigenous peoples of Lowland South America, who tend to impose aesthetic elaboration on objects of ceremonial or practical use." Thus, also in the brochures, Roopnaraine notes that Tancredo's multidimensional work is a form of innovation debunking "another incorrect image of Amerindian art: that it merely cleaves to iterative forms and standard media."

Roopnaraine's goal is to have viewers see Tancredo's work as an Indigenous aesthetic practice understood evolutionarily within western concepts of what constitutes high artistic value. His defense of Tancredo's work reveals some of the problems with strictly designating Indigenous cultural production as art. To argue that Tancredo's work is innovative, Roopnaraine simultaneously has to suggest that it is *more* than its Indigenous origins. As indicated in the arguments of Chiricahua Apache art historian Nancy Marie Mithlo, a deeply problematic post-Indian status rescues Tancredo's art from its overidentification as craft. Moreover, Roopnaraine's essential elevation of Tancredo's work *as* art reflects what Mithlo sees as a co-optation to the terms and economies of western artistic cultural production. As art, Tancredo's work is only realized in the conflict between his Indianness and art. Roopnaraine's defense is thus still caught within two dominant perspectives of viewing Indigenous cultural production that are based in anti-indigeneity. Mithlo writes, "The exposure of narrowly restrictive strategies of debate—including the rejection of standard fine arts categories of reception ("no word for art in my language") and the assimilation of these same fine arts concepts ("I'm an artist first and an Indian second," or post-Indianness) is critical for advancing more accurate terms of engagement."[28] Despite Roopnaraine's argument that the work must be viewed within an Indigenous context, the internal distinction between craft and art against which he must work reinstitutes the dialectic of labour and work that makes Tancredo's figures valuable for the gallery/museum itself.

With these cautions in mind, I do not want to undermine Roopnaraine's description of Tancredo's stunning work, of which even a photographic depiction cannot do justice to its scale or intricacy, nor his plea that it be viewed in its own context. However, I suggest that Tancredo's artistry is a material or plastic arts practice that is not simply the aesthetic recreation of Indigenous life. It reproduces (like the 40,000 GPS points in chapter 6) or depicts Indigenous labour as a sovereign phenomenon, resisting its representation as art—its (metaphoric) conscription for accumulation in the dialectic. This sovereignty becomes lost precisely because of the western interpretive practices that Roopnaraine criticizes. Moreover, emerging out of the failure of balata bleeding and selling to function as a sufficient source of income, what Tancredo does with essentially surplus or leftovers of the balata commodity is to *reconvert* an economy or industry of accumulation into one of subsistence, within the terms of his own labour as a sovereign Indigenous practice. In the previously mentioned brochure, Tancredo even notes that his work with balata, including teaching it as craft, allows him to not "work as hard on the farm." Thus, Tancredo's depictions themselves are not mediated by extra-Indigenous elements. Tancredo critically facilitates for us the recovery of Indigenous labour from its Conversion, in this case to craft, within the labour-work dialectic (for postcolonial nationalism), reinvigorating that labour as sovereign and sustaining.

Craft—as a term applied to Indigenous practices of making products that have been useful to their livelihoods, which sustain their sovereignties within communities, and have become objects for tourist consumption (e.g., the matapee for processing cassava)—is a deliberate way of rendering Indigenous labour invisible *as* unproductive labour. Moreover, the reduction of Tancredo's work to craft prevents the realization of his aesthetic practice as a doubling of sovereignty in the land. Additionally, we are faced with the problem that to recover it *as craft* invokes Indigeneity's temporal pre-position to Creole culture and identity, but to recover it *as art* also facilitates its continued Conversion to forms of value. Thus, the problem Roopnaraine actually identifies is how the perception of Tancredo's own artistic labour as craft happens in terms of the evolutionary colonial perspective on indigeneity, which reasserts itself as an organizing desire for the representative capacity of Castellani House and the museums to which it is likened in the postcolonial nation-state. Tancredo's work and its *representation* as art is therefore a moment of both metaphoric conscription (acceptable simulation) and metonymic rupture (unacceptable break).

As a practice of representation (i.e., as symbolic practice), Tancredo's work is held in a space made possible by the articulation of coloniality's spatial practices with those of postcoloniality. Castellani House is on coastal land that, as Rodney reminded us (by deploying settler/conquistadorial desire in his labour analysis, as I argued), was not that of Indigenous Peoples. Castellani House thus initiates several kinds of displacement through which Tancredo's work has meaning or makes sense. First, the displacement of land: the work showing the occurrence of Indigenous sovereignty is in a fundamentally anthropological-colonial cum national space existing through the very abrogation or deferral of that sovereignty. Second, the displacement of Indigenous labour itself, which is read in the Castellani House as a cultural, anthropological space in terms of the distance between its organization and creation under British colonialism, and the objective status conferred on indigeneity by the national status of Castellani House. This distance allows for the object (Indigenous life and labour) to be represented in the first place.

The final displacement is the doubling of Indigenous labour. Tancredo's work is like the practice of mapping; the doubling in a different form of a topography of sovereignty. It is metonymic rather than metaphoric, contained by these forms of relation and exceeding them where substitution of the part for the whole breaks down. However, as a physically intensive artistic practice, it is reduced to unproductive labour in a space designed to represent such labors, to represent Indigenous bodily actions after and through their Conversion. The representation of Tancredo's work as craft within the national sphere (read: Independence over Sovereignty) positions it on the left side of the labour-work division, tying its meaning to the postcolonial nation's public sphere through the division itself. Thus, the art gallery or museum is a space not of productive work, but only of the kinds of labour that need to be sustained by corporate or private donation, government grants, and so on. These labours must be sustained by the surplus of productive work, and their productive potential exists as culture to secure the narrative of the nation as Creole patrimony.

We need to approach Tancredo's and other Indigenous work in terms of how it refers to itself, its own antecedents and contemporaries, rather than in terms of the metaphoric-metonymic management that incorporates Indigenous labour's difference within structures of relationality to other arts rather than to other Indigenous labours. We need to access Indigenous labour's specific forms of doubling as a renewal of Indigenous sovereignties and develop an at least partial (nonappropriative) interpretive context for articulating it. By sustaining the difference of Indigenous labour, its objective status as *not*-labour, the museum/gallery space relies on the mechanisms of contiguity to establish a paradigmatic or metaphoric relation that undermines Indigenous sovereignty by presenting a representation of Tancredo's labour as unproductive or nonaccumulative *before* it can be read as sovereign and thus already governed by other strategies of doubling. Tancredo's work, however, both re-presents and continues pre-contact, sovereign labour practice that manipulates the very objects of Indigenous labour conversion away from value. He shares this with African American/ diasporic artists Jean-Michel Basquiat and Thornton Dial, allowing their artistic production to collectively function as a site of refusal and sovereign labour practice.

In 2006, the Museum of Fine Arts in Houston (MFAH) exhibited the works of African American artists Thornton Dial (1928–2016) and Jean-Michel Basquiat (1960–1988; of Haitian and Puerto Rican descent).[29] Basquiat, famous for his postmodern and neoexpressionist drawings and paintings, has been referred to as a postcolonial, Afrofuturistic artist. In contrast, Dial, a former farmworker, carpenter, bricklayer, welder, and steelworker, is known for mixed-media creations that have at times been described as "folk," "spiritual," and postmodern (where postmodern actually seems to mean for Dial simplistic or derivative).[30] With Dial's less well-known work in one building in an exhibit titled "Thornton Dial in the 21st Century," alongside Gee's Bend quilts to reinforce this perspective on Dial's work, and Basquiat's in another, patrons moved from the heavy, cloying fumes of Dial's metals, plastics, and found objects such as shoes, goat carcasses, and a Ken doll to Basquiat's work. With the latter, it was not the effluvia of chemicals but the unrelenting layering of images and words that assaulted visitors.

The MFAH's simultaneous display of these artists' works made stark the contrast between Basquiat's discursive style and Dial's tactile, heavy materialism. Had the museum placed Dial's, Basquiat's, and Gee's Bend's works in the same space, then race would have been their overarching context, and the art would have been designated collectively as black.[31] Without doing so, the MFAH imposed another, less obvious limit on the work by spatially separating what could be deemed the twentieth-century southern, rural black American condition from the northern, urban black American and diasporic condition. By situating their art in different locations and reinforcing Dial's difference from Basquiat, the museum unwittingly displayed their works through the very split that is internal to the function of accumulation: labour and work. Although both collections are commodities in the art world, where Basquiat's was more highly regarded and valued than Dial's for decades, it reinforced black work as the production context of Dial's art. In other words, it reinforced the prior transformation of blacks and the accumulative function of their bodily labours, whereas the weightlessness of Basquiat's discursivity had seemingly transcended that function to circulate differently from Dial's. However, I suggest that the works themselves contain possibilities for a new language for black labour and a new approach to its objects. In particular, that language emerges precisely from the chronology of my museum visit as I encountered Basquiat's work *after* Dial's.

In Basquiat's work, the image that interests me is *50 Cent Piece* from the Daros Suite. Created in 1982–83, these thirty-two drawings were acquired from Basquiat as a single group. This piece can be read in several possible ways, but I foreground, as a caution, three different ways of framing and hence deploying the dialectic's conscripting function to his work. First, the postcolonial reading sees him as working in the "third or intertextual space of form" that rejects origins and privileges juxtaposition even as Basquiat is simultaneously read as a black, authentic street artist.[32] This reading affirms Basquiat's paintings as resisting the logocentrism we bring to most cultural products; in his painting we cannot find any single essential meaning, which he denies through "incoherence." This reading uses the references in the painting to the Occupation of Haiti; François Duvalier; a side view of a 50 cent piece; a side view of Marcus Garvey; a brain X-ray photo; the US occupation of Haiti; the Royal Sugar Corporation; industrialization; the Back to Africa movement; rum, sugar, bananas; homogenization; the Federal Reserve; the underdeveloped world and to civilize (both references deliberately obscured); and, finally, salt. In particular, the latter has so many external references (e.g., forms of currency, the saltwater of the Atlantic Ocean, salted meats and fish given as rations to the enslaved) that it displaces what it represents, allowing for multiple meanings to coincide in its depiction. Basquiat's use of (the biblical) Noah's ark instead of the slave ship makes visible the ship's conditions of possibility—black subordination in the post-diluvial narrative dividing earth's people into redeemed and fallen—through metonymy and deferral as the ark doubles and defers the slave ship rather than engages its overrepresentation and overdetermination of post-chattel black life. In its single frame and lack of chronological depiction, the painting suggests no progression between alternate states of repression and revolution (e.g., Russian czars together with Marcus Garvey's Back to Africa movement). Overall, the postcolonial reading exploits the piece's displacement of time as linear/progressive and its indication of power's constant reproduction. The piece thus plays with power as postcolonial critique does.

A second possible reading is the work's critique of empire, in which the anti- anti-logocentrism facilitating the postcolonial studies approach reveals a critique of empire depicting a structuring paradox or contradiction that shapes Caribbean reality. This paradox, unrecognized because it is articulated definitively as mere historical fact, is that the Americas began to liberate themselves at the end of (rather than after) two empires. First, at the end or decline (read: transformation) of the European empire(s) they helped create, and then at the end of the American empire, so North America literally ends at the Caribbean and Latin America, forcibly incorporating their economies (by the North American Free Trade Agreement [NAFTA], for instance) as earlier empires have done. The Caribbean is therefore caught between two imperial attitudes—Columbus and Monroe/Roosevelt—and three moments: the rise and decline of European imperialism, the rise (and dare we hint at the decline) of American imperialism, and the transformation of global wealth in Empire's economic order, conceptualized by Michael Hardt and Antonio Negri. This paradox of coloniality that ties the Caribbean to empire consequently forces the Caribbean to "repeat"—to recall Antonio Benítez-Rojo—itself and its history for the First World. By repetition I refer to twentieth-century colonial invasions, euphemized as either interventions or regime changes, such as those of Grenada, Haiti, and the Dominican Republic, repeating fifteenth and sixteenth centuries' imperial incursions; the reenactments in the Virgin Islands of the Danish transfer of power to the United States, repeating the denial of political sovereignty under colonial rule; the annual recreation of Columbus's landfall on Trinidad; and similar reenactments of real and symbolic imperial power.

Moreover, these repetitions are considered ahistorical, occurring within Empire's new universal time and culture, which has surpassed that of European modernity and emerged to devour the history that produced it. As Hardt and Negri famously decry, "Empire exhausts historical time, suspends history, and summons the past and future within its own ethical order."[33] Even the first African American president of the United States, Barack Obama, drew on the now-abstracted notion of the end of history, a logic produced by empire itself, situating it alongside the discourse of market deregulation in the 1990s.[34] Consequently, less than fifty years after the emergence of viable, independent Caribbean and African states from

European control, the nation-state and the political sovereignty it guaranteed ceases to matter, partly because capitalism's racialist logic requires it to be an underdeveloped receptor for First World goods contributing to First World nations' wealth. The repetition of imperial history thus becomes instrumental in producing Caribbean and Latin American states as underdeveloped, poor populations whose own wealth would contradict the structuring "classificatory schema" of the present economic order.[35] Basquiat's repeated yet different representations (of the ark, for instance) gesture toward this repetition of empire, which is possible because—unlike in the postcolonial reading—it resists a view of colonial modernity that historian Frederick Cooper cautions against, which binds colonization in every instance to a discourse or project of modernization.[36]

The final, (Afro)futuristic reading that provided the initial context for this exploration of their work brings us to questions about how we see the text's space and time. The fact that the painting demands to be read simultaneously vertically and horizontally not only rejects linearity, but creates a dimensional rearrangement that is newly productive for black futures. In this reading, *50 Cent Piece* resists time both as play (postcolonial) and as an adjunct of blackness (empire), suggesting instead that black futures are in no way pre- or overdetermined by black pasts. However, questions remain: What does this reading or possibility for black expression and black being emerge from? Is it possible only out of a rendering of the past or present as incoherent or "semiotic wilderness," or only out of the exhaustion of other possible readings as the limit of a critique of power?[37] In this case, Afro futures are ineffably tied to the narrative of the end of history, depending on the subordination of black work through the reengineering of signs that can reproduce it. Blacks' positive relationship to time and space would then emerge singularly from the displacement of (or resistance to) black work, leaving us wondering, Where does black labour go in Afro futures? Must these futures supersede the labour that built them?

I encountered Basquiat's work not on its own terms (if this is possible in the museum's artificial structure), but after or through Dial's, and this route leads me to reject all three readings above. In the museum, I went, perfectly haphazardly, from Dial's work to Basquiat's even though the museum and art world place Dial—who was still producing work at the time, including on 9/11 and Obama's election—before Basquiat, in the sense that Basquiat's work is seen as contemporary, unlike Dial's. Thus, we come to Basquiat after Dial as a chronological problem of black labour cleaved into accumulative and nonaccumulative forms. Dial brings a material critique of Reconstruction-era black American labour into the present, extending it into the contemporary period of fictitious capital, which presents poverty without labour and all that goes with it (e.g., the redistribution of commodities during riots as *looting*, as fundamentally illegal rather than just reparation).

That critique, however, is partly undermined by the work's function as art and the prohibitions of museum spaces, so although Dial's work is tactile, we are not allowed to *touch* the wire brushes, peach basket, ironing board, Ken doll, decomposing carcasses, tire, wood, shoes, paintbrushes, rope, or wire in *Lost Farm (Billy Goat Hill)* (see figure C.1). Visitors are thus limited to a visual consumption of Dial's (found) objects, which literally leap off the canvas, such as the rusted car he reclaims as art by chopping it up for a series of pieces called *Driving to the End of the World*. Thus, a particular irony surrounds work that not only critiques black subordination, as he does in numerous works like *Construction on the Victory*, but also imagines black freedom as an outright possibility. Ironically, though, Basquiat's semiotics references black work (slavery) more directly than Dial's, who invokes loss. The literal "lost farm" is not the agricultural lands blacks lost, but the active losing of any mode of recuperation for that farm to exist as an object of accumulation. He thus accumulates the loss of the semiotics of the thing itself on the canvas, eroding the language of its expression, its containment.

The conditions of production for Dial's work, however, reveal the ever-present limits of black resistance and the ways our labour is always conscripted even before its occurrence. Bill Arnett, a white collector who funded southern black artists, paid for Dial's work. Arnett's and then the museum's capture of its aesthetic means that whatever labour Dial put into it is turned into its accumulative form when the work becomes a commodity. Moreover, Arnett's pre-funding of the work ensures that what Dial produces is always already valuable, always already part of a particular economy no matter what labour is put into it. This partial compulsion of Dial's work simulates his labour as a former factory worker, making it newly productive. Dial cannot leave black work's accumulative function in the past even as he fundamentally refashions it. He seemingly cannot leave behind the reinscription of capital, which Basquiat abandons for the semiotic wilderness. Thus, the work either rejects a specific problem within capital, which reinscribes Marxist labour history and its particular outcome, or falls into that divide between work and pleasure, work and aestheticism. It is almost as though the heavy materialism of Dial's art literally weights

FIGURE C.1: Thornton Dial, *Lost Farm (Billy Goat Hill)*, 2000.
© Estate of Thornton Dial.

it down. Dial's labour on things is thus always superseded by his work on the commodity as that which must be realized out of black work. However, Dial, I argue, does something to the commodity's time (and hence its value) with his labour, whose disruptive potential both rejects black subordination through the compelling of black work and resists the negative relation between indigeneity and blackness.

In the 2011 forum "Hard Truths: The Art of Thornton Dial" at the Indianapolis Museum of Art, Fred Moten offered in his presentation, "An Ecology of (Eloquent) Things," a black radical engagement with Dial's work. Placing it within the radical tradition, Moten argues that just as the tradition engages Marxist critique at its point of "exhaustion" by racial capital, Dial's work achieves a "critical transcendence of private property," and that Dial rejects the split between private property, or wealth, and poverty.[38] Moten goes further to say that Dial's "refusal of the disposable" and "incorporation of the fact of decomposition" means that he "makes things out of things," challenging Marx's idea of man's "mastery" over nature. Moten's analysis, using Cedric Robinson's work, is critical in foregrounding an alternative approach to both blackness and black work. Through Moten, we can read Dial's work beyond any simple resistance to its conscription. It offers a new language for thinking about the commodity and labour. If, as I suggested, Dial works on or against time, and Moten argues that he incorporates decomposition in making things out of things, then Dial fundamentally demonstrates black labours' productive capacity as both prior and parallel to capitalist political economy. It shows that *as* or having *been* commodities, blacks retained a relationship to their labour that literally destroys the commodity as a common object of the human.

In *Capital*, Marx clarifies that value in a commodity is determined not by the time it takes to produce it but by labour power. He writes that use values are only such "because human labour in the abstract has been embodied or materialised in it. . . . The labour, however, that forms the substance of value, is homogenous human labour expenditure of one uniform labour power."[39] However, the commodity also produces time (or a particular kind of relationship to it) as an effect of labour power, and changes and entrenches our relationship to time as one of alienation. Marx writes, "The labour time socially necessary is that required to produce an article under the normal conditions of production, and with the average degree of skill and intensity prevalent at the time."[40] Unremunerated black chattel work, however, could not abide by this limit of only what is socially necessary, and therefore posed a problem for value itself.

Even as their own conversion to value shores up the system of value, this failure of the enslaved to abide by the limit of what is socially necessary indicates the excess of the unacceptable part of conquistadorial desire in the function and position of the master, which will transition into the bourgeois class. At the end of slavery, blacks were literally mandated to convert to underpaid waged labour. In Guyana, for example, it happened through apprenticeship, which prohibited the refusal to work (read: idleness). In Texas, the decree that ended slavery stated, "The freedmen are advised to remain quietly at their present homes and work for wages" because "they will not be . . . supported in idleness either there or elsewhere."[41] This was an attempt to legitimize the desire that required their lack of remuneration, but because it was excessive, postslavery black labour continued to be devalued and exploited. In short, in becoming and functioning as enslaved people working on the settler-master's goods, blacks are prohibited from the master's relationship to time, which is based on accumulation. After slavery, the prohibition must remain because it is intrinsic to the evolution of value and the management of settler-master desire.

Death and Elimination (the latter applying to all forms of indigeneity) are flexible, atemporal structures reinforcing the commodity's linear time by managing (through black and native bodies) the position of lack or failure in the commodity, its literal decay (as opposed to its consumption). They are thus necessary for the forms of value contained by the commodity. The commodity defers its own decay when it circulates, but Dial removes that deferral, collapsing the antagonistic relationship of blackness and indigeneity in a space that serves as the ark of black unfolding into different relationships. Dial effectively reworks time in the commodity, reworking the very thing for which black and native labours have been converted: our relationship to labour from both the nonaccumulative side of the dialectic and its remainder. The commodity that we cannot possess works on us, but Dial works on the commodity after the exhaustion of its use value as an expression of a normative relationship between labour power and value, showing us how to change our relationship to time and thus to it.

Moreover, enslaved blacks are alienated from time as an effect of labour. This is the "unowned differential, differentiated thing itself that we hold out to one another in the bottom under our skin for the general kin."[42] Black becoming is not just against property but prior to it, Moten suggests by using Robinson. Thus, it becomes in and against any kind of relation, even negation. Instead, black labour produced the "eloquence" necessary to the growth of that metonymic crop we saw in Pruitt. Many discussions of Dial's work and its consumption within the art world constantly reinsert it back into the very split between private property and poverty that Moten says it transcends. However, Dial's actual labour—as a volitional engagement with discarded items—neither observes it nor reproduces its articulating structures, use and exchange value, precisely because in pieces like *Lost Farm* the objects he utilizes do not *become*. His work rejects the forms of conversion and abstraction necessary to the commodity. The semiotic field of value, its necessary overrepresentation, in essence, cannot be sustained in the work itself. Dial thus destroys the architecture of value that the dialectic produces, which is extended even in anticapitalist, Marxist criticism (see chapter 1). However, he also does something else that fundamentally pushes back against the overrepresentation of the productive function of (anti)blackness' antagonism to (anti)indigeneity. His work goes further than most to address this structural problem as part of the elaboration of black labour.

In his piece *Buffalo Man* (People have learned from the Indian) (1992), made primarily of wood rather than the multivariate reclaimed objects of many of his other works, Dial imagines freedom as a relational aspiration of blacks and Indigenous Peoples. The work is described as one that "honors the Native American, represented in a profile image inspired by the 'Indian head' or 'buffalo' nickel of Dial's youth. Clusters of birds and disguised forms of tigers identify the common reach for freedom that Native Americans share with African Americans."[43] *Buffalo Man* introduces several questions about Dial's work, particularly regarding what it transcends. Dial suggests a learning rather than *taking* from indigenous Peoples; what does this learning—from outside the economy of taking or theft—mean for black labour and its futures? In depicting this shared aspiration for native and black freedoms, what translation of Indigenous sovereignties or rights-based claims does Dial's piece enact? Does the *symbolic* of the native in this piece, which comes from a form of monetary exchange (the coin), achieve the same critical transcendence of value discussed above and is this the only point at which blackness can have a relationship to indigeneity in which the state and its rights structures are not the limit? Is this the same reconciliation of the difference between wealth and poverty, the always already of the critical outcome/interpretation?

I ask these questions because of the opposed structures of time as history and space as nature in the work of Sioux activist and writer Vine Deloria Jr.[44] Deloria identified Black civil rights struggles as orientated toward settler civil society's institutional structures and thus as connected with time (i.e., notions of progress tied to the literal accumulation of rights), by contrast to native peoples, who are interested in rights that are concerned with space and nature.[45] If the freedoms Dial envisions or visualizes concern rights, then the work itself might transcend a split internal to capital but not the core, a priori split of the antagonism between black and native bodies in the labour-work dialectic. However, I find in the work a specific operation of metonymy that achieves a critical displacement, although Dial essentially mimics the coin: the distortion of the image is a strategic form of misrepresentation allowing for relationality without overdetermination.

FIGURE C.2: Thornton Dial, *Buffalo Man (People Have Learned from the Indian)*, 1992. © Estate of Thornton Dial.

Dial has said he works only with "materials that have been used by people," essentially operating at the limit of the distinction between use and exchange value.[46] His work is thus not only a language of transcendence, but one of negation expressed through a positive valuation of the decay of use. Both use and exchange value have a temporal dimension, and what is instructive about Dial's and Basquiat's work together is that they resist it. Basquiat's drawings work against the semiotic field in which the time of black subordination operates/is arranged. Dial works on time (specifically, modern time): decayed, not disappeared, shown only through its wear. In this wearing of time, Dial represents the future of black labour as a working in/on time itself: precisely the moment of possibility of alliance with native struggles for land-based sovereignties.

Conceptually, Dial's and Basquiat's works suggest that it is not about removing black labour or transcending it, but about turning it toward the architecture of time—dismantling it, wearing it down. In doing this, Dial essentially changes the terms of value, giving us a new language for having or possession. On the one hand, if we see Dial's work as superseding the poverty versus wealth split, then we say that it exists only through accumulation and thus does not transcend the "split" between labour and work, which is its condition of existence. However, Dial demonstrates that something actually remains of black labour in the making of things that does not depend on what those things become—be they commodities or literally exhausted (use) values woven into the museum market's exchange circuit. The prohibition against touching, feeling, or holding Dial's work in the museum is actually the point where value reasserts itself phenomenologically, reimposing the human as relation to property (see Moten, Hartman) as the only point of contact with the world.

Together, Dial's and Basquiat's works offer not just a new symbolic expression of black labour, but a phenomenology of black labour. Read *after* Dial, Basquiat's critique of European and US spatial and economic imperialism in works like *50 Cent Piece* reveals how empire flattens out the labour involved in its creation, normalizing the class divisions that are the precise vehicle for its criticism. Dial's critique of southern black labour and alienation in works like *Lost Farm (Billy Goat Hill)* and of American consumerism in *American $* provide a criticism of culture and empire without reproducing the division of labour or abstracting labour. More importantly, Dial does not make the transcendence of black labour necessary for us to exit modernity. He does not suggest that black labour is unrepresentable in Afro futures, but opens up a project space allowing indigenous and Afro futures to return. Dial's work shows us work's reconversion to labour through the creation of this heavy materialism and, as Moten says, the making of things out of things. Basquiat's work gives us new language for this making of things outside accumulation regimes because, like Dial's, it also defers the commodity. The semiotic play is also a way of representing the commodity without allowing us to have any (stable) access to the objects or things they represent. Together, Dial and Basquiat undo the time of black labour's conversion and of political economic language/critique, which traps black labour in the labour-work dialectic.

The MFAH's simultaneous exhibition of these works bridged the real and affective differences between Basquiat and Dial through either race or taste. Yet it is precisely the break between them that gives us new possibilities for the political and economic language of black labour. If, for example, Dial doubles things, then what we see is not the commodity form central to Marxist analysis, but ineffable objects instead. And because of Basquiat's reordering of time, markets' linear progression does not govern the product of Dial's labour. While Dial's heavy materialism and history literally as a labourer would close him off from Afro futures' temporality, his work actually shows ways of positioning those futures in terms of that same immanence that exists as an alternative possibility for the involuntary, postcolonial settler state (see chapter 4).

Both black and Indigenous sovereignties are continually sacrificed to the nation-state's constitutional freedoms through the broad conscription of capital's economies and descriptive languages through repetition. Therefore, the involuntary settler state's independence rests on the deferral of sovereignty for the Indigenous population. The state's contingent liberty—the maintenance of separate, colonially derived policies governing Indigenous Peoples' lives in the Americas—should be read as the ever-vanishing or retreating edge of sovereignty, as opposed to freedom/independence, for the Caribbean state. A black political economy focused on our labour breaks the moment of repetition of the labour-work division that pits our work against Indigenous sovereignties and leaves open the possibility of our historical and contemporary relation with Indigenous Peoples.

Out of new histories we can imagine new possibilities for the state and Indigenous sovereignties to be writ large, and for the sovereignty of black labour. If sovereignty is enacted at the level of the body, land, and language, rather than granted, then the works discussed above reflect it. Reengaging Moten, Dial's and Basquiat's art is literally the performance of no-thing—whether material or grammatical (given the decentered nature of both)—*as* some-thing. They undo the opposition between black optimism and Afropessimism, between, in Moten's words on Dial, "something" and "no-thing," respectively. Basquiat and Dial work from the death of the thing, of value, illustrating Jared Sexton's point that black death is in fact not opposed to black life, but, as he says elaborating Moten, "black life is *lived* in social *death*."[47]

Moreover, particularly Dial's work on the death of things allows us to return to and reread Tancredo's balata sculpture in terms of its difference from and relation to black art. To recall, Tancredo initially worked with leftover or surplus material, before balata's conversion as a natural product into a good for international markets. Tancredo thus works from a kind of surplus *before* the "thing," the commodity itself, while Dial, using found objects that had either been commodities (e.g., a doll) or never entered the commodity circuit (e.g., a goat carcass), works on or *after* the thing. This, on its face, is the temporal division that the labour-work dialectic institutes around Indigenous and black labours. Moreover, it reflects the differing relationships to things we share where there is a priorness to the thing that Indigenous being retains, while black being is overdetermined by or as the thing itself. However, if we read Dial and Tancredo as working from different ends of things themselves, from the death of its nonexistence and the death after its existence, we come to the possibility of a new phenomenology of things and, together with Basquiat's work, a language of semantic refusal that resists dialectics.

The dialectic breaks down in Tancredo's, Basquiat's, and Dial's works where two possibilities emerge: one for a new language for a radical tradition that does not resuscitate the labour-work divide, and another for refashioning our forms of Independence(s) away from their antagonism with Indigenous sovereignties. In specific, they all reject the conquistadorial desire our bodily conversions were made to support, rerouting us instead toward our nonaccumulative labours for sovereign being. The works support not the end of history, but that of Independence as a mode of sustaining accumulation, allowing us to posit the sovereignties of our labours. In the involuntary settler state of the South and in the settler North, we must go beyond our (Fanonian) rejection of recognition and embrace both the constant revolution of a radical tradition temporally unbound by slavery and the rebellion of permission evidenced in Dial's work, for instance. We must engage in forms of asking and encounter with Indigenous peoples and their titled and unceded lands as we unfold our flesh between "dirt and soil," and *ark* out of the illicit prohibition of touch, into the conscious pleasure of what can be felt.

PREFACE

1 The quotation is from Bulkan, who refers to Creoles as "settlers" as well; "Struggle for Recognition," 368. See also Trotz and Roopnaraine, "Angles of Vision."
   Dei has challenged Lawrence and Dua's work as well as Mamdani's, to claim that
   North American blacks cannot be settlers. Not only does the structural nature of
   anti-blackness mean that blacks can only be implicated but not complicit with
   the settler project, but "only white bodies have ever succeeded in deploying Terra
   Nullius." Dei, *Reframing Blackness*, 111. I agree with Dei on this point.

2 In *Creole Indigeneity*, I discuss the sociocultural use of the term *Creole*. Here, I
   use it to designate primarily, though not exclusively, the descendants of formerly
   enslaved blacks and indentured South Asians.

3 I use raison d'être here *as* and as *more than* a particular kind of ontological statement. It is *not* equivalent to the totality of what Creoles, particularly blacks, have
   become. It refers to both the material reality of black chattel bodies in the Americas and the idealistic efforts to have them serve as the "other" for the humanity
   of colonial, European man. These efforts focused on replacing Indigenous, black
   cosmogonic belonging with an ontological statement that tied and delimited it
   within Judeo-Christian subjectivity. The purpose of black being was then recast
   from being for itself within African cosmogonic systems to being for others or
   working for the well-being of Man/the human and of the colony, which aspires to
   be a state. In other words, black ontology, where it is not an oxymoron, becomes
   limited to work for Man's selfhood. I take seriously Frantz Fanon's statements
   that "every ontology is made unavailable in a colonized and civilized society"
   (*Wretched of the Earth*, 109). Moreover, whites' inhabiting of humanity always

forecloses black ontology by instituting a particular concept of Man, a genre, as Sylvia Wynter would say, for which blacks are necessarily "liminal"; (white) Man and black (human) are always opposed and irreconcilable grammars. In colonies like Guyana, blacks negotiated their raison d'être, or ontological statement, via Indigenous Peoples. This negotiation, I argue, is a co-constitutive element of their legal relationship with the latter. (For more on Man and the genres of the human, see Wynter, "Columbus and the Poetics," and McKittrick, *Sylvia Wynter*.)

4 Aileen Moreton-Robinson writes in *The White Possessive* of development as applied to Indigenous Peoples: "Development and aid are tied to achieving modernity and progress as well as white morals and values" (*White Possessive*, Loc 2840).

5 Guyana's Amerindian Act, as I discussed in *Creole Indigeneity*, designates who can be said to be Indigenous, legally superseding how Indigenous Peoples determine and practice belonging based on their own kinship structures.

6 Many analytic categories we employ as academics reinforce the divisions I seek to bridge between blacks and Indigenous Peoples. They are simply not applicable to many black and native ways of existing and interpreting the world. One of the best examples of this absolute difference is Chinua Achebe's *Things Fall Apart*. More contemporary discussions from within native (American) studies include Watts, "Indigenous Place-Thought," and Todd, "Indigenous Feminist's Take.?

7 See Introduction for explanation of term *weaver*.

INTRODUCTION

1 Although both enslaved black and indentured South Asian work has been linked with the evolution of the postcolonial nation-state and the radical and resistant anticolonial labour histories essential to its genesis, this book is primarily concerned with the relationship between Indigenous and black labour. I discuss South Asian indenture in *Creole Indigeneity*. Kamala Kempadoo argues against linking black chattel slavery to indenture, suggesting that the latter is more closely related to sex-trafficking and "modern slavery." See Kempadoo, "'Bound Coolies.'"

2 Although more strict definitions of franchise colonialism exist, I refer to Caribbean colonies of resource extraction and exploitation that utilized black chattel slavery as franchise colonies. Throughout the manuscript, the term "franchise" marks a distinction from settler colonies/colonialism even as I seek to have us read them relationally.

3 For the prior arrival thesis, see *Creole Indigeneity*.

4 I quote Zakiyyah Iman Jackson to specify the particular kind of racialization to which blacks are subject as distinct from other forms of racialization (*Becoming Human*, 93). I also acknowledge the resonances between my work and Tiffany Lethabo King's, as we are both concerned with the links and breaks among the black radical tradition, Afropessimism, and Indigenous studies, and we are both interested in the impasses of blackness and indigeneity around land, labour, and the human. Even where our analyses overlap in very differently oriented projects (King's is focused on the body, "porosity," and fungibility), it is purely coinci-

dental, and I do not read or critique these overlaps. In this project, my interest in labour, grammar, and being has evolved directly out of my first book, and I am deeply grateful that *Beyond Constraint* sits in such good company. I am even more grateful because the work of King and the other writers listed here makes the book less like a fish out of water than *Creole Indigeneity* was when it was first published.

5 King, *Black Shoals*, ix.

6 Lowe, *Intimacies of Four Continents*.

7 Byrd et al., "Predatory Value," 5.

8 Byrd et al., "Predatory Value," 6.

9 In *Creole Indigeneity* I discuss Cheddi Jagan's Marxism. For other work on Marxism's role in Caribbean politics and labour organizing, see Slack, "Charles W. Mills"; Maingot, *Race, Ideology, and the Decline*; Munroe, "Contemporary Marxist Movements" and *Marxist "Left" in Jamaica*.

10 Taylor, From #BlackLivesMatter to Black Liberation, 215–16 (my emphasis).

11 Césaire, Discourse on Colonialism, 78.

12 Depestre, "Interview with Aimé Césaire," 85.

13 Depestre, "Interview with Aimé Césaire," 85.

14 Depestre, "Interview with Aimé Césaire," 85–86.

15 See Wilderson, Afropessimism.

16 See Taylor, *From #BlackLivesMatter to Black Liberation*, chapter 7.

17 In an oft-quoted passage, Fanon writes: "In the colonies the economic infrastructure is also a superstructure. The cause is effect: You are rich because you are white, you are white because you are rich. This is why a Marxist analysis should always be slightly *stretched* when it comes to addressing the colonial issue. . . . In the colonies, the foreigner imposed himself using his cannons and machines [and he] . . . always remains a foreigner. . . . The ruling species is first and foremost the outsider from elsewhere, different from the indigenous population, 'the others.'" *Wretched of the Earth*, loc. 658 (my emphasis).

18 Cedric Robinson will see this last point as also peculiar to the race-capital Matrix in *Black Marxism*, nearly twenty years after Fanon, writing: "capitalism was less a catastrophic revolution (negation) of feudalist social orders than the extension of these social relations into the larger tapestry of the modern world's political and economic relations" (*Black Marxism*, 10). The distinctions that constitute the material base of society or "infrastructure" relations (forces of production) for Fanon, as distinct from but interconnected with its "superstructure" (noneconomic institutions), matter less in an account of social change in the colonies. For the operative elaboration of the distinction between base (infrastructure in Fanon) and superstructure, see Harman, "Base and Superstructure." Importantly, base and superstructure are not discrete or disarticulated. Drawing on Marx's recognition of this, Walter Rodney notes this at the outset of *How Europe Underdeveloped Africa* (6), and this fact in Marx's work has allowed Sylvia Wynter to consistently argue that "the mode of economic production" determines how we are human. McKittrick, ed., *Sylvia Wynter*, loc. 5584–88.

19 Fanon uses the term "settler" in *Wretched of the Earth*.

20 See Williams, *Capitalism and Slavery*; Silva, *Toward a Global Idea*.

21 For God's function to "extrahumanly" mandate the social structure of Christian Europe, see Wynter, "Columbus and the Poetics" and McKittrick, ed., *Sylvia Wynter*. Fanon refers to this external, validating element of social and economic relations to which he correlates race. Wynter argues that race replaced God and thus functions in the same way.

22 See Taylor, *From #BlackLivesMatter to Black Liberation*, chapter 7.

23 Homi Bhabha uses "Manichean" in his introduction to *The Wretched of the Earth* (2004). Constance Farrington's translation (1963) puts the term in Fanon's text itself.

24 Fanon (2004), loc. 664–70. In a separate work I talk briefly about the ontological versus the phenomenological Fanon in these books (Jackson, "Colonialism"). See also Fanon's "Why We Use Violence."

25 Taylor, *From #BlackLivesMatter to Black Liberation*, 206.

26 Coulthard, "The Colonialism of the Present." This phrasing in the piece's title echoes Means's claim that "for America to live Europe must die."

27 Alfred uses the term "partnership." "Sovereignty," 45.

28 Marx quoted in Taylor, *From #BlackLivesMatter to Black Liberation*, 206.

29 Coulthard and Simpson. "Grounded Normativity," 251.

30 Coulthard and Simpson, "Grounded Normativity," 252.

31 Means, "For America to Live, Europe Must Die!." The controversy concerns Means's acting and style of activism. See Stripes, "Strategy."

32 Means, "For America to Live, Europe Must Die!."

33 Wynter deliberately refers to herself as a "weaver" in rejection of a positioning as a humanist or philosopher.

34 Wynter, "Columbus and the Poetics," 275 (my emphasis). See also her "'No Humans Involved.'" The question remains: Do possibilities for disalienation exist for groups that refuse either to move through and into capitalist world-historical positions or to see these positions as the horizon of their humanity? If so, what would those possibilities look like?

35 See Wynter, "Columbus and the Poetics." In my conversation with Wynter on June 15, 2017, she referred to the Judeo-Christian cosmogony as spatial (with regard to the heavens) and the new bourgeois one as temporal (with regard to Darwinian evolution and the descent of man).

36 Wynter, "'No Humans Involved.'"

37 McKittrick, ed., *Sylvia Wynter*, loc. 1049–54 (my emphasis). In *Infrapolitical Passages*, Williams's critique of Marx aligns with Wynter's (see Williams, 39). See also Wynter, "The Ceremony Must Be Found," for the human same and human other as "Sameness/Difference."

38 Lindahl, "Caribbean Diversity and Ideological Conformism," 58–59.

39 Lindahl elaborates Caribbean Marxism's additional limits, positing that at the time of his writing, it is in fact on the "decline" precisely because of these limits, a position that sociologist Maingot also shared. Maingot, *Race, Ideology, and the*

Decline. See Henry, *Caliban's Reason*, for both a critique of Caribbean Marxism and criticisms of it such as Lindahl's.

40 McKittrick, ed., *Sylvia Wynter*, loc. 1043.

41 Wilderson, "Gramsci's Black Marx," 226. Wilderson writes that while "The worker calls into question the legitimacy of productive practices, the slave calls into question the legitimacy of productivity itself," 231. I discuss Wilderson in later chapters.

42 See, for example, the Guyana Independence Act of 1966. http://www.legislation.gov.uk/ukpga/1966/14/enacted. See also https://guyanachronicle.com/2016/05/14/our-first-Independence-day/.

43 For another example, consider the first prime minister of the Democratic Republic of Congo, Patrice Lumumba, who spoke in 1960 of the brutal repression of black freedom, famously characterizing such transfers of power not as a stage in colonial development after the necessary tutelage of colonized people, as Belgium would, but as a struggle "filled with tears, fire and blood." Lumumba, "Speech at the Ceremony."

44 For instance, though independent since 1966, Barbados retained the British monarch as head of state until November 2021, when it finally became a Republic after decades of decolonization measures.

45 The Public Archive, "Detours and Distance: An Interview with J. Michael Dash." https://thepublicarchive.com/?p=3134. For Barbados: https://www.pbs.org/newshour/world/barbados-becomes-a-republic-after-bidding-farewell-to-british-monarchy.

46 "There is the mistaken belief black people achieved power with independence," he argued, "but a black man ruling a dependent state within the imperialist system has no power. He is simply an agent of the whites in the metropolis, with an army and police force designed to maintain the imperialist way of things." Rodney, "Black Power," in *Groundings*, 11.

47 See, for example, the structural adjustment programs of the World Bank and the International Monetary Fund implemented in the region in the late 1970s.

48 See Nkrumah's *Neo-Colonialism*. For a range of critiques of postcoloniality, see Appiah, "Is the Post"; Shohat, "Notes on the 'Post-Colonial'"; McClintock, "Angel of Progress" and *Imperial Leather*; Spivak, *Critique of Postcolonial Reason*; Mishra and Hodge, "What Is Postcolonialism?"; Chibber, *Postcolonial Theory*; Dirlik, "Postcolonial Aura."

49 For a discussion of the settler as a rights-bearing subject, see Ben-zvi, *Native Land Talk*. My focus is on the function of the settler with regard to cultivation, so I do not focus on definitions that see the settler as a figure that evolves later in colonization projects, such as in the post-Independence United States.

50 Hartman, *Scenes of Subjection*, 21.

51 Wynter charts this shift across her work.

52 In *Maya Cultural Heritage*, McAnany identifies the same depiction of Indigenous Peoples in Latin America, although the histories of forced work in Latin America have a different mode of representation for Indigenous Peoples as a peasantry.

53 In *Red, White, and Black*, Wilderson is preoccupied with blacks' and Indigenous Peoples' "ontological" "grammar of suffering." My discussion neither derives from nor engages Wilderson's work within a specific genre (film), or that which is "submerged in speech" (31). I am interested in grammar that does not derive from discursive arrangements per se, but has a material ground that the discursive relationships evolve to secure. The grammar I discuss here is neither an after to a specific event nor a priorness. It is co-constitutive of the event itself, in this case, that of putting in place the regime of accumulation for transforming black and Indigenous bodies and as such the possibility for capital accumulation. The event is thus only a nodal point within a larger structure.

54 Wynter's discussion of cosmogonies is relevant here. In McKittrick, ed., *Sylvia Wynter*, she defines a cosmogony as "origin myth" (927) or "origin narrative" (957). Cosmogonies are governing systems of belief that generate social orders specific to the peoples who hold them. In this text and in, for instance, "Columbus and the Poetics," Wynter foregrounds two crucial points for this work. The first is the general way in which, through conquest, black people and natives would come to be governed by Eurocentric cosmogonies: how they knew themselves as human would be supplanted by another system in which they could not be recognized as fully human. The second is that European-based cosmogonies shifted from being theocentric to "biocentric" (1594). Although religion was the primary difference among peoples prior to the discoveries of the mid- to late fifteenth century, this categorical difference becomes supplanted by biology as the form of racial difference.

55 In the introduction to *Formations of United States Colonialism*, Goldstein remarks that the imposition of a new time is a mechanism of domination of Indigenous Peoples.

56 For white, "possessive logics," see Moreton-Robinson, *White Possessive*.

57 For one such history of Guyana, see my discussion of Vere T. Daly in *Creole Indigeneity*.

58 Wilderson, *Afropessimism*, 227.

59 Wilderson, *Afropessimism*, 14, 16, 217, 222.

60 Wilderson, *Afropessimism*, 241.

61 This argument reformulates the discussion of dialectics in *Creole Indigeneity*, where I outline how the master-slave dialectic moves Indigenous and black peoples into relation in order to produce the Creole citizen as a native subject who then deploys the colonially based settler-native relation (theorized in this book) in order to hold power over Indigenous Peoples.

62 Hartman, *Scenes of Subjection*, 65. For the slave as the threshold of political representation (while man functions as the figure who can be represented within political structures), see, for example, Agamben, *Homo Sacer*; Patterson, *Slavery and Social Death*; Aristotle, "Politics: Book 1." Moreover, the rights denied enslaved persons in the constitutions of slaver nations reflect this incapacity for political representation that is the enslaved person. What's critical here is Wilderson's argument that the imbrication of slaveness and blackness means that the black (today and in the past) is incapable of true political representation.

63 I am struck by the fact that the protests over George Floyd's death bear out black freedom's and Indigenous sovereignty's relational nature. His death and the Black Lives Matter protest sparked worldwide protest against oppression. But in the United States, in particular, they led to a new wave of native protest against settler coloniality, and these together effected, finally, the consideration of removing the Redskins name and logo from the Washington State football team. While this is far afield from the issues of postcolonial governmentality, it shows the interconnected nature of black and Indigenous oppression and freedom.

64 See work by Wolfe. Scholars working in Indigenous Studies have complicated this model to focusing on how this perspective, in its singularity, also deploys the settler colonial knowledge apparatus. See, for instance, work by O'Brien. Settler colonialism not just relies on real or cultural violence to Indigenous Peoples, but is a mode of colonialism born out of the crucible of empire as an anterior and future formation. It has consistently perpetrated the violent remaking of indigeneity and Indigenous sovereignty in international and national politics through a variety of contractual strategies such as treaty making, the redefining of sovereign polities through legal mechanisms external to them, and the production and deployment of anti-Indigenous, settler knowledge formations. See Goldstein, ed., *Formations of United States Colonialism*.

65 Barker, "For Whom Sovereignty Matters," 1.

66 See, for example, Morales, "Coronavirus Infections Continue to Rise on Navajo Nation," NPR.org, May 11, 2020, https://www.npr.org/sections/coronavirus-live -updates/2020/05/11/854157898/coronavirus-infections-continue-to-rise-on-navajo -nation, and "As Coronavirus Cases Rise, Navajo Nation Tries to Get Ahead of Pandemic," NPR.org, April 4, 2020, https://www.npr.org/2020/04/04/826780041/as -coronavirus-cases-rise-navajo-nation-tries-to-get-ahead-of-pandemic.

67 Felicia Fonseca, Carolyn Kaster, and Tim Sullivan, "Inside the Navajo Nation as It Endures the Coronavirus Outbreak," AP.org, May 22, 2020, https://leads.ap.org /best-of-the-states/navajo-nation-in-lockdown.

68 Hollie Silverman et al., "Navajo Nation Surpasses New York State for the Highest Covid-19 Infection Rate in the US," CNN.com, May 18, 2020, https://edition.cnn .com/2020/05/18/us/navajo-nation-infection-rate-trnd/index.html.

69 In chapter 6, I discuss metaphor as a legal strategy.

70 *Auxiliary* here refers to the categorization and function of words such as "would" and "shall."

71 Barker and Alfred write of how the use of tribe and nation to define Indigenous Peoples in US law has signaled their difference from and hence subordination to states. See Barker, "For Whom Sovereignty Matters," 10–11; Alfred, "Sovereignty," 35.

72 See O'Malley, "Indigenous Governance," and Simpson, *Mohawk Interruptus*, 7.

73 See work by Bruyneel, Simpson, and Coulthard, among others.

74 See the Declaration and its discussion in Moreton-Robinson, *White Possessive*. The Declaration should supersede the right of any state to inhibit Indigenous freedoms, but individual states still grant titles or recognize nations.

75 Betasamosake Simpson, *As We Have Always Done*, loc. 2907, 2924

76 See Barker's discussion of the UN Declaration.

77 Moreton-Robinson, *White Possessive*, 385.

78 Moreton-Robinson, *White Possessive*, 623.

79 See her elaboration in chapter 9 around a reading of Foucault's *Society Must Be Defended*: loc. 2568–2577, 2586, 2647, 2664, 2682.

80 Steve Newcomb, "Indigenous Sovereignty and the Political Subordination of Our Nations," *Indian Country Today*, March 27, 2017. Newcomb writes, "Indigenous sovereignty means a form of sovereignty under a system of domination."

81 Simpson, *Mohawk Interruptus*, 10.

82 Simpson, *Mohawk Interruptus*, 11.

83 Simpson, *Mohawk Interruptus*, 23.

84 See Williams, *American Indian in Western Legal Thought*. I use pre- and post-conquest to refer to the end of the fifteenth century, but the canonical, legal discussions at that time responded to earlier conquests.

85 Barker, "For Whom Sovereignty Matters," 20, 21.

86 Alfred, "Sovereignty," 33.

87 Alfred, "Sovereignty," 34–35.

88 Moreover, the concept developed out of "values and objectives that put it in direct opposition to the values and objectives found in most traditional indigenous philosophies." Alfred, "Sovereignty," 43.

89 Alfred, "Sovereignty," 44–47.

90 Betasamosake Simpson, *As We Have Always Done*, loc. 203.

91 Betasamosake Simpson, *As We Have Always Done*, loc. 366.

92 Betasamosake Simpson, *As We Have Always Done*, loc. 1798 and 1838.

93 See her discussion of Nanabush (loc. 934), and the section "I Am Not a Nation State" (loc. 180).

94 "To the Best of Our Knowledge," https://www.ttbook.org/interview/wisdom-corn-mother, May 31, 2020. For more on Kimmerer, see *Braiding Sweetgrass*.

95 See Hintzen, *Costs of Regime Survival*; Knight, *The Caribbean*; Rodney, *Groundings*, chapter 3.

96 Keeping in mind that Indigenous Peoples in the United States and Canada are subject to forms of state-sponsored and other kinds of anti-Indigenous violence, in Latin America, Indigenous Peoples (and non-Indigenous activists) face even more openly violent forms of repression for their rights activism. Over seven hundred activists, mostly Indigenous and black, have been killed in Columbia since 2016. The Garifuna (Garinagu) leader Antonio Bernárdez of the Punta Piedra community was murdered in 2020, and Lenca activist Berta Caceras, winner of the 2015 Goldman Environmental Prize and the founder of COPINH, the Consejo Cívico de Organizaciones Populares e Indígenas de Honduras, was murdered in 2016. For more on how the Garifuna claim Indigenous status and negotiate relations between indigeneity and blacks, see Anderson, *Black and Indigenous*. They exist in tense relation to more traditionally defined Indigenous groups such as the Maya.

97 http://copinhenglish.blogspot.com/p/who-we-are.html.

98 https://today.caricom.org/2015/10/30/ccj-grants-historic-constitutional-relief-to
    -maya-people/.

99 See Amerindian Act; Bulkan, "Struggle for Recognition," 373.

100 Guyana's Department of Public Information, "National Toshaos Council—Highest
    Representative Body for Indigenous Peoples in Guyana," last modified October 2,
    2012, https://dpi.gov.gy/national-toshaos-council-highest-representative-body-for
    -indigenous-peoples-in-guyana/.

101 Bulkan, "Struggle for Recognition," 371.

102 Griffiths and La Rose, *Searching for Justice*, 18.

103 Gregory and Vaccaro include a list of sources reflecting how Guyana's com-
    promised state governmentality is similar to that of Latin America. "Islands of
    Governmentality," 347.

104 Gregory and Vaccaro, "Islands of Governmentality," 348. Their deployment of
    the trope of islands speaks directly to the abrogation of Indigenous sovereignty
    regarding land rights. The archipelagic trope traps the Caribbean in a reduc-
    tive, globally consumable language tied to the regimes of touristic, trade, and
    other forms of exploitation in the global economy. On the other hand, the renam-
    ing of "spaces of governmentality" as islands highlights the circumscription of
    Indigenous sovereignty. While it seems to make the case for the need to see the
    issues facing Indigenous Peoples in Guyana through the lens of Latin America
    and Indigenous peoples in other areas of Amazonia, it also suggests a distinctly
    Caribbean governing mechanism.

105 Gregory and Vaccaro, "Islands of Governmentality," 348. Trotz and Roopnaraine
    also note the need to dominate. See *Creole Indigeneity* on this issue.

106 Gregory and Vaccaro, "Islands of Governmentality," 349.

107 See Alexander Zaitchik, "How Conservation Became Colonialism: Indigenous
    people, Not Environmentalists, Are the Key to Protecting the World's Most
    Precious Ecosystems," *Foreign Policy*, July 16, 2018, https://foreignpolicy.com/2018
    /07/16/how-conservation-became-colonialism-environment-indigenous-people
    -ecuador-mining/.

108 Iwokrama International Centre for Rainforest Conservation and Development,
    "About Us," https://iwokrama.org/about-us/; "Our Work," https://iwokrama.org
    /our-work/. Iwokrama bears similarity to the protected areas of the Cofan dis-
    cussed in Zaitchik, "How Conservation Became Colonialism."

109 Iwokrama International Centre, "About Us."

110 Both Barker and Alfred, for instance, respectively note how Indigenous Peoples
    are positioned as "welfare recipients" through a "patronizing faux altruism"
    designed to produce and reinforce forms of dependency and compel integration
    into the states within which Indigenous nations are located. Barker, "For Whom
    Sovereignty Matters," 16; Alfred, "Sovereignty," 44–45.

111 Gregory and Vaccaro, "Islands of Governmentality," 352.

112 Gregory and Vaccaro, "Islands of Governmentality," 352.

113 Gregory and Vaccaro, "Islands of Governmentality," 352.

114 Gregory and Vaccaro, "Islands of Governmentality," 353.

115 See Bulkan, "Struggle for Recognition."

116 Bulkan, "Struggle for Recognition," 377.

117 See my discussion of the Rupununi Rebellion in *Creole Indigeneity*.

118 Betasamosake Simpson, *As We Have Always Done*, loc. 2849.

119 Betasamosake Simpson, *As We Have Always Done*, loc. 744.

120 Betasamosake Simpson, *As We Have Always Done*, loc. 751 (my emphasis).

121 Alfred, "Sovereignty," 41.

122 Betasamosake Simpson, *As We Have Always Done*, loc. 456, 488. See also work by Jodi Byrd.

123 Moreton-Robinson, *Possessive Whiteness*, loc. 497–505. See also Vine Deloria Jr., *God Is Red*.

124 Moreton-Robinson, *Possessive Whiteness*, loc. 634.

125 Moreton-Robinson, *Possessive Whiteness*, 3728, 3739.

126 Moreton-Robinson, *Possessive Whiteness*, 3723.

127 I've made this point in earlier work, and it is supported by Moreton-Robinson, who argues, "States regulate and discipline Indigenous peoples on the basis of our different status and rights claims in ways that do not threaten their sovereignty" (*Possessive Whiteness*, loc. 3634).

128 Moten, *Stolen Life*, loc. 816–30.

1. CONVERSION

1 For a historical account of the growth of enslaved black populations and the political and economic conditions that supported the breeding of enslaved peoples, see Sublette and Sublette, *American Slave Coast*, and Smithers, *Slave Breeding*. For perspectives beyond that of the United States, see also Donoghue, *Black Breeding Machines*, and Morgan, *Laboring Women*. The reproduction or growth of the black population in the Americas occurs alongside the documented decline of the Indigenous population, as outlined, for instance, in Denevan, *Native Population*. The relationality of black growth and native decline must be theorized not as a retroactive, causal legitimation of slavery but as a direct result of the institution of native slavery, black slavery, as well as of the encomienda and the repartimiento as anti-black *and* anti-indigenous labour systems that legitimized non-chattel slavery. More importantly, despite black reproduction, no system valued black or Indigenous life, but all represent a specific devaluing of each that is tied to the manner in which blacks and native peoples needed to be productive for accumulative regimes.

2 In addition, see Marx's discussion of labour and nature in chapter 7 of *Capital*, volume 1.

3 I refer to forced removals, treaty making, creating reservations, and titling lands that may or may not have been the ancestral homes of specific native peoples in the Americas.

4 When Césaire writes in the long poem "Notebook of a Return to the Native Land" of enslaved blacks' embodied labour ("not an inch of this world devoid of my fin-

gerprint"), what he eclipses is that not an inch of the land that these buildings are on is devoid of Indigenous prior belonging, settlement, and related decisions and choices about such, as well as forms of labour. It is also not devoid of that labour that has been accumulated within the black body and that is not, and cannot, be fully coextensive with the object of work in the Americas, that is, the structures of the built environment of colonialism. Césaire writes, "not an inch of this world devoid of my fingerprint and my calcaneus on the spines of skyscrapers and my filth in the glitter of gems!" (20). My claim here about what we do or do not designate as Indigenous land, and as such may have to cede to Indigenous Peoples, echoes Betasamosake Simpson's argument that "every piece of North America is Indigenous land." *As We Have Always Done*, loc. 3086.

5 Nichols, "Disaggregating Primitive Accumulation," 22. Byrd et al. use Nichols, among others, to theorize "debt" as an ongoing mode of dispossession for Indigenous Peoples and other racialized Peoples.

6 Nichols, "Disaggregating Primitive Accumulation," 22.

7 Nichols, "Disaggregating Primitive Accumulation," 24.

8 Nichols, "Disaggregating Primitive Accumulation," 26.

9 Nichols, "Disaggregating Primitive Accumulation," 24. For Marx, primitive accumulation is multivariate and notably violent: "In actual history it is notorious that conquest, enslavement, robbery, murder, briefly force, play the great part." Marx, *Capital*, volume 1: 11516–24.

10 Nichols, "Disaggregating Primitive Accumulation," 27.

11 Nichols, "Disaggregating Primitive Accumulation," 27.

12 Although still at times retaining the land-labour distinction, Yusoff also recognizes this form of black dispossession as a relation to land by identifying it as "another form of spacial extraction" (*Billion Black Anthropocenes*, 3, 6).

13 See Wilderson, *Red, White and Black*.

14 Rodney, *Groundings*, 74.

15 For black Death, see Hartman, *Scenes of Subjection*; Wilderson, *Red, White and Black*; and Sexton, "The Social Life of Social Death." Prior texts that lead to this position include those by Fanon and Patterson. Native death is marked as ontologically different from black death. It constitutes removal, Elimination, and (we must add) non-chattel slavery, and changes the articulation of death/Death to Death/Elimination. These deaths are thus understood (as I see it through Afropessimism) in relation which is critical because, as I argue, anti-blackness and anti-indigeneity have been developed as structurally necessary to each other within capitalist social and political structures. Thus, I do not see these deaths as separating blacks from Indigenous Peoples as though one group is more oppressed than the other. While we do need to mark distinctions, these deaths must always be understood in their relation *through* the marking of their definitive ontological differences.

16 For prisons as extensions of the slave ship hold, see Sharpe, *In the Wake*, 21, 27, 75, and elsewhere.

17 Arendt, *The Human Condition*, 7, 8. Arendt gives this definition when elaborating what she terms the *Vita Activa*.

18 Montag, "Necro-Economics," 10–11; Mbembe, "Necropolitics," 19. Mbembe does not directly source his understanding of the labour-work break from Arendt, relying on her *Origins of Totalitarianism* instead of *Human Condition*.

19 Moore, "The Rise of Cheap Nature."

20 Arendt, *Human Condition*, 29, 88. Indeed, Arendt elaborates the condition of excision informing Agamben's conceptualization of *homo sacer*.

21 Arendt, *Human Condition*, 87, 86. We could even argue that *homo politicus* manages the valorization of labour as its new mode of exclusion. In one way, Arendt anticipates Wynter's criticism of Marx on the function of ownership as both are interested in what is served by the failure to look to the real function of ownership and that of the misreading of labour as and for work.

22 Marx, *Capital*, volume 1: 2629.

23 Marx, *Capital*, volume 1: 2678.

24 https://www.marxists.org/archive/marx/works/1863/theories-surplus-value/ch04.htm.

25 Arendt, *Human Condition*, 101.

26 Arendt, *Human Condition*, 99, 125.

27 Arendt, *Human Condition*, 115, 116, 124.

28 A rather basic example of this is the COVID-19 pandemic in which the replication (read: accumulation) of the virus forced countries to go into lockdown and essentially shut down portions of their economies. The catastrophic human effects of these shutdowns were job losses or the literal loss of livelihood. The virus thus laid bare how the ability of the labour process to continue unimpeded is tied to the ability of life itself to continue unimpeded. The virus introduced a purely biological regime of accumulation that directly impeded the capitalist one and the ways in which it is tied to individuals' ability to live/reproduce themselves, until the market could begin to commodify the virus through, for example, the production of personal protective equipment, disinfectants, and so on.

29 Arendt, *Human Condition*, 86.

30 See chapter 2 of McKittrick, ed., *Sylvia Wynter* for her elaboration of the term "homo narrans." See Foucault, *Birth of Biopolitics* and *Order of Things*.

31 A shorthand way of understanding Wynter here is to think of biological man as something that exists, is invented, after the sign (language, discourse, myth) of man. Wynter elaborates that this is a specifically Darwinian process: it is not universal but particularly western. Only the sign of man (man as understood through discourse, language, myth, etc.) can be said to be a universal process that occurs according to each specific people's cosmogony. McKittrick, ed., *Sylvia Wynter*, chapter 2.

32 Wilderson, *Afropessimism*, 227, 248.

33 Afropessimist writers are clear about the requirement of black death. Here I am interested in thinking about it in terms of political economy rather than ontology. For more, see the work of Wilderson, Sharpe, and James and Costa Vargas.

34 See Wilderson, *Red, White and Black* and *Afropessimism*. In a particularly cogent summary of his work, Hart writes that for Wilderson, "antiblackness (slavery, the afterlife of slavery, and social death) describes the relationship between the

collective subject that he variously calls human, settler, and master, that is, white people, and the collective object that he calls slave, that is, black people." Hart, "Constellations," 20.

35 Hart, "Constellations," 20 (emphasis in original). See Wilderson, *Red, White and Black*, 25. See also Wilderson, "The Prison Slave," 25.

36 Wilderson, *Red, White and Black*, 38. See chapter 1 in general for the distinction between "contingent" and "gratuitous."

37 He writes, "At every scale—the soul, the body, the group, the land, and the universe— [the Settler and the 'Savage'] can both practice cartography, and although at every scale their maps are radically incompatible, their respective 'mapness' is never in question. This capacity for cartographic coherence is the thing itself, that which secures subjectivity for both the Settler and the 'Savage' and articulates them to one another in a network of connections, transfers and dis-placements." Wilderson, *Red, White and Black*, 181.

38 Wilderson, *Red, White and Black*, 159.

39 Wilderson, *Afropessimism*, 16, 42, 197. Blacks thus not only are closed off from these forms of grievance and representation, but remain phobic objects that threaten both settler *and* native sovereignties. See his reading of the film *Skins* in *Red, White and Black*.

40 Wilderson, *Afropessimism*, 164. The term *homunculi* here is from Pagden's discussion of Juan Gines de Sepulveda's attack on the Indigenous Peoples of the new world, ("Introduction," loc. 388). Wynter quotes Pagden for her use of homunculi to mark the specific degree of less than human status for Indigenous Peoples as different from Eruopeans and blacks. She writes, "While 'indios' and 'negros,' Indians and Negroes, were to be both made into the Caliban-type referents of Human Otherness to the new rational self-conception of the West, there was also, there-fore . . . a marked differential in the degrees of subrationality, and of not-quite-human-ness, to which each group was to be relegated within the classificatory logic of the West's ethnocultural field." Wynter, "Usettling the Coloniality," 300. She does not use the term *infrahumans* in this essay. It's also important to note that infra/human is still a relation to the human, just one of abjection, as Zakiyyah Iman Jackson would argue.

41 Wilderson, *Afropessimism*, 191–98.

42 See chapter 5 of Wilderson, *Afropessimism*.

43 UN Declaration on the Rights, 3.

44 UN Declaration on the Rights, 3.

45 UN Declaration on the Rights, 7.

46 Las Casas, *Short Account*, 922–27 (my emphasis). The Portuguese priest Fernando Oliveira campaigned against black enslavement for profit in the sixteenth century, deploying arguments similar to Las Casas's about the lack of a just (war) cause for enslavement. However, it's unclear if he saw them as having a "right" to resist. See Orique, "Comparison of the Voices," 2014. Right in Las Casas is not a casual usage and must be read in terms of his knowledge of canon law.

47 See work by Menezes and Bulkan.

48 It is always already deferred because full humanity (in western terms) for Indigenous Peoples would be dependent on their rejection of their own sovereignty.

49 Hart, "Constellations," 23. Wilderson develops this position in *Red, White and Black*, arguing that Indigenous Peoples are "half-alive" because they retain a capacity for representation within civil society's structures of redress (48). This assertion is built around Wilderson's argument that blacks are overdetermined by the ontological closures of "accumulation and fungibility," while Indigenous Peoples are defined by "sovereignty and genocide" (chapters 1 and 2). Byrd utilizes the undead as a descriptive analytic for colonialism, writing, "Zombie imperialism is the current manifestation of a liberal democratic colonialism that locates biopower at the intersection of life, death, law, and lawlessness . . . where death belongs more to racialized and gendered multitudes and killing becomes 'precisely targeted'" (*Transit of Empire*, 228). More needs to be done to think through Byrd's concept of the undead with Wilderson's of the fully Dead black and half-dead savage as states of being that are continuously produced for nonwhites and which index different relationships with the state with regard to life and politics.

50 See discussion of Achebe's *Things Fall Apart*.

51 See the discussion of South Africa in Arendt, *Origins of Totalitarianism*. For workers, see pp. 194 and 205. Throughout the book Arendt uses the terms "savage tribe," "native savages," and "black savages." Similarly to her assumption of biopolitical subjecthood in *Human Condition*, in *Origins of Totalitarianism* her analysis cannpt rise above the fact and appearance of racism in European thought, which structures her attempt to reveal and challenge it. For her understanding of the term savage, see Mbembe, "Necropolitics."

52 Moten writes, "Biopolitics is already given in the figure of the political animal; that the move from natural history to biology is a held trajectory; that the regulation of generativity is already given in the idea of a natural kind. . . . What's interesting and implicit here . . . is the political subject as a natural kind, the political subject as the subject of natural history, natural history as a field that is presided over by the political animal" ("Blackness and Nothingness," 775).

53 Moten, "Blackness and Nothingness," 739 (emphases in original).

54 Moten, "Blackness and Nothingness," 750.

55 I have chosen not to engage Mbembe's discussion of the political animal in "Necropolitics" here. The well-known concept of man as political animal stems from Aristotle's work, a discussion of which is beyond the scope of this book.

56 Moten, *The Universal Machine*, loc. 2267.

57 McKittrick, ed., *Sylvia Wynter*, 20.

58 Dumont, "not just a platform for my dance," 65.

59 "Potential" signals how Indigenous Peoples function differently as subjects of right and representation than blacks. I distinguish political animals (man capable of rationality and representation) from infrahumans (blacks). In *Becoming Human*, Jackson, like Fanon, Moten, myself, and many others, also differentiates this concept of man that is specific to the human from blacks. She makes a critical distinction between the concept of man as a political animal and the animal that is bracketed off from the former, which she argues is the black. In essence, she

argues that the black is the index for the later concept of the animal that emerges from the fifteenth century to the Enlightenment. This crucial intervention suggests broader, necessary revision within the field of political economy to address this specific concept of the black/blackness. My discussion here is limited to the concept of the political animal as it emerges in Aristotle and as it is engaged in Arendt and in Moten's critique of her work.

60 For failed market identities, see Mamdani, "Beyond Settler and Native." I discuss this concept substantially in *Creole Indigeneity*.

61 See Jackson, *Creole Indigeneity*. The symbolic economy precedes the imposition of physical, economic structures.

62 Columbus, "First Voyage," 8.

63 Columbus, "First Voyage," 10.

64 A long tradition views Indigenous Peoples both as possessing an abundance for their needs and as not possessing reason nor the right kind of labour to transform their land (through work) to their property. This tradition is key to various justifications for their subordination and the usurpation of their lands. See Williams's discussion of Franciscus de Victoria in *American Indian in Western Legal Thought*, 104. John Winthrop refers to Indigenous lands without certain evident forms of development as "waste lands"; see his "General Observations.". In describing the Puritans' arrival at Cape Cod, William Bradford writes in his "History of 'Plimoth Plantation'" of the encountered lands as "wilderness, full of wild beasts & willd men" (chapter 9, http://www.gutenberg.org/files/24950/24950-h/24950-h.htm). The perception of these lands as wild or waste filled with "wild men" enabled Europeans to frame Indigenous lands as abundant and excessive because untamed, as not having been imbued with the productive forms of labour that turn excess (read: waste) into scarcity. Kimmerer argues that "abundance" reflects Indigenous labour that is organized according to different principles, knowledge, and technologies and a practice of not taking more than is necessary. See "Honorable Harvest" in *Braiding SweetgGrass*.

65 Columbus, "First Voyage," 8.

66 Columbus, "First Voyage," 14.

67 Not only did Columbus first land in the modern-day Bahamas, but as Las Casas details, Indigenous Peoples were transported as slaves between mainland Latin America and the Caribbean islands. For a discussion of Conversion's role in the English empire (in a Protestant rather than Catholic context), see Gerbner, *Christian Slavery*.

68 For the evolution of the concept of Just War, see Williams, *The American Indian*.

69 See Polanco, *Indigenous Peoples*, and Reséndez, *Other Slavery*. In Mexico, Conversion led to the invisibility of Indigenous labour within urban centers and intense exploitation outside those areas, while in Peru, it resulted in greater increase of African enslaved peoples and more protections for Indigenous Peoples who actively manipulated their vassalage. See Bennett, *Africans in Colonial Mexico*, and O'Toole, *Bound Lives*.

70 See Azurara, *Chronicle*, and Bennett, *Africans in Colonial Mexico*. For more on Conversion and the operation of the Catholic Church in Latin America, see Schwaller, *Church in Colonial Latin America*.

71 See "Inter Caetera." The "Inter Caetera" was the first of several bulls on Spain's right in the Americas. See Orique, "Comparison of the Voices," for a list of the others.

72 Columbus, "First Voyage," 12.

73 Columbus, "First Voyage," 14.

74 *Encomendero* refers to someone on whom the Spanish crown conferred a grant of (Indian) labour. It is one cog in the encomienda system.

75 For more on Las Casas's conversions, see Lampe, "Las Casas and African Slavery." See Orique and Roldan-Figueroa, eds., *Bartolome de las Casas*, for Las Casas's various roles and titles. For the processes that converted Indigenous Peoples into feudal subjects, see Williams, *American Indian in Western Legal Thought*. For the ways in which enslaved peoples were also defined by forms of feudalism, see Ben-zvi, *Native Land Talk*.

76 Wynter, "New Seville: Part One," 26 (emphasis in original). For the specific factors that influenced his conversion, see Valdivia Giménez, "Reason, Providence, and Testimony." See Lantigua, "Religion within the Limits," for how he understood features of native culture, like human sacrifice, that were used to justify their sub-jugation. See also Brunstetter, "Las Casas and the Concept," for the complexities and history of Las Casas's "just war" arguments.

77 See Wynter, "New Seville: Part One," and Pierce, "Bartolomé de las Casas." Many scholars date Las Casas's proposition of black slavery to a 1516 "Memorial de Re-medios," but I have access only to the 1518 text. Thanks to Fr. David Orique for the reference to Las Casas, "Memorial de remedios." The 1516 "Memorial" predates the order in the year of the second "Memorial" to bring in enslaved blacks, who of course would already have been converted to Christianity. In a 1518 "cedula" to the Governer of Bresa (Lorenzo de Gorrevod), the King of Spain granted "permis-sion" "to take to the Indies, the islands and the mainland of the ocean sea already discovered or to be discovered, four thousand negro slaves both male and female, provided they be Christians." Bresa is ordered to "make any arrangements with traders or other persons to ship the said slaves, male or female, directly from the isles of Guinea and other regions from which they are wont to bring the said ne-groes to these realms and to Portugal." In the order, the king emphasizes that the enslaved "have become Christians" before reaching the Americas. See "Permission Granted to the Governor of Bresa," 41–42. Lampe argues that Las Casas was not responsible for introducing transatlantic black slavery (beginning in 1501, well be-fore his 1516 "Remedios"). He also argues that when he began his third conversion to the idea of black humanity, Las Casas was the first to condemn black slavery. See Lampe, "Las Casas and African Slavery."

78 Las Casas, "Memorial de remedios," 33–34 (my emphasis). Las Casas would later propose that an even greater number (hundreds) of blacks be granted to Spanish colonizers. See Lampe, "Las Casas and African Slavery," 427.

79 In *Capital*, Marx writes that surplus labour (as opposed to surplus value or relative-surplus value) does not originate with capital(ism). *Capital*, loc. 3493

80 The term "ecclesiastical plantation" has been used in various contexts and senses; for a nineteenth-century instance, see Pillsbury, *Acts*. For another, see Larson, "Enslaved Malagasy."

81 Fanon, *Wretched of the Earth*, loc. 658.

82 Wynter, "New Seville: Part Two," 47.

83 Las Casas, *Short Account*, loc. 724–33. This book has multiple titles and editions. For access reasons, I have chosen to use the Penguin edition entitled *A Brief Account of the Destruction of the Indies*, which is available as an audio file from LibriVox and from Project Gutenberg, in addition to other versions of the text. This edition is translated from the 1552 print version. The analysis here could be extended by a discussion of his *In Defense of the Indians*, but I was unable to obtain an accessible copy in time for this project. Charles V eventually heeded Las Casas and other such advocates by passing "The New Laws of the Indies for the Good Treatment and Preservation of the Indians" in 1542–43.

84 Las Casas, *Short Account*, 757.

85 Las Casas, *Short Account*, 782. See also 799.

86 Las Casas, *Short Account*, 765.

87 Chaplin, "Race," 174, 176, 184.

88 Las Casas, *Short Account*, 815.

89 Las Casas, *Short Account*, 1613.

90 Las Casas, *Short Account*, 1707.

91 Las Casas, *Short Account*, 1557, 940, 943, 949, 1435.

92 Las Casas, *Short Account*, 2224, 790.

93 Las Casas, *Short Account*, 1168, 1176.

94 Las Casas, *Short Account*, 1346.

95 This chapter discusses how a specific colonial text institutes the labour-work division. It is not meant to survey Indigenous forms of labour in the Americas.

96 Spanish soldiers were so "impressed . . . by the defenses" in one of the kingdoms of Guatemala that they slept outside its walls. Indigenous Peoples dug large "pits" in the earth to thwart Spanish progress but were themselves buried in them. Las Casas, *Short Account*, 1335.

97 Las Casas, *Short Account*, 1461

98 Las Casas, *Short Account*, 1449.

99 Las Casas, *Brief Account*, 1036.

100 Hartman, *Lose Your Mother*, 111.

101 The term "machine" is from Benitez-Rojo's work.

102 See Columbus's first letter.

103 Simpson, *Mohawk Interruptus*, 101. Locke's *Second Treatise* distinguishes what is held in "common" from that which becomes property through appropriate labour. Locke, *Two Treatises*, 80. John Winthrop expressed this position earlier (1629) by claiming, "That which is common to all is proper to none. This savage people ruleth over many lands without title or property; for they enclose no ground, neither have they cattell to maintayn it, but remove their dwellings as they have occasion, or as they can prevail against their neighbours." Winthrop, "General Observations.". Thanks to Yael Ben-zvi for pointing me to Winthrop and a few nineteenth-century sources.

104 For theorization of elimination, see Wolfe, "Structure and Event."

105 Las Casas, *Short Account*, 1799, 1883.

106 Las Casas, *Short Account*, 1876–85. The term "perished" I take from 943.

107 Welburn, *Roanoke and Wampum*, 25–26 (emphasis in original).

108 Welburn, *Roanoke and Wampum*, 30.

109 Welburn, *Roanoke and Wampum*, 27.

110 Yusoff and Chaplin note that even before chattel slavery, black bodies were thought to have "properties" (Yusoff, *Billion Black Anthropocenes*, 14) of "bodily durability" (Chaplin, "Race," 179). The process of adding value either reveals or turns what is perceived as inherent into productive form as value.

111 Wynter, "Columbus and the Poetics."

112 See Moore and Yusoff for the Anthropocene's pre-eighteenth-century origins. For primitive accumulation, see the discussion of Nichols's work above and Coulthard and Simpson's "Grounded Normativity," 252. I discuss Coulthard's work on primitive accumulation in chapter 4.

113 McKittrick, ed., *Sylvia Wynter*, 22. Marx's *Capital* is its own object lesson: commodities do speak as and through the economist and the theorist (loc. 1119).

114 Marx, *Capital*, loc. 367–75.

115 Harvey, *Companion*, 32.

116 Here I disagree with Wilderson's claim that blacks (alone) made the commodity (see beginning of *Red, White and Black*) because I argue that this relationship of indigeneity and blackness actually produces it.

117 See Buck-Morss, *Hegel, Haiti, and Universal History*.

118 Marx cited in Taylor, *From #BlackLivesMatter to Black Liberation*, 206. For a different discussion of the slave and slavery in Marx, see Sorentino, "Abstract Slave."

119 Byrd et al., "Predatory Value," 8. Although the authors refer to the nineteenth century, antebellum use of "slave-backed bonds," their language generally applies to Indigenous and black people used as coerced labour that could literally be packaged (here read as not only enslaved blacks, but also the creation and transfer of encomiendas) and sold as goods beginning in the sixteenth century.

120 Harvey, *Companion*, 30.

121 Harvey, *Companion*, 17.

122 I paraphrase the title of Derek Walcott's poem "The Sea Is History."

123 See Wilderson, *Afropessimism*, 41–46, 160–64.

124 Wilderson, *Afropessimism*, 221.

125 For examples of Las Casas's recognition of Indigenous sovereignty over their lands, see *Short Account*, 893, 1089.

126 Wilderson, *Afropessimism*, 227.

2. TOWARD A MIDDLE PASSAGE/METHODOLOGY

1 Benítez-Rojo, *Repeating Island*, 5.

2 "Ocean sea" refers to the title (Admiral of the Ocean Sea) Columbus requested as part of his overall reward for encountering "new" lands. His yoking of these words anticipates the actual yoking of the Caribbean Sea and Atlantic Ocean with subse-

quent explorations and black and Indigenous slave trading. The term "ocean sea" is frequently used in early chronicles of exploration from the fifteenth century on.

3 See DeLoughrey, *Routes and Roots*.

4 Wright, *Physics of Blackness*, 540–47, 2810. Wright asserts that Afropessimism is oriented by middle passage modes of knowing, articulating blackness in terms of progress and/or lack of progress.

5 Wright, *Physics of Blackness*, 724–28.

6 Dark waters is indentured Indians' naming of the Atlantic (Kala pani) passage.

7 Wright, *Physics of Blackness*. See her chapter 1 for discussion of horizontal (inclusive space and time) and vertical (hierarchical and restrictive) configurations of blackness.

8 King, *The Black Shoals*, 4.

9 Wright, *Physics of Blackness*, 103, 407.

10 See her use and discussion of the term in *Physics of Blackness*, Chapters 1 and 2.

11 For my engagement with Sharpe's concept in terms of blackness and indigeneity, see Barchiesi and Jackson, "Introduction."

12 Wright, *Physics of Blackness*, 352.

13 https://www.britannica.com/place/Anegada-Passage.

14 http://www.svpartyoffive.com/2017/05/07/anegada-passage-a-bitch-times-two/.

15 https://www.lexico.com/es/definicion/anegar.

16 Rose Ciotta, "The Slender Passage to Anegada Is Awash with Danger," *Buffalo News*, September 29, 1996, https://buffalonews.com/news/the-slender-passage-to-anegada-is-awash-with-danger/article_5c5e6bdb-b326-54ee-b662-85f1aeafe52d.html.

17 Laurencin et al., "Polyphased Tectonic Evolution." The authors note that these other geologic formations aren't fully deterministic of the Passage.

18 Las Casas, *Short Account*, 851, 1437, 943. Basting refers to the repeated "sprinkling" of oil on an Indigenous man so that his feet would burn uniformly.

19 Jackson, Z. I., *Becoming Human*, 86–88. Plasticity es an extant term that Jackson adapts and elaborates in order to explore how black infrahumanity is, to some extent, epiphenomenal for and in the production of the human. (See p. 12, p. 20 and p.47) I am arguing not that Indigenous Peoples are subject to such anti-black plasticity, but that they are subjected to forms of plasticity that are consequential for their Elimination and that impact the formation of blackness. The links here need to be further explored.

20 See, e.g., Linebaugh and Rediker, *Many-Headed Hydra*, 27.

21 Gilroy, *The Black Atlantic*, 38.

22 Sánchez-Godoy, "'We Never Could Understand,'" 169.

23 Smith, "Other Atlantics," 247, 262.

24 Edwards, "The Uses of Diaspora," 61 (emphasis in original).

25 Edwards, "The Uses of Diaspora," 63. He doubts "that such oceanic frames can be thought of as separate in any consistent manner," arguing that "the term diaspora, in [its] interventionist sense ... allow[s] us to think beyond such limiting geographic frames, and without reliance on an obsession with origins."

26 Edwards, "The Uses of Diaspora," 46, 52, and 64.

27 Edwards extends the concept of decalage across later work. See Edwards, *The Practice of Diaspora: Literature, Translation, and the Rise of Black Internationalism.*

28 Edwards, "The Uses of Diaspora," 66.

29 Edwards, "The Uses of Diaspora," 61.

30 Zeleza, "Rewriting the African Diaspora," 37.

31 Zeleza, "Rewriting the African Diaspora," 40, 38 (my emphasis). See Chrisman's "Beyond Black Atlantic and Postcolonial Studies," "Journeying to Death," and "Rethinking Black Atlanticism" (which Zeleza cites).

32 Zeleza, "Rewriting the African Diaspora," 36.

33 Zeleza, "Rewriting the African Diaspora," 42. Scientific study places the origin of human life in Africa, so all human racial, ethnic, or cultural groups are in effect the dispersal of African populations.

34 Morgan and Greene, "Introduction," 8.

35 Bushnell, "Indigenous America and the Limits," p. 191.

36 Bushnell, "Indigenous America and the Limits," p. 191. She gives a "recent consevative estimate" of the New World's Indigenous population "on the eve of Columbus's first voyage": "46,800,000–53,800,000" people (192).

37 Bushnell, "Indigenous America and the Limits," 194.

38 Bushnell, "Indigenous America and the Limits," 203.

39 Cohen, "Was There an Amerindian Atlantic?," 398.

40 Cohen, "Was There an Amerindian Atlantic?," 409, 394.

41 Stam and Shohat, *Race in Translation*, xviii.

42 Stam and Shohat, *Race in Translation*, xv.

43 Stam and Shohat, *Race in Translation*, 3.

44 Stam and Shohat, *Race in Translation*, 6.

45 Stam and Shohat, *Race in Translation*, 18.

46 Weaver, *The Red Atlantic*, loc. 88.

47 Weaver, *The Red Atlantic*, loc. 102.

48 Weaver, *The Red Atlantic*, loc. 308.

49 Weaver, *The Red Atlantic*, loc. 369.

50 Weaver, *The Red Atlantic*, loc. 444.

51 Weaver, *The Red Atlantic*, loc. 499.

52 Weaver, *The Red Atlantic*, loc. 102. As example, he cites Foreman's *Indians Abroad, 1493–1938* and Vaughan's *Transatlantic Encounters*, which "catalog and discuss every known Native from the Americas who traveled to one or another colonial metropole."

53 Las Casas, *Short Account*, 815.

54 Las Casas, *Short Account*, 918–27.

55 Las Casas, *Short Account*, 943, 1463.

56 Las Casas, *Short Account*, 1142–50.

57 Las Casas, *Short Account*, 1420.

58 Las Casas, *Short Account*, 1761, 1752.

59 Las Casas, *Short Account*, 1761.

60 See Wilderson, chapter 1, Z. I. Jackson's work, and King for theorization of the forms of vulnerability and porosity to which black bodies are uniquely subjected. See also Byrd et al. for their reference to bodily porosity.

61 Marx, *Capital*, loc. 3461. This concept from Marx should not be confused with later formations such as *vampire capitalism*. See Kennedy, Vampire Capitalism. *Wétiko* comes from Forbes, *Columbus and Other Cannibals*. I return to it later.

62 Fisher, "'Dangerous Designes'" notes that Indigenous slavery has been understudied despite some pioneering early work and growing research. Indigenous slavery in Latin America is both obscured by and made possible through early implementation of the repartimiento and encomienda systems. See Gallay, *Indian Slavery*; Simpson, *Encomienda in New Spain*; Sherman, *Forced Native Labor*; Bryant, *Rivers of Gold*. For Indigenous slavery in the non-Hispanophone Caribbean, see Gallay, *Indian Slave Trade*; and Chaplin, "Enslavement of Indians." It is impossible to provide an exhaustive list of sources on Indigenous enslavement. It is also important to note early black enslavement in the Iberian Peninsula (Spain/Portugal) and the enslavement of Indigenous Peoples there. See Russell-Wood, *Black Man in Slavery*, and van Deusen, *Global Indios*. For a perspective that complicates black slavery together with indigeneity, see Restall, *Black Middle*; Vinson, *Before Mestizaje*; Rout, *African Experience*; and Wheat, *Atlantic Africa*.

63 Fisher, "'Dangerous Designes.'" The final Act is titled "An Act of Explanation to the Act of Negroes, and to Prohibit the Bringing of Indians to This Island," although it was initially crafted, as Fisher argues, in direct response to the threat of black rebellion, and its immediate goal was to restrict not all Indigenous slave labour but only that labour considered to be problematic (109–10, 118). Fisher makes the case for understanding Indigenous enslavement together with black enslavement, writing that the Barbados "assembly feared that with the introduction of New England Natives, 'greater mischief may happen to this Island then [*sic*] from any Negroes'" (115). I could not consider Stone's work for this book because of the time of its publication (2021).

64 Fisher references the Pequot War (1636–38) and King Phillip's War (1675–78).

65 See Reséndez, *Other Slavery*, chapter 12.

66 In 1542, as a result of Las Casas's and others' work, Charles V issued the New Laws (The New Laws of the Indies for the Good Treatment and Preservation of the Indians, Promulgated by the Emperor Charles the Fifth, 1542–1543) to protect Indigenous Peoples in Spanish America. The laws did not end Indigenous enslavement and ill treatment, and were soon repealed. Following the 1550 Valladolid debate, Indigenous Peoples were granted vassalage. According to Reséndez, the laws "prohibited the granting of new encomiendas, forbade colonists to compel Natives to carry loads against their will, and prevented Spaniards from forcing Indians to dive for pearls." As "free vassals," "Indian[s could not] be made into . . . slave[s] *under any circumstance* including wars, rebellions, or when ransomed from other Indians" (46). For an online source of the laws, see https://babel.hathitrust.org/cgi /pt?id=mdp.35112204863734&view=1up&seq=11 and https://sourcebooks.fordham .edu/mod/1542newlawsindies.asp. Although vassalage separated Indigenous and

black peoples, it was in various places applied as a category to blacks, though not with the broad consequences for Indigenous Peoples. See Díaz, *Virgin, the King*, and Hatfield, *Boundaries of Belonging*. See also Graubart, "Slaves and Not Vassals."

67 Reséndez, *Other Slavery*, 8.

68 Reséndez, *Other Slavery*, 96.

69 Reséndez, *Other Slavery*, 5.

70 Reséndez, *Other Slavery*, 10. See in particular the chapters "Pull of Silver" and "Contractions and Expansions." For another perspective on the Thirteenth Amendment, see DuVernay, *13th*.

71 Reséndez, *Other Slavery*, 24

72 Reséndez, *Other Slavery*, 23.

73 Reséndez, *Other Slavery*, 17.

74 Reséndez, *Other Slavery*, 23.

75 Reséndez, *Other Slavery*, 23–24.

76 Reséndez, *Other Slavery*, 28.

77 For cosmogony, see Wynter's works.

78 Reséndez, *Other Slavery*, 45, and see the chapter "Caribbean Debacle."

79 Reséndez, *Other Slavery*, 4.

80 Reséndez, *Other Slavery*, 43, 95, 71.

81 Jackson uses the term "black-ened" in *Becoming Human* to index the processes through which Indigenous Africans and their descendants are remade through the logics and practices of anti-blackness. It is a specific engagement, as I read it here with Afropessimist understandings of phenomenological blackness. Wilderson uses the term "black (ened)" in "Gramsci's Black Marx," which I discuss in chapter 3.

82 Schwartz, "Indian Labor," 44.

83 See Jackson, *Creole Indigeneity*, chapter 2.

84 Warren, *New England Bound*, loc. 79.

85 Warren, *New England Bound*, loc. 141.

86 Warren, *New England Bound*, loc. 78.

87 Warren, *New England Bound*, loc. 196–205.

88 Warren, *New England Bound*, loc. 594.

89 Warren, *New England Bound*, loc. 858.

90 Warren, *New England Bound*, loc. 997.

91 Warren, *New England Bound*, loc. 1788.

92 Warren, *New England Bound*, loc. 443.

93 Warren, *New England Bound*, loc. 1496.

94 Reséndez, *Other Slavery*, 40.

95 Reséndez, *Other Slavery*, 37.

96 Arguably, all black attempts to flee the plantation are a resurfacing of this eliminated (native) labour.

97 While black resistance to and occupation of positions outside slavery in the colonial era constitute various forms of freedoms, I distinguish them from land-based sovereignties such as those achieved by Maroon groups and which

are recognized by international law, as in the UN Declaration on the Rights of Indigenous Peoples. A rich literature on Anglophone slavery demonstrates how blacks remade themselves and carved out freedoms. For a collection considering this in Latin America, see Landers, *Slaves, Subjects, and Subversives*, particularly the chapter "*Cimarrón* and Citizen." It is also important to recall that black thinkers like Walter Rodney did not see black postcolonial states as necessarily free and sovereign because of the capitalism's social, political, and economic constraints, which secure whiteness as ontologically sovereign and materially dominant.

98 Warren, *New England Bound*, loc. 1419.

99 Warren, *New England Bound*, loc. 1851, see n. 89.

100 Warren, *New England Bound*, loc. 2002.

101 In the Caribbean, that work is more than just incidentally settler colonial because enslaved and indentured peoples remained and inherited the fruits of that initial labour and transformation of land.

102 Schwartz, "Indian Labor," 55.

103 Schwartz, "Indian Labor," 45–46.

104 Melamed, personal communication, September 12, 2018.

105 See Fraser, *Capitalism's Crisis*.

106 Forbes, *Columbus and Other Cannibals*, loc. 70. Forbes uses *wétiko*, the Cree word for cannibal to argue that cannibalism is the European consumption of the "lives and possessions" of others under imperialism.

107 For black and Indian poverty, see Gafar, "Poverty, Income Growth, and Inequality."

108 For Wilderson, this is "late capital's over-accumulation crisis," which he elaborates for blacks, who he says "are meant to be warehoused and die" ("Gramsci's Black Marx," 238). I argue that this is true for both blacks and Indigenous Peoples.

109 Moten, *Black and Blur*, 205

110 Nichols, "My Black Triangle," 673. This chapter begins and ends with a reference to gender. Though central to understanding the transformations of blackness in the Americas, gender is beyond the scope of this study.

3. LEFT LIMITS AND BLACK POSSIBILITIES

1 Bushnell, "Indigenous America," 203.

2 Rodney, *History of the Guyanese*, 2–3. I quoted this passage in *Creole Indigeneity*, but have continued to think about how it works, so I revisit it here.

3 Rodney, *History of the Guyanese*, 2. In *Groundings*, Rodney argues that Indigenous wealth (gold) made Europeans rich, without discussing how this wealth was extracted from the land nor who extracted it (13). Indigenous Peoples are thus still collapsed with the land, rather than function as agents within it. Throughout *Groundings*, Rodney refers to native genocide rather than native labour. This may be the limit of a singularly Caribbean perspective, but it also reasserts the pre-position.

4 See Barker, "For Whom Sovereignty Matters," 8, for a discission of Locke.

5 For a discussion of *terra nullius* as necessary for the imposition of nonnative sovereignties, see Moreton-Robinson, *White Possessive*, loc. 2730.

6 Sexton, "Social Life of Social Death," 10. For Sexton, as for other Afropessimist and black optimist texts, not only can blackness not be represented within normative analytic terms, but the problem of blackness itself jeopardizes the operation of thought as an expression of self/subject.

7 Rodney, *How Europe Underdeveloped Africa*, 12.

8 For settler colonialism as a "structure," see Wolfe, "Settler Colonialism and the Elimination of the Native."

9 1516 refers to the first time Las Casas is supposed to have proposed importing blacks to take the place of native peoples, prior to the 1518 text quoted in chapter 1.

10 For historical work on the Caribbean and global markets, see Thompson, *Haunting Past*; Beckles, *Natural Rebels*; Bolland, *Politics of Labour*, and others.

11 Barchiesi and Jackson, "Introduction," 4.

12 See Wynter, "Ceremony Must Be Found."

13 Wilderson, "Gramsci's Black Marx," 228.

14 Wilderson, "Gramsci's Black Marx," 233.

15 Wilderson, "Gramsci's Black Marx," 230.

16 In *Red, White and Black*, Wilderson is clear that the enslaved person's fundamental condition is "accumulation and fungibility" rather than "exploitation and alienation" (14).

17 See *Red, White and Black*, 6, 151.

18 Wilderson, "Gramsci's Black Marx," 230. At the start of *Red, White and Black*, Wilderson provocatively states that blacks essentially "gave birth to the commodity" (2). I don't disagree, but I argue that the commodity, as a repository of use and exchange values, is a particular expression of a process that transformed *both* blacks and Indigenous Peoples' literal bodies. To lose sight of either one is the point at which anti-blackness or anti-indigeneity resurfaces in our work.

19 Wilderson, "Gramsci's Black Marx," 237.

20 Williams, *Capitalism and Slavery*, loc. 89. It can be argued that Williams simply follows and elaborates Marx's observations in *Capital* about the role enslaved black people played in the rise of both capital (through claims about primitive accumulation) and even consciousness of worker exploitation. Marx, for instance, writes that "the veiled slavery of the wage workers in Europe needed, for its pedestal, slavery pure and simple in the new world" (*Capital*, loc. 12185).

21 The history of a place like New Orleans is relevant here as descendants of formerly enslaved peoples have re-rooted themselves and were uprooted through Hurricane Katrina and more recently Hurricane Sally.

22 Wilderson, "Gramsci's Black Marx," 237. See Wilderson, *Red, White and Black* for structural adjustment, as well as Warren's elaboration of the concept in "Onticide."

23 In the *Futures of Black Radicalism*, Robinson reinforces the centrality of culture and Indigenous African belief systems as the originary point for resistance to the forms of bondage of colonialism and capitalism.

24 Mignolo, "Delinking." See Robinson and Robinson, "Preface," *Futures of Black Radicalism*, loc. 107.

25 These texts include Gilroy, *Ain't No Black* (1987) and *Against Race* (2002), Roediger, *Class, Race, and Marxism* (2017), and Mills, *From Class to Race* (2003). These works (including those published later) reflect over a decade of work and are preoccupied not strictly with capitalism's role in black subordination but with the structural relationship of race to capital and class formation. Mills notes that the original work on race and class informing this 2017 work predates his more well-known book, *Racial Contract*. Several chapters in Roediger's book were previously published as early as 2006. The time of these texts shows the simultaneity rather than chronology of development of a historical materialism for racial capitalism.

26 "Marx had not realized fully that the cargoes of labourers also contained African cultures. . . . It would be through the historical and social consciousness of these Africans that the trade in slaves and the system of slave labour was infected with its contradiction" (Robinson, *Black Marxism*, xiv). In *How Europe Underdeveloped Africa*, Walter Rodney refers to racism as one of capitalism's "irrationalities," 11.

27 See Davies, *Left of Karl Marx*.

28 Robinson, *Black Marxism*, xxx, 2. Robinson refers to the "inadequacies of Marxism." See also Fanon, *Wretched of the Earth*, 40.

29 Hart, "Constellations," 15. I disagree with Hart on this point; see chapter 4.

30 Hart, "Constellations," 15.

31 The word "sentient" refers to Wilderson, *Red, White and Black*.

32 Moten, *Black and Blur*, 9.

33 Robinson, *Black Marxism*, xxx.

34 Robinson, *Black Marxism*, xxx.

35 Robinson, *Black Marxism*, xxx.

36 Robinson, *Black Marxism*, xxx.

37 Robinson, Black Marxism, xxx.

38 Robinson, *Black Marxism*, 99–100.

39 Robinson, *Black Marxism*, 117.

40 Robinson, *Black Marxism*, 126 (my emphasis).

41 Robinson, *Black Marxism*, 187.

42 Robinson, *Black Marxism*, 287.

43 Robinson, *Black Marxism*, 187. In *Creole Indigeneity*, I discuss Hegel's idea that cultural proximity to European culture is redemptive. As I discussed in chapter 1, Arendt's "savage" is an irredeemable position.

44 Robinson, *Black Marxism*, 140.

45 Robinson, *Black Marxism*, 201.

46 Robinson, *Black Marxism*, 170.

47 Robinson, *Black Marxism*, 170.

48 Robinson, *Black Marxism*, 125.

49 See Ciccariello-Maher, *Decolonizing Dialectics*.

50 Robinson, *Black Marxism*, 81.

51 Fanon, *Black Skin*, Loc 1334.

52 O'Brien, "Tracing Settler Colonialism's Eliminatory Logic," 251–52.

53 Kelley, "Rest of Us," 267.

54 Kelley, "Rest of Us," 268.

55 Kelley, "Rest of Us," 269.

56 Kelley, "Rest of Us," 269.

57 Kelley, "Rest of Us," 269.

58 Kelley, "Rest of Us," 271 (emphasis in original).

59 Robinson, *Black Marxism*, 145. See "The Property" in James, *Black Jacobins*.

60 See, for instance, Linda Villarosa, "Why America's Black Mothers and Babies Are in a Life-or-Death Crisis," *New York Times*, April 11, 2018, https://www.nytimes .com/2018/04/11/magazine/black-mothers-babies-death-maternal-mortality.html, and Mattie Quinn, "Why Texas Is the Most Dangerous U.S. State to Have a Baby," Governing.com, April 17, 2017, https://www.governing.com/topics/health-human -services/gov-maternal-infant-mortality-pregnant-women-texas.html.

61 In *In the Wake*, Sharpe, through Hartman's and Spillers's works, argues that the black woman's womb was "turned into a factory producing blackness as abjection much like the slave ship's hold and the prison, and turning the birth canal into another do-mestic Middle Passage with Black mothers, after the end of legal hypodescent, still ushering their children into their condition; their non/statism their non/being-ness" (74). The fact that black women's wombs as a kind of "hold" reproduced the a priori of slave status, and that black women also withhold their wombs through deliberate pregnancy termination, distinguishes birth in slavery from the lack of reproduction as strict Elimination in part because, following Sharpe, "what is also being birthed is" "anagrammatical blackness," a form of rupture within the production of black-ness as nonbeing (75). I therefore read black women's violently imposed sterility as formal Elimination, and the birthing of black bodies in slavery as anti-blackness, though the latter is still premised on dispossession and must incorporate elimina-tory mechanisms to discipline blacks and ensure that slave offspring who have made the passage through the amniotic *sea*, rather than the Columbian ocean-sea, come to know their ontological lack. Sharpe's concept of the womb as middle pas-sage should be placed in conversation with Wynter, "Beyond Miranda's Meanings," where she writes that we were never to reproduce ourselves. Wynter refers both to Caliban's lack of a (hetero) mate and to the reproduction of ourselves as sover-eign beings. This *prohibition* on reproduction that supersedes any act of physical reproduction makes birthing by enslaved women a middle passage. That passage is literally the process by which value is added to black bodies, so by calling black enslaved women's wombs machines, Sharpe signals how the process of adding value (a form of converting black bodies) had to be ongoing rather than temporally fixed in the past. Spillers elaborated on the black women's womb as the amniotic sea of the middle/passage by discussing what it means for black women to reproduce outside pre-capture kinship structures and what it means for their offspring to not belong to any gendered progenitor: "the captive female body locates precisely a moment of converging political and social vectors that mark the flesh as a prime commodity of exchange." Spillers, "Mama's Baby," 75. For black women's resistance to reproduction, see Beckles, *Natural Rebels*. See also chapter 1, note 1.

62 Robinson, *Black Marxism*, 151.

63 Robinson, *Black Marxism*, 151.

64 Wolfe, "Structure and Event," 123.

65 Las Casas secured a form of vassalage for Indigenous Peoples that represented the moment of capacity, I argue, for representation. Blacks lack this, even where they are converted to Christianity before being transported for chattel slavery. Vassalage is thus the pre-political position necessary for particular forms of Otherness to be recuperated within western political and legal systems. This does not mean that Indigenous Peoples have full representation, only that there is a moment in which they are literally given an analogue status that can serve to enact it later.

66 Robinson, *Black Marxism*, 72.

67 Robinson, *Black Marxism*, 73. This "negation" as tension in black radical thought that does not allow for any singular position with regard to, in this instance, Marxist political economy is clear in Rodney's *Groundings*. It is also evident in, as Barchiesi points out in conversation, a range of writings including Cruse's response to Aptheker's *Documentary History* in "Revolutionary Nationalism," the left journalist Claudia Jones's work, and even earlier in W. E. B. DuBois's writings. See also Sexton's argument that "black life is not lived in the world that the world lives in, but it is lived underground, in outer space." Sexton, "Social Life of Social Death," 28, and "Ante-Anti-Blackness."

68 In his preface to the 2000 edition, Robinson writes, "The Black Radical Tradition was an accretion, over generations, of collective intelligence gathered from struggle" (*Black Marxism*, xxx).

69 Robinson, *Black Marxism*, 72.

70 Robinson, *Black Marxism*, 121.

71 Robinson, *Black Marxism*, 133.

72 Robinson, *Black Marxism*, 134.

73 See discussion in *Creole Indigeneity*.

74 Robinson, *Black Marxism*, 177 (emphases in original).

75 Robinson, *Black Marxism*, 184.

76 Robinson, *Black Marxism*, 99.

77 Robinson, *Black Marxism*, 141.

78 Robinson, *Black Marxism*, 138–39.

79 Robinson, *Black Marxism*, 152 and 154.

80 Robinson, *Black Marxism*, 143.

81 For "citational practice," see Vimalassery, Pegues, and Goldstein, "Introduction."

82 Robinson, *Black Marxism*, 165.

83 Robinson, *Black Marxism*, 166.

84 See, for example, Robinson, *Black Marxism*, 164–65, 194.

85 Robinson, *Black Marxism*, 168.

86 Robinson, *Black Marxism*, 168.

87 Robinson, *Black Marxism*, 170.

88 Mills, *From Class to Race*, 128.

89 Mills, *From Class to Race*, 129.

90 Mills, *From Class to Race*, 129. Mills mobilizes the extinction thesis in relation to not only black plantation work, but also black elimination. See Mills, *From Class to Race*, 118, note 14.

91 Moreton-Robinson, *White Possessive*, xix.

4. AGAINST THE GRAIN

1 There is a way in which Rodney's death, the death of other labour activists and workers, and threats against those such as my great uncle Gordon Todd, mentioned in *Creole Indigeneity*, haunt my life and work and shaped their trajectory in ways I am only now beginning to understand. I remain humbled by the breadth of Rodney's engagement with black struggle in Africa, the United States, and the Caribbean; his intellectual curiosity; and his commitment to staying in struggle, what Coulthard might even see as a kind of "grounded normativity" from the material tradition, even where the ground (Guyana, Jamaica) was blatantly hostile to him and his family.

2 Prescod, "Guyana's Socialism," 117, 121. Osuna also addresses Rodney's criticism of his own class position and the need to work against it. See Oscuna, "Class Suicide." Rodney is even more clear on this in *Groundings*.

3 See Fanon, *Wretched of the Earth*, and Rodney, *Groundings*.

4 See "About Walter Rodney," the Walter Rodney Foundation, https://www .walterrodneyfoundation.org/biography/; Commission of Inquiry Report on Rodney's death, https://www.walterrodneyfoundation.org/coi; and Campbell, *Improper Life*. For this representation of anti-elite socialism in contrast to Burnham's state socialism, see Prescod, "Guyana's Socialism," 125, 128.

5 Rodney says, "The contradictions of international capital . . . are reflected in a sharper and sharper manner in the dependencies in Third World countries," and "It's in that context of the defensive posture of capitalism and of its ideology at this stage that one must see the recourse to socialist slogans and policies." Prescod, "Guyana's Socialism," 113, 114. See Wynter, "Columbus and the Poetics."

6 For Hart, see "Constellations."

7 Rodney, *Groundings*, 10–11. See also Césaire, *Discourse on Colonialism*. Rodney's articulation anticipates a perspective that Jared Sexton summarizes from Blackburn, *Making of New World Slavery*, where Blackburn identifies the definitive link that chattel slavery established between private property and black enslavement. See Sexton, "Social Life of Social Death," 17.

8 Wilderson states that because Marxists "try to show how violence is connected to production, . . . they are not really thinking about the violence of slavery comprehensively" (*Afropessimism*, 224; see also 216, 222–23). Rodney is more aligned with Afropessimism than it might seem because he too identifies blackness as a slave status within capital (*Groundings*, 16). However, for Rodney, political economy *can* explain anti-black violence because capitalism is predicated on anti-blackness.

9 See Jackson, "To Be Anti-Black" and "Killing *Us* Softly."

10 Prescod, "Guyana's Socialism," 123

11　Prescod, "Guyana's Socialism," 124. Rodney also says that "we are in a better position to judge what a socialist society would look like, and we know that, qualitatively, the first essential is working-class power." Prescod, "Guyana's Socialism," 123–24.

12　Prescod, "Guyana's Socialism," 117.

13　This is Roland Barthes's approach to ideology, which Silverman contrasts to Althusser's more complex understanding. Silverman, *Subject of Semiotics*, 30. See also Althusser, "Ideology and Ideological State Apparatuses."

14　I am thinking here of Césaire's Caliban, who has to "spit" out the colonizer, Prospero. Both Rodney and Césaire depict the double-edged nature of ideological struggle. Césaire, *A Tempest*, 60 (Act III, scene V).

15　Prescod, "Guyana's Socialism," 114.

16　Prescod, "Guyana's Socialism," 114.

17　Kelley, "Foreword," xvi.

18　Williams, *Capitalism and Slavery*, 9.

19　Robinson, *Black Marxism*, 241. For more on James, see McClendon, *C. L. R. James's Notes*.

20　For James's life, see his *History of Pan African Revolt*, and Forsdick and Høgsbjerg, eds., *Black Jacobins Reader*.

21　Robinson, *Black Marxism*, 265.

22　Robinson, *Black Marxism*, 272. See also Depestre, "Interview with Aimé Césaire," and his *Letter to Maurice Thorez* (secretary and head) resigning from the French Communist Party in 1956.

23　Robinson, *Black Marxism*, 274.

24　Robinson, *Black Marxism*, 276.

25　Williams, *Capitalism and Slavery*. See, for instance, how time functions as the difference between slavery and indenture (374).

26　Robinson, *Black Marxism*, 276–77.

27　James, *Black Jacobins*, 47.

28　See Foucault, *Security, Territory, Population*.

29　James, *Black Jacobins*, 3.

30　James, *Black Jacobins*, 4

31　James, *Black Jacobins*, 4.

32　In her biographic essay on James, Grimshaw notes this about his interest in Thackery. See Anna Grimshaw, "C. L. R. James: A Revolutionary Vision for the 20th Century," Marxists.org, https://www.marxists.org/archive/james-clr/biograph .htm.

33　James, *Black Jacobins*, 7 (my emphasis).

34　James, *Black Jacobins*, 56.

35　James, *Black Jacobins*, ix. James portrays the economic book of "pre-revolutionary San Domingo" thus: "Between 1764 and 1771 the average importation of slaves varied between ten and fifteen thousand. In 1786 it was 27,000, and from 1787 onwards the colony was taking more than 40,000 slaves a year," 55.

36　James, *Black Jacobins*, 8, 56.

37　James, *Black Jacobins*, 14.

38 James, *Black Jacobins*, 20.

39 James, *Black Jacobins*, 15.

40 James, *Black Jacobins*, 16–17.

41 James, *Black Jacobins*, 85–86.

42 James, *Black Jacobins*, 86.

43 James, *Black Jacobins*, 90.

44 James, *Black Jacobins*, 94.

45 See *Tragedy of Henri Christophe*. If we return to Foucault on the evolution of the state, we can suggest that Henri Christophe's failure was not simply because he was a despot who essentially reinstituted slavery, as Césaire's play indicates. His failure is because both the French and Haitian revolutions when viewed through the capitalist forces or mechanisms of accumulation that helped to engender them (enslavement, etc.) are the mechanisms by which the modern state seeks to emerge as a constitutional entity rather than just an economic one.

46 James, *Black Jacobins*, 101.

47 See Rodney, *History of the Guyanese*, 131.

48 James, *Black Jacobins*, 43.

49 Rodney, *History of the Guyanese*, 2.

50 Prescod, "Guyana's Socialism," 118 (emphasis in original).

51 In his interview with Prescod, Rodney identifies four groups that composed the WPA: the African Society for Cultural Relations, the Indian Political Revolutionary Association, the Working People's Vanguard Party M-L (Marxist-Leninist), and the Ratoun group (university group). He names the last two as Marxist.

52 Prescod, "Guyana's Socialism," 122.

53 Prescod, "Guyana's Socialism," 127.

54 Rodney speaks about race: "These groups came together in response to at least two important pressures. One was a new demand to overcome a racist-oriented politics, to break with the divisiveness of race as a fact of organization, so that both ASCRIA and IPRA collaborated on issues such as the landless squatters, of both Indian and African descent. The question was dealt with in class terms rather than racial terms." Prescod, "Guyana's Socialism," 120.

55 Fanon, *Wretched of the Earth*.

56 Rodney, "African History," 67.

57 Rodney, "African History," 72–73.

58 Rodney, "African History," 71.

59 Rodney, "African History," 73.

60 Rodney, "African History," 73.

61 Rodney, "African History," 75, 78.

62 Rodney, "African History," 79.

63 Rodney, "African History," 78.

64 Rodney, "African History," 79.

65 Rodney, "African History," 80.

66 Recall Rodney's assertion that capitalism is anti-black. See Sexton, "The Social Life of Social Death," 35. Thanks to Franco Barchiesi for leading me to this formulation in Sexton.

67 Byrd et al. note, "Remarkably for Marx, while slavery, forced relocations, colonization, and imperialism are levers of the industrial mode of production, they are not
constitutively an aspect of what he terms the 'enslavement of workers.' In the first
volume of *Capital*, the figure of the enslaved worker is instead reserved for the
European immigrant and his relatives, the internal vagabond, the propertyless,
the former serf" ("Predatory Value," 6).

68 Knight, *Caribbean*, 120–21.

69 Wynter, "Beyond Miranda's Meanings," 114–15. Spillers also notes this absence of
a mate in "Mama's Baby," 65.

70 This emphasis on culture over ontology is generally also held to be a problem in Afropessimist thought. In "Social Life of Social Death," Sexton discusses the problems
of construing blackness in terms of statelessness or in terms of culture (37 n. 1).

71 See the discussion of Spillers in chapter 6. This reproduction that represents a
slippage, a difference and a transformation within and without the strictures of
phobia, has been noted and designated across Black studies. It is the core of Creole cultural studies and is philosophically captured through theorizations of the
"insurgent" (para) ontological from Spillers to Moten to Hartman to Sexton and
others.

72 For the distinction between human difference and blacks sameness, see Warren,
"Onticide."

73 Rodney, *History of the Guyanese*, 16.

74 Rodney, *History of the Guyanese*, 33.

75 Rodney, *History of the Guyanese*, 33.

76 Rodney, *History of the Guyanese*, 18.

77 Rodney, *History of the Guyanese*, 31.

78 Rodney, *History of the Guyanese*, 43.

79 Rodney, *History of the Guyanese*, 33, 48.

80 Rodney, *History of the Guyanese*, 36, 44.

81 Rodney, *History of the Guyanese*, 51, 58.

82 Rodney, *History of the Guyanese*, 2.

83 Singh, "On Race,'" 842, 893.

84 Singh, "On Race," 1186.

85 Singh, "On Race," 868.

5. "MARXIAN AND NOT MARXIAN"

1 Henry, *Caliban's Reason*, 139.

2 Henry, *Caliban's Reason*, 140.

3 Henry, *Caliban's Reason*, 140.

4 See Scott, "Re-Enchantment of Humanism."

5 Henry labels her "poststructuralist" while crediting her with avoiding its "es-
sentializing tendencies" through "supplementary relations with Marxism and
Pan-Africanism" (*Caliban's Reason*, 118–19). I agree that poststructuralism has been
influential in her work, but her relationship to the field is less derivate.

6 Scott, "Re-Enchantment of Humanism," 142.

7   Scott, "Re-Enchantment of Humanism," 134–35. "Native" here refers to the pecu-
    liarity of nonwhite colonized labour rather than particularly Indigenous American
    identity.
8   I elaborate refusal as a rejection of something into which one has already been
    compelled. Since Wynter was a Marxist *until* she was not, I see her critique not
    as an outside one but as one that reflects prior entanglement with and action
    through Marxist ideology.
9   Currently, *Black Metamorphosis* exists as a typed manuscript with handwritten cor-
    rections. It cannot be converted using OCR so that I can have audio access as per
    my disability.
10 Wilderson, *Afropessimism*, 170.
11 See Nash, "On the Beginning"; Jackson, *Becoming Human*; and Weheliye, *Habeas
    Viscus*.
12 Wynter, "Beyond Miranda's Meanings," 116. This is Wynter's spelling in the essay.
13 Wynter, "Beyond Miranda's Meanings," 118, 120.
14 Wynter, "Columbus and the Poetics," 255. Although the earth was the center of
    other "spheres," it was still subordinate to the ultimate sphere associated with
    divinity. This is an Aristotelian view that Wynter outlines in the essays. See also
    Jackson, "Colonialism."
15 Wynter, "Beyond Miranda's Meanings," 116.
16 Wynter, "Beyond Miranda's Meanings," 117.
17 For "chaos," see Wynter, "Ceremony Must Be Found."
18 See Davies, *Left of Karl Marx*; and Jones, "End to the Neglect."
19 Wynter, "Beyond Miranda's Meaning, 113.
20 McKittrick, ed., *Sylvia Wynter*, loc. 987 (emphasis in original).
21 Wynter, "Beyond Miranda's Meaning," 119.
22 See Giroux, "Reading Hurricane Katrina."
23 Malthus, *Principle of Population*, 50.
24 Malthus, *Principle of Population*, 60, 46.
25 Malthus, *Principle of Population*, 85.
26 Darwin, *Descent of Man*, loc. 889 and 912.
27 Malthus, *Principle of Population*, 14–15.
28 Malthus, *Principle of Population*, 37.
29 Malthus, *Principle of Population*, 28.
30 Wynter, "Columbus and the Poetics," 269 (emphasis in original).
31 See Giroux, "Reading Hurricane Katrina," on disposability.
32 Wynter, "Columbus and the Poetics," 276.
33 Wynter, "Beyond Miranda's Meanings," 120 ("Marxian and not-Marxian"); 119
    ("gender, and not-gender").
34 Wynter, "Beyond Miranda's Meanings," 116. "Degodded" is Wynter's term to signal
    the stripping of cosmogonic origin from blacks who were enslaved, and the secular
    turn in Europe. See "1492: A New World View" and "Unsettling the Coloniality."
35 Wynter, "Beyond Miranda's Meanings," 115.
36 Wynter, "Beyond Miranda's Meanings," 124, n. 27.
37 Wynter, "Beyond Miranda's Meanings," 118.

38 Wynter, "New Seville: Part One," 26 (emphasis in original). "Land-labour ratio" is the term she uses in the essays. See, for example, p. 30.

39 Wynter, "New Seville: Part One," 29.

40 Wynter, "New Seville: Part One," 28.

41 Wynter, "New Seville: Part One," 29 (emphasis in original).

42 Wynter, "New Seville: Part One," 29 (emphasis in original).

43 Wynter, "New Seville: Part One," 31.

44 Wynter, "New Seville: Part One," 30.

45 Wynter, "New Seville: Part Two," 49–50.

46 Wynter, "New Seville: Part Two," 50.

47 Wynter, "New Seville: Part Two," 50.

48 Wynter, "New Seville: Part Two," 50, 49.

49 Wynter, "New Seville: Part Two," 50.

50 Wynter, "New Seville: Part One," 30.

51 Wynter, "Jonkonnu in Jamaica," 35.

52 See *Creole Indigeneity*.

53 Wynter, "Jonkonnu in Jamaica," 35, emphasis added.

54 Wynter, "Jonkonnu in Jamaica," 36.

55 Wynter, "Jonkonnu in Jamaica," 37.

56 Wynter, "Jonkonnu in Jamaica," 36.

57 Wynter, "Jonkonnu in Jamaica," 36.

58 Wynter, "Jonkonnu in Jamaica," 39.

59 Wynter, "Jonkonnu in Jamaica," 38 (my emphasis).

60 Wynter, "Jonkonnu in Jamaica," 41.

61 Wynter, "Jonkonnu in Jamaica," 39.

62 Wynter, "Jonkonnu in Jamaica," 41.

63 Wynter, "Jonkonnu in Jamaica," 47.

64 Wynter, "Jonkonnu in Jamaica," 37.

65 For the original definition of autopoiesis, see Maturana and Varela, *Autopoiesis and Cognition*. Wynter adapts their term to describe how we systemically (re)produce ourselves as (genres of the) human materially and narratively in such a way that the fact of this reproduction is mostly unavailable to us because it would represent a rupture. See McKittrick, ed., *Sylvia Wynter*.

66 Melamed, "Racial Capitalism," 76.

67 Byrd et al., "Predatory Value," 135.

68 A good deal of theorizing focuses on black "flesh," with which the concept of skins is in dialogue, although I do not utilize that term nor use it to elaborate a psycho-analytic state. See Warren, "Onticide," and Spillers, "Mama's Baby."

69 Fanon, *Black Skin*, loc. 1360, 1367.

70 See Lamming, *Castle of My Skin*, and Paquet, "Foreword."

71 See Hughes, "House in the World."

72 Spillers, "Mama's Baby," 67–68. Here Spillers theorizes the slave-making process, but she also discusses how black women exist "*in the flesh*" as reproductive machines (animals) within slavery (79, 80).

73 Haraway, "Staying with the Trouble," 48.

74 See Crist, "Poverty of Our Nomenclature."

75 Moore, "Introduction: Anthropocene or Capitalocene?," 6.

76 Moore, *Capitalism in the Web of Life*, Loc 2538.

77 Moore, *Capitalism in the Web of Life*, 190.

78 Moore, "The Rise of Cheap Nature," 92.

79 Vergès, "Racial Capitalocene," 1616.

80 Vergès, "Racial Capitalocene," 1589 (my emphasis).

81 Yusoff, *Billion Black Anthropocenes*, 9.

82 Yusoff, *Billion Black Anthropocenes*, 8.

83 Karera, "Blackness and the Pitfalls," 32, 34, 44, 47.

84 My description of it as neo-Darwinian is based on Yusoff's outlining of its symbolic and mythic properties; *Billion Black Anthropocenes*, chapter 1.

85 Compost is discussed in Haraway's work. On genres of the human, see Wynter's work. Ironically, or fittingly for capitalism, the composting of human remains is a legalized form of burial service that is, of course, not free, but transactional. It also costs more than the cheapest method of disposing remains, cremation, and as such is still tied to degrees of graduated economic access. See, for instance: https://www.smithsonianmag.com/smart-news/california-has-legalized-human-composting-180980809/

86 Haraway, "Staying with the Trouble," 51.

87 Karera, "Blackness and the Pitfalls."

88 Haraway, "Staying with the Trouble."

89 See Linda Villarosa, "Why America's Black Mothers and Babies Are in a Life-or-Death Crisis." *The New York Times* Magazine, April 11, 2018. https://www.nytimes.com/2018/04/11/magazine/black-mothers-babies-death-maternal-mortality.html.

90 See Wynter, "Columbus and the Poetics," 254 (emphasis in original). This outside perspective may in fact be a diminishing or vanishing point in the face of capitalist integration. It is the point that I think Coulthard wants to retain for Indigenous resistance and sovereignty, and which Recognition refuses. For this critique of Haraway, see Jenny Turner, "Nothing Natural," *London Review of Books*, January 23, 2020, https://www.lrb.co.uk/the-paper/v42/no2/jenny-turner/nothing-natural. In conversation, Barchiesi, who directed me to Turner, suggests that Haraway essentially says that the problem of the Anthropocene is not really consumption, but excessive (re)production of bodies of color.

91 Coulthard, "Colonialism of the Present."

92 Coulthard, "Colonialism of the Present." See also *Red Skin, White Masks*, loc. 3198, for a summary of his position.

93 Coulthard, "Colonialism of the Present." Indeed, after George Floyd's murder, we had had to become more aware in the United States of the forms of state-sponsored eliminatory discipline of black bodies and Indigenous bodies and the use of carceral structures to accomplish this as well. In the United States, for example, Indigenous women are incarcerated at six times the rate of white women. See "Mitch Jones on Fracking's Hazards, Matt Sutton on Drug War's Victims," Fairness and Accuracy in Reporting, October 23, 2020, https://fair.org/home/mitch-jones-on-frackings-hazards-matt-sutton-on-drug-wars-victims/.

94 See Ta-Nehisi Coates, "The Case for Reparations," *Atlantic*, June 2014; Villarosa, *Under the Skin*.

95 See Coulthard, "Colonialism of the Present."

96 Coulthard and Simpson, "Grounded Normativity," 254

97 Coulthard and Simpson, "Grounded Normativity," 253 (my emphasis).

98 Coulthard, *Red Skin, White Masks*, loc. 3296.

99 Coulthard, *Red Skin, White Masks*, loc. 473–74.

100 Coulthard, *Red Skin, White Masks*, loc. 3233–43.

101 Coulthard, *Red Skin, White Masks*, loc. 405.

102 I am borrowing "reenchanted" from Scott, "Re-Enchantment of Humanism."

103 Coulthard, *Red Skin, White Masks*, loc. 2808–17.

104 Coulthard, *Red Skin, White Masks*, loc. 2948.

105 Coulthard, *Red Skin, White Masks*, loc. 3081.

106 Coulthard, *Red Skin, White Masks*, loc. 3181.

107 See Moten, *Consent Not to Be a Single Being* trilogy.

108 Johnson and Lubin, "Introduction," loc 395.

109 Robinson and Robinson, "Preface." See also loc. 196.

110 Johnson and Lubin, "Introduction," loc. 245; Robinson and Robinson, "Preface," loc. 170.

111 Vergès, "Racial Capitalocene," 1634–42.

112 Scott, "Re-Enchantment of Humanism," 141.

113 Wynter, "Jonkonnu in Jamaica," 38–39.

114 The relation I imagine here is therefore something else, something not confined to that of properly political subjects.

115 Yusoff, *Billion Black Anthropocenes*, 15.

6. WORK AS METAPHOR, LABOUR AS METONYMY

1 Guyana, Act No. 6 of 2006, 5.

2 Guyana, Act No. 2 of 1980, 33.

3 For "truth," see Baudrillard, *Jean Baudrillard: Selected Writings*.

4 I use libido not simply as sex drive, but as a broader psychic urge or desire intrinsic to human action and compulsion, or will to act/be. Columbus and his contemporaries expressed a desire that was both political and ontological. This desire is transformed or expressed over time as a literal sexual desire *for* the other (particularly the black) and to *be* the other (the native), as McClintock's *Imperial Leather* demonstrates and as Deloria's *Custer Died* makes clear, respectively. Thus, libidinal is about a primary political plane of expression and a secondary or adjacent sexual plane of expression tied to racialization and (settler) colonialism.

5 See Jackson, "Baptism of Soil."

6 See Wynter, "Columbus and the Poetics."

7 Azurara, *Chronicle*, chapter 18.

8 Gimenez Valdivia also deliberately associates Las Casas with the conquistadores, writing that prior to 1514, "nothing oriented Las Casas's heart towards the issue of justice" ("Reason, Providence, and Testimony," 312). For his ownership of

blacks, see Lampe, "Las Casas and African Slavery." Although they are considered vastly different, Cortes and Las Casas were at one point indeed "friends" (Restall, "'There Was a Time'"). I read friendship as a mode of complicity of feeling with regard to this shared desire for wealth that I am charting as foundational.

9 Yusoff, *Billion Black Anthropocenes*, 10.

10 See "Towards a Politics of Accountability: Caribbean Feminisms, Indigenous Geographies, Common Struggles," Antipode Online, November 2017, https://antipodeonline.org/201516-recipients-2/iwa-1516-gahman/.

11 "Jean La Rose, 2002 Goldman Prize Winner," GoldmanPrize.org, https://www.goldmanprize.org/recipient/jean-la-rose/.

12 See McKittrick, *Demonic Grounds*; Goeman, *Mark My Words*; and Ben-zvi, *Native Land Talk*.

13 Pearce and Louis, "Mapping Indigenous Depth," 108–9, 113.

14 Pearce and Louis, "Mapping Indigenous Depth," 113.

15 Wapichan territory also extends to the Upper Essequibo basin. For the location, see the prize's case study at Equator Initiative, "South Central People's Development Association," https://www.equatorinitiative.org/2017/05/29/south-central-peoples-development-association/.

16 Amazon Conservation Team, "Amazon Tribes Use Mapping Technologies to Empower Cultural Stewardship of Ancestral Lands," https://www.amazonteam.org/amazon-tribes-use-mapping-technologies-to-empower-cultural-stewardship-of-ancestral-lands/; see also Kimberley Brown, "How Drones and GPS Are Helping People in Ecuador Save the Amazon," *Pacific Standard*, April 16, 2019, https://psmag.com/environment/how-drones-and-gps-are-helping-indigenous-people-save-the-amazon; and Reuters, "Interactive Map Can Help Indigenous Peoples Secure Land Rights," VOA News, November 19, 2015, https://www.voanews.com/a/indigenous-peoples-given-interactive-map-to-help-secure-land-rights/3065328.html.

17 See Pearce and Louis, "Mapping Indigenous Depth," 110, on Indigenous mapping practices as forms of "process cartography" that differ from more object- or "product"-oriented western mapping practices. They borrow the term from Rundstrom, "Mapping, Postmodernism."

18 Scott Wilson, "In Gaza, Lives Shaped by Drones," *Washington Post*, December 3, 2011, https://www.washingtonpost.com/world/national-security/in-gaza-lives-shaped-by-drones/2011/11/30/gIQAjaP6OO_story.html; Robert Mackey, "Secret Israeli Report Details Errors in Deadly Drone Strike," August 11, 2018, Intercept.com, https://theintercept.com/2018/08/11/israel-palestine-drone-strike-operation-protective-edge/; Palestinian Center for Human Rights website, https://www.pchrgaza.org/en/; Zolan Kanno-Youngs, "U.S. Watched George Floyd Protests in 15 Cities Using Aerial Surveillance," *New York Times*, June 19, 2020, https://www.nytimes.com/2020/06/19/us/politics/george-floyd-protests-surveillance.html. See Jackson "Killing *Us* softly" for Haiti drone reference.

19 The prize system seems divided between those awarding primarily First World actors for both discovery and activism, and those awarding Third and Fourth World actors for their efforts to save the environment. "List of Environmental Awards," Wikipedia.org, https://en.wikipedia.org/wiki/List_of_environmental_awards.

20 Equator Initiative, "What We Do," https://www.equatorinitiative.org/about/what-we-do/.

21 See the language used by Ervin, manager of the Global Programme on Nature for Development, United Nations Development Programme: "The Equator Initiative . . . ensures a connection is made between local actors on the ground, national governments and international policy makers" (Equator Initiative, "What We Do").

22 Equator Initiative, "All Winners," https://www.equatorinitiative.org/equator-prize/all-winners/.

23 See Sobel, *Longitude*.

24 For Columbus's use of dead reckoning and other navigational methods, see Peck, "Theory versus Practical Application."

25 See, for example, Twain, *Journey around the World*; Stevenson, *In the South Seas*; Conrad, *Heart of Darkness*. Guadalupi and Shugaar, *Latitude Zero*.

26 See Wynter, "Poetics of the *Propter Nos*"; Azurara, *Chronicle*; Nussbaum, *Torrid Zones*.

27 I am thinking of the English monarchy's contemporary role and of the countries comprising the British Commonwealth.

28 Equator Initiative, "South Central People's Development Association," case study.

29 Equator Initiative, case study.

30 Equator Initiative, case study, 7; Protected Areas Trust (Guyana), "Kanuku Mountains Protected Area," https://protectedareastrust.org.gy/protected-areas/kanuku-mountains/.

31 "Community mapping teams create territorial maps that are used to make land claims and devise collective land use plans for the forest, mountain, savannah and wetland ecosystems that fall within the territory of the 17 Wapichan communities. More than 100 intercommunity agreements have been reached on the sustainable use of natural resources, the protection of wildlife and the conservation of forests" (Equator Initiative, "South Central People's Development Association" Case Study). Also on p. 8 of project summary.

32 Equator Initiative, case study, 12.

33 The case study reads: "In 1994, former President of Guyana, Cheddi Jagan, *challenged* the Wapichan people to provide evidence to show how they use the land and the communities' ability to manage, develop, and administrate the local natural resources. In *response*, SCPDA initiated several actions" (Equator Initiative, case study, 8 [my emphasis]).

34 Equator Initiative, case study, 4.

35 Equator Initiative, case study, 6. This condition puts the British in an agential position, but as Bulkan has illuminated, this clause or condition of independence was won through the successful and coordinated lobbying of Indigenous Peoples prior to independence in 1966 (Bulkan, "Struggle for Recognition").

36 Equator Initiative, case study, 6. For the amount of land requested by Indigenous Peoples and the land recommended for titling by the Commission, see Colchester et al., *Mining and Amerindians*.

37 Equator Initiative, case study, 10.

38 Forest Peoples Programme, "Wapichan People in Guyana Present Territorial Map and Community Proposals to Save Ancestral Forests," February 20, 2012, https://

www.forestpeoples.org/en/topics/participatory-resource-mapping/news/2012/02
/wapichan-people-guyana-present-territorial-map-an.

39 Forest Peoples Programme, "Wapichan People."

40 United Nations, Guyana, Announcement of Equator Prize Winner.

41 Moreover, according to Fredericks, "The lands legally handed to the communities take up a portion just about quarter of the land the Wapichan people actually
use" ("How the Wapichan"). https://guyanachronicle.com/2015/12/20/how-the
-wapichan-people-won-the-equator-prize/

42 According to the 2016 article in *National Geographic*, over "20 indigenous groups"
"create land-use maps covering more than 44 million acres for tribal use in developing reserve management plans" (Amazon Conservation Team, "Amazon Tribes
Use Mapping Technologies").

43 Amazon Conservation Team, "ACT Pilots Open Data Kit (ODK) to Enable Indigenous Partners to Seamlessly Collect Field Data in Their Native Language,"
https://www.amazonteam.org/act-pilots-open-data-kit-odk-to-enable-indigenous
-partners-to-seamlessly-collect-field-data-in-their-native-language/.

44 Equator Initiative, case study.

45 Amazon Conservation Team, "ACT Pilots Open Data Kit."

46 Amazon Conservation Team, "ACT Pilots Open Data Kit."

47 Brown, "How Drones and GPS."

48 Brown, "How Drones and GPS."

49 I am thinking here of Heidegger's concept of proper and improper relationships
to technology. See Campbell, *Improper Life*.

50 *OED*, "metonymy," https://www-oed-comview/Entry/117328.

51 Mbembe, "Necropolitics," 28.

52 See Voloshinov, "The Study of Ideologies"; Barthes, *Elements of Semiology*, 1967;
Fromm, "Marxism, Psychoanlysis, and Reality"; Wyk, "Psychoanalysis, Marxism";
Pavón-Cuéllar, *Marxism and Psychoanalysis*.

53 Silverman, *Subject of Semiotics*, 124–26, 52.

54 Wilderson, *Red, White and Black*, 70–78.

55 Wilderson, *Red, White and Black*, 88.

56 Wilderson, *Red, White and Black*, 92, 77.

57 Spillers, "Mama's Baby," 67, 69, 72.

58 Silverman, *Subject of Semiotics*, 55, 72, 54. I thank Bob Griffin for directing me to
this work of Silverman.

59 Silverman, *Subject of Semiotics*, 68, 72.

60 Silverman, *Subject of Semiotics*, 85, 82, 87, 73 (social).

61 Silverman, *Subject of Semiotics*, 61, 87 (my emphasis).

62 Silverman, *Subject of Semiotics*, 87.

63 Silverman, *Subject of Semiotics*, 99.

64 Silverman, *Subject of Semiotics*, 104–5.

65 Silverman, *Subject of Semiotics*, 106.

66 Silverman, *Subject of Semiotics*, 110, 111.

67 Silverman, *Subject of Semiotics*, 110.

68 Silverman, *Subject of Semiotics*, 113.

69 Silverman, *Subject of Semiotics*, 115–16.

70 Silverman, *Subject of Semiotics*, 120.

71 See Foucault, "Two Lectures."

72 Wynter, "Columbus and the Poetics," 254–55.

73 See Polanco, *Indigenous Peoples*, 28.

74 Cortés, *Hernán Cortés*, 76.

75 Cortés, *Hernán Cortés*, 64.

76 Yusoff writes of the tastes associated with slavery, such as sugar: "a desire that launches that point into existence." *Billion Black Anthropocenes*, 14. See also McClintock, *Imperial Leather*, and Gikandi, *Slavery and the Culture*. I shift from the precise concern with markets and matter (geology) to the semiotic. Moten writes about things and thingliness in the *Consent Not to Be as Single Being* trilogy.

77 Cortés, *Hernán Cortés*, 79. See also Columbus, *Four Voyages*.

78 Columbus's greed and brutality allows me to use him as an initiative point for the conquistadorial habit in the Americas, although he was not considered a true conquistador like later explorers.

79 Silverman, *Subject of Semiotics*, 113.

80 Silverman, *Subject of Semiotics*, 115–16.

81 Silverman, *Subject of Semiotics*, 9.

82 Warren also theorizes this inability to desire ourselves, by reading Hortense Spillers's work where he describes the condition of sameness or "undifferentiation" to which blacks/enslaved people are subject and in which, lacking subjectivity, the black "cannot desire but is, instead, *desired* on" (Warren, "Onticide," 398 [emphasis in original]).

83 In chapter 5, this reading of the environment is sustained particularly by Yussof's work. It is also sustained by work like Z. I. Jackson's on the animal, both suggesting that what is marked off as different from the animal to the geological are the expression of an internal system of meaning making, not a true external difference.

84 Equator Initiative, "Equator Prize 2015 Award Ceremony," https://www.equatorinitiative.org/2017/06/08/equator-prize-2015-award-ceremony/.

85 Equator Initiative, "Equator Prize 2015 Award Ceremony."

86 Griffiths and La Rose, "Searching for Justice," 38 (my emphasis).

CODA

1 Pruitt, "Mississippi Gardens."

2 Byrd et al., "Predatory Value," 11.

3 Byrd et al., "Predatory Value," 11.

4 Moten, "An Ecology of (Eloquent) Things," YouTube, https://www.youtube.com/watch?v=10RKOhlMmKQ.

5 Hale, "*Resistencia para que?*," 198.

6 Hale, "*Resistencia para que?*," 195.

7 Hale, "*Resistencia para que?*," 195.

8   See Penniman, *Farming While Black*; Soul Fire Farm, https://www.soulfirefarm.org
    /; Black Family Land Trust, "Savage Farm," https://www.bflt.org/savage-farm.html.

9   Darity and Mullen, *From Here to Equality*, 13-14.

10 Hurricane Katrina caused a mass uprooting of poor, particularly black peoples.
    Because its level of devastation was engineered through the failure of effective
    social politics and modes of governmental neglect, as Henry Giroux argues, I sug-
    gest that it should be understood as a mechanism of removal for the settler state.
    See Giroux, "Reading Hurricane Katrina." For Seneca Village, see Smith, *How
    the Word*. Greenwood and Tulsa are not singular examples of black uprooting.
    For discussion of Greenwood and similar black enclaves, see the interview with
    Garrett-Scott, "We Know about Tulsa—But What Happened to Other Black Wall
    Streets?," NPR.org, June 15, 2021, https://www.npr.org/podcasts/478859728/think. For
    Elaine, Arkansas, see Anderson, *Second*; Lancaster, *Elaine Massacre and Arkansas*.

11 For a discussion of American overseas expansion, see Immerwahr, *How to Hide*.

12 See Coates, "Case for Reparations," *Atlantic*, June 2014. For the reparations bill in
    the US Congress (H.R. 40): https://www.congress.gov/bill/116th-congress/house
    -bill/40.

13 See caricomreparations.org. For Guyana's similar demand for reparations, see
    Aamna Mohdin, "Guyana's President Asks European Slave Traders' Descendants
    to Pay Reparations," *Guardian*, August 25, 2023, https://www.theguardian.com
    /world/2023/aug/25/guyanas-president-asks-european-slave-traders-descendants
    -to-pay-reparations.

14 Hanchard, *Party/Politics*, 263.

15 In *How the Word*, Smith discusses Angola prison, the site of a former slave planta-
    tion, where predominantly black prisoners were forced to cultivate cotton for 7
    cents per day. This reveals the carceral for blacks not strictly as a place of waste or
    Death, but as a mechanism to *make* the black body productive.

16 Sharpe references Deloughrey's formulation of an "arc" to describe the structures
    of racism in the United States. Sharpe, *In the Wake*, 3

17 The Gallery hosted the thirtieth annual exhibit of the "Guyana Women Artist's
    Association," titled "The Journey of Persistence and Endurance." For more about
    the house, see "Castellani House: A Historical and Architectural Synopsis," *Guy-
    ana Chronicle*, August 30, 2014, https://guyanachronicle.com/2014/08/30/castellani
    -house-a-historical-and-architectural-synopsis/.

18 Al Creighton, "The National Gallery at 25," *Stabroek News*, May 27, 2018, https://
    www.stabroeknews.com/2018/05/27/sunday/arts-on-sunday/the-national-gallery
    -at-25/; "Castellani House, Guyana," Facebook, https://www.facebook.com/pages
    /Castellani-House-Guyana/838305056259229.

19 "Guyana Museums," Explore Guyana, https://exploreguyana.org/guyana-museums
    /. See McDougall and Davidson, *Roth Family*.

20 Spencer Papers, Pitt Rivers Museum, https://www.prm.ox.ac.uk/spencer-papers.

21 See Subraj Singh, "Celebrating Indigenous Art in Indigenous Heritage Month,"
    Guyana Chronicle, September 18, 2016, https://guyanachronicle.com/2016/09/18
    /celebrating-indigenous-art-in-indigenous-heritage-month/.

22 Albuquerque, "Objects, Histories and Encounters," 126, 130.

23 Albuquerque, "Objects, Histories and Encounters"; Visit Rupununi, "The Story of Balata," Facebook, June 6, 2017, https://www.facebook.com/visitrupununi/posts /the-story-of-balata-commercial-balata-latex-harvesting-started-in-guyanaregion -9/452976648376601/.

24 Albuquerque, "Objects, Histories and Encounters," 125

25 "Balata Artist George Tancredo Now Working to Teach a New Generation," *Guyana Times International*, August 25, 2011, https://www.guyanatimesinternational .com/balata-artist-george-tancredo-now-working-to-teach-a-new-generation/. I include this article, which contains the same information about Tancredo's collection, but my source is the curator of Castellani House, Ohene Koama.

26 "Celebrating Indigenous Art in Indigenous Heritage Month," *Guyana Chronicle*, September 18, 2016, https://guyanachronicle.com/2016/09/18/celebrating -indigenous-art-in-indigenous-heritage-month/.

27 "Indigenous Nations," Ministry of Amerindian Affairs, https://moaa.gov.gy /amerindian-nations/.

28 Mithlo, "No Word for Art," 120–21.

29 The ideas here developed from that 2006 exhibit, a later Dial exhibit in Louisiana, and a conference paper I presented at the American Studies Association in 2011 titled "Basquiat after Dial: The Ark of Black Diaspora Labor."

30 "Thornton Dial," Black History in America, https://www.myblackhistory.net /Thornton_Dial.htm.

31 Tate, "Thornton Dial," discusses black art's cultural context, and how it leads to the works' dismissal and devaluing.

32 See Dimitriadis and McCarthy, *Reading and Teaching*.

33 Hardt and Negri, *Empire*, 11.

34 Obama, *Dreams from My Father*, x.

35 Wynter, "Columbus and the Poetics," 274–75.

36 Cooper, *Colonialism in Question*.

37 Mercer, ed., *Exiles, Diasporas and Strangers*.

38 Moten, "Ecology."

39 Marx, *Capital*, loc. 325–32.

40 Marx, *Capital*, loc. 336–42.

41 Michael Davis, "National Archives Safeguards Original 'Juneteenth' General Order," National Archives News, June 19, 2020, https://www.archives.gov/news /articles/juneteenth-original-document.

42 Moten, "Ecology."

43 Description of Thornton Dial's *Buffalo Man: People Have Learned from the Indian*, Souls Grown Deep website, https://www.soulsgrowndeep.org/artist/thornton-dial /work/buffalo-man-people-have-learned-indian.

44 Deloria, *God Is Red*, 57.

45 Deloria, *God Is Red*, 47.

46 Tate, "Thornton Dial," 23.

47 Sexton, "Social Life of Social Death," 29 (emphasis in original).

Bibliography

Achebe, Chinua. *Things Fall Apart*. London: Penguin Group, 1996 (1958).

Agamben, Giorgio. *Homo Sacer: Sovereign Power and Bare Life*. Translated by Daniel Heller-Roazen. Stanford, CA: Stanford University Press, 1998 (1995).

Albuquerque, Sara. "Objects, Histories and Encounters: British Guiana Seen through Balata." *Fronteiras: Journal of Social, Technological and Environmental Science* 7, no. 1 (2018): 124–41.

Alexander VI, Pope. Inter Caetera, 1493. In *Papal Encyclicals Online*.

Alfred, Taiaiake. "Sovereignty." In *Sovereignty Matters: Locations of Contestation and Possibility in Indigenous Struggles for Self-Determination*, edited by Joanne Barker, 33–50. Lincoln: University of Nebraska Press, 2006.

Althusser, Louis. "Ideology and Ideological State Apparatuses (Notes towards an Investigation)." In *Lenin and Philosophy and Other Essays*, 127–86. New York: Monthly Review Press, 1971.

Anderson, Carol. *The Second: Race and Guns in a Fatally Unequal America*. New York: Bloomsbury, 2021.

Anderson, Mark. *Black and Indigenous: Garifuna Activism and Consumer Culture in Honduras*. Minneapolis: University of Minnesota Press, 2009.

Appiah, Kwame Anthony. "Is the Post- in Postmodernism the Post- in Postcolonial?" *Critical Inquiry* 17, no. 2 (1991): 336–57.

Arendt, Hannah. *The Human Condition*. Chicago: University of Chicago Press, 1998 (1958).

Arendt, Hannah. *The Origins of Totalitarianism*. New York: A Harvest Book, 1994 (1951).

Aristotle. "Politics: Book 1." In *Aristotle: The Complete Works*. ᴋᴛʜᴛᴋ, 1998.

Armitage, David. "Three Concepts of Atlantic History." In *The British Atlantic World, 1500–1800*, edited by David Armitage and Michael J. Braddick, 11–27. New York: Palgrave Macmillan, 2009.

Azurara, Gomes Eannes de. *The Chronicle of the Discovery and Conquest of Guinea*, vol. 1. Translated by Raymond Charles and Edgar Prestage Beazley. New York: Burt Franklin, 2011 (1896).

Barchiesi, Franco, and Shona N. Jackson. "Introduction." *International Labor and Working Class History* 96 (2019): 1–16.

Barker, Joanne. "For Whom Sovereignty Matters." In *Sovereignty Matters: Locations of Contestation and Possibility in Indigenous Struggles for Self-Determination*, edited by Joanne Barker, 1–31. Lincoln: University of Nebraska Press, 2006.

Barthes, Roland. *Elements of Semiology*. Translated by Annette and Colin Smith Lavers. New York: Hill and Wang, 1973 (1964).

Baudrillard, Jean. *Jean Baudrillard: Selected Writings*. Edited by Mark Foster. Stanford, CA: Stanford University Press, 2001.

Beckles, Hilary McDonald. *Natural Rebels: A Social History of Enslaved Black Women in Barbados*. New Brunswick, NJ: Rutgers University Press, 1989.

Benítez-Rojo, Antonio. *The Repeating Island: The Caribbean and the Postmodern Perspective*. Translated by James Maraniss. Durham, NC: Duke University Press, 1996.

Benjamin, Thomas. *The Atlantic World: Europeans, Africans, Indians, and Their Shared History, 1400–1900*. New York: Cambridge University Press, 2009.

Bennett, Herman L. *Africans in Colonial Mexico: Absolutism, Christianity, and Afro-Creole Consciousness, 1570–1640*. Bloomington: Indiana University Press, 2003.

Ben-zvi, Yael. *Native Land Talk: Indigenous and Arrivant Rights Theories*. Lebanon, NH: Dartmouth College Press, 2018.

Bolland, O. Nigel. *The Politics of Labour in the British Caribbean: The Social Origins of Authoritarianism and Democracy in the Labour Movement*. Berkeley: University of California Press, 2001.

Bradford, William. *Bradford's History "Of Plimoth Plantation."* Boston: Wright and Potter, 1898.

Brunstetter, Daniel R. "Las Casas and the Concept of Just War." In *Bartolome de las Casas, O.P.: History, Philosophy, and Theology in the Age of European Expansion*, edited by David Thomas Orique and Rady Roldan-Figueroa, 218–42. Leiden: Koninkliike Brill, 2019.

Bruyneel, Kevin. *The Third Space of Sovereignty: The Postcolonial Politics of U.S.-Indigenous Relations*. Minneapolis: University of Minnesota Press, 2007.

Bryant, Sherwin K. *Rivers of Gold, Lives of Bondage: Governing through Slavery in Colonial Quito*. Chapel Hill: University of North Carolina Press, 2014.

Buck-Morss, Susan. *Hegel, Haiti, and Universal History*. Pittsburgh: University of Pittsburgh Press, 2009.

Bulkan, Janette. "The Struggle for Recognition of the Indigenous Voice: Amerindians in Guyanese Politics." *The Round Table* 102, no. 4 (2013): 367–80.

Bulkan, Janette, and Arif Bulkan. "'These Forests Have Always Been Ours': Official and Amerindian Discourses on Guyana's Forest Estate." In *Indigenous Resurgence in the*

Contemporary Caribbean: Amerindian Survival and Revival, edited by Maximilian C. Forte, 135–54. New York: Peter Lang, 2006.

Bushnell, Amy Turner. "Indigenous America and the Limits of the Atlantic World, 1493–1825." In *Atlantic History: A Critical Appraisal*, edited by Jack P. Green and Philip D. Morgan, 191–222. New York: Oxford University Press, 2009.

Byrd, Jodi A. *The Transit of Empire: Indigenous Critiques of Colonialism*. Minneapolis: University of Minnesota Press, 2011.

Byrd, Jodi A., Alyosha Goldstein, Jodi Melamed, and Chandan Reddy. "Predatory Value: Economies of Dispossession and Disturbed Relationalities." *Social Text* 36, no. 2 (135) (2018): 1–18.

Campbell, Timothy C. *Improper Life: Technology and Biopolitics from Heidegger to Agamben*. Minneapolis: University of Minnesota Press, 2011.

CARICOM Reparations Commission. "TEN POINT ACTION PLAN." *Africology: The Journal of Pan African Studies*, 9, no. 5 (2016): 115–19.

Césaire, Aimé. *Letter to Maurice Thorez*. Paris: Présence Africaine, 1957.

Césaire, Aimé. *Discourse on Colonialism*. Translated by Joan Pinkham. New York: Monthly Review Press, 2000 (1955).

Césaire, Aimé. "Notebook of a Return to the Native Land." In *Aimé Césaire, the Collected Poetry*, edited by Clayton Eshleman, and Annette Smith, 32–85. Berkeley: University of California Press, 1983. Original edition, 1939.

Césaire, Aimé. *A Tempest: Based on Shakespeare's The Tempest, Adaptation for a Black Theatre*. Translated by Richard Miller. New York: TCG Translations, 2002 (1969).

Césaire, Aimé. *The Tragedy of King Christophe*. Translated by Ralph Manheim. New York: Grove Press, 1969 (1963).

Chaplin, Joyce E., "Enslavement of Indians in Early America: Captivity without the Narrative." In *The Creation of the British Atlantic World*, edited by E. Mancke and C. Shammas. Baltimore: Johns Hopkins University Press, 2005.

Chaplin, Joyce E. "Race." In *The British Atlantic World, 1500–1800*, edited by David Armitage and Michael J. Braddick, 173–90. New York: Palgrave Macmillan, 2009 (2002).

Chibber, Vivek. *Postcolonial Theory and the Specter of Capital*. London: Verso, 2013.

Chrisman, Laura. "Beyond Black Atlantic and Postcolonial Studies: The South African Differences of Sol Plaatje and Peter Abrahams." In *Postcolonial Studies and Beyond*, edited by Suvir Kaul et al. Durham, NC: Duke University Press, 2005.

Chrisman, Laura. "Journeying to Death: Gilroy's Black Atlantic." *Race and Class* 39, no. 2 (1997): 51–64.

Chrisman, Laura. "Rethinking Black Atlanticism." *The Black Scholar* 30, nos. 3–4 (2000): 12–17.

Ciccariello-Maher, George. *Decolonizing Dialectics*. Durham, NC: Duke University Press, 2017.

Cohen, Paul. "Was There an Amerindian Atlantic? Reflections on the Limits of a Historiographical Concept." *History of European Ideas* 34, no. 4 (2008): 388–410.

Colchester, Marcus, Jean La Rose, and Kid James. *Mining and Amerindians in Guyana: Final Report of the APA/NSI project on "Exploring Indigenous Perspectives on Consultation and Engagement with the Mining Sector in Latin America and the Caribbean."* Ottawa: North-South Institute/L'Institut Nord-Sud, 2002.

Columbus, Christopher. "First Voyage of Columbus: Letter of Columbus." In *The Four Voyages of Columbus: A History in Eight Documents, Including Five by Christopher Columbus, in the Original Spanish, with English Translations*, edited by Cecil Jane, 2–19. New York: Dover, 1988 (1493).

Cooper, Frederick. *Colonialism in Question: Theory, Knowledge, History.* Berkeley: University of California Press, 2005.

Cortés, Hernán. *Hernán Cortés, Conqueror of the Aztecs: Five Letters 1519–1526.* Edited by Francis A. MacNutt. New York: Routledge, 2017 (1908).

Coulthard, Glen. "The Colonialism of the Present: An Interview with Glen Coulthard," edited by Andrew Bard Epstein. *Jacobin*, 2015. https://www.jacobinmag.com/2015/01/indigenous-leftglen-coulthard-interview/.

Coulthard, Glen. "For Our Nations to Live, Capitalism Must Die." *Unsettling America: Decolonization in Theory and Practice* (blog). November 5, 2013. https://unsettlingamerica.wordpress.com/2013/11/05/for-our-nations-to-live-capitalism-must-die/.

Coulthard, Glen Sean. *Red Skin, White Masks: Rejecting the Colonial Politics of Recognition.* Minneapolis: University of Minnesota Press, 2014.

Coulthard, Glen, and Leanne Betasamosake Simpson. "Grounded Normativity/Place-Based Solidarity." *American Quarterly* 68, no. 2 (2016): 249–55.

Crist, Eileen. "On the Poverty of Our Nomenclature." In *Anthropocene or Capitalocene? Nature, History, and the Crisis of Capitalism*, edited by Jason W. Moore, 14–33. Oakland, CA: PM Press, 2016.

Darity, William A., Jr., and A. Kirsten Mullen. *From Here to Equality: Reparations for Black Americans in the Twenty-First Century*, 2nd Edition. Chapel Hill: University of North Carolina Press.

Darwin, Charles. *The Descent of Man and Selection in Relation to Sex.* London: John Murray, 1874 (1871).

Dash, Michael. "Detours and Distance: An Interview with J. Michael Dash. *The Public Archive*, 2012. https://thepublicarchive.com/?p=3134.

Davies, Carole Boyce. *Left of Karl Marx: The Political Life of Black Communist Claudia Jones.* Durham, NC: Duke University Press, 2008.

Dei, George J. Sefa. *Reframing Blackness and Black Solidarities through Anti-Colonial and Decolonial Prisms.* Cham: Springer, 2017.

Deloria, Vine, Jr. *God Is Red: A Native View of Religion.* Golden, CO: Fulcrum, 2003 (1973).

DeLoughrey, Elizabeth. *Routes and Roots: Navigating Caribbean and Pacific Island Literatures.* Honolulu: University of Hawai'i Press, 2007.

Denevan, William M. *The Native Population of the Americas in 1492.* 2nd ed. Madison: University of Wisconsin Press, 1992.

Depestre, René. "An Interview with Aimé Césaire." In *Discourse on Colonialism*, 79–94. New York: Monthly Review Press, 2000 (1955).

Deusen, Nancy E. van. *Global Indios: The Indigenous Struggle for Justice in Sixteenth-Century Spain*. Durham, NC: Duke University Press, 2015.

Díaz, María Elena. *The Virgin, the King, and the Royal Slaves of El Cobre: Negotiating in Colonial Cuba, 1670-1780*. Stanford CA: Stanford University Press, 2000.

Dimitriadis, Greg, and Cameron McCarthy. *Reading and Teaching the Postcolonial: From Baldwin to Basquiat and Beyond*. New York: Teachers College Press, 2001.

Dirlik, Arif. "The Postcolonial Aura: Third World Criticism in the Age of Global Capitalism." *Critical Inquiry* 20, no. 2 (1994): 328–56.

Donoghue, Eddie. *Black Breeding Machines: The Breeding of Negro Slaves in the Diaspora* Bloomington, IN: AuthorHouse, 2008.

Dumont, Marilyn. "Not Just a Platform for My Dance." In *A Really Good Brown Girl*, 46. London, Ontario: Brick Books, 1996.

DuVernay, Ava, dir. *13th*. 100 min. English. USA: Netflix, 2016.

Edwards, Brent Hayes. *The Practice of Diaspora: Literature, Translation, and the Rise of Black Internationalism*. Cambridge, MA: Harvard University Press, 2003.

Edwards, Brent Hayes. "The Uses of Diaspora." *Social Text* 19, no. 66 (2001): 45–73.

Elliot, J. H. "Atlantic History: A Circumnavigation." In *The British Atlantic World, 1500–1800*, edited by David Armitage and Michael J. Braddick, 223–49. Houndmills, Basingstoke, UK: Palgrave Macmillan, 2009 (2002).

Fanon, Frantz. "Why We Use Violence: Address to the Accra Positive Action Conference, April 1960." In *Alienation and Freedom*, edited by Jean Khalfa and Robert J. C. Young, loc. 12305–414. London: Bloomsbury Academic, 2020 (1960).

Fanon, Frantz. *The Wretched of the Earth*. Translated by Constance Farrington. New York: Grove Press, 1963.

Fanon, Frantz. *The Wretched of the Earth*. Translated by Richard Philcox. Commentary by Jean Paul-Sartre and Homi K. Bhabha. New York: Grove Press, 2004 (1963).

Farred, Grant. "The Unsettler." *South Atlantic Quarterly* 107, no. 4 (2008): 791–808.

Fisher, Linford D. "'Dangerous Designes': The 1676 Barbados Act to Prohibit New England Indian Slave Importation." *The William and Mary Quarterly* 71, no. 1 (2014): 99–124.

Forbes, Jack D. *Columbus and Other Cannibals: The Wétiko Disease of Exploitation, Imperialism, and Terrorism*. New York: Seven Stories Press, 2008 (1979).

Forsdick, Charles, and Christian Høgsbjerg, eds. *The Black Jacobins Reader*. Durham, NC: Duke University Press, 2017.

Foucault, Michel. *The Birth of Biopolitics: Lectures at the Collège de France, 1978–1979*. Translated by Graham Burchell, edited by Michel Senellart. New York: Picador, 2008 (2004).

Foucault, Michel. *On the Government of the Living: Lectures at the Collège de France, 1979–1980*. Translated by Graham Burchell, edited by Michel Senellart. New York: Picador, 2014 (2012).

Foucault, Michel. *The Order of Things: An Archaeology of the Human Sciences*. New York: Vintage, 1994 (1970).

Foucault, Michel. *Security, Territory, Population: Lectures at the Collège de France, 1977–1978*. Translated by Graham Burchell, edited by Michel Senellart. New York: Picador, 2007 (2004).

Foucault, Michel. *Society Must Be Defended: Lectures at the Collège de France, 1975–1976.* Translated by David Macey. New York: Picador, 2003 (1997).

Foucault, Michel. "The Subject and Power." In *Michel Foucault: Power*, edited by James D. Faubion, 326–48. New York: New Press, 2000 (1994).

Foucault, Michel. "Two Lectures: Lecture Two January 14, 1976." In *Power/Knowledge: Selected Interviews and Other Writings 1972–1977*, edited by Colin Gordon, 78–108. New York: Pantheon Books, 1980.

Fraser, Nancy. "Capitalism's Crisis of Care." *Dissent* 63, no. 4 (2016): 30–37.

Fromm, Erich. "Marxism, Psychoanalysis and Reality." In *Marxist Internet Archive*, 2011. https://www.marxists.org/archive/fromm/works/1966/psychoanalysis.htm.

Gafar, John. "Poverty, Income Growth, and Inequality in Some Caribbean Countries." *The Journal of Developing Areas* 32, no. 4 (1998): 467–90.

Gallay, Alan, ed. *Indian Slavery in Colonial America.* Lincoln: University of Nebraska Press, 2009.

Gallay, Alan. *The Indian Slave Trade the Rise of the English Empire in the American South, 1670–1717.* New Haven, CT: Yale University Press, 2002.

Gerbner, Katharine. *Christian Slavery: Conversion and Race in the Protestant Atlantic World.* Philadelphia: University of Pennsylvania Press, 2018.

Gikandi, Simon. *Slavery and the Culture of Taste.* Princeton, NJ: Princeton University Press, 2011.

Gilroy, Paul. *The Black Atlantic: Modernity and Double-Consciousness.* Cambridge, MA: Harvard University Press, 1993.

Gimenez Valdivia, Ramon Dario. "Reason, Providence, and Testimony in the Conversion of Bartolome de Las Casas: A Theological Reading." In *Bartolome de las Casas, O.P.: History, Philosophy, and Theology in the Age of European Exapansion*, edited by David Thomas Orique and Rady Roldan-Figueroa, 310–24. Leiden: Brill, 2019.

Giroux, Henry A. "Reading Hurricane Katrina: Race, Class, and the Biopolitics of Disposability." *College Literature* 33, no. 3 (2006): 171–96.

Glare, P. G. W., ed. *Oxford Latin Dictionary.* Oxford: Oxford University Press, 2000 (1982).

Goeman, Mishuana. *Mark My Words: Native Women Mapping Our Nations.* Minneapolis: University of Minnesota Press, 2013.

Goldstein, Alyosha. "Introduction: Toward a Genealogy of the U.S. Colonial Present." In *Formations of United States Colonialism*, edited by Alyosha Goldstein, 1–31. Durham, NC: Duke University Press, 2014.

Graubart, Karen. "As Slaves and Not Vassals: Interethnic Claims of Freedom and Unfreedom in Colonial Peru." *Población y sociedad* 27, no. 2 (2020): 30–53.

Green, F. Ray H. *Aboriginal Indian Committee-Interim Report.* Georgetown, Demerara: Department of Land and Mines, 1946.

Gregory, Gillian, and Ismael Vaccaro. "Islands of Governmentality: Rainforest Conservation, Indigenous Rights, and the Territorial Reconfiguration of Guyanese Sovereignty." *Territory, Politics, Governance* 3, no. 3 (2015): 344–63.

Griffiths, Tom, and Jean La Rose. "Searching for Justice and Land Security: Land Rights, Indigenous Peoples and Governance of Tenure in Guyana." Forest Peoples

Programme and Amerindian Peoples Association, 2014. https://www.forestpeoples
.org/sites/default/files/publication/2014/06/guyanasection1.pdf.

Guadalupi, Gianni, and Antony Shugaar. *Latitude Zero: Tales of the Equator*. New York: Carroll and Graf, 2002.

Guyana, Government of. Act No. 2 of 1980: Constitution of the Co-operative Republic of Guyana Act, 1980.

Guyana, Government of. Act No. 6 of 1976: Amerindian Act 1976. Laws of Guyana, 1998. Original edition, 1976.

Guyana, Government of. Act No. 6 of 2006: Amerindian Act 2006. Laws of Guyana, 2006.

Guiana, Government of British. The Amerindian Ordinance, 1951: An Ordinance to Make Provision for the Good Government of the Amerindian Communities of the Colony (1953).

Hale, Charles R. "*Resistencia para que?* Territory, Autonomy, and Neoliberal Entanglements in the 'Empty Spaces' of Central America." *Economy and Society* 40, no. 2 (2011): 184–210.

Hanchard, Michael. *Party/Politics: Horizons in Black Political Thought*. Oxford: Oxford University Press, 2006.

Haraway, Donna J. "Anthropocene, Capitalocene, Plantationocene, Chthulucene: Making Kin." *Environmental Humanities* 6 (2015): 159–65.

Haraway, Donna J. "Staying with the Trouble: Anthropocene, Capitalocene, Chthulucene." In *Anthropocene or Capitalocene? Nature, History, and the Crisis of Capitalism*, edited by Jason W. Moore, 34–76. Oakland, CA: PM Press, 2016.

Haraway, Donna J. "Staying with the Trouble: Making Kin in the Cthulucene." YouTube, April 25, 2017, https://www.youtube.com/watch?v=GrYA7sMQaBQ.

Hardt, Michael, and Antonio Negri. *Empire*. Cambridge, MA: Harvard University Press, 2000.

Harman, Chris. "Base and Superstructure." *International Socialism* 2, no. 32 (1986): 3–44. https://www.marxists.org/archive/harman/1986/xx/base-super.html.

Hart, William David. "Constellations: Capitalism, Antiblackness, Afro-Pessimism, and Black Optimism." *American Journal of Theology and Philosophy* 39, no. 1 (2018): 5–33.

Hartman, Saidiya V. *Lose Your Mother: A Journey along the Atlantic Slave Route*. New York: Farrar, Straus and Giroux, 2008.

Hartman, Saidiya V. *Scenes of Subjection: Terror, Slavery, and Self-Making in Nineteenth-Century America*. New York: Oxford University Press, 1997.

Harvey, David. *A Companion to Marx's Capital*. London: Verso, 2018.

Hatfield, April Lee. *Boundaries of Belonging: English Jamaica and the Spanish Caribbean, 1655–1715*. Philadelphia: University of Pennsylvania Press, 2023.

Hegel, Georg W. F. *The Philosophy of History*. Translated by J. Sibree. New York: Prometheus Books, 1991.

Henry, Paget. *Caliban's Reason: Introducing Afro-Caribbean Philosophy*. New York: Routledge, 2000.

Hintzen, Percy. *The Costs of Regime Survival: Racial Mobilization, Elite Domination and Control of the State in Guyana and Trinidad*. Cambridge: Cambridge University Press, 1989.

Hughes, Langston. "House in the World." In *The Collected Poems of Langston Hughes*, edited by Arnold Rampersad, 138. New York: Alfred A. Knopf, 1994 (1931–40).

Immerwahr, Daniel. *How to Hide an Empire: A History of the Greater United States*. New York: Picador, 2019.

Jackson, Shona N. "The Baptism of Soil: Rooplall Monar and the Aesthetics of the Kala Pani Modern." *Journal of Caribbean Literatures* 6, no. 3 (2010): 9–21.

Jackson, Shona N. *Creole Indigeneity: Between Myth and Nation in the Caribbean*. Minneapolis: University of Minnesota Press, 2012.

Jackson, Shona N. "Colonialism." In *Keywords for African American Studies*, edited by Erica R. Edwards, Roderick A. Ferguson, and Jeffrey O. G. Ogbar, 51–57. New York: New York University Press, 2018.

Jackson, Shona N. "The 'Inadequacies of Marxism' or Black Labor's Pessimism." Introduction to *International Labor and Working-Class History* no. 96 (Fall 2019): 1–16.

Jackson, Shona N. "Indigeneity and African Belonging in the New World." UNESCO General History of the African Diaspora (forthcoming).

Jackson, Shona N. "Killing *Us* Softly: Conversion and the Arc of Black Death in the Americas." *Aztlán: A Journal of Chicano Studies* 46, no. 2 (Fall 2021): 161–78.

Jackson, Shona N. "Movement and Time: A Diasporic Response to Grounded Light." *American Quarterly* 71, no. 2 (2019): 343–52.

Jackson, Shona N. "Postcolonial Biopolitics and the Hieroglyphs of Democracy." In *Biopolitics-Geopolitics-Life; Settler States and Indigenous Presence*, edited by René Dietrich and Kerstin Knopf. Durham, NC: Duke University Press, 2023.

Jackson, Shona N. "To Be Anti-Black Is to Be Anti-indigenous: Reflections on Emancipation." *Stabroek News* (Georgetown, Guyana), July 28, 2014.

Jackson, Shona N. "Violence or Counterdiscourse? A Review of *Decolonizing Dialectics* by George Ciccariello-Maher." *Antipode: A Radical Journal of Geography* (2018): 1–13. https://radicalantipode.files.wordpress.com/2018/04/book-review_jackson-on-ciccariello-maher.pdf.

Jackson, Zakiyyah Iman. *Becoming Human: Matter and Meaning in an Antiblack World*. New York: New York University Press, 2020.

James, C. L. R. *The Black Jacobins: Toussaint L'Ouverture and the San Domingo Revolution*. New York: Vintage Books, 1989 (1963).

James. C. L. R. *A History of Pan-African Revolt*. Binghamton, New York: PM Press, 2012 (1938, 1969).

James, Joy, and João Costa Vargas. "Refusing Blackness-as-Victimization: Trayvon Martin and the Black Cyborgs." In *Pursuing Trayvon: Historical Contexts and Contemporary Manifestations of Racial Dynamics*, edited by George Yancy and Janine Jones, 193–205. Lanham, MD: Lexington Books, 2012.

Johnson, Gaye Theresa, and Alex Lubin. "Introduction." In *Futures of Black Radicalism*, edited by Gaye Theresa Johnson and Alex Lubin, loc. 221–418. London: Verso, 2017.

Jones, Claudia. "An End to the Neglect of the Problems of the Negro Woman!" *Political Affairs*, June 1949: 3–19.

Karera, Axelle. "Blackness and the Pitfalls of Anthropocene Ethics." *Critical Philosophy of Race* 7, no. 1 (2019): 32–56.

Kauanui, J. Kēhaulani. "Tracing Historical Specificity: Race and the Colonial Politics of (In)Capacity." *American Quarterly* 69, no. 2 (2017): 257–65.

Kelley, Robin D. G. "Foreword." In *Black Marxism: The Making of the Black Radical Tradition*, xi–xxvi. Chapel Hill: University of North Carolina Press, 2000.

Kelley, Robin D. G. "The Rest of Us: Rethinking Settler and Native." *American Quarterly* 69, no. 2 (2017): 267–76.

Kempadoo, Kamala. "'Bound Coolies' and Other Indentured Workers in the Caribbean: Implications for Debates about Human Trafficking and Modern Slavery." *Anti-Trafficking Review* 9 (2017): 48–63. https://www.antitraffickingreview.org/index .php/atrjournal/article/view/263/252.

Kennedy, Paul. *Vampire Capitalism: Fractured Societies and Alternative Futures*. London: Palgrave Macmillan, 2017.

Kimmerer, Robin Wall. *Braiding Sweetgrass: Indigenous Wisdom, Scientific Knowledge and the Teachings of Plants*. Minneapolis: Milkweed Editions, 2013.

King, Tiffany Lethabo. *The Black Shoals: Offshore Formations of Black and Native Studies*. Durham, NC: Duke University Press, 2019.

Knight, Franklin W. *The Caribbean: The Genesis of a Fragmented Nationalism*. New York: Oxford University Press, 1990 (1978).

Lamming, George. *In the Castle of My Skin*. Ann Arbor: University of Michigan Press, 1991 (1953).

Lampe, Armando. "Las Casas and African Slavery in the Caribbean: A Third Conversion." In *Bartolome de las Casas, O.P.: History, Philosophy, and Theology in the Age of European Expansion*, edited by David Thomas Orique and Rady Roldan-Figueroa, 421–36. Leiden: Brill, 2019.

Lancaster, Guy, ed. *The Elaine Massacre and Arkansas: A Century of Atrocity and Resistance, 1819–1919*. Little Rock, AR: Butler Center Books, 2018.

Landers, Jane G., and Barry M. Robinson, ed. *Slaves, Subjects, and Subversives: Blacks in Colonial Latin America*. Albuquerque: University of New Mexico Press, 2006.

Lantigua, David. "Religion within the Limits of Natural Reason: The Case of Human Sacrifice." In *Bartolome de las Casas, O.P.: History, Philosophy, and Theology in the Age of European Expansion*, edited by David Thomas Orique and Rady Roldan-Figueroa, 280–309. Leiden: Brill, 2019.

Larson, Pier M. "Enslaved Malagasy and 'Le Travail de la Parole' in the Pre-Revolutionary Mascarenes." *The Journal of African History* 48, no. 3 (2007): 457–79.

Las Casas, Bartolomé de. "Memorial de remedios para las Indias (1518)." In *Obras Escogidas de Bartolomé de Las Casas: Opúsculos, cartas, y memoriales*, edited by Juan Pérez de Tudela Bueso, vol. 5: 5–27. Madrid: BAE, 1958.

Las Casas, Bartolomé de. *A Short Account of the Destruction of the Indies*. Translated and edited by Nigel Griffin. London: Penguin Books, 2004 (1542).

Laurencin, M., B. Marcaillou, D. Graindorge, F. Klingelhoefer, S. Lallemand, M. Laigle, and J. F. Lebrun. "The Polyphased Tectonic Evolution of the Anegada Passage in the Northern Lesser Antilles Subduction Zone." *Tectonics* 36, no. 5 (2017): 945–61.

Lindahl, Folke. "Caribbean Diversity and Ideological Conformism: The Crisis of Marxism in the English-Speaking Caribbean." *Social and Economic Studies* 43, no. 3 (1994): 57–74.

Linebaugh, Peter, and Marcus Rediker. *The Many-Headed Hydra: Sailors, Slaves, Commoners and the Hidden History of the Revolutionary Atlantic*. London: Verso, 2000.

Locke, John. *Two Treatises of Government and A Letter Concerning Toleration*. Digireads .com Publishing, 2009.

Lowe, Lisa. *The Intimacies of Four Continents*. Durham, NC: Duke University Press, 2015.

Lumumba, Patrice. "Speech at the Ceremony of the Proclamation of the Congo's Independence." In *Patrice Lumumba, The Truth about a Monstrous Crime of the Colonialists*, 44–47. Moscow: Foreign Languages Publishing House, 1961.

Maingot, Anthony P. *Race, Ideology, and the Decline of Caribbean Marxism*. Gainesville: University Press of Florida, 2015.

Malthus, Thomas Robert. *An Essay on the Principle of Population*. London: J. Johnston, 1798.

Mamdani, Mahmood. "Beyond Settler and Native as Political Identities: Overcoming the Political Legacy of Colonialism." *Comparative Studies in Society and History* 43, no. 4 (2001): 651–64.

Marx, Karl. *Capital (Das Kapital)*, vols. 1–3. Chicago: Musaicum Books, 2018.

Marx, Karl. "Preface." In *A Contribution to the Critique of Political Economy*. Moscow: Progress, 1977 (1859).

Matthew, Restall. "'There Was a Time When We Were Friends': Las Casas and Cortes as Monstrous Doubles of the Conquest Era." In *Bartolome de las Casas, O.P.: History, Philosophy, and Theology in the Age of European Expansion*, edited by David Thomas Orique and Rady Roldan-Figueroa, 58–70. Leiden: Brill, 2019.

Maturana, H.R., and F.J. Varela. *Autopoiesis and Cognition: The Realization of the Living*. Dordrecht: Springer Netherlands, 1980.

Mayer, Marc, ed. *Basquiat*. New York: Merrell Publishers and the Brooklyn Museum, 2005.

Mbembe, Achille. "Necropolitics." *Public Culture* 15, no. 1 (2003): 11–40.

Mbembe, Achille. "Provisional Notes on the Postcolony." *Africa: Journal of the International African Institute* 62, no. 1 (1992): 3–37.

McAnany, Patricia A. *Maya Cultural Heritage: How Archaeologists and Indigenous Communities Engage the Past*. Lanham, MD: Rowman and Littlefield, 2016.

McBrien, Justin. "Accumulating Extinction: Planetary Catastrophism in the Necrocene." In *Anthropocene or Capitalocene? Nature, History, and the Crisis of Capitalism*, edited by Jason W. Moore, 116–36. Oakland, CA: PM Press, 2016.

McClendon, John H. III *C. L. R. James's Notes on Dialectics: Left Hegelianism or Marxism-Leninism?* Lanham, MD: Lexington Books, 2005.

McClintock, Anne. "The Angel of Progress: Pitfalls of the Term 'Post-Colonialism.'" *Social Text* 31–32 (1992): 84–98.

McClintock, Anne. *Imperial Leather: Race, Gender and Sexuality in the Colonial Contest*. New York: Routledge, 1995.

McDougall, Russell, and Iain Davidson, eds. *The Roth Family, Anthropology, and Colonial Administration*. New York: Routledge, 2008.

McKittrick, Katherine. *Demonic Grounds: Black Women and the Cartographies of Struggle*. Minneapolis: University of Minnesota Press, 2006.

McKittrick, Katherine, ed. *Sylvia Wynter: On Being Human as Praxis*. Durham, NC: Duke University Press, 2015.

Means, Russell. "For America to Live, Europe Must Die!" Black Hills International Survival Gathering, 1980.

Melamed, Jodi. "Racial Capitalism." *Critical Ethnic Studies* 1, no. 1 (2015): 76–85.

Menezes, Mary Noel. *British Policy towards the Amerindians in British Guiana, 1803–1973.* Oxford: Clarendon Press, 1977.

Mercer, Kobena, ed. *Exiles, Diasporas and Strangers.* Boston: Iniva/MIT Press, 2008.

Mignolo, Walter D. "Delinking: The Rhetoric of Modernity, the Logic of Coloniality and the Grammar of De-Coloniality." *Cultural Studies* 21, nos. 2–3 (2007): 449–514.

Mills, Charles W. *From Class to Race: Essays in White Marxism and Black Radicalism.* Lanham, MD: Rowman and Littlefield, 2003.

Mills, Charles W. "Black Radical Liberalism or Black Marxism?" *Radical Philosophy Review* 25, no. 3 (2022): 277–92.

Ministry of Indigenous Peoples Affairs [Ministry of Amerindian Affairs]. *The New Amerindian Act: What Will It Do for Amerindians?* Georgetown: Guyana Government Information Agency [GINA], 2005.

Mishra, Vijay, and Bob Hodge. "What Is Postcolonialism?" *New Literary History* 36, no. 3 (2005): 375–402.

Mithlo, Nancy Marie. "No Word for Art in Our Language? Old Questions, New Paradigms." *Wicazo Sa Review* 27, no. 1 (2012): 111–26.

Montag, Warren. "Necro-Economics: Adam Smith and Death in Life of the Universal." *Radical Philosophy* 134 (2005): 7–17.

Moore, Jason W. *Capitalism in the Web of Life: Ecology and the Accumulation of Capital.* London: Verso, 2015.

Moore, Jason W. "Introduction: Anthropocene or Capitalocene? Nature, History, and the Crisis of Capitalism." In *Anthropocene or Capitalocene? Nature, History, and the Crisis of Capitalism,* edited by Jason W. Moore, 1–12. Oakland, CA: PM Press, 2016.

Moore, Jason W. "The Rise of Cheap Nature." In *Anthropocene or Capitalocene? Nature, History, and the Crisis of Capitalism,* edited by Jason W. Moore, 78–115. Oakland, CA: PM Press, 2016.

Moore, Sophie Sapp, Monique Allewaert, Pablo F. Gómez, and Gregg Mitman. "Plantation Legacies." *Edge Effects,* January 22, 2019.

Moreton-Robinson, Aileen. *The White Possessive: Property, Power, and Indigenous Sovereignty.* Minneapolis: University of Minnesota Press, 2015.

Morgan, Jennifer L. *Laboring Women: Reproduction and Gender in New World Slavery.* Philadelphia: University of Pennsylvania Press, 2004.

Morgan, Philip D., and Jack P. Greene. "Introduction: The Present State of Atlantic History." In *Atlantic History: A Critical Appraisal,* edited by Jack P. Greene and Philip D. Morgan, 3–34. Oxford: Oxford University Press, 2009.

Morgensen, Scott Lauria. "The Biopolitics of Settler Colonialism: Right Here, Right Now." *Settler Colonial Studies* 1, no. 1 (2011): 52–76.

Moten, Fred. *Black and Blur (Consent Not to Be a Single Being).* Durham, NC: Duke University Press, 2017.

Moten, Fred. "Blackness and Nothingness (Mysticism in the Flesh)." *The South Atlantic Quarterly* 112, no. 4 (2013): 737–80.

Moten, Fred. "The Case of Blackness." *Criticism* 50, no. 2 (2008): 177–218.

Moten, Fred. "An Ecology of (Eloquent) Things." Paper presented at Hard Truths: A Forum on Art and the Politics of Difference, Indianapolis Museum of Art, April 11, 2011.

Moten, Fred. *Stolen Life (Consent Not to Be a Single Being)*. Durham, NC: Duke University Press, 2018.

Moten, Fred. *The Universal Machine (Consent Not to Be a Single Being)*. Durham, NC: Duke University Press, 2018.

Munroe, Trevor. *The Marxist "Left" in Jamaica, 1940-1950*. Mona, Jamaica: University of the West Indies, 1977.

Munroe, Trevor. "Contemporary Marxist Movements: Assessing WPJ Prospects in Jamaica." *Social and Economic Studies* 36, no. 3 (1987): 1–35.

Nash, Jennifer C. "On the Beginning of the World: Dominance Feminism, Afropessimism and the Meanings of Gender." *Feminist Theory* 23, no. 4 (2022): 556–74.

Newcomb, Steve. "Indigenous Sovereignty and the Political Subordination of Our Nations." *Indian Country Today* (blog). March 27, 2017.

Nichols, Grace. "My Black Triangle." In *I Have Crossed an Ocean: Selected Poems*, 81. Hexham: Bloodaxe Books, 2014.

Nichols, Robert. "Disaggregating Primitive Accumulation." *Radical Philosophy* 194 (2015): 18–28.

Nkrumah, Kwame. *Neo-Colonialism: The Last Stage of Imperialism*. London: Thomas Nelson, 1965.

Nussbaum, Felicity A. *Torrid Zones: Maternity, Sexuality, and Empire in Eighteenth-Century English Narratives*. Baltimore: Johns Hopkins University Press, 1995.

Obama, Barack. *Dreams from My Father: A Story of Race and Inheritance*. New York: Three Rivers Press, 2004 (1995).

O'Brien, Jean M. "Tracing Settler Colonialism's Eliminatory Logic in *Traces of History*." *American Quarterly* 69, no. 2 (2017): 249–55.

O'Malley, Pat. "Indigenous Governance." *International Journal of Human Resource Management* 25, no. 3 (1996): 310–26.

Orique, David Thomas. "A Comparison of the Voices of the Spanish Bartolomé de Las Casas and the Portuguese Fernando Oliveira on Just War and Slavery." *E-Journal of Portuguese History* 12, no. 1 (2014): 87–118.

Osuna, Steve. "Class Suicide: The Black Radical Tradition, Radical Scholarship, and the Neoliberal Turn." In *Futures of Black Radicalism*, edited by Gaye Theresa Johnson and Alex Lubin, loc. 425–802. London: Verso, 2017.

O'Toole, Rachel Sarah. *Bound Lives: Africans, Indians, and the Making of Race in Colonial Peru*. Pittsburgh: University of Pittsburgh Press, 2012.

Pagden, Anthony, ed. *Hernán Cortés: Letters from Mexico*. New Haven, CT: Yale University Press, 1986.

Pagden, Anthony. "Introduction." In *A Short Account of the Destruction of the Indies*, loc. 144–607. London: Penguin Books, 2004 (1992).

Paquet, Sandra. "Foreword." In *In the Castle of My Skin*, ix–xxxiii. Ann Arbor: University of Michigan Press, 1983.

Patterson, Orlando. *Slavery and Social Death: A Comparative Study*. Cambridge, MA: Harvard University Press, 1982.

Pavón-Cuéllar, David. *Marxism and Psychoanalysis: In or against Psychology?* New York: Routledge, 2017.

Pearce, Margaret Wickens, and Renee Pualani Louis. "Mapping Indigenous Depth of Place." *American Indian Culture and Research* 32, no. 3 (2008): 107–26.

Peck, Douglas T. "Theory versus Practical Application in the History of Early Ocean Navigation." *Terrae Incognitae* 34, no. 1 (2002): 46–59.

Penniman, Leah. *Farming While Black: Soul Fire Farm's Practical Guide to Liberation on the Land*. White River Junction, VT: Chelsea Green, 2018.

Pierce, Brian. "Bartolomé de las Casas and Truth: Toward a Spirituality of Solidarity." *Spirituality Today* 44, no. 1 (1992): 4–19.

Pillsbury, Parker. *Acts of the Anti-Slavery Apostles*. Concord, NH: Clague, Wegman, Schlicht, 1883.

Polanco, Héctor Díaz. *Indigenous Peoples in Latin America: The Quest for Self-Determination*. Translated by Lucia Rayas. New York: Routledge, 2018 (1997).

Prescod, Colin. "Guyana's Socialism: An Interview with Walter Rodney." *Race and Class* 18, no. 2 (1976): 109–28.

Pruitt, Stephanie. "Mississippi Gardens." In *The Ringing Ear: Black Poets Lean South*, edited by Nikky Finney, 158. Athens: University of Georgia Press, 2007.

Reséndez, Andrés. *The Other Slavery: The Uncovered Story of Indian Enslavement in America*. New York: Houghton Mifflin Harcourt, 2016.

Restall, Matthew. *The Black Middle: Africans, Mayas, and Spaniards in Colonial Yucatan*. Stanford, CA: Stanford University Press, 2009.

Robinson, Cedric J. *Black Marxism: The Making of the Black Radical Tradition*. Chapel Hill: University of North Carolina Press, 2000 (1983).

Robinson, Cedric J., and Elizabeth P. Robinson. "Preface." In *Futures of Black Radicalism*, edited by Gaye Theresa Johnson and Alex Lubin, loc. 62–215. London: Verso, 2017.

Rodney, Walter. "African History in the Service of the Black Liberation." *Small Axe* 10 (2001): 66–80.

Rodney, Walter. *The Groundings with My Brothers*. Edited by Asha T. Rodney and Jesse J. Benjamin. London: Verso, 2019 (1969).

Rodney, Walter. *A History of the Guyanese Working People, 1881–1905*. Baltimore: Johns Hopkins University Press, 1981.

Rodney, Walter. *How Europe Underdeveloped Africa*. London: Verso, 2018 (1972).

Rout, Leslie B., Jr. *The African Experience in Spanish America*. Princeton, NJ: Markus Wiener, 2003 (1976).

Rundstrom, R. A. "Mapping, Postmodernism, Indigenous People and the Changing Direction of North American Cartography." *Cartographica* 28, no. 2 (1991): 1–12.

Russell-Wood, A. J. R. *The Black Man in Slavery and Freedom in Colonial Brazil*. Houndmills, Basingstoke, Hampshire: Palgrave Macmillan, 1982.

Sanchez-Godoy, Ruben A. "'We Never Could Understand Why the Black Man Did Not Come to Us': Early African-Amerindian Subjectivities in Miguel Cabello Balboa's

Verdadera Descripción de la Provincia de Esmeraldas (1583)." *Comparative Literature Studies* 49, no. 2 (2012).

Sanders, Andrew. "Protected Status and the Amerindians of Guyana: A Comparative Examination." *Social and Economic Studies* 44, nos. 2–3 (1995): 125–41.

Schwaller, John F., ed. *The Church in Colonial Latin America*. Wilmington, DE: Scholarly Resources, 2000.

Schwartz, Stuart B. "Indian Labor and New World Plantations: European Demands and Indian Responses in Northeastern Brazil." *The American Historical Review* 83, no. 1 (1978): 43–79.

Scott, David. "The Re-Enchantment of Humanism: An Interview with Sylvia Wynter." *Small Axe* 8 (2000): 119–207.

Sexton, Jared. "Ante-Anti-Blackness: Afterthoughts." *Lateral* 1 (2012). https://csalateral .org/issue/1/ante-anti-blackness-afterthoughts-sexton/.

Sexton, Jared. "The Social Life of Social Death: On Afro-Pessimism and Black Optimism." *InTensions* 5 (2011): 1–47.

Sharpe, Christina. *In the Wake: On Blackness and Being*. Durham, NC: Duke University Press, 2016.

Sherman, William L. *Forced Native Labor in Sixteenth-Century Central America*. Lincoln: University of Nebraska Press, 1979.

Shohat, Ella. "Notes on the 'Post-Colonial.'" *Social Text* 31–32 (1992): 99–113.

Silva, Denise Ferreira da. *Toward a Global Idea of Race*. Minneapolis: University of Minnesota Press, 2007.

Silverman, Kaja. *The Subject of Semiotics*. New York: Oxford University Press, 1983.

Simpson, Audra. *Mohawk Interruptus: Political Life across the Borders of Settler States*. Durham, NC: Duke University Press, 2014.

Simpson, Leanne Betasamosake. *As We Have Always Done: Indigenous Freedom through Radical Resistance*. Minneapolis: University of Minnesota Press, 2017.

Simpson, Lesley Byrd. *The Encomienda in New Spain: The Beginning of Spanish Mexico*. Berkeley: University of California Press, 1950.

Singh, Nikhil Pal. "On Race, Violence, and 'So-Called Primitive Accumulation.'" In *Futures of Black Radicalism*, edited by Gaye Theresa Johnson and Alex Lubin, loc. 809–1204. London: Verso, 2017.

Slack, Gregory. "Charles W. Mills: Black Radical Liberalism or Black Marxism?" *Radical Philosophy Review*. https://doi.org.10.5840/radphilrev20221118131. November 23, 2022.

Smallwood, Stephanie E. *Saltwater Slavery: A Middle Passage from Africa to American Diaspora*. Cambridge, MA: Harvard University Press, 2008.

Smith, Brady. "Other Atlantics: Cape Verde, *Chiquinho*, and the Black Atlantic World." *Comparative Literature Studies* 49, no. 2 (2012): 246–64.

Smith, Clint. *How the Word Is Passed: A Reckoning with the History of Slavery across America*. New York: Little, Brown, 2021.

Smithers, Gregory D. *Slave Breeding: Sex, Violence, and Memory in African American History*. Gainesville: University Press of Florida, 2012.

Sobel, Dava. *Longitude: The True Story of a Lone Genius Who Solved the Greatest Scientific Problem of His Time*. New York: Bloomsbury, 2007.

Sorentino, Sara-Maria. "The Abstract Slave: Anti-Blackness and Marx's Method." *International Labor and Working-Class History* 96 (2019): 17–37.

Spain. "Permission Granted to the Governor of Bresa for Four Thousand Slaves." In *Documents Illustrative of the History of the Slave Trade to America*, edited by Elizabeth Donnan, 41–42. Washington, DC: Carnegie Institution of Washington, 1930.

Spain [Council of the Indies/Charles V]. *The New Laws of the Indies for the Good Treatment and Preservation of the Indians, Promulgated by the Emperor Charles the Fifth, 1542–1543*. London: Chiswick Press, 1893 (1542–43).

Spillers, Hortense J. "Mama's Baby, Papa's Maybe: An American Grammar Book." *Diacritics* 17, no. 2 (1987): 64–81.

Spivak, Gayatri Chakravorty. *A Critique of Postcolonial Reason: Toward a History of the Vanishing Present*. Cambridge, MA: Harvard University Press, 1999.

Stam, Robert, and Ella Shohat. *Race in Translation: Culture Wars around the Postcolonial Atlantic*. New York: New York University Press, 2012.

Stripes, James. "A Strategy of Resistance: The 'Actorvism' of Russell Means from Plymouth Rock to the Disney Studios." *Wicazo Sa Review* 14, no. 1 (1999): 87–101.

Sublette, Ned, and Constance Sublette. *The American Slave Coast: A History of the Slave-Breeding Industry*. Chicago: Lawrence Hill Books, 2016.

Tate, Greg. "Thornton Dial: Free, Black, and Brightening Up the Darkness of the World." In *Hard Truths/The Art of Thornton Dial*, edited by Joanne Cubbs and Eugene W. Metcalf, 23–35. New York: Indianapolis Museum of Art and DelMonico Books, 2011.

Taylor, Keeanga-Yamahtta. *From #BlackLivesMatter to Black Liberation*. Chicago: Haymarket Books, 2016.

Thompson, Alvin O. *The Haunting Past: Politics, Economics and Race in Caribbean Life*. New York: Routledge, 2015.

Todd, Zoe. "An Indigenous Feminist's Take on the Ontological Turn: 'Ontology' Is Just Another Word for Colonialism." *Journal of Historical Sociology* 29, no. 1 (2016): 4–22.

Trotz, Alissa, and Terry Roopnaraine. "Angles of Vision from the Coast and Hinterland of Guyana." In *Anthropologies of Guayana: Cultural Spaces in Northeastern Amazonia*, edited by Neil L. Whitehead and Stephanie Alemán, 235–53. Tucson: University of Arizona Press, 2009.

Turner, Jenny. "Nothing Natural." *London Review of Books* 42, no. 2 (2020). January 23. https://www.lrb.co.uk/the-paper/v42/no2/jenny-turner/nothing-natural.

United Kingdom, Parliament. Guyana Independence Act 1966.

United Nations. Announcement of the Equator Prize Winner: South Central People's Development Association, 2015.

United Nations Development Programme, Equator Initiative. *Equator Initiative Case Studies: South Central People's Development Association: Guyana*, 2018.

United Nations General Assembly. *United Nations Declaration on the Rights of Indigenous Peoples*, 2007.

University of Guyana, Amerindian Research Unit. *Amerindian Concerns: A Compilation from the Written Submissions Received by the Amerindian Research Unit from*

Amerindian Village Councils in Preparation for the National Conference of Amerindian Representatives. 1994.

Vergès, Françoise. "Racial Capitalocene." In *Futures of Black Radicalism*, edited by Gaye Theresa Johnson and Alex Lubin, loc. 1473–681. London: Verso, 2017.

Villarosa, Linda. *Under the Skin: The Hidden Toll of Racism on American Lives and on the Health of Our Nation.* New York: Penguin, 2022.

Vimalassery, Manu, Juliana Hu Pegues, and Alyosha Goldstein. "Introduction: On Colonial Unknowing." *Theory and Event* 19, no. 4 (2016).

Vinson, Ben III. *Before Mestizaje: The Frontiers of Race and Caste in Colonial Mexico.* New York: Cambridge University Press, 2018.

Vizenor, Gerald Robert. *Manifest Manners: Postindian Warriors of Survivance. (Narratives on Post Indian Survivance).* Lincoln: University of Nebraska Press, 1999 (1993).

Voloshinov, Valentin Nikolaevich. "The Study of Ideologies and Philosophy of Language." In *Marxism and the Philosophy of Language.* New York: Seminar Press, 1973 (1929).

Walcott, Derek. "The Sea Is History." In *Selected Poems: Derek Walcott*, edited by Edward Baugh, 137–39. New York: Farrar, Straus and Giroux, 2007.

Warren, Calvin. "Onticide: Afro-Pessimism, Gay Nigger #1, and Surplus Violence." *GLQ: A Journal of Lesbian and Gay Studies* 23, no. 3 (2017): 391–418.

Warren, Wendy. *New England Bound: Slavery and Colonization in Early America.* New York: Liveright, 2016.

Watts, Vanessa. "Indigenous Place-Thought and Agency amongst Humans and Non-Humans (First Woman and Sky Woman Go on a European World Tour!)." *Decolonization: Indigeneity, Education and Society* 2, no. 1 (2013): 20–34.

Weaver, Jace. *The Red Atlantic: Indigenes and the Making of the Modern World, 1000–1927.* Chapel Hill: University of North Carolina Press, 2014.

Weheliye, Alexander G. *Habeas Viscus: Racializing Assemblages, Biopolitics, and Black Feminist Theories of the Human.* Durham, NC: Duke University Press, 2014.

Welburn, Ron. *Roanoke and Wampum: Topics in Native American Heritage and Literatures.* New York: Peter Lang, 2001.

Wheat, David. *Atlantic Africa and the Spanish Caribbean, 1570–1640.* Chapel Hill: University of North Carolina Press, 2016.

Wilderson, Frank B., III. *Afropessimism.* New York: Liveright, 2020.

Wilderson, Frank B., III. "Gramsci's Black Marx: Whither the Slave in Civil Society?" *Social Identities* 9, no. 2 (2003): 225–40.

Wilderson, Frank B., III. "The Prison Slave as Hegemony's (Silent) Scandal." *Social Justice* 30, no. 2 (92) (2003): 18–27.

Wilderson, Frank B., III. *Red, White and Black: Cinema and the Structure of U.S. Antagonisms.* Durham, NC: Duke University Press, 2010.

Williams, Eric. *Capitalism and Slavery.* Chapel Hill: University of North Carolina Press, 1994 (1944).

Williams, Gareth. *Infrapolitical Passages: Global Turmoil, Narco-Accumulation, and the Post-Sovereign State.* New York: Fordham University Press, 2021.

Williams, Robert A., Jr. *The American Indian in Western Legal Thought: The Discourses of Conquest*. New York: Oxford University Press, 1990.

Winthrop, John. "General Observations: Higginson Copy." *Papers of the Winthrop Family, Volume 2*. Boston: Massachusetts Historical Society. https://www.masshist.org/publications/winthrop/index.php/view/PWF02d073#PWF02d073.

Wolfe, Patrick. "Settler Colonialism and the Elimination of the Native." *Journal of Genocide Research* 8, no. 4 (2006): 387–409.

Wolfe, Patrick. *Settler Colonialism and the Transformation of Anthropology: The Politics and Poetics of an Ethnographic Event*. London: Cassell, 1999.

Wolfe, Patrick. "Structure and Event: Settler Colonialism, Time, and the Question of Genocide." In *Empire, Colony, Genocide: Conquest, Occupation, and Subaltern Resistance in World History*, edited by A. Dirk Moses, 102–32. New York: Berghahn Books, 2008.

Wright, Michelle M. *Physics of Blackness: Beyond the Middle Passage Epistemology*. Minneapolis: University of Minnesota Press, 2015.

Wyk, Johan van. "Psychoanalysis, Marxism, and Semiology: Identity, Value and the Sign." *Psychology in Society* 20 (1995): 36–41.

Wynter, Sylvia. "1492: A New World View." In *Race, Discourse, and the Origin of the Americas: A New World View*, edited by Sylvia Wynter, Vera Lawrence Hyatt, and Rex Nettleford, 5–57. Washington, DC: Smithsonian Institution Press, 1995.

Wynter, Sylvia. "Beyond Miranda's Meanings: Un/Silencing the 'Demonic Ground' of Caliban's 'Woman.'" In *The Black Feminist Reader*, edited by Joy James and T. Denean Sharpley-Whiting, 109–27. Malden, MA: Blackwell, 2000.

Wynter, Sylvia. "The Ceremony Must Be Found: After Humanism." *boundary* 2 12, no. 3 (1984): 19–70.

Wynter, Sylvia. "Columbus and the Poetics of the *Propter Nos*." *Annals of Scholarship* 8, no. 2 (1991): 251–86.

Wynter, Sylvia. "Jonkonnu in Jamaica." *Jamaica Journal* 4, no. 2 (1970): 34–48.

Wynter, Sylvia. "New Seville and the Conversion Experience of Bartolomé de Las Casas, Part One." *Jamaica Journal* 17, no. 2 (1984): 25–32.

Wynter, Sylvia. "New Seville and the Conversion Experience of Bartolomé de Las Casas, Part Two." *Jamaica Journal* 17, no. 3 (1984): 46–55.

Wynter, Sylvia. "'No Humans Involved': An Open Letter to My Colleagues." *Forum N.H.I.: Knowledge for the 21st Century* 1, no. 1 (1994): 42–73.

Wynter, Sylvia. "Unsettling the Coloniality of Being/Power/Truth/Freedom: Towards the Human, after Man, Its Overrepresentation—An Argument." *CR: The New Centennial Review* 3, no. 3 (2003): 257–337.

Yusoff, Kathryn. *A Billion Black Anthropocenes or None*. Minneapolis: University of Minnesota Press, 2018.

Zeleza, Paul Tiyambe. "Rewriting the African Diaspora: Beyond the Black Atlantic." *African Affairs* 104, no. 414 (2005): 35–68.

Index

Italicized page numbers indicate maps

Achebe, Chinua, 56, 298n6
"An Act of Explanation to the Act of Negroes" (Fisher), 317n63
Africa, 113, 127, 299n18; Caribbean linked with, 73; human life originating in, 316n33; independence in, 172; religious practices of, 212–13
African enslavement, Indian enslavement contrasted with, 106
African history, black people impacted by, 178
"African History in the Service of Black Liberation" (Rodney), 178
African peoples, Robinson distinguishing, 152–53
Africans and the Industrial Revolution in England (Inikori), 93
African societies, civilization conformed to by, 178
Afropessimism, 5, 160, 188, 308n33, 324n8; anti-blackness grappled with by, 131; black and natives differentiated in, 80; black Death and, 58–59, 143; black left engaged with by, 182; Césaire echoing, 8; culture emphasized by, 327n70; middle passage orienting, 315n4; psychoanalysis troubled by, 258–59; Wright on, 315n4; Wynter contrasted with, 195

Agamben, Giorgio, 52
Albuquerque, Sarah, 279
Alfred, Taiaiake, 27, 28, 303n71
Algeria, Fanon on, 9
Amazon Conservation Team, 246
Amazon River basin, 246
American $ (Dial), 293
The American Indian and Western Legal Thought (Williams, R.), 61
American slavery, enslaved Indigenous Peoples originating, 98
American Studies Association (ASA), 145, 223
Amerindian Act, in Guyana, 197n5, 236–37, 250
Amerindian Peoples Association (APA), 30, 244
Amerindian Research Unit, at University of Guyana, 31
amniotic *sea*, 147, 322n61
Anegada (island), 88
Anegada Passage (geological formation), 88–90, *89*, 121
Angola prison, 336n15
Anguilla (island), 88
Anthropocenes, 77, 314n112; Capitalocene contrasted with, 218; Haraway on, 330n90; Vergès challenging, 228–29; Wynter critiquing, 219; Yusoff critiquing, 232

anti-blackness, 132, 308n33; Afropessimism grappling with, 131; anti-indigeneity and, 4–5; in capital accumulation, 136; capitalism and, 160, 324n8, 326n66; of capitalist political economy, 127; Coulthard resurrecting, 226; in Indigenous thought, 81; in labour category, 131

anti-black violence, 160

anticapitalist critique, Indigeneity in, 221

anti-indigeneity, 132; anti-blackness and, 4–5; within black radical tradition, 188; Wilderson reinscribing, 131; toward workers, 177

APA (Amerindian Peoples Association), 30, 244

Arawakan (Indigenous group), 125–26, 209

Arendt, Hannah, xv, xix, 116, 191, 310n51; on labour, 51–52; on labour-work dialectic, 78; Marxism critiqued by, 48–50; Moten critiquing, 57; political economy limiting, 52; on "savages," 56; Wynter anticipated by, 308n21. *See also individual works*

Aristotelian view, Wynter outlining, 328n14

ark, art displaced by, 277–80

Arnett, Bill, 287

art: ark displacing, 277–80; craft contrasted with, 279–81; cultural context of black, 337n31; Indigenous labour as, 279–81. *See also* Basquiat, Jean-Michel; Dial, Thornton

ASA (American Studies Association), 145, 223

As We Have Always Done (Betasamosake Simpson), 28

Atkinson, J. Sharon, 244

Atlantic (ocean) "dark waters," 92–95, 97–101, 315n6; black, 115; Europe impacting, 83–84; Indigenous Peoples in, 96; middle/passage contrasted with, 121; red, 100–101, 113–15

Atlantic history: Bushnell critiquing, 96; critical approaches to, 92; Indigenous forced labour and, 101–2; Indigenous Peoples marginalized by, 97–98; labour-work dialectic influencing, 120

Atlantic History (Greene and Morgan), 96

Atlantic studies, racialism reinscribed by, 84–85

Australia, 36

Bahamas, 311n67

Baldwin, Alec, 267

Barbados, 105, 301n44

Barchiesi, Franco, 129–30, 323n67

Barker, Joanne, 25, 27, 303n71

Barthes, Roland, 325n13

Basquiat, Jean-Michel, 283, 295; Dial contrasted with, xxii, 292–93; empire critiqued by, 285; *50 Cent Piece* by, 284–86, 293

Becoming Human (Jackson, Z.), 298n4, 318n81

Belize, 30

Benítez-Rojo, Antonio, 83, 100

Bernárdez, Antonio, 304n96

Betasamosake Simpson, Leanne, 28, 34–35, 223

"Beyond Miranda's Meanings" (Wynter), 181–82, 195–99

Bhabha, Homi, 200n23

A Billion Black Anthropocenes or None (Yusoff), 77, 218–19

biology: nature distinguished from, 202–3; racial categories and, 198; religion supplanted by, 302n54

biopolitical categories, as inadequate for blacks, 214–15

biopolitics, 27, 53; blackness and, 56; Indigenous cultural symbols facilitating, 239; Indigenous Peoples managed with, 237–38; Moten on, 310n51

The Birth of Energy (Daggett), 48

black aesthetic, xvii

Black and Blur (Moten), 119

The Black Atlantic (Gilroy), 93, 100

black Atlantic studies, linguistic myopia of, 93–94

black bodies, 4, 317n60; capital transformed into by, 131, 141, 144, 147; Death of, 143–44; durability associated with, 314n110; European man contrasted with, 297n3; exploitation of, 45; land cleared of, 5, 45, 148

black culture, 206–7

black death, 308n33; Moten on, 294; native death differentiating, 307n15; slavery aiming toward, 45; Wynter complicating, 213–14

black Death, 53, 55, 155; Afropessimism and, 58–59, 143; black exploitation and, 128–29; Indigenous half death in relation to, 58–59, 80; native Elimination contrasted with, 5; resistance through, 232; Wynter on, 212

black enslavement: Conversion justifying, 64–65; Indigenous enslavement developing into, 110; Oliveira against, 309n46

black exploitation, black Death and, 128–29

Black Family Land Trust (collective endeavor), 275

The Black Feminist Reader (book), 197

black "flesh," skins contrasted with, 329n68

black freedom, postcolonial independence in conflict with, 24

black growth, native decline contrasted with, 306n1

black identity, elimination informing, 143

black indigenization, Wynter theorizing on, 210

The Black Jacobins (James), 166–67, 171

black labour, 151, 272, 292–93; black radical tradition recovering, 157; black work contextualizing, 152–53; Indigenous labour contrasted with, 2, 14, 79, 81–82, 112–15, 118–19, 256; land reorganized by, 43; native labour with, 92; surplus value and, 104; as work, 80

black left, 133; Afropessimism engaging with, 182; Marxism pressured by, 6; political economy reinscribed by, 132

black liberation, Marx and, 14

Black Lives Matter protests, 303n63

black Marxism, xix–xx

Black Marxism (Robinson), xviii, 134–40, 147–51, 166, 211, 299n18

Black Metamorphosis (Wynter), 192–95, 328n9

blackness, 87, 178, 320n6; biopolitics and, 56; black women producing, 322n61; capital development not overdetermining, 141; Conversion co-making, 85; humanness contrasted with, 53; indigeneity delinked from, 273; Robinson on, 154. *See also* antiblackness; "the negro"

black people, 301n46; African history impacting, 178; Hurricane Katrina uprooting, 336n10; labour sourced from, 148

black political economy: outside capitalism, 272; Death as beginning of, 188–89; Indigenous death and, 165; Indigenous labour within, 139–40; labour history emerged from by, 130; labour-work dialectic broken by, 294; against liberal structures, 159–60

black proletarianization, Rodney on, 185

black radical tradition, 137–38; antiindigeneity within, 188; black labour recovered in, 157; indigeneity within, 122, 235; Indigenous Peoples excluded from, xi–xii, 160–61; labour-work dialectic within, 141; marronage extending, 150; middle/passage methodology reading, 161; Robinson on, 323n68; skins insisted on by, 227–28

black resistance, limits of, 287

blacks, 309n39; Afropessimism differentiating between natives and, 80; biopolitical categories as inadequate for, 214–15; commodities birthed by, 320n18; Conversion failing, 149; culture reproduced by, 182; Elimination of, 222–23; geographic space lacked by, 54; labour associated with, 44–45; Middle Passage linked with, 72; middle/passage transforming, 71; natives delinked from, 62–63; in postcolonial states, 22–23; pre-positions separating Indigenous Peoples and, 92, 128; racialization of, 298n4; removal of, 275; reparations not received by, 275; settlers contrasted with, 297n1; slavery depriving, 54; workers not representing, 155. *See also* enslaved blacks; "the negro"

The Black Shoals (King), 86

Black Skin, White Masks (Fanon), 223–25

black slavery: Indigenous slavery compared with, 111; Las Casas proposing, 312n77, 320n9; native genocide disarticulated from, 3

black sovereignty, reparations not reinstituting, 277

black struggle, culture differentiating, 180

black subjects, indigenization producing, 215

black women: blackness produced by, 322n61; gender and, 199, 205, 231; Spillers discussing, 329n72; superexploitation of, 200; symbolic order expelling, 197

black work, 272; black labour contextualized by, 152–53; Indigenous labour contrasted with, 134; native labour contrasted with, 130

bodies, black. *See* black bodies

bodies, Indigenous. *See* Indigenous bodies

bonds, slave-backed, 314n119

bourgeois class, conquistadorial desire in, 289–90

Bresa (governor), 312n77

A Brief Account of the Destruction of the Indies (Las Casas), 313n83

British, Dutch superseded by, 175–76

Buckley, Cedric, 251–52

Buck-Morss, Susan, 76

Buffalo Man (Dial), 291–92

Bulkan, Janette, 31, 333n35

Burnham, Forbes, 278

Bushnell, Amy Turner, 74, 96–97, 125

Byrd, Jodi A., 310n49

Caceras, Berta, 304n96
Caliban (fictional character), 181, 197–202, 206–7
capital: black bodies transforming into, 131, 141, 144, 147; commodities transforming into, 50; Elimination producing, 147; ontological function of, 13–14; over-accumulation crisis of, 319n108
Capital (Marx), 50, 75–76, 289, 320n20, 327n67
capital accumulation, 130; anti-blackness in, 136; Conversion necessitated for, 75; workers resisting, 177
capital development, blackness not overdetermined by, 141
capitalism, 53, 218; anti-blackness and, 160, 324n8, 326n66; black political economy outside, 272; Fanon on, 299n18; race in relation to, 231n25; racial, 136, 216; Robinson challenging, 134–35; Rodney discussing, 324n5
Capitalism and Slavery (Williams, E.), 11, 93, 131, 160
capitalist political economy: anti-blackness of, 127; scarcity in, 196–206; Wynter critiquing, 193–95
capitalist system, peasantry attacking, 172–73
Capitalocene, xix–xx, 218, 220, 229
Captives of Conquest (Stone), 105
Caribbean: Africa linked with, 73; Columbus writing on, 59; independence in, 17; North America contrasted with, 31–32. *See also individual areas*
Caribbean capitalist teleology, political economy rejecting, 174
Caribbean Community (CARICOM) Reparations Commission, 276
Caribbean labour history: indigeneity in, 105; Indigenous slavery ignored by, 110; native labour within, 194; Rodney shifting, 183
CARICOM (Caribbean Community) Reparations Commission, 276
cartography, Indigenous, 245
Castellani, Cesar, 278, 281–82
Castellani House, 278–79, 336n17
Center for Native Peoples and the Environment, at SUNY College of Environmental Science and Forestry, 29
Césaire, Aimé, 7–8, 15, 22, 306n4
Charles V (emperor), 66, 313n83, 317n66
chattel slavery, 272, 324n7

Chrisman, Laura, *The Black Atlantic* critiqued by, 93
Christian monarchs, Conversion mandated by, 60–61
Christophe, Henri, 326n45
The Chronicle of the Discovery and Conquest of Guinea (Azurara), 242
Chthulucene, 219–20
Ciccariello-Maher, George, 141
civilization, African societies conforming to, 178
class, race and, 9, 231n25
class identity, freedom linked to, 12
class interests, Conversion expressing, 208–9
climate change, Indigenous sovereignty and, 267–68
Coc, Cristina, 244
Cofán (Indigenous group), mapping by, 253
Cohen, Paul, 97
colônia (Latin term), 18–19
colonial dispossession, labour relationships disrupted by, 222
colonialism, 7, 18–19, 45–46, 142, 250, 298n2. *See also* settler colonialism
colonial metropoles, natives traveling to, 316n52
colonists, mulattoes usurping, 173
colonization, settlers and, 301n46
colonus (Latin term), 18–19
Columbian error, 59, 68, 79, 90, 106, 181
Columbus, Christopher, 106, 263, 311n67; Caribbean written on by, 59; conquistadors compared with, 242, 335n78; desire expressed by, 261–62, 331n4; Indian slaves valued by, 108; Indigenous labour observed by, 60; ocean sea and, 314n119; as slaver, 107
"Columbus and the Poetics of the *Propter Nos*" (Wynter), 198–99, 203–4, 261–62, 302n54
commodities: blacks birthing, 320n18; capital transformed into by, 50; value of, 289
Communist Party, 7, 8
compelled labour, 185–86
composting, of human remains, 330n85
Condé, Maryse, 182
Confederación Nacional de Organizaciones Campesinas Indigenas y Negras (Ecuador), 13
Confederación Sindical Única de Trabajadores Campesinos de Bolivia (CSUTCB), 13
Congress of Black Writers, 177

conquistadorial desire, xxi, 255, 262, 264, 273; in bourgeois class, 289–90; labour-work dialectic expressing, 4, 243; political-economic system influenced by, 259, 261

conquistadorial habit, xxi, 88, 242, 335n78

conquistadors: Columbus compared with, 242, 335n78; Las Casas associated with, 331n8; as masters, 108, 112

Conrad, Joseph, 247

conscription methods, the state evolving, 274

conservation, 246; Indigenous labour subordinated by, 253; as neoliberal governmentality, 32–33; within sovereignty, 252

Constitution, of Guyana, 236

Constitution, of the United States, 106

consumptive labour, 117–18

conversion, 152; of Indigenous bodies, 113; of Indigenous Peoples, 108; to value, 73–74; to waged labour, 289–90

Conversion, 79, 195, 235–36, 265; black enslavement justified by, 64–65; blackness co-made by, 85; blacks failed by, 149; capital accumulation necessitating, 75; Christian monarchs mandating, 60–61; class interests expressed by, 208–9; desire managed with, 264; through hieroglyphs, 239; indigeneity co-made by, 85; of Indigenous labour, 255, 311n69; Indigenous Peoples linked with, 63, 68–69, 72, 90–91, 104, 110–11; labour-work dialectic and, xiv, 59; mapping exceeding, 245; middle/passage and, 101–2; Middle Passage shaped by, xvi–xvii, 46–47; as religious and economic phenomenon, 4–5

Cooper, Frederick, 286

COPINH (NGO), 30

Cortés, Hernán, 262–63

cosmogonies, Wynter defining, 302n54

cotton, slaves and, 271–72

Coulthard, Glen, 12, 14, 196; anti-blackness resurrected by, 226; Fanon read by, 224–25; primitive accumulation rethought by, 221–22; proletarianization rejected by, 11; Recognition refused by, 223. See also individual works

COVID-19 pandemic, 25, 275, 308n28

craft, 279–81

Creole (term), sociocultural use of, 297n2

Creole citizens, master-slave dialectic producing, 301n61

Creole identity, Middle Passage limiting, 87

Creole Indigeneity (Jackson, S.), xi, 36, 84, 240, 297n2

Creole labour, Indigenous labour contrasted with, xii

Creoles, Indigenous Peoples deprived by, xii

Crutzen, Paul, 217

CSUTCB (Confederación Sindical Única de Trabajadores Campesinos de Bolivia), 13

cultivation, settler-master delinked from, 19–20

cultural discourse, 240

cultural production, Indigenous, 280

cultural symbols, Indigenous, 239

culture, 239; Afropessimism emphasizing, 327n70; black, 206–7; blacks reproducing, 182; black struggle differentiated by, 180; Haitian Revolution propelled by, 167

Curtain, Philip, 148

Daggett, Cara New, 48

dance, as labour, 213

dance, Jonkonnu, 212–13

"'Dangerous Designs'" (Fisher), 317n62–63

dark waters. See Atlantic (ocean) "dark waters"

Dash, Michael, 18

death: Indigenous, 165; native, 307n15; perpetual, xviii, 144. See also black death

Death, 114; of black bodies, 143–44; black political economy beginning with, 188–89; Elimination compared with, 5–6, 143–44, 148, 290; representation tied to, 129

decolonization, of Barbados, 301n44

Deer Island, Natick Indians in, 114

Dei, George J. Sefa, 297n1

Deloria, Vine, Jr., 291

DeLoughrey, Elizabeth, 86

Depestre, René, 7

The Descent of Man (Malthus), 202

desire, 260; behind accumulation, 255–56; Columbus expressing, 261–62, 331n4; Conversion managing, 264; labour-work dialect managing, 263–64; libido and, 331n4; psychoanalysis uncovering, 243. See also conquistadorial desire

Dial, Thornton, 283, 287–88, 290–92; Basquiat contrasted with, xxii, 292–93; within radical tradition, 288–89; Tancredo contrasted with, 294–95. See also individual works

Disaggregating Primitive Accumulation (Nichols, R.), 43

Discourse on Colonialism (Césaire), 7

dispossession, 128–29; black, 258–59, 307n12; colonial, 222; exploitation and, 43; land, 107–8; primitive accumulation featuring, 43–44

Documentary History (Aptheker), 323n67

domestic work, middle-class status and, 231–32

doubling: of Indigenous labour, xx, 241–42, 282; by Indigenous Peoples, 244–45; as poetic unconscious, 240; of settler-master, 115

A Dream of My Ancestors and the Past (Tancredo), 279

Driving to the End of the World (Dial), 287

Dumont, Marilyn, 57–58

Dutch, British superseding, 175–76

Dutch Guiana, 105

Eanes de Azurara, Gomes, 242

"An Ecology of (Eloquent) Things" (Moten), 288–89

the economic, the political contrasted with, 49–50

economic development, narratives of, 177

economic dominance, of settlers, 9–10

economic right, political right contrasted with, 19–20, 24

Edwards, Brent Hayes, 91, 94–96

Elaine (Arkansas), 275

elimination, 143–46

Elimination, 71–72, 114, 134; of blacks, 222–23; capital produced through, 147; Death compared with, 5–6, 143–44, 148, 290; Greenwood neighborhood subject to, 275; James describing, 169–71; as middle/passage, 142; native, 5; reparations and, 276; resistance responded to with, 171; Robinson elaborating on, 146; settler colonialism featuring, 144–45

empire, Basquiat critiquing, 285

encomienda systems, 106, 312n74, 317n52

encomienderos, 208, 312n74

enslaved blacks: inability to reproduce of, 147–48, 170, 181; indigeneity lost by, 55; labour of, 42–43, 306n4; time alienating, 290–91; work of, 127; Wynter on, 328n34. *See also* black enslavement

enslaved Indigenous Peoples: American slavery originating with, 98; in Barbados, 105; bodily injury of, 90–91

enslaved labour, "the negro" managing, 142–43

enslaved persons: plantations destroyed by, 172–73; representation of, 302n62; as "surrogate," 19

epiphenomenal time, 86

Equator Initiative, 247–49, 251

Equator Prize, xx, 247–49, 267–68, 332n15, 332n19; map of winners of, *248*, 254

Equiano, Olaudah, 258

"Española, Cuba, Sant Juan y Jamaica" (Las Casas), 62–63

An Essay on the Principle of Population (Malthus), 201–2

Europe, Atlantic impacted by, 83–84

European economy, Indigenous Peoples subordinating, 69

European man, black bodies contrasted with, 297n3

European system, Indigenous Peoples subordinated in, 112

exchange value, 75–77, 290, 292, 320n18

exploitation: of black bodies, 45; black Death and black, 128–29; dispossession and, 43; super-, 200

extermination, plasticity generated by, 90

extinction, 69–70, 140; Reséndez not challenging, 109; Robinson explaining, 139; sovereignty denied through, 220

Fanon, Frantz, 11, 15, 217, 227, 299n17, 300n23; on Algeria, 9; on capitalism, 299n18; Coulthard reading, 224–25; Marx rejected by, 10; Wynter reading, 13. *See also individual works*

Farrington, Constance, 200n23

Federal Reserve, US, 275

female subjectivity, signification recovering, 258

feminism, 199

50 Cent Piece (Basquiat), 284–86, 293

Fisher, Linford D., 317nn62–63

Floyd, George, 303n63, 330n93

Forbes, Jack D., 117, 319n106

Forbes Burnham regime, 159

forced labour, plasticity generated by, 90

Forest Peoples Programme, 31

Foucault, Michel, 52, 261, 326n45

franchise colonialism, 45–46, 142, 298n2

Fredericks, Guy, 278

Fredericks, Nicholas, 251–52

freedom: black, 24; class identity linked to, 12; Indigenous, 28–29

French Revolution, 168
Freud, Sigmund, 259–60
From Class to Race (Mills), 154–55, 231n25
funerals, resistance and, 213–14
The Futures of Black Radicalism (Robinson), 134, 228, 320n23

Garifuna (Indigenous group), 244, 274, 304n96
Gaza (Palestine), 275
gender, 199–201, 205, 230–31, 319n110
geographic space, blacks lacking, 54
Georgetown, in Guyana, 32
Gilroy, Paul, 93; Edwards rejecting, 94–95; Weaver critiquing, 99–100; Zeleza differentiated from, 119. *See also individual works*
Giroux, Henry, 336n10
Global Change Newsletter (Crutzen and Stoermer), 217
GOIP. *See* Guyanese Organization of Indigenous Peoples
Goldman Environmental Prize, 244
Gomes, Patrick, 251
Goodall, Jane, 267–68
Google Earth, 247
Goveia, Elsa, 192
grammar, 17–25, 243, 302n53
Gramsci, Antonio, 131
Greene, Jack P., 96
Greenwood neighborhood, in Tulsa (Oklahoma), 275–76, 336n10
Gregory, Gillian, 32
Griffiths, Tom, 31, 268
grounded normativity, 216, 222–24, 232, 324n1
grounded relationality, 216–17
The Groundings with My Brothers (Rodney), 45, 232n67, 319n3
Guatemala, 313n96
Guiana, Dutch, 105
Guyana, xx–xxi, 159, 163, 278–79; Amerindian Act in, 197n5, 236–37, 250; coastal region of, 126–27; Constitution of, 236; Georgetown in, 32; Indigenous sovereignty in, 30–38; Low Carbon Development Strategy of, 250; Ministry of Indigenous Peoples Affairs of, 279; plantations on, 175; Rupununi–Region 9 in, 246; Sawari Wa'o Village in, 31; socialism in, 176–77. *See also* Rodney, Walter
Guyana Women Artist's Association, 336n17

Guyanese Organization of Indigenous Peoples (GOIP), 31

Haitian Revolution, 99, 147, 166–67, 172
Hale, Charles R., 274
Hanchard, Michael, 277
Haraway, Donna J., 220–21, 330n90
Hardt, Michael, 285
"Hard Truths" (forum), 288
Harris, Wilson, 193
Hart, William David, 53–56, 137, 308n33
Hartman, Saidiya V., 24, 131, 143
Henry, Paget, 192–93, 327n5
hieroglyphs, 235, 238–39
Hispaniola (island), 113
history, Atlantic. *See* Atlantic history
A History of the Guyanese Working People (Rodney), 125, 175, 181, 212
A History of the Upper Guinea Coast (Rodney), 176
homunculi, 54–55, 91, 268–69, 279, 309n40
How Europe Underdeveloped Africa (Rodney), 127, 299n18
How the Word (Smith), 336n15
human action, within political economy, 57–58
The Human Condition (Arendt), 48
human life, Africa originating, 316n33
humanness, blackness contrasted with, 53
human remains, composting of, 330n85
human rights approach, Indigenous issues and, 249
Hurricane Katrina, 275, 320n21, 336n10
Hurricane Sally, 320n21

immanence/imminence, 173–74
incarceration, of Indigenous women, 330n93
In Defense of the Indians (Las Casas), 313n83
indenture, South Asian, 298n1
independence: in Africa, 172; in Caribbean, 17; land-labour dialectic codified by, 82; postcolonial, 2, 24; power distinguished from, 301n46; settle colonialism not dismantled by, 23; settler grammars of, 17–25; sovereignty and, 16–17
Indian enslavement, African enslavement contrasted with, 106
Indian legal status, Indigenous enslavement not stopped by, 109
Indian slaves, Columbus valuing, 108

indigeneity: in anticapitalist critique, 221; blackness delinked from, 273; within black radical tradition, 122, 235; in Caribbean labour history, 105; Conversion co-making, 85; enslaved blacks losing, 55; labour resisted through, 206–15; openings to, xix, xxii, 3, 122, 125, 135, 141, 156, 161, 221, 235; productive work in tension with, 129; settler colonialism rejected by, 174. *See also* anti-indigeneity

indigenization, 210, 215

"Indigenous America and the Limits of the Atlantic World, 1493–1825" (Bushnell), 125

Indigenous bodies: conversion of, 113; Indigenous sovereignty exercised by, 30; slave codes targeting, 111

Indigenous cartography, 245

Indigenous cultural production, 280

Indigenous cultural symbols, biopolitics facilitated by, 239

Indigenous death, black political economy and, 165

Indigenous enslavement, 105–6; black enslavement developing from, 110; Indian legal status not stopping, 109; Reséndez chronicling, 107

Indigenous forced labour, Atlantic history and, 101–2

Indigenous freedom, 28–29

"Indigenous Geographies and Caribbean Feminisms" (conference), 243–44

Indigenous half death, black Death in relation to, 58–59, 80

Indigenous issues, human rights approach to, 249

Indigenous labour, 3, 175; abundance associated with, 59, 311n64; as art, 279–81; black labour contrasted with, 2, 14, 79, 81–82, 112–15, 118–19, 256; within black political economy, 139–40; black work contrasted with, 134; Castellani House displacing, 282; Columbus observing, 60; conservation subordinating, 253; consumption motivating, 116–17; Conversion of, 255, 311n69; Creole labour contrasted with, xii; doubling of, xx, 241–42, 282; enslaved, 11; European need obscuring, 67; as invisible, 64–65; labour history reducing, xiii, 135; labour-work dialect reducing, 239–40; Las Casas writing on, 67–68; mapping and, 245–46, 253–54; radical tradition excluding, xvii, 1,

78, 125; representation of, 268–69; before resistance, 186; sugar market developed through, 209; work and, 108–9; Wynter on, 209

Indigenous Law Institute, 27

Indigenous Palestinians, Israeli government assaulting, 275

Indigenous Peoples, 20–21; in Atlantic, 96; Atlantic history marginalizing, 97–98; biopolitics managing, 237–38; black radical tradition excluding, xi–xii, 160–61; Conversion linked with, 63, 68–69, 72, 90–91, 104, 110–11; conversion of, 108; Creoles depriving, xii; doubling by, 244–45; European economy subordinated by, 69; European system subordinating, 112; labour history excluding, 49; land associated with, 44–45; lobbying by, 333n35; middle/passage and, 70–73; Middle Passage and, 118–19; nature transformed by, 42; peasantry equated with, 301n52; plantation labour without, xv; plasticity subjecting, 315n19; as political subjects, 54–55; postcolonial states subordinating, 18; pre-positions dislocating, 132; pre-positions separating blacks and, 92, 128; purchase and sale of, 73–74; regulatory measures on, 37; reparations entitled to, 55; representation of, 310n49, 310n59; rights of, 26, 54, 303n74; Sepulveda attacking, 309n40; social well-being excluding, 70; Spanish soldiers and, 313n96; Thirteenth Amendment not freeing, 106; unproductive labour linked with, 78–79; US subordinating, 303n71; without value, 106; vassalage of, 61, 109–10, 168, 317n66, 323n65; welfare and, 305n110; work by, 66–67. *See also* enslaved Indigenous Peoples; mapping; natives; Wapichan peoples; *See also specific Indigenous groups*

Indigenous removals, slave trade contrasted with, 113–14

Indigenous self-determination: Indigenous sovereignty contrasted with, 27; land rights and, 30–31; mapping supporting, 245

Indigenous slavery: black slavery compared with, 111; Caribbean labour history ignoring, 110; repartimiento systems obscuring, 317n52; Robinson not accounting for, 140

Indigenous sovereignty, 35–36, 74; climate change and, 267–68; complexities of, 25; in Guyana, 30–38; Indigenous bodies exercis-

ing, 30; Indigenous self-determination
contrasted with, 27; island trope reducing, 305n104; the law misrepresent-
ing, 240; metaphor impacting, 256–57;
Moreton-Robinson on, 26–27; postcolonial
independence in conflict with, 2, 24; postcolonial states and, 33–34; relational nature
of, 303n63; reparations not reinstituting,
277; rights transformed into by, 236; settler
states in relation to, 29–30
Indigenous thought, anti-blackness in, 81
Indigenous women, incarceration of, 330n93
Indigenous work, Las Casas on, 103–4
infrahumans, 54–55, 79–81, 141, 178, 231,
268–69
Inikori, Joseph, 93
In Search of Lost Time (Proust), 260–61
In the Castle of My Skin (Lamming), 216–17
In the Wake (Sharpe), 322n61
involuntary settlerhood, xii, 165–66
island trope, Indigenous sovereignty reduced
by, 305n104
Israeli government, Indigenous Palestinians
assaulted by, 275
Iwokrama Centre for Rainforest Conserva-
tion, 32

Jackson, Shona N., xi, 36, 84, 240, 297n2.
    See also individual works
Jackson, Zakiyyah Iman, 298n4, 318n81,
    335n83. *See also individual works*
Jagan, Cheddi, 299n9, 333n33
Jamaica Journal (journal), 62
James, Cyril Lionel Robert, xvii–xix, 137, 163,
    232, 325n35; citation of, 164; Elimination
    described by, 169–71; Marxism broken from
    by, 174; Robinson on, 166–67; Williams
    contrasted with, 167–68. *See also individual
    works*
Johnny, Angelbert, 251
Jones, Claudia, 192, 200, 231, 323n67
Jonkonnu dance, Wynter describing, 212–13
"Jonkonnu in Jamaica" (Wynter), 195, 210–11
"The Journey of Persistence and Endurance"
    (exhibit), 336n17

Karera, Axelle, 219
Kelley, Robin D. G., 135, 145–46
Kempadoo, Kamala, 298n1
Kimmerer, Robin Wall, 29, 311n64
King, Tiffany Lethabo, 3, 86

Knight, Franklin, 181, 183–84
Koama, Ohene, 337n25
Kogi (Indigenous group), 252

labour: abstract *versus* concrete, xix–xx;
    Arendt on, 51–52; black people as source of,
    148; blacks associated with, 44–45; com-
    pelled, 185–86; consumptive, 117–18; dance
    as, 213; of enslaved blacks, 42–43, 306n4;
    indigeneity resisting, 206–15; land dispos-
    session in relation to, 107–8; peasantry dis-
    tinguished from, 185; productive, 75–76; as
    resistance, 185–86, 206–15; waged, 289–90;
    of Wapichan peoples, 251; work distin-
    guished from, xv–xvi, 42–49, 52, 56–58, 69,
    77, 128–29, 167, 173, 187. *See also* black labour;
    Indigenous labour; land-labour dialectic;
    native labour; unproductive labour
labour history, 102–3; Barchiesi critiquing,
    129–30; black political economy emerging
    from, 130; Indigenous labour reduced by,
    xiii, 135; Indigenous Peoples excluded from,
    49; pre-positions structuring, 164. *See also*
    Caribbean labour history
labour relationships, 222, 229
labour-work dialectic, 112, 132–33, 215–16;
    Arendt on, 78; Atlantic history influenced
    by, 120; black political economy breaking,
    294; within black radical tradition, 141; con-
    quistadorial desire expressed in, 4, 243; as
    conquistadorial habit, 242; Conversion and,
    xiv, 59; desire managed through, 263–64;
    Indigenous labour reduced by, 239–40;
    Marx expressing, 77; meaning imposed by,
    265; radical tradition not resuscitating, 295;
    representation used by, 235–36; settler co-
    lonialism under, 273–74; as symbolic order,
    257–58; as symbolic practice, 261; Wynter
    critiquing, 191
Lacan, Jacques, 258–59
Lamming, George, 216–17
land, 126; black bodies cleared from, 5, 45, 148;
    black labour reorganizing, 43; Indigenous
    Peoples associated with, 44–45; mapping
    doubling, 244–45; native people separated
    from, 42–43; nature contrasted with, 211;
    Pruitt reenvisioning, 273; as *terra nullius*,
    127; Wapichan peoples protecting, 249
land claims, mapping making, 333n31
land dispossession, labour in relation to,
    107–8

land-labour dialectic, 41–44, 46, 157; independence codifying, 82; pre-positions supporting, 22; sovereignty linked to, 34; Wynter critiquing, 206–7

land-labour ratio, primitive accumulation accounted for in, 207–8

land rights, 24, 30–31

La Rose, Jean, 31, 244

Las Casas, Bartolomé de, 55, 61, 69–72, 81, 264–65, 309n46; black slavery proposed by, 312n77, 320n9; conquistadors associated with, 331n8; *In Defense of the Indians* by, 313n83; as encomiendero, 208; Indigenous labour written on by, 67–68; on Indigenous work, 103–4; "Memorial de Remedios" by, 231n77; representation and, 323n65; Reséndez contrasted with, 108; slavery described by, 102–3; Wynter discussing, 62–65, 207–8. *See also individual works*

Latitude Zero (Conrad), 247

the law, Indigenous sovereignty misrepresented by, 240

left, black. *See* black left

legal status, Indian, 109

Lesser Antilles (island group), 88

liberal structures, black political economy against, 159–60

libido, desire and, 331n4

Lindahl, Folke, 300n39

linguistic myopia, of black Atlantic studies, 93–94

Llanos de Moxos (Indigenous group), 125, 128

Locke, John, 71, 313n103. *See also individual works*

Lost Farm (Billy Goat Hill) (Dial), 287–90, 293

Louis, Renee Pualani, 245, 252

Low Carbon Development Strategy, of Guyana, 250

Lowe, Lisa, 3

Lucayos (Indigenous group), 113

Lumumba, Patrice, 301

Macusi (Indigenous group), 278–79

Making of New World Slavery (Blackburn), 324n7

Malthus, Thomas Robert, 201–2

man: black bodies contrasted with European, 297n3; political animal contrasted with, 310n59; Wynter, Sylvia on, 308n31

Manichean (Indigenous group), 200n23

Manifest Manners (Vizenor), 143

mapping, by Indigenous Peoples, xx–xxi, 255; by Cofán, 253; Conversion exceeded by, 245; impacts of, 251; Indigenous labour and, 245–46, 253–54; Indigenous self-determination supported by, 245; as labour practice, 242; land claims made with, 333n31; land doubled through, 244–45; *National Geographic* discussing, 334n42; political economy broken down by, 245; representation of, 166–67; rights secured through, 251–52

Maroon (Indigenous group), 246, 274, 318n97

marronage, black radical tradition extended by, 150

Marronage, slavery exceeded by, 153

Marx, Karl, xv, 8, 43–44; black liberation and, 14; Fanon rejecting, 10; labour-work dialectic expressed by, 77; Nichols reenvisioning, 46; on primitive accumulation, 307n9; productive labour emphasized by, 75–76; radical tradition repeating, 16; Williams elaborating on, 320n20; Wynter on, 14–15. *See also individual works*

Marxian critique, Rodney exceeding, 179

Marxism, 6–7, 12, 75, 191; Arendt critiquing, 48–50; black, xix–xx; black left pressured by, 6; of Jagan, 299n9; James breaking from, 174; limits of, 14–16, 300n39; universality of ownership extended by, 15; Wilderson on, 324n8; Wynter critiquing, 228, 328n8

master position, sovereign power of, 263

masters, conquistadors as, 108, 112

master-slave dialectic, Creole citizens produced by, 301n61

Maya Leaders Alliance (Belize), 30, 244

Mayor, Mireya, 246

Mbembe, Achille, 48, 257, 310n55

McAnany, Patricia A., 301n52

McKittrick, Katherine, 200

meaning, labour-work dialect imposing, 265

Means, Russell, 12

Melamed, Jodi, 116, 117

"Memorial de Remedios" (Las Casas), 231n77

metaphor, 240, 260–61; Indigenous sovereignty impacted by, 256–57; metonymy and, 241, 255; simulation structuring, xx

metonymy, 260–61, 282; metaphor and, 241, 255; simulation structuring, xx

MFAH (Museum of Fine Arts in Houston), xxii, 283–84, 293–94

middle-class status, domestic work and, 231–32

middle/passage, 86, 103–6; Atlantic contrasted with, 90, 121, 315n4; blacks transformed by, 71; Conversion and, 101–2; Elimination as, 142; Indigenous Peoples and, 70–73; Middle Passage contrasted with, 91; Moten on, 119; within radical tradition, 133–34; womb as, 322n61

Middle Passage: blacks linked with, 72; Conversion shaping, xvi–xvii, 46–47; Creole identity limited by, 87; Indigenous Peoples and, 118–19; middle/passage contrasted with, 91

middle passage epistemology, 84–85

middle/passage methodology, xvii, 5, 92; black radical tradition read with, 161; Mills read through, 156–57; relations privileged by, 91

middle passage narratives, Jackson, S., critiquing, 84

Mills, Charles, 154–57, 208, 231n25. *See also individual works*

Ministry of Indigenous Peoples Affairs, of Guyana, 279

"Mississippi Gardens" (Pruitt), 271–73

Mithlo, Nancy Marie, 280

Mohawk Interruptus (Simpson), 71

Montag, Warren, 48

Moore, Jason W., 49, 218, 229

Moreton-Robinson, Aileen, 197n4; on Indigenous sovereignty, 26–27; possessive logics conceptualized by, 155; on postcoloniality, 36. *See also individual works*

Morgan, Philip D., 96

Moten, Fred, 37, 53, 137, 310n59, 335n76; Arendt critiqued by, 57; on biopolitics, 310n51; on black death, 294; on middle/passage, 119. *See also individual works*

Movimento dos Trabalhadores Rurais Sem Terra (MST) (Brazil), 13

mulattoes, colonists usurped by, 173

Museum of Fine Arts in Houston (MFAH), xxii, 283–84, 293–94

"My Black Triangle" (Nichols, G.), 120

Natick Indians, in Deer Island, 114

National Geographic (magazine), 246, 334n42

the native, "the negro" in tension with, 225–26

native death, black death differentiated from, 307n15

native decline, black growth contrasted with, 306n1

native Elimination, black Death contrasted with, 5

native genocide, black slavery disarticulated from, 3

native labour: with black labour, 92; black work contrasted with, 130; within Caribbean labour history, 194

native people, land separated from, 42–43

native racialism, Robinson exploring, 138–39

natives: Afropessimism differentiating between blacks and, 80; blacks delinked from, 62–63; colonial metropoles traveled to by, 316n52; enslavement of, 87–88; workers transcending, 223–24

nature, 267–68; biology distinguished from, 202–3; Indigenous Peoples transforming, 42; land contrasted with, 211; population governed, 202

Navajo Nation, COVID-19 pandemic impacting, 25

"Necropolitics" (Mbembe), 310n55

Negri, Antonio, 285

"the negro," 317n63; enslaved labour managed through, 142–43; financial motives creating, 138–39; the native in tension with, 225–26

neoliberal development goals, territorial claims served by, 274

neoliberal governmentality, 31–33

Newcomb, Steve, 27

New England Bound (Warren), 105

The New Laws of the Indies for the Good Treatment and Preservation of the Indians, 106, 317n66

New Orleans (Louisiana), Hurricane Sally impacting, 320n21

"New Seville and the Conversion Experience" (Wynter), 195

Nichols, Grace, 120, 211

Nichols, Robert, 42–43, 46, 210

North America, Caribbean contrasted with, 31–32

"Notebook of a Return to the Native Land" (Césaire), 306n4

"Not Just a Platform for My Dance" (Dumont), 57–58

Obama, Barack, 285

O'Brien, Jean M., 145

ocean sea (term), 83, 88, 314n119

Oliveira, Fernando, 309n46

The Origins of Totalitarianism (Arendt), 56

The Other Slavery (Reséndez), 105
Oxford English Dictionary, 19
Oxford Latin Dictionary, 18–19

Pagden, Anthony, 74, 309n40
Palestinians, Indigenous, 275
Palmer, Colin, 95
Papal Bull (Alexander VI), 61
Party/Politics (Hanchard), 277
Patterson, Orlando, 131
Pearce, Margaret Wickens, 245, 252
peasantry, 171; capitalist system attacked by, 172–73; Indigenous Peoples equated with, 301n52; labour distinguished from, 185
periodization, Robinson rejecting, 151–52
plantation labour, without Indigenous Peoples, xv
Plantationocene, 218, 220
plantations, 19–21, 181, 336n15; enslaved persons destroying, 172–73; on Guyana, 175; productive work compelled by, 184
plasticity, Indigenous Peoples subjected to, 315n19
plural crossings, reading for, xvii
poetic unconscious, doubling as, 240
Polanyi, Karl, 211
the political, the economic contrasted with, 49–50
political animal, man contrasted with, 310n59
political economic critique, of workers, 206
political-economic system, conquistadorial desire influencing, 259, 261
political economy, 49–50, 277–78; Arendt limited by, 52; black left reinscribing, 132; Caribbean capitalist teleology rejected by, 174; human action within, 57–58; mapping breaking down, 245; radical tradition reinscribing, 132; representation in, 244–45; Rodney on, 324n8. *See also* black political economy; capitalist political economy
political right, economic right contrasted with, 19–20, 24
political subjects, Indigenous Peoples as, 54–55
political theory, work prioritized by, 50
Portuguese, Tupinamba encountered by, 116
possessive logics, 27, 37, 155–56
postcolonial independence, 2, 24
postcolonial states: blacks in, 22–23; Indigenous Peoples subordinated in, 18; indigenous sovereignty and, 33–34

power, independence distinguished from, 301n46
pre-positions, xviii, xxi, 16–17, 20, 23, 243; blacks and Indigenous Peoples separated by, 92, 128; Indigenous Peoples dislocated through, 132; labour history structured by, 164; land-labour dialectic supported by, 22; representation and, 235–36; Rodney employing, 127; temporal, 21, 140, 243, 281
primitive accumulation, 46, 75, 106; Coulthard rethinking, 221–22; dispossession as feature of, 43–44; land-labour ratio accounting for, 207–8; Marx on, 307n9
private property, chattel slavery linked with, 324n7
productive labour, 75–76, 117–18
productive work, 81; indigeneity in tension with, 129; plantations compelling, 184; unproductive labour delinked from, xiv–xv, 46, 49, 77–80, 128
proletarianization: black, 185; Coulthard rejecting, 11; Means rejecting, 12
proletariat, 171, 185
proto-master, 107, 263
proto-settler, 112, 261, 263
Proust, Marcel, 260–61
Pruitt, Stephanie, 271–73, 277–78. *See also individual works*
psychoanalysis, 257; Afropessimism troubling, 258–59; black dispossession not characterized by, 258–59; desire uncovered through, 243; as semiotic practice, 264

race, 98, 145–46, 154–55; capitalism in relation to, 231n25; class and, 9, 231n25; Rodney speaking on, 326n54
Race in Translation (Stam and Shohat), 98
racial capitalism, 136, 216
racial categories, biology and, 198
racialism: Atlantic studies reinscribing, 84–85; native, 138–39; "savages" transferred, 139
racialization, 98, 298n4
radical tradition: Dial within, 288–89; Indigenous labour excluded from, xvii, 1, 78, 125; labour-work dialectic not resuscitated by, 295; limits of, 183; Marx repeated by, 16; middle/passage within, 133–34; political economy reinscribed by, 132; Robinson articulating, 156–57; Wynter included in, xix, 189, 229–30. *See also* black radical tradition
Recognition, 196, 223

Red, White, and Black (Wilderson), 53–54, 131, 302n53, 310n49, 320nn16–17

red Atlantic, 100–101, 113–15

The Red Atlantic (Weaver), 14, 99

Red Skin, White Masks (Coulthard), 14, 223–24

Redskins (former football team name), 303n63

religion, biology supplanting, 302n54

religious practices, African, 212–13

reparations: blacks not receiving, 275; black sovereignty not reinstituted with, 277; Elimination and, 276; Indigenous Peoples entitled to, 55; Indigenous sovereignty not reinstituted with, 277

Reparations Commission, of Caribbean Community, 276

repartimiento systems, 106, 317n52

The Repeating Island (Benítez-Rojo), 83

representation, 256–57, 281–82, 301n52; Death tied to, 129; of enslaved persons, 302n62; of Indigenous labour, 268–69; of Indigenous Peoples, 310n49, 310n59; labour-work dialectic using, 235–36; Las Casas and, 323n65; of mapping, 166–67; political, 302n62; in political economy, 244–45; pre-positions and, 235–36; slippage demonstrated by, 327n71

reproduction, Wynter describing, 329n65

Reséndez, Andrés, 100, 105–6; extinction not challenged by, 109; Indigenous enslavement chronicled by, 107; Las Casas contrasted with, 108; Schwartz corroborating with, 110. *See also individual works*

resistance: through black Death, 232; Elimination as response to, 171; funerals and, 213–14; Indigenous labour before, 186; labour as, 185–86, 206–15; limits of black, 287

"Revolutionary Nationalism" (Jones), 323n67

"Rewriting the African Diaspora" (Zeleza), 95

rights: of Indigenous Peoples, 26, 54, 303n74; Indigenous sovereignty transforming into, 236; land, 24, 30–31; mapping securing, 251–52; Wapichan peoples struggling for, 250

rights activism, violence against, 304n96

Roanoke and Wampum (Welburn), 72

Robinson, Cedric, 142–45, 150, 182–83, 228, 289, 320n23; African peoples distinguished by, 152–53; on blackness, 154; on black radical tradition, 323n68; capitalism challenged by, 134–35; Elimination elaborated on by, 146;

extinction explained by, 139; Hart on, 137; Indigenous slavery not accounted for by, 140; on James, 166–67; labour relationships emphasized by, 229; native racialism explored by, 138–39; periodization rejected by, 151–52; radical tradition articulated by, 156–57; Rodney not considered by, 163–64. *See also individual works*

Rodney, Walter, xvii–xix, 18, 69, 125, 159–61, 176; on black proletarianization, 185; capitalism discussed by, 324n5; Caribbean labour history shifted by, 183; citation of, 164; death of, 324n1; Marxian critique exceeded by, 179; perspectival categories of existence questioned by, 180–81; on political economy, 324n8; pre-positions employed by, 127; race spoken on by, 326n54; Robinson not considering, 163–64; slavery described by, 126; socialism defined by, 162; socialist society envisioned by, 325n11; on working people, 184. *See also individual works*

Roediger, David, 223

Roopnaraine, Terry, 279–81

Roth, Edmund, 278

Routes and Roots (DeLoughrey), 86

Royal Agricultural and Commercial Society, 278

Rupununi–Region 9, in Guyana, 246

St. Augustine (Trinidad and Tobago), 243

Saltwater Slavery (Smallwood), 121

Sánchez-Godoy, Ruben A., 94

San Domingo, 170, 325n35

São Jorge da Mina (trading post), 107

Sartre, Jean-Paul, 224–25

Saussure, Ferdinand de, 257, 265

"savages," 55; Arendt on, 56; population distinguished from, 203; racialism transferred to, 139; the settler contrasted with, 309n37

Sawari Wa'o Village, in Guyana, 31

scarcity, in capitalist political economy, 196–206

SCF (Survey of Consumer Finances), by US Federal Reserve, 275

Schwartz, Stuart B., 110, 115–16

SCPDA (South Central People's Development Association), xxi, 247–49, 333n33

"Searching for Justice and Land Security" (La Rose and Griffiths), 268

Second Treatise (Locke), 313n103

self-determination, Indigenous. *See* Indigenous self-determination

Seneca Village (New York), 275–76

Sepúlvada, Juan Ginés de, 81, 309n40

settler colonialism, 27, 303n64; Betasamosake Simpson critiquing, 34–35; Elimination featured by, 144–45; franchise colonialism contrasted with, 45–46, 142, 298n2; independence not dismantling, 23; indigeneity rejecting, 174; labour-work dialectic under, 273–74; sovereignty and, 35

settler grammars, of independence, 17–25

settlerhood, involuntary, xii, 165–66

settler-master, cultivation delinked from, 19–20

settlers: blacks contrasted with, 297n1; colonization and, 301n46; economic dominance of, 9–10; "savages" contrasted with, 309n37

settler states, Indigenous sovereignty in relation to, 29–30

Sexton, Jared, 323n67, 327n70

Shakespeare, William, 181–82, 197–200, 205

Sharpe, Christina, 86–87, 109, 322n61, 336n16

Shohat, Ella, 98–99

A Short Account of the Destruction of the Indies (Las Casas), 65–66

A Short History (Las Casas), 74, 102

Silva, Denise Da, 206

Silverman, Kaja, 257–61, 265. *See also individual works*

Simpson, Audra, 26, 27, 29, 71. *See also individual works*

simulation, metaphor and metonymy structured by, xx

Singh, Nikhil Pal, 188

skins, 217, 226; black "flesh" contrasted with, 329n68; black radical tradition insisting on, 227–28; racial capitalism elaborated on by, 216

slave-backed bonds, 314n119

slave codes, Indigenous bodies targeted by, 111

slaver, Columbus as, 107

slavery, 19, 250; American, 98; black death as aim of, 45; blacks deprived by, 54; chattel, 272, 324n7; Las Casas describing, 102–3; Marronage exceeding, 153; Rodney describing, 126; Warren on, 111. *See also* black enslavement; black slavery; Indigenous enslavement; Indigenous slavery

slaves: cotton and, 271–72; Indian, 108; San Domingo importing, 325n35; workers

contrasted with, 301n41. *See also* black enslavement; Indigenous enslavement

slave ships, hold of, 53–54

slave trade, Indigenous removals contrasted with, 113–14

Smallwood, Stephanie, 121

Smith, Brady, 94, 336n15

socialism, 162–63, 179; in Guyana, 176–77; Means critiquing, 12; Rodney defining, 162. *See also* Marxism

socialist platforms, 7

socialist society, Rodney envisioning, 325n11

"Social Life of Social Death" (Sexton), 327n70

Social Text (journal), 3, 216, 273

social well-being, Indigenous Peoples excluded from, 70

Soul Fire Farm (collective endeavor), 275

South Asian indenture, 298n1

South Central People's Development Association (SCPDA), xxi, 247–49, 333n33

sovereign power, of master position, 263

sovereignty, 7; Alfred rejecting, 28; black, 277; conservation within, 252; extinction denying, 220; independence and, 16–17; land-labour dialectic linked to, 34; Maroon granted, 318n97; settler colonialism and, 35. *See also* Indigenous sovereignty

Sovereignty Matters (Barker), 27

Spanish soldiers, Indigenous Peoples and, 313n96

Spillers, Hortense, 258–59, 322n61, 329n72

Stalin, Joseph, 8

Stam, Robert, 98–99

the state, conscription methods evolved by, 274

Stoermer, Eugene, 217

Stolen Life (Moten), 37

Stone, Erin Woodruff, 105

The Subject of Semiotics (Silverman), 258

sugar market, Indigenous labour developing, 209

SUNY College of Environmental Science and Forestry, Center for Native, Peoples and the Environment at, 29

superexploitation, of black women, 200

Suriname, 253, 274

surplus value, black labour and, 104

Survey of Consumer Finances (SCF), by US Federal Reserve, 275

Swann's Way (Silverman), 260–61

symbolic order: black women expelled by, 197; dialectic as, xxi–xxii; labour-work dialect as, 257–58

Tancredo, George, xxii, 278–83, 294–95, 337n25. *See also individual works*
Taylor, Keeanga-Yamahtta, 7, 8
technology, Wapichan peoples using, 246, 252–54, 267
The Tempest (Shakespeare), 197–200, 205
territorial claims, neoliberal development goals served by, 274
Things Fall Apart (Achebe), 298n6
Thirteenth Amendment, of US Constitution, 106
"Thornton Dial in the 21st Century" (exhibit), 283
time, 86, 290–91
Time, 134
Todd, Gordon, 324n1
Traces of History (Wolfe), 145–46
Trinidad and Tobago, 243
Trio (Indigenous group), 253
Trotsky, Leon, 151
Tulsa (Oklahoma), 275–76, 336n10
Tupinamba (Indigenous group), 116
Turner, Jenny, 221

UN (United Nations), 26, 54, 303n74
the unconscious, Silverman elaborating on, 259–60
UN Declaration on the Rights of Indigenous Peoples (UNDRIP), 26, 54, 303n74
United Nations (UN), 26, 54, 303n74
United States (US): Constitution of, 106; Federal Reserve of, 275; Indigenous Peoples subordinated in, 303n71
The Universal Machine (Moten), 57
University of Guyana, Amerindian Research Unit at, 31
University of the West Indies (St. Augustine), 243
unproductive labour: craft associated with, 281; Indigenous Peoples linked with, 78–79; productive work delinking from, xiv–xv, 46, 49, 77–80, 128
US. *See* United States
use value, 75–77, 289–90

Vaccaro, Ismael, 32
Valdivia, Gimenez, 331n8

value: of commodities, 289; conversion to, 73–74; exchange, 75–77, 290, 292, 320n18; Indigenous Peoples without, 106; surplus, 104; use, 75–77, 289–90
vassalage, of Indigenous Peoples, 61, 109–10, 168, 317n66, 323n65
Vergès, Françoise, 218, 228–29
violence, against rights activism, 304n96
violence, anti-black, 160
Virgin Islands, 88
Vizenor, Gerald, 143
Voloshinov, Valentin, 257

waged labour, conversion to, 289–90
Wallerstein, Immanuel, 210
Walter Roth Museum of Anthropology, 278
Wapichan peoples (Indigenous group), xxi, 333n31; labour of, 251; land protected by, 249; rights struggled for by, 250; technology used by, 246, 252–54, 267; territory of, 332n15
Warren, Wendy, 100, 105, 111–15
"Was There an Amerindian Atlantic?" (Cohen), 97
Wayana (Indigenous group), 253
Weaver, Jace, 14, 99–101
Welburn, Ron, 72
welfare, Indigenous Peoples and, 305n110
western man, reinvented as biological, 52
wétiko phase, 117
whiteness, postcoloniality depending on, 36–37
The White Possessive (Moreton-Robinson), 197n4
white supremacy, 155
Wilderson, Frank D., III, 15, 22–23, 80–81, 155; anti-indigeneity reinscribed by, 131; grammar preoccupying, 302n53; Hart on, 53–56, 308n33; Lacan critiqued by, 258–59; on Marxism, 324n8; Williams echoed by, 131–32. *See also individual works*
Williams, Eric, 183–84; James contrasted with, 167–68; Marx elaboured on by, 320n20; Wilderson echoing, 131–32. *See also individual works*
Williams, Robert A., Jr., 27, 61
Winthrop, John, 311n64, 313n103
Wolfe, Patrick, 71, 132, 143–48
womb, as middle/passage, 322n61
women, black. *See* black women
women, incarceration of Indigenous, 330n93

work: black labour as, 80; of enslaved blacks, 127; Indigenous labour and, 108–9; by Indigenous Peoples, 66–67; labour distinguished from, xv–xvi, 42–49, 52, 56–58, 69, 77, 128–29, 167, 173, 187; political theory prioritizing, 50. *See also* black work; labour-work dialectic; productive work

workers, 187; anti-indigeneity toward, 177; blacks not represented by, 155; capital accumulation resisted by, 177; natives transcended by, 223–24; political economic critique of, 206; the slave contrasted with, 301n41

working people, Rodney on, 184

Working People's Alliance (WPA), 162, 176, 326n51

The Wretched of the Earth (Fanon), 136, 300n23

Wright, Michelle, 84–86, 315n4

Wynter, Sylvia, 117–18, 130, 232, 297n3, 300n35; Afropessimism contrasted with, 195; Anthropocenes critiqued by, 219; Arendt anticipating, 308n21; Aristotelian view outlined by, 328n14; "Beyond Miranda's Meanings" by, 181–82, 195–99; on black Death, 212; black death complicated by, 213–14; black "indigenization" theorized on by, 210; capitalist political economy critiqued by, 193–95; cosmogonies defined by, 302n54; disalienation questioned by, 300n24; on enslaved blacks, 328n34; Fanon read by, 13; gender interpreted by, 201, 230–31; Henry critiquing, 192–93; on Indigenous labour, 209; Jonkonnu dance described by, 212–13; labour-work dialectic critiqued by, 191; land-labour dialectic critiqued by, 206–7; Las Casas discussed by, 62–65, 207–8; on man, 308n31; on Marx, 14–15; Marxism critiqued by, 228, 328n8; radical tradition including, xix, 189, 229–30; reproduction described by, 329n65; Wallerstein relied on by, 210. *See also individual works*

Yusoff, Kathryn, 77, 218–19, 232, 307n12, 335n76, 335n83

Zeleza, Paul Tiyambe, 94–96, 119